THE KURRAJONG TREE

The Kurrajong Tree

Loves and Lives of Three Women
in Colonial Australia

⁂

ELINOR MARTIN

Eastcot Publications

2012

Copyright © 2012 by Elinor Martin

All rights reserved. No part of this publication may be reproduced, stored in a retrieval system, or transmitted, in any form or by any means, without prior written permission of the publisher.

Eastcot Publications
West Vancouver, B.C.
elinorandstewart@shaw.ca

Layout and design: Vancouver Desktop Publishing Centre Ltd.
Cover image(s): Kurrajong tree photo by Helen Bowly; Elizabeth Barnes photo courtesy of Doreen Higgins; Rebecca and Susannah's photos from Dr. William Miller's collection
Proofreading: Naomi Pauls, Paper Trail Publishing
Map page 10: Shire of Cootamundra
Author photo: Brenda Brunton

The publisher has made every effort to request permission for images reprinted in this book and will be pleased to credit additional sources in future editions.

Library and Archives Canada Cataloguing in Publication
Martin, Elinor, 1932–
    The kurrajong tree : loves and lives of three women in colonial Australia / Elinor Martin.

Includes bibliographical references.
ISBN 978-0-9878243-0-1

    1. Barnes, Elizabeth, 1802–1886. 2. Nixon, Rebecca, 1836–1920. 3. Gordon, Susannah, 1851–1927. 4. Women pioneers—New South Wales—Biography. 5. New South Wales—Biography. I. Title.

DU172.A2M37 2012   994.402092'2   C2012-900821-4

Printed in Canada by Printorium Bookworks. Second printing.

*To the memory of my father, Dr. William Miller,
whose collection of memorabilia and knowledge
of his ancestors inspired this book.*

*And for my granddaughter, Sonya Jane Jorgenson-Martin,
in remembrance of her colonial ancestors
Elizabeth, Rebecca and Susannah.*

Contents

Barnes and Miller Family Chart / 8

Modern Map of Cootamundra Area / 10

Preface / 11

ELIZABETH

In Sunshine and Safety / 13

REBECCA

To Own a Farm / 107

SUSANNAH

From Love to Love / 241

Epilogue / 405

Acknowledgements / 409

Illustration Credits / 411

Appendix: Family Charts / 412

Glossary / 418

Sources and References / 422

About the Author / 428

Barnes and Miller Families

JOHN BARNES m. 1833 **ELIZABETH KING ELLEN**
(1812–1863)   (1802–1886)
Bletsoe,   Shaftesbury,
Bedfordshire   Dorsetshire
Issue: Thomas Alfred, John Frederick, George Robert, William John, Edward Prior **"Ted"**, Elizabeth Mary Maria "Beth"

WILLIAM MILLER m. 1813 **MARGARET MARY MASKELYNE TOOMER**
(1779–1861)   (1788–1862)
Poole,   Newbury, Berkshire
Dorsetshire
Issue: William, Mary Jane, Joseph, Elizabeth, Thomas Nevil, **John**, Sophia

JOHN MILLER m. 1857 **REBECCA NIXON**
(1824–1881)   (1836–1920)
Margate, Kent   Drumquin, Tyrone

Issue: Mary Jane, Emily Elizabeth, John James **"J.J."**, **William**, Margaret Mary Maskelyne, Sarah Ann, Eliza Gore Gilmour, Jessie Annie, Compton South, Alexander Archibald **"Alick"**, Edward Lanfear, Nevil Maskelyne

EDWARD PRIOR BARNES m. 1873 **SUSANNAH MARIA GORDON**
(1844–1900)   (1851–1927)
Sydney, NSW   London, England

Issue: Susie Ellen **"Nellie"**, Lilla Maria, Eva, **Hilda** Prior, Ivy Fenner "Goog", Bertha Jane "Peeler", Edward Gordon, Twin sons (stillborn), Edward John, Lewis Ernest "Mickey", Elfrida Mary, Florence Esther

NELLIE, HILDA and SUSANNAH BARNES married WILLIAM, ALICK and J.J. MILLER

WILLIAM m. 1894 **NELLIE BARNES**
(1863–1944)   (1874–1927)
Pejar,   Cootamundra,
NSW   NSW

ALICK m. 1900 **HILDA BARNES**
(1873–1941)   (1879–1977)
Goulburn,   Cootamundra,
NSW   NSW

J.J. m. 1902 **SUSANNAH MARIA (GORDON) BARNES**
(1860–1950)   (1851–1927)
Berrima,   London, England
NSW

Issue: Clive "Bon", Bertha Gordon, Coramundra, William **"Bill"**, Elinor Susie "Lel", Croydon Sydney, Lionel Gordon, Myee Wilga Australia, Huntley Edward

Issue: Joan Alexandra, Selwyn Archibald "Boyd", Ivy Hilda

No issue.

WILLIAM **"Bill"** MILLER (1900–1989) Cootamundra, NSW   m. 1930   MARTHA MARGARET JANE "Reta" OLIVER (1904–1992) Toronto, Canada

Issue: Margaret **Elinor,** David Croydon, William Clarke, Stephen Clive

STEWART WILLIAM MARTIN (1927–) Ladner, Canada   m. 1958   MARGARET **ELINOR** MILLER (1932–) Vancouver, Canada

Issue: David William, Elizabeth Jane

DAVID WILLIAM MARTIN (1961–) North Vancouver, Canada   m. 1989   TANYA LEAH JORGENSON (1960–) Vancouver, Canada

Issue: Sonya Jane

Compiled by M. Elinor (Miller) Martin, West Vancouver, Canada, 2011. The families of Elizabeth Barnes, Rebecca Miller and Susannah Miller are listed in more detail in the Appendix.

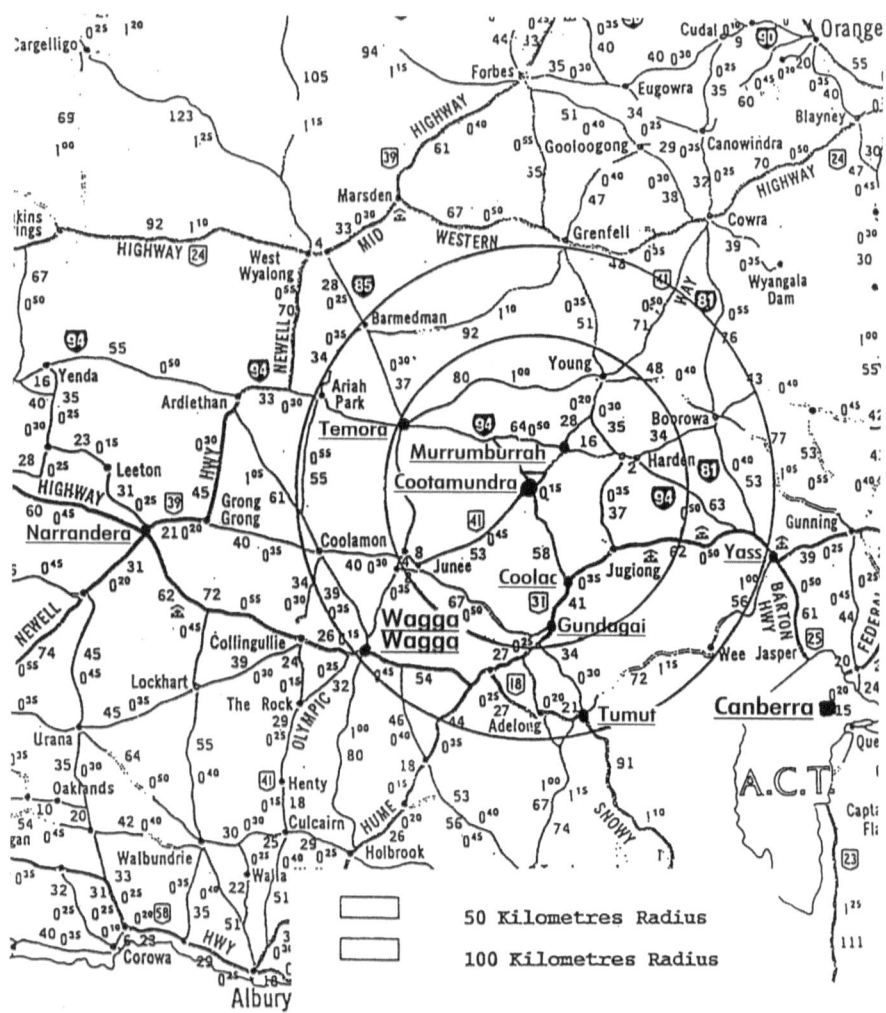

Modern map of Cootamundra area (The Shire of Cootamundra)

Preface

In 1840 Elizabeth King Ellen Barnes, my great-great-grandmother, her husband and three young sons sailed as cabin class passengers from London, England, to the colony of New South Wales, where they planned to establish a farm. Elizabeth was described at the time as having deep blue eyes, pleasant features and a youthful figure that belied her childbearing and her thirty-eight years.

In 1854 Rebecca Nixon, my great-grandmother, a sturdy seventeen-year-old farm girl, left County Tyrone, Ireland, to work in New South Wales. She was amongst 258 Irish assisted immigrants in steerage, all of them bound for employment in the colony as agricultural labourers or house servants.

In 1873 Susannah Maria Gordon, also my great-grandmother, departed from England as the only unaccompanied female cabin class passenger on her voyage to the colony. An energetic twenty-one-year-old, she was chaperoned by the Captain's wife from London to Sydney, where she was to marry a son of Elizabeth Barnes.

In setting out for the distant colony, each woman left behind forever her relatives and friends and all that was certain in her life. In 1874 Elizabeth, Rebecca and Susannah met at Cootamundra, a town on the western slopes of New South Wales, where their lives were irrevocably joined.

The nineteenth-century author of *The Pastoral Possessions of New South Wales, 1889,* William Hanson, wrote in his author's note that he "had long cherished a wish to undertake the congenial work involved in the present enterprise." I, too, had long cherished such a wish. I grew up in a family where stories of our ancestors were told and retold; by the age of ten I knew the various marriage connections between the colonial Barnes and Miller families.

One impression from these Australian stories became dominant: the stories featured the exploits of the men. Scant attention was paid to the accomplishments of the Barnes and Miller women; one of the Miller daughters, for example, was the first person in the town of Cootamundra to graduate from university, a fact never mentioned yet one that came to light during my research for *The Kurrajong Tree*. My "congenial work," I decided, must focus on my female ancestors.

I wondered about the circumstances that prompted Elizabeth, Rebecca and Susannah to abandon the country of their birth and courageously sail to an alien land on the other side of the world. What did they experience on their voyages? When they settled in the colony, what problems did they face? What sort of marriages did they have? What were their interests and talents? I discovered that they had thirty-three children; under what conditions did they give birth to those children, and how did they cope with the deaths of ten of them? Years later, what made three branches of the family suddenly emigrate to Canada? These and many other questions prompted me to investigate the lives of the Barnes and Miller women in colonial New South Wales.

Beyond the verifiable facts in a family history, all else is conjecture. *The Kurrajong Tree* is thus a fictionalized but, I trust, plausible account based on research into my ancestors' colonial lives. I assure my readers that no fictitious event or character in the story is intended to reflect the life of any person living or dead. The historical figures and my ancestors, reputable and otherwise, are portrayed to the best of my knowledge, and I ask forgiveness for any errors or omissions.

My "congenial work" now introduces you to Elizabeth, Rebecca and Susannah.

Elizabeth

IN SUNSHINE
AND SAFETY

On England's shore I saw a pensive band,
With sails unfurl'd for earth's remotest strand...
—THOMAS CAMPBELL, "LINES ON THE DEPARTURE OF
EMIGRANTS FOR NEW SOUTH WALES"

In 1788 the British government claimed the eastern part of the Australian continent as a repository for criminals, thereby laying the foundation of the colony of New South Wales. The mother country soon learned that the colony possessed valuable resources and set out to profit by their development. Not all former felons, however, were productive workers, and if New South Wales were to prosper, a population of solid citizens was required. Attracting settlers to grow crops to feed the colony and raise sheep to supply British woollen mills became a priority.

Attributes of the advertised agricultural properties were often exaggerated, yet many Britons, including John and Elizabeth Barnes, were inspired by the advertisements and applied for grants offered as inducements to prospective farmers. Whatever their backgrounds in Britain, thousands of Free Settlers set out to become farmers in the colony.

In 1840 British emigrants reached New South Wales by sailing for five months on an ocean voyage of sixteen thousand miles. Their scant knowledge of the destination and ignorance of the hazards along the way did not discourage the Free Settlers, who had high hopes for their new life in the spacious colony.

***

Some forty-six years later, in 1886, the following letter, which had been intended for two of her granddaughters, was found amongst the possessions of the late Elizabeth King Ellen Barnes.

December 15th, 1885

My Dearest Nellie and Lilla,
I have often spoken of incidents during my voyage out to the colony and I am pleased you have enjoyed my sketches done whilst on the ship. At long last I have put pen to paper and recorded the complete story for you to read when you are a little older.

As I look back on the voyage, it was an interesting adventure, taken all in all, with unusual sights to see and much to learn. The Abbotsford brought me to this vast land and to years of great happiness as well as painful sorrow.

Old age is overtaking me, my darlings, and I regret not having the strength to write of my life in the colony. I have faith that in the future someone will tell the tale of my years spent in New South Wales.

As always, my dearest granddaughters, I remain your loving Grandmamma,

Elizabeth King Ellen Barnes

Attached to this letter was Elizabeth's story, which began in 1840 in London.

ONE

Promised Land

I stood at the port rail in the dim light of a November dawn and looked on London for the last time. The *Abbotsford* slipped her lines, and two noisy tugboats belching smoke towed our ship, with her sails furled, out into the current of the Thames. The margin of murky river water widened between our ship and the shore until the great city disappeared into smoke-laden fog.

The *Abbotsford* swayed down the river, hauled by the tugboats churning a path for her down to the sea. The smoke from their funnels stung my eyes, and the stench and sight of human and animal wastes floating in the river made me gag. I clutched the rail with one hand and my stomach with the other and prayed silently to God for His comfort.

At the starboard rail your Uncle George, who was a ten-month-old baby, sat in your Grandpapa's arms whilst your uncles Thomas and John, ages four and three, perched on the shoulders of two seamen who were showing them the vessels on the river. Apparently oblivious to smoke and smells, my husband and young sons listened to their knowledgeable guide, the Ship's Surgeon, as he commented on the barges, tugboats and ships crowding the Thames on the ebb tide.

The tugboats veered off and the river pilot departed over the side before the *Abbotsford* set sail beyond Greenwich. Her canvas, now billowing, carried her through the estuary and out to the sea. Northeast winds lifted the barque towards the Strait of Dover, and the Captain, pleased with the speed of departure, shared his satisfaction with the helmsman. The waters beneath us, which had been dark and filthy in the river, turned green, and ocean swells smacked the ship's hull.

My queasiness abruptly turned to violent nausea, and I disgraced myself over the rail. John took charge of the children on deck whilst the Surgeon helped me to our cabin. He pulled open the heavy door for me, reached into a copious coat pocket and took out a handful of hard biscuit.

"Chew that, Mrs. Barnes, to stave off the nausea," he said, but I was beyond chewing anything. Clutching a bedpost to steady myself, I struggled to remove my travelling clothes and pull on a flannel shift. When I pushed open the small window in the cabin, blustery winds chilled me through. I curled up on the narrow bed, my head pounding and my arms holding my heaving stomach.

I had been so keen to emigrate, yet the journey had scarcely begun and I was already unable to manage. Dreams of a home of our own in a sunny, spacious country were a world away from this wretched misery. And what if I couldn't survive the thousands of miles ahead? With tears streaming, I uttered a prayer of desperation and gave in to another bout of vomiting.

London streets soaked in sooty rain and smothered in fog had deadened my spirits. Not just the London weather, but Cheapside itself caused me distress, its footpaths full of thieves, drunks and street-corner trollops. A walk to do the daily shopping was unsettling, even dangerous, for a woman and her small children.

As often as London weather allowed, I braved the streets and walked with my young sons to a small fenced park near Saint Paul's Cathedral. There Thomas and Johnny played with a ball whilst I sat knitting for my expected baby. On the way home one day, I passed a shipping agent's office and, as I had done before, paused for a moment to read a printed notice in the window.

This time I opened the agency door to have my two little boys captivated at once by a stuffed kangaroo in a corner. A man in a grey frock coat came forward to greet me. With his bald head, round eyes and thin-lipped mouth, he had a fishlike appearance.

"Good afternoon, Madam." His eyes assessed me and the children.

"You wish to emigrate, no doubt. I can direct you to the most excellent cabin class accommodation on the finest of ships."

"Thank you, but I merely came in to enquire whether I might have a copy of the notice in the window."

"Of course, Madam." He pulled open the shallow top drawer of his desk and removed a large printed sheet. "That will be a ha'penny. Write your name and address here, please." He placed a register in front of me.

I had not expected to have to pay or sign for anything, but I supposed he did not want triflers. I handed him a ha'penny, then wrote my name and my address, 111 Wood Street, Cheapside, in his register.

"This agency is always at your service, Madam."

I thanked him and folded the notice into a pocket of my cape. When I had dragged Thomas and Johnny away from the stuffed kangaroo, the three of us set out again for Wood Street.

That evening I settled the boys into bed as usual, Thomas clutching his little stuffed horse and Johnny his stuffed lion, said their prayers with them and kissed them goodnight. With the notice from the shipping agent's office in my hand, I went through to the small sitting room in the flat above our shop.

"What's all this, then?" said John, when I held out the large printed sheet.

"It's from a shipping agency, a description of opportunities in the colony of New South Wales," I said. "We could have the lease of farmland and a home of our own for an annual fee of ten pounds plus a ha'penny for each pastured animal. We've often said we'll never be able to afford our own home here. Think of the children, John. They'll have fresh air, sunshine and space to romp and grow! And your sister lives in the colony."

"I'm a merchant, Elizabeth, not a farmer, and Susan lives at Sydney, undoubtedly miles from any farmland."

"You could learn to be a farmer, I'm sure! You'll admit our shop is less of a paying proposition than in your uncle's time. Back then Cheapside was a respectable part of London. It's becoming a desperate place to do business and raise our children." John had come from a village in Bedfordshire, and I had been born in Dorsetshire; both of us had pleasant memories of living in the English countryside.

"I agree it's not the country life we knew," said John, who had long been aware of my determination to get away from Cheapside. "What sort of property do they have on offer?"

"It says here, 'Each property is arable, attractive, and may be expanded after three years.' It tells about the bounty system, too. 'Married able-bodied migrants under the age of thirty may apply to the Colonial Office for an outright grant of thirty pounds plus five pounds for each child.' That would surely help in paying for our passage and establishing our home."

No matter my enthusiasm or the decline of his business in Cheapside or the fact that his sister lived in New South Wales, John could not see himself as a farmer, especially in a strange land on the other side of the world. But I persisted. "I'm going to write to the Colonial Office to ask them to send us the applications," I said. John looked at me indulgently, shook his head and went back to reading *The Times*.

My mind was set on starting life anew and offering our sons the sort of freedom I had enjoyed in Dorsetshire as a child. At eight and thirty years of age, I was ten years older than my husband, yet that difference had not seemed important until now. I wanted to emigrate before my age affected my ability to adapt to strange surroundings, although I would never say so.

The applications arrived, and after I had completed them, I left them on the sideboard for John to sign. He ignored them. I waited whilst the January days dragged on, but I said nothing more.

My walks to the park would soon come to an end. I was showing, even in my most voluminous skirts. In fact, the birth was not far off, and I was more than a little anxious. I had lost twin baby girls the previous year, and I could only hope and pray for an easy confinement and a healthy infant this time. I knew only too well that for weeks I would be restricted to the flat, where the boys would become cranky and quarrelsome. One frosty January afternoon, despite the impending birth, I bundled up the boys for a walk to the little fenced park near Saint Paul's Cathedral.

Thieves abounded in Cheapside, and I walked quickly, a child by each hand, aware that I could be jostled at any time and have my purse stolen. When we arrived at the park, I lifted the latch on an iron gate coated in hoarfrost. I was always relieved to reach this sanctuary.

I settled myself on my usual bench—and looked up into the muzzle of a gun. A wild-eyed, pockmarked youth was aiming a pistol at my face. Thomas and Johnny clutched at my skirts. "Gimme y'r money!" For one fleeting moment I thought to refuse the robber, snatch up the children and race for the gate. Instead, I reached beneath my cape and brought out my purse. The thief grabbed it and ran.

As he struggled to open the latch on the gate, the gun went off. The shot ripped through the folds of my skirts, missing Thomas by inches. By the time I had regained my wits, the thief had vanished. I hurried my terrified children out of the park and homeward through the crowded streets.

"That puts paid to the matter!" said John, white-faced as he paced around the sitting room. "No cowardly whelp will rob my wife at gunpoint, nor will my children be shot at when they go out to play! Where are those applications for New South Wales? I'm sure to qualify as a bounty migrant."

After the Colonial Office had ascertained our medical status and our good character, John, age eight and twenty, received bounty migrant papers as a Free Settler in New South Wales. We knew the colony had been founded by transported convicts, including felons from London, but that fact escaped us entirely as we dreamed of owning our own home and having a life far away in sunshine and safety. A life of shadows and perils, too, as time was to tell.

Whilst I tended to the boys and our vigorous newborn son, George, who had arrived three days after that frightening experience in the park, John went off to the Colonial Office for brochures on farming and maps of New South Wales. I yearned to live in countryside like the Dorset downs, and the information we pored over indicated that available farmland in the interior near the Yass River should satisfy my longings.

Our departure was set for autumn. All cautious passengers, we had learned, endeavoured to acquire as much knowledge as possible about ships and their officers before booking passage. John spent his spare time talking to agencies, touring vessels at the Thames docks, and meeting Captains and Ship's Surgeons.

Meanwhile, I engaged a tailor to fashion a travelling outfit for each of us: a burgundy costume for me with a hidden pocket inside its petticoat for my inheritance of fifty pounds, a frock coat and twill trousers for John, and little sailor suits for the boys. I began to stitch our tropical clothing myself. Memories of my dear papa in his wool draper's shop, his needle flashing, his whittling knife carving intricate buttons, offered me inspiration. All the while, I read newspaper stories alarmingly illustrated with sketches of doomed ships wrecked on the southern coast of our destination.

"I've found us a ship, my dear," said John one October evening. "She's called the *Abbotsford* and she's sailing the third week of November. I've booked a cabin on the port side for us. Extra expense, I know, but I've been down in some steerage compartments, and we'll not travel that way."

"I'm grateful, John. We'll appreciate the privacy and space of a cabin, I'm sure. But I've been reading some disturbing newspaper articles about voyages to New South Wales. Are you sure we can trust the Captain of this ship to get us there safely?"

"The Captain of the *Abbotsford* is a sober, God-fearing Scot, very proud of his ship's record. The Ship's Surgeon is also a Scot and looks to be a responsible fellow. We'll be in good hands." I could do nothing but accept my husband's judgment.

In the following week John fortuitously received this letter from his sister.

Parkside, Redfern
Sydney
New South Wales
June 29th, 1840

My Dear Brother John,
Your letter of the 1st of February arrived today. I am thrilled by your intention to emigrate! I had thought never to see you again and now I anticipate your arrival with great happiness! You and your family must, of course, stop with us at Sydney before you set out for your farm. Robert and I have ample room in our home and we look forward to offering you our hospitality. I admire your courage in leasing a property on the western slopes of the colony. Grand country, I have heard, and open to expansion of your holdings, but so far away from Sydney! Visit with us for as long as you like before you begin your journey westward.

Do accept my congratulations on your new son and give my warmest regards to your dear wife Elizabeth. I look forward to meeting her and the children.

Please write to me the moment you know which ship you are taking and your intended arrival date so that I may watch the Arrivals notices in the newspaper and be at dockside to welcome you. I shall have this letter delivered at once to Port Jackson and placed on the fastest ship leaving today.

With heartfelt joy, I remain your loving sister,

Susan

In 1833 John's younger sister, Susanna Eliza, known as Susan, had been amongst 200 courageous British women who had left England on the barque *Bussorah Merchant*, hoping for a better life in New South Wales. In 1837 she had married a Sydney solicitor and, according to her twice-yearly letters, led a comfortable life. John wrote to her immediately and posted the letter on the largest full-rigged vessel sailing for New South Wales that day, one that was sure to reach Sydney before we did.

On Wednesday evening, the 18th of November, 1840, we boarded the *Abbotsford*. Although I was eager to emigrate, I had to fight back tears because I knew I was leaving the land of my birth forever. No sooner had I boarded the ship than the combined odours of oiled decks, brass polish and fresh tar nauseated me. I smiled wanly at the Captain when he stepped forward to introduce himself and show us to our accommodation.

A bearded master mariner of stocky build with a strong, weather-beaten countenance, Captain Cameron was clad in a navy coat with two vertical rows of polished brass buttons. His Captain's hat with its faded gold braid was as weathered as his face and hands. He walked confidently about the ship, his gait rolling a little from side to side. I followed him cautiously, realizing with discomfort that I was sensitive to the motion of the vessel, even at dockside.

"The *Abbotsford* is a barque of four hundred seven tons," explained Captain Cameron, his blue eyes reflecting pride in his vessel. I had no idea what such information meant. Whilst I admired the polished fittings and clean decks, I thought the ship very small for such a long journey. "This cabin on the port side is one of the best. It offers you the full benefit of ocean breezes as well as shelter from the western sun in the Atlantic." The cabin looked much too cramped for the five of us. Privacy we would have. Space was not an option offered.

"How many people will sail with us, Captain, and will our voyage be as lengthy as I have heard?" I asked.

"The *Abbotsford* will carry twelve in her cabins, Madam, including the Surgeon, nine in steerage, eighteen of a crew and a cargo of general merchandise. We'll have you all at Port Jackson in Sydney Harbour within five months."

"And what is your provisioning for this voyage?" My question brought a somewhat condescending smile from the Captain.

"We sail with fresh water, bread, vegetables and fruit, Madam, and stop often to replenish our stores. Livestock will be kept forward in steerage—chickens for their eggs and meat, goats to supply milk, and two geese for Christmas."

I was pleased to hear him speak of fresh food. My particular concern was for the family's nourishment during five months at sea, and

I was suckling a baby and therefore needed to eat well. I supposed we would become accustomed to the odours and noises of animals and the smells of oil, brass polish and tar.

As I looked around the small ship, out of a hatchway came a portly man with a pink face and the most amazing ginger eyebrows, a bushy contrast to his sparse sidewhiskers and wispy fringe of ginger hair. The Captain introduced the Ship's Surgeon, Mr. Bruce, who seemed delighted to meet us.

"I see you have three bairns with you, Mrs. Barnes. They'll have a grand time aboard the *Abbotsford*! We'll sail away from grey old England and show you enough glorious sights to last you a lifetime. You'll arrive at the colony safely and in the best of health."

Thomas and Johnny were active, inquisitive lads, eager to see every corner of the ship, and I suddenly wondered whether I could keep them safe, even with John's help. Troubled by thoughts of spending five months in a cramped ship's cabin, I moved towards the rail overlooking the wharf. How could I possibly take care of our three little children in all kinds of weather over thousands of miles of ocean? The Captain, seeming to sense my distress, said, "Should you require assistance with the children, Mrs. Barnes, help can be found amongst those in steerage."

We spent that evening placing our belongings in our cabin. The little room contained a washstand and two three-foot-wide beds, supposedly enough space for two persons in each. All our goods were with us in the cabin, small as it was. We had brought our cradle for the baby, the carpet from our sitting room for the cabin floor, my rocking chair and a chamber pot. Our best wash basin and jug we placed on the washstand and our looking glass on the wall above.

We had also brought a number of other goods: a tin box with a small ham, a few apples, some hard cheese and tins of oatcakes, a metal bathing tub, and a trunk that contained a change of bedding, additional clothing, my knitting and embroidery supplies, dishes and cooking utensils for our new home, John's books, brochures, maps and his favourite pepper mill. At the last moment I had placed in the trunk two small watercolours from the sitting room, one of the village of Milton Abbas in Dorsetshire and the other of Saint Paul's Church at Bedford. Under the beds were our two portmanteaux with immediate needs.

Whilst I tried to settle our excited children, John helped a seaman lash down the cradle, rocking chair and trunk. In a frame fastened to the wall near the door of the cabin were Captain's Standing Orders as they applied to passengers. Everything from mealtimes to cleaning routines to use of the decks and the dining saloon was listed in neat lettering. A well-organized ship, I reckoned, as I read the Captain's Orders.

Before supper that evening, John answered a knock on our door and found the Surgeon issuing an invitation. "You've not yet met your fellow cabin passengers. Come along to the dining saloon, and we'll have a wee dram together." John and I wondered if this were to be a nightly ritual. It turned out to be so.

"Hiram Dartnell," said a thick-set man with greying, pomaded hair who offered a large, soft hand, "and my good wife, Dorcas. I'm a schoolmaster from Fulham. These young ladies are our daughters, Chloe, Judith and Esther." The solemn girls stood close to their mother.

"I'm Amos Winters," said the other cabin passenger, an earnest young man. "I was a clerk in a bank in Southwark." I caught him looking at the Dartnell girls.

The Dartnells and Amos Winters, we learned, were also Free Settlers who had applied to lease farmland in the colony. "Such a grand opportunity," said Dorcas Dartnell. "We'll be living at Parramatta, just fifteen miles from Sydney, close enough for the girls to meet people of quality."

None of us had ever lived on a farm, but we spent that evening sharing our plans for farming the spacious, sunny acres of New South Wales.

TWO

The Abbotsford

As Captain Cameron tacked his ship into the English Channel, I vomited myself dry. John and the boys stayed on deck that first day, getting their balance on a tossing ship and watching sailors climb through rigging to unfurl sails. John carried George to me to nurse and murmured his sympathies, but he did not remain in the cabin. When he and the boys joined me at nightfall, I was faint from heaving and wished only for the ultimate release from my suffering, a quiet death. I roused myself enough to beg God's forgiveness for such a sinful thought.

At sunrise John fetched the Surgeon to the cabin, now putrid with the stench of my vomit. I was drooped over the basin, moaning and weeping in misery. I had abandoned baby George, who had added his full nappy to the foulness of the cabin and howled in his cradle. Mr. Bruce felt my brow and, satisfied that I had no fever, reached into his pocket to pull out another handful of hard biscuit.

"You've not been chewing my biscuit, Mrs. Barnes. You have to put something down to throw something up, else you'll injure yourself with the dry heaves." With his bushy eyebrows knitted in a deep frown, he left the cabin. I groaned. I could no more swallow his hard biscuit than stand upright.

The Surgeon soon returned, followed by a slight young girl with clear grey eyes and waves of dark hair. "Mrs. Barnes, this is Rachel Gibson from Newtownards in County Down. She'll see you right." The girl's ready smile quite eased my despair. Rachel rescued my raging baby and cheerfully clucked at him as she changed his nappy.

"You'll tend to Mrs. Barnes and her bairn and their linen," Mr. Bruce told the girl, who now held a squirming George astride her hip. As he gave her instructions for our care, the girl from Newtownards nodded at him and smiled at me. Having put me in Rachel's care, the Surgeon left the cabin. I retched yet again. Rachel held the basin for me and sponged my brow whilst I heaved. To supplement my waning supply of milk, she fetched goat's milk mixed with boiled water for George. She fed, bathed and dressed the baby, and changed my soiled shift and bed linen. "Now then," she said, "as soon as I've rocked the bairn to sleep, I'll get to the washing. We have more sea water than we'll ever need, and there's a washtub in steerage and a clothesline on deck. Sure an' it'll all be done in no time."

By late that afternoon I felt somewhat rested, although hours of retching had left my throat burning and my chest and stomach aching. I came awake from a doze to discover Rachel standing beside me, holding a hard biscuit and a beaker of pale green liquid. "The Surgeon says I'm to see to it you take these. There's many in steerage just like you, Mrs. Barnes, and 'tis only the Surgeon's biscuit that's keeping them from the pain you're in." She handed me the beaker and began to break the biscuit into pieces.

"This drink looks vile, Rachel. What is it?"

"'Tis lime juice, and I took great care in squeezing the limes. You'll find no pips in the juice."

"Thank you very much, but I don't believe I'll have any just now."

"You'll be doing as you're told, begging your pardon. You've been retching for hours but not throwing up a thing. I say you'll feel much better when you throw up Mr. Bruce's vile green drink and hard biscuit." I didn't know which hurt me more: forcing down lime juice and biscuit, or laughing at Rachel's prescription for feeling better.

"'Tis lucky you are to be a cabin passenger, Mrs. Barnes. You have lime juice for your health in place of that queer scurvy grass we have to chew in steerage." The mere thought of chewing grass put my head over the basin again. When the Irish girl gently sponged my face, I said to her, "You have the knack of caring for people, Rachel. How old are you?"

"Just on sixteen. I'm the eldest of ten on the farm, seven of us girls. My Da' said he had more than enough women around him and told me to go an' find my own way. I do miss my Mam." I patted the girl's hand. "Come and work for us in the colony, why don't you?"

"'Tis a lovely idea, Mrs. Barnes, but I'm to be housekeeper to Mr. Garvey, a landowner at Camden, south of Sydney. His wife died in childbirth, and he's been left with five young ones under the age of ten." I could only hope that whoever the widower Garvey was, he would not take advantage of this attractive young girl. Rachel's courage in setting out to assume responsibility for a household with five children had earned my admiration.

My husband and eldest sons, all with steady stomachs, spent hours watching sailors climb aloft and helmsmen keep the ship downwind. Like most fathers, John had spent little time with his children and was enthusiastic in sharing their discoveries. They were a healthy, happy trio on deck whilst I was a wan, miserable passenger in bed.

Strong westerly winds and heavy swells flung the barque southward across the Bay of Biscay, leaving me convinced my stomach would never settle. I tried to accustom myself to the ship's upward slope over each swell, her downward pitch into each trough and her incessant rolling and tossing. I nibbled pieces of hard biscuit to keep my digestion at ease and ventured out on deck. Clutching the rail whilst focusing my eyes on the horizon helped ease my nausea, and the sun and wind brightened my complexion. Dorcas Dartnell and her daughters sat in a sheltered corner clutching parasols and wearing gloves and high collars. "Elizabeth, if I may speak frankly," said Dorcas, "your complexion will suffer if you do not seek shelter. I have always advised my girls to keep themselves protected from the elements. Men prefer delicate skin on a woman, believe me." I smiled at Dorcas and continued to stand at the rail, the sun bronzing my face and arms, the ocean breezes swinging my braided hair. With the fresh air I began to enjoy my food again, and my milk was now sufficient to enable me to suckle George successfully.

"You'll not be needing me any more," said Rachel in the cabin one afternoon as I sat in my rocking chair with the baby at my breast. "On the contrary," I replied, "we'd like to employ you for the entire voyage, if you're willing. My husband is quite weary of minding Thomas and Johnny."

"I'd be pleased to help you, Mrs. Barnes. I'll go and see to the boys at once. Caring for young ones is no job for a man."

Our first stop for provisions was at Tenerife, the largest of the Canary Islands off the coast of Morocco, where the air was clear, the breezes gentle. Having arranged for Rachel to accompany us, we went ashore, thankful for land under our feet once more. Volcanic beaches beckoned us to remove boots and stockings and wade ankle-deep in warm tidal pools. Swarthy natives, draped in layers of strange clothing and speaking an incomprehensible language, were eager for our trade, and whilst wandering through a market, John and I purchased two wool travel blankets. The Surgeon had advised us to bargain for every item, but being merchants ourselves, we could not put much heart into it.

On the approach to Tenerife, Cook's offerings had become so meagre that our last meal consisted of salted beef and a hard-boiled egg with a hard biscuit soaked in a beaker of tea with goat's milk; my handy food tin provided my family with a little extra. The *Abbotsford* left Tenerife with chickens to replace the ones consumed, plus bananas, oranges, onions, pumpkins, rice, newly baked bread and plenty of wine and fresh water. Mr. Bruce now had an ample supply of limes, even for those in steerage.

One bright day as we sailed southward from Tenerife, Dorcas was having a nap, and the Dartnell girls and I were sharing a midafternoon pot of tea in the saloon. The Second Officer, Mr. Perry, a Welshman, appeared at the door carrying scissors and red and green paper. "I wonder," he said shyly, "if I might ask you ladies to decorate the saloon for Christmas." Not realizing Christmas would be upon us so soon, I experienced a rush of homesickness and wondered if the Dartnell girls felt the same.

For Christmas worship on deck, the crewmen were smartly turned out, as were cabin and steerage passengers, wearing Sunday best. Captain Cameron conducted the worship service; Hiram Dartnell and Amos Winters read the Collect and Epistle from *The Book of Common Prayer*; the Captain read the Gospel; the Surgeon preached a brief homily on the Nativity, and John led the closing prayers.

In our decorated dining saloon that afternoon, the officers and cabin passengers ate roast goose, mashed potatoes, pumpkin baked with onions, giblet gravy, boiled Christmas pudding with rum sauce, and for afters, oranges and bananas. With Canary Islands wine we toasted the health of young Queen Victoria and the voyage of the *Abbotsford,* and much to everyone's delight, Mr. Bruce played Christmas music with festive enthusiasm on his harmonium. Aboard a small ship on a vast ocean, miles away from the churches of London and centuries away from the crèche at Bethlehem, we sang "O Come, All Ye Faithful." In bed that night, I wondered how we would spend our next yuletide, our first in New South Wales.

Propelled by the northeast trade winds, the *Abbotsford* sailed southwestward on the Canaries Current. Spanking breezes billowed the canvas and sent the barque surging onward.

Now that our curiosity about shipboard life had been satisfied, we began to realize the monotony of a five-month voyage. On calm evenings John and I played cards, draughts or dominoes in the saloon with Amos Winters and the Dartnell family, and during the long daylight hours, weather permitting, we all sat on deck and told stories of our lives, or read aloud to one another. The cabin passengers came supplied with instructive material from the Colonial Office, and a shelf in the dining saloon contained brochures on agricultural topics, which included information about raising sheep and cattle.

I had a pleasant, if reserved, companion in Dorcas Dartnell. She was a ladylike creature who fussed about her appearance, which I thought a pointless preoccupation on the deck of a sailing ship. In one of our conversations about establishing our new homes, Dorcas declared, "Hiram and I might apply for assisted immigrants to help us, like the Irishmen in steerage, although that could be a long wait. Perhaps we'll ask the authorities for prisoners to be assigned to us, which, I believe, is commonly done. We've read that convicts' offences were sometimes trivial, but can any man or woman be trusted after a life hardened by transportation and imprisonment?"

Dorcas's question was one I had never considered. I preferred not to think about transported convicts, but rather to envision New South Wales as a spacious land of sunshine and safety for my family. Trust in God, I told myself, and do not brood over the unknown.

On most days the chickens and goats were brought up from below to be confined in a fenced space on deck whilst their quarters were swept clean. Thomas and Johnny were delighted because the only animals they had ever seen were horses in the streets and stray cats and dogs. When Sam, the farm lad who tended the animals, allowed the children to feed the chickens and goats, they chortled with glee. John usually stood near the livestock pen on the pretext of supervising the boys, although in fact he used the opportunity to put questions to Sam about farming. In a lilting Irish brogue the young man delivered pithy opinions on many agricultural subjects. John, a scholarly sort of man, later compiled careful notes, especially on grain and sheep, which he had decided were to be the focus of his farming at Yass.

The ocean offered an interesting array of birds and sea life, and I filled my sketchbook with "Creatures of the Seas." Flocks of gulls occasionally appeared, eager to scoop up the food scraps Cook threw overboard. Flying fish soared above the waves, sometimes landing fatally on deck. Dolphins danced in our wake, and young sharks swam close to the surface. John, Amos and Hiram had a fine time devising ways to hook them. Thomas and Johnny wanted to join in the fishing, and one auspicious morning the two of them were able to catch a small shark. They proudly carried it down to Cook to bake for dinner.

Dorcas Dartnell and I spent endless hours together. That same morning, whilst the boys were catching the small shark, Dorcas was crocheting one of many antimacassars; all upholstered chairs in the Dartnell household would be protected fron Hiram's pomaded hair.

I was reading aloud from an agricultural brochure on cows. Both of us were determined to learn all we could on this subject. I would be responsible for the cow on our farm, and Dorcas and Hiram intended to establish a dairy farm.

Our Surgeon, although a jovial sort of man, was clearly dedicated to his shipboard responsibility: the health of all persons on the *Abbotsford*. Twice each week, two limes were delivered to our cabin, and I was to share their juice amongst the five of us to prevent scurvy. The children's reaction to lime juice was identical to mine. One afternoon I mentioned that all three boys were refusing the sour drink.

"Mrs. Barnes," Mr. Bruce snapped at me, his eyebrows bristling, "should you not put that juice into those bairns twice each week, I'll not be responsible for their deaths from scurvy. I've never yet had a passenger nor a crewman succumb to the disease. Scurvy is a dreadful malady of swollen, bleeding gums, distressing skin blotches, wretched weakness and often fatal consequences. It can be prevented by eating fresh vegetables and fruit. You are aware such provisions are in short supply on a long voyage, and you must understand that my limes are essential in maintaining your good health!" My compliance was thus assured. From then on I spooned lime juice into us twice each week, despite any protests about the taste.

We noticed that the First and Second Officers had a large share of the ship's duties, which they performed without complaint in all sorts of weather. These included seeing that the *Abbotsford* was scrubbed down every third day, provisions were carefully rationed, and the entire ship, including the shining brass, was properly maintained.

In a corner of the deck, the First Officer, Mr. Arnold, kept a nursery of small shrubs, which he tended carefully and tied up securely in blustery weather. He explained they were for his garden and his neighbours' gardens at Ashfield in West Sydney, where his wife and three children lived. His collection, brought from his parents' garden in Kent, included hazelnut bushes, rhododendrons and azaleas, and in boxes of wood shavings, daffodil bulbs, gladioli corms and dahlia tubers.

When he realized John and I were interested in his work, Mr. Arnold showed us his large stock of seeds, sorted alphabetically in individual packets. Later in the voyage he seeded several trays of Kentish earth, which sprouted seedlings in readiness for planting at Ashfield.

I said to him one evening, "Would you be kind enough to teach me how to sow seeds and care for them in my kitchen garden? I've never planted a garden, and unless I learn to grow vegetables, my family will be ill-nourished." My sister Jane had always tended to the kitchen garden at home in Dorsetshire, whilst I had devoted myself to caring for our younger brothers and sisters. "I'd be delighted, Mrs. Barnes," Mr. Arnold responded. "Tomorrow afternoon I'll bring my packets to the saloon and suggest the best methods of planting and cultivation."

The next day Mr. Arnold laid out a bewildering array of tiny seeds on the dining table. In the days to come, the sea-going botanist provided many lessons on keeping a kitchen garden. Chloe Dartnell joined me, and we each filled a notebook with his instructions.

The Second Officer, Mr. Perry, took it upon himself to become the boys' tutor. Young as they were, Thomas and Johnny could soon tie knots, demonstrate hitches and bends, and tell nautical time by counting the striking of bells in each watch. They told everyone that when they grew up, they were going to be sailors.

Whenever he was free from duties, Mr. Perry often sat in a corner of the main deck singing sea chanties to Thomas and Johnny whilst he whittled pieces of a broken spar into square and round designs. I have forever held in my memory the three of them sitting cross-legged in the sunshine, the boys reciting "The Sailor's Alphabet," "A is for anchor, B is for bowsprit, C is for capstan . . . ," as they caught the shavings falling from Mr. Perry's carvings. I was delighted the boys were learning their alphabet, but then he taught them songs about pirates and famous sea battles: "Eighty-eight Sir Francis Drake" and "Nelson's Death and Victory." John thought it was a good way for the boys to learn a bit of history. I considered the ballads far too adult for my young children.

"Mamma," said Thomas one night when I had finished saying his prayers with him, "the *Abbotsford* shouldn't be called a ship, you know." I didn't understand what he was talking about. "She doesn't have three square-rigged masts like a real ship. Her mizzen-mast is fore-and-aft rigged, and that makes her a barque."

"Ah," I replied, recognizing Mr. Perry's Welsh tones in my small son's explanation. "I'll call the *Abbotsford* a barque from now on." Thomas nodded his approval.

On Sunday mornings in calm weather, the entire ship's company came on deck in best dress for Matins. Mr. Bruce's harmonium was lifted outside, and everyone sang hymns in thankful praise for the *Abbotsford*'s smooth voyage. "All Hail the Power of Jesus' Name," "Jesus Shall Reign Where'er the Sun" and "Rejoice, the Lord Is King" rang out across the seas.

The *Abbotsford* put in at the Cape Verde Islands off the coast of West Africa for provisions and continued onward to the equator. When I noticed our vessel was sailing more westward than southward, I told the First Officer I did not think we would reach the Cape of Good Hope this way. He was amused and promised an explanation at the table after dinner. On a chart he pointed out the prevailing winds crucial to our steady progress across the seas.

"The northeast trade winds are carrying us towards the coast of Brazil, where we'll put in at Rio de Janeiro for provisions. From there we'll pick up the southwest trades for our voyage across to the Cape of Good Hope. Attempting to sail directly southward through the doldrums off the coast of Africa, with no winds to aid our passage, would prove a miserable, frustrating experience." I still thought that crossing the Atlantic twice was a tiresome way to reach New South Wales.

One calm evening, in honour of our passing to the southern hemisphere, seamen strung lanterns over the main deck and brought the harmonium from the dining saloon. Captain Cameron, usually a master mariner immersed in his work, appeared as King Neptune, resplendent in a cloak of purple and gold. Those in steerage were included in the festivities, and on command of King Neptune, each person had to forfeit a talent to the equator crossing by performing for the entire company. John told an anecdote about a vicar of Bletsoe and a publican's daughter, which does not bear repeating here. To the Surgeon's accompaniment I sang a ballad about a lover and his lass, and Judith Dartnell followed with a dramatic recitation of "The Tyger" by William Blake. Rachel danced an Irish jig, and so it went until all had earned their way across the equator and our three sons lay sleeping in our arms in the dark velvet warmth of the tropical night.

By next morning, despite our Captain's best intentions, our barque had slipped out of the trade winds and into the doldrums of the Atlantic Narrows. Her drifting plight, so contrary to our experience thus far, was nerve-wracking. With her sails hanging steaming, the *Abbotsford* lay motionless on a flat, shimmering ocean. Soaked in perspiration and nauseated by the heat, we opened our cabin doors and windows and languished in the suffocating atmosphere.

Below decks the unbearable heat and stifling air compelled the steerage passengers to come up and rest and eat under canvas awnings. The animals, listless under their shelters on deck, added their odours and noises to the heavy air. Whilst I tried to amuse my fretful children in the sticky cabin, I had far too much time to ponder once more our decision to leave England. Although the voyage had been an easy passage compared with others I had read about, the sheer length of the journey was wearying. And now we drifted aimlessly in this merciless heat and humidity.

On the fourth evening the thick air was stirred by slight breezes, and Captain Cameron gave brisk orders to his sailors and helmsman. The steaming canvas gradually filled, and bearing slowly southwestward, the *Abbotsford* eventually picked up the Brazil Current and proceeded down the coast to Rio de Janeiro. Set ashore, we wandered around Rio whilst the vessel was scrubbed down, rigging and sails checked, and food and water replenished. We purchased straw hats and, along with Rachel, strolled the streets and parks of the colourful Portuguese town. In Rio we celebrated George's first birthday with a picnic. Mr. Bruce, who had come with us, identified some of the strange vegetation and even stranger birds, macaws and toucans in particular.

Meanwhile, Mr. Arnold disappeared from the ship; a few days later he returned in a dray laden with bundles of grapevines and collections of orange trees. "We have contracts for orange trees with orchardists in the Macquarie Towns," he said, "and a vineyard in the Hunter Valley has ordered grapevines. They'll be pleased with this selection." Amos Winters helped the First Officer secure the trees and vines on deck, and the two men became engaged in a continuing conversation about orange trees. Amos the bank clerk was heading for the orchard country west of Sydney.

We left Rio and, driven by the gusty southwest trades, sailed towards southern Africa. Through the daylight hours we watched albacore mackerel hunt flying fish and send them soaring into the air to escape. Thomas and Johnny, browned by the sun and wind, were thoroughly at home on the *Abbotsford* and enthralled by the work of the crew. The young sailors who scrambled up through the rigging held their greatest interest. Incessant questions from our small boys tried the patience of some older crewmen. Not at all dismayed by their gruffness, Thomas and Johnny called them "ruffty-tuffty sailors."

Late one afternoon I arose from a rest and whilst Rachel comforted little George, who was feverish from teething, I went out on deck to enjoy the warm breezes and the *Abbotsford* sailing gently over rippling waters. John and the two boys were nowhere in sight. I finally found my husband in a corner, deep in conversation with Amos Winters. "What have you done with the boys?" I demanded. "They're perfectly all right, my dear," said John. "Two young sailors told me they would take care of them."

Suddenly, Thomas's voice came from a great distance. "Mamma, Mamma, look up here! I can see all the way across the ocean!" Then I heard Johnny. "Me, too, Mamma! Look where I am!" Shading my eyes with my hands, I strained to look up amongst the sails, my heart beating fearfully fast. Tied to the backs of two barefoot young sailors, our children were on their way up a mast.

"Bring those boys down at once!" I shouted in sheer fright. I held my breath as the sailors paused and nimbly descended. They set Thomas and Johnny before me, but not before giving the children a conspiratorial wink. I marched our sons up to their father. "John Barnes! Rachel left these children in your care, but you'd rather talk to Amos than watch over them. You know they must be kept under strict supervision!" Then I strode off to the cabin, aware that I had embarrassed my husband in front of Amos Winters. That evening I apologized to both of them. For the rest of the way across the South Atlantic, I had to listen to Thomas and Johnny grumble that they would never learn to be sailors, and it was all my fault.

As our vessel rolled onward to Cape Town, Captain Cameron and the Ship's Carpenter began to prowl the barque and swing out over her gunwales in slings to scrutinize her hull. Watching the Captain, I knew something was not right. Before we left London, I had questioned my husband's faith in the man's competence, and now I prayed that the experienced master mariner would be able to solve any problem and ensure our safe passage to Port Jackson.

THREE
Onward to Sydney

One golden evening the great tableland dominating Cape Town came into view. We were expecting our vessel to spend a few days anchored in Table Bay, but at dinner Captain Cameron announced we would be there for three weeks whilst the barque's caulking was sealed with fresh tar. The days becalmed in scorching heat, he told us, had dried out the hull. "Tar has noxious fumes," he said, "and I'm advising you to seek accommodations ashore. You'll be reimbursed by the shipping agency." His passengers' annoyance was obvious, but, to be honest, I was more relieved than annoyed.

Next day, having been rowed ashore with the other cabin passengers, we set out to find a place to stay. We had vouched for Rachel, who was happy to be going with us because steerage passengers, bound for indenture, were to remain on board as usual. "The Cape has a particular attraction for ship jumpers," commented Mr. Bruce. "Assisted immigrants have tried to abandon ship here and disappear into the veldt of southern Africa rather than report to their assigned work in New South Wales. The Captain has the responsibility of delivering them to their rightful employers."

We strolled through Cape Town looking for a house to let and decided on a delightful residence with a thatch roof. The cottage, situated on the lowest reaches of the tableland, had an elaborate bell-shaped gable and half-doors opening onto a back garden surrounded with ferns. Similar furnished cottages seemed readily available, and we learned that Cape residents made a practice of letting their homes to ships' passengers because vessels often put in for lengthy repairs.

Our stay at the Cape was blissful. We relaxed in the warm, dry air of southern Africa and made use of the ample fresh water for drinking, bathing and washing clothes. Any clothing Rachel had washed in sea water had become laden with salt, and humidity had dampened and mildewed most of our belongings. Rachel, with the children playing happily around her, did our laundry and cooked for the family as John and I lazed in the garden or climbed the lower slopes of the tableland. I felt guilty enjoying myself whilst Rachel did all the chores, but when I tried to help the girl, I was told there was no need. "I'm enjoying myself, too, Mrs. Barnes!" she told me. "'Tis a grand house this is, and I've only three bairns to care for, not like the nine at home." She suggested I go for another walk.

We were enjoying breakfast in the garden one morning when a seaman delivered the message that passengers were to be aboard next day. The *Abbotsford*, scrubbed down and shipshape, reeked of new tar. We learned that in addition to her usual provisions, she had taken on fresh mutton and beef. Mr. Arnold had increased his collection as well. "Let me show you my latest treasures," he said. "These are bougainvillaea vines, and here I have some unusual ferns. I've also added a ram and three ewes to our livestock. They're excellent specimens of the Afrikaaner fat-tail, ordered by a grazier at Parramatta, who will cross-breed them with merinos."

Whilst his seamen stood by the capstans ready to weigh anchor, an impatient Captain Cameron addressed the assembled passengers. "Our first weeks at sea should follow routine, but on our approach to the Australian continent, be prepared for heavy weather." Having said all that he intended to say, he gave brisk orders to his crew, and the *Abbotsford* sailed for Port Jackson in Sydney Harbour.

Our vessel rounded the Cape and headed eastward, driven by strong westerly winds that carried her across the great expanse of the southern Indian Ocean. Here the days dragged interminably. Stories of our pasts had been told, plans for our futures revealed, publications from the Colonial Office and brochures from the dining saloon shelf read aloud and discussed. Amiable as we all were, we nevertheless had to make a deliberate effort to get along with one another.

With hopes of distracting us, the Surgeon pointed out in the clear waters the colourful schools of tropical fish. John and I spent hours with the children and Rachel watching the dolphins that played in the barque's wake leap in dripping arcs to match the motion of our vessel. One afternoon a large bird with an enormous wingspan floated from the clouds and wheeled around the mainmast. "An albatross," said Mr. Bruce, as the gigantic creature dipped low over the swells and swept out of sight. It left so quickly I had to sketch its graceful intrusion from memory. Days like this, I mused, made the whole voyage worthwhile. We would always remember the "glorious sights" promised by Mr. Bruce, and I now felt a kinship with all seafarers who roamed the oceans of the world.

My euphoria, however, was short-lived. The *Abbotsford* was proceeding under bleak skies into chilling gusts. The First Officer, helped by the Ship's Carpenter, began spending any free moments fencing his trees into deck corners and fastening canvas over them to keep away the salt spray. Smaller plants filled every cranny of his cabin.

Meanwhile, we huddled in our cabin under our wool travel blankets in all our warm clothing. My apprehension about upcoming "heavy weather" left me gripped by headaches. John, always more stoic than I was, reminded me that we were in the good hands of an experienced Captain.

The officers had often commented that ours had been an especially smooth voyage. Now the winds were fierce—more forceful than we had ever felt them. The main deck was awash, and any crewman who crossed it had to cling to a line strung amidships. The children, no longer able to play outside, were bad-tempered. I worried about my family's safety and my queasy stomach as we headed into rising seas. My anxiety made my headaches worse.

Whilst the Captain held course at latitude forty degrees south, the ocean suddenly turned vicious, plunging the barque into deep hollows and tossing her up onto foam-laden crests. Erratic winds stretched the canvas screamingly taut, then dropped, only to crack the sails full again. Barely able to control my nausea, I curled up in bed and said a silent prayer for sailors sent aloft to trim sails and for Rachel, confined below with the other steerage passengers.

That night a storm hit the *Abbotsford*. It threw us from our beds and tore the cradle from its lashings. In the booming darkness John and I gathered our frantic children into our narrow bed whilst the barque rolled and pitched. Thunder growled overhead as our trunk lurched loose and smashed into the rocking chair. Our looking glass, basin, jug and chamber pot crashed into fragments.

Dawn brought no respite. Through the roar we heard the Surgeon shouting, "I'm coming in!" John pulled back the bolts, and a seaman accompanying Mr. Bruce hauled against the winds and heaved the door open. The seaman, who was responsible for our part of the ship, had a coil of rope slung across his body and carried a lantern and a canvas bag of tools. The two men staggered across the sill and the door slammed shut, but not before I saw a frightening wall of water rising up behind.

"Let me give each of you a wee look over," said Mr. Bruce. "I wouldn't want any harm to come to you in this blow." With shutters latched over the window, the cabin was in complete blackness, and the seaman held up the lantern so that the Surgeon could peer at us. "Only bruises, nary a thing broken," he declared, and instructed us to remain in bed. The seaman inspected the damage done to the cabin, gathered up shards of glass and pottery and secured our belongings. He promised to return with another basin, jug and chamber pot.

Torrents of water poured over the *Abbotsford* as she careened into mountainous seas. John and I spent the day praying. We strained to hear the regular clang of the ship's bell, hoping for reassurance of our safety. I suddenly recalled reading about convicts lashed into steerage hammocks during a storm and shuddered when I thought of Rachel and her friends confined below. Although not lashed to their beds, they were battened down in a steerage compartment, helpless in the airless darkness and doomed if the *Abbotsford* should founder. I begged God to give them courage.

The Surgeon came with limes and biscuits, but in these raging seas nausea had quite overwhelmed me. I clung to a bedpost and retched into the basin. John, his body aching from bracing himself in the bed, struggled to keep his crying children close against him. The stench of vomit and excrement in the closed cabin was insufferable. I had horrifying doubts the *Abbotsford* would ever reach Port Jackson.

John prayed aloud for God's protection. "Merciful Saviour, we beg thee to hear us in our hour of need. In the name of thy Son, Jesus Christ, deliver us to a safe haven. Amen." He repeated the prayer many times. Surely our Gracious Father would not doom us all to an ocean grave.

Each time the Surgeon came to check on us that day, we caught glimpses of looming headlands, ominous under tumbling clouds and jagged lightning. The surf boiled over black outcroppings and poured onto a desolate coast. This was the treacherous southern edge of the continent, graveyard of so many ships, and despite the helmsman's determined efforts to bear off from shore, the storm was driving our barque closer to the reefs.

"Have faith!" said Mr. Bruce. "I've known the *Abbotsford* to escape worse storms." The Surgeon's words were of some comfort as I recalled with terror newspaper articles about migrants who had drowned along this coast. One illustration had shown the skeletons of scores of ships scattered at the bottom of rain-swept cliffs. The *Abbotsford* heaved and groaned, and I prayed that every timber in her hull would stay in place. Then I thought of our responsible, cautious Captain and said a silent prayer of thanks for his meticulous seamanship.

"The pumps are still churning," reported Mr. Bruce the next morning, "although crewmen on pump duty are far gone with exhaustion. The masts are holding firm, but if the *Abbotsford* is to outrun this storm, the Captain will have to risk sacrificing canvas." The master mariner took the risk, and we could hear sails snapping open and screaming when howling winds stretched them taut. I prayed for the sailors who were ordered to climb up into the savagery of the storm to unfurl canvas. Mere moments later, we felt the barque lunge forward with a new surge of power.

As abruptly as the *Abbotsford* had been seized by the storm, she pulled free of its force. John offered a prayer of gratitude to God for saving us all from certain death. "Thou hast heard our petitions, Gracious Saviour, and we give thee humble and hearty thanks for thy great mercy. Amen." Meanwhile, the rains continued and the sturdy *Abbotsford* rolled and pitched, but she sailed steadily onward. Rachel appeared at our door, scooped up the three children and kissed them. "Praise be to God!" she said. "Down in that blackness, I thought I'd been called for!"

The passengers were a pale-faced, hungry and filthy lot as the *Abbotsford*, battered but still sound, made her way towards Van Diemen's Land. Setting ourselves to rights, we washed our clothes and cleaned our quarters and then slept long hours. No lives had been lost, and our church service on the next calm day was the most fervent of all. Captain Cameron read a Collect of thanksgiving from Prayers to be Used at Sea, and passengers and crew sang "O God, Our Help in Ages Past."

Towering in front of us on a blustery afternoon in mid-March were the strangely fluted black cliffs of the Tasman Peninsula on Van Diemen's Land. The *Abbotsford* was sailing into Port Arthur, destination of thousands of convicts. Flocks of seabirds swirled above us when our vessel settled at anchor.

"No one goes ashore," announced Captain Cameron. "This is a penal settlement and not safe for any of us. Chandlers will send out fresh provisions. Keep clear of the ruffians bringing supplies aboard. They're emancipated felons and a nasty lot."

Whilst the *Abbotsford* rode at anchor in the harbour, the Captain and his officers supervised ex-convicts who carried food and gear up a rope ladder. Crewmen swarmed over the vessel checking canvas, rigging and fittings, and making repairs. Thomas, Johnny and George were enchanted with the activity; John and I thanked God the boys were alive and fit to enjoy it.

In his rare free moments the First Officer struggled to repot his plants and trees on deck. I came upon him one afternoon carrying trays of wilted seedlings from his cabin and throwing them overboard. "Oh, no! You must be able to save them, Mr. Arnold!" I exclaimed. "I regret that I cannot, Mrs. Barnes," he replied. "They've been too many days without care. Only one voyage in three is entirely calm enough for me to deliver plantings to my good wife." He trudged back to his cabin to continue his task.

The progress of the *Abbotsford* towards Sydney became intermittent when the barque began to struggle against the Australian Current around the southeastern coast of New South Wales. Impatient to start our new lives in the colony, we found those last few days endless. Yet on the shining morning of April 5th, 1841, we awakened to find the *Abbotsford* gliding on an incoming tide past golden sandstone cliffs guarding the entrance to Sydney. The haven of our prayers was within sight, and I offered silent thanks to our Heavenly Father for our family's safe arrival. We dressed quickly and stood at the rails in the glow of an autumn sunrise.

As our vessel entered the calm waters, the Surgeon pointed out the sights on the low hills of the city: residential bungalows in orderly rows, taller commercial buildings in the central area, the massive Hyde Park Barracks and the graceful spire of Saint James Church. Small steam tugboats, as smoky as those on the Thames, chugged out to meet the *Abbotsford* and guide her to a berth in the vast harbour.

No sooner had the barque been made secure at Port Jackson in Sydney Harbour than she was boarded by colonial authorities. They examined passengers and crew, checked our papers and those of the *Abbotsford* itself. When we learned of vessels moored out in the harbour in quarantine because of illness aboard, we were openly thankful to Mr. Bruce for his conscientious care, lime juice and all.

Whilst Rachel and I packed up the family's smaller belongings, John and a seaman crated the larger pieces, or what was left of them. The cradle could be repaired and the carpet cleaned, but our looking glass, jug, basin, chamber pot and my rocking chair would have to be replaced, expenditures I had not anticipated.

In the evening John and I joined Amos Winters and the Dartnells for a farewell supper in the saloon. In the midst of songs, speeches and toasts, Rachel brought Thomas, Johnny and George from the cabin to be embraced by everyone. John gave Rachel an envelope with five pounds for her devoted assistance.

"You're a gem, Rachel," I said. "Here's my address at Sydney. Please write to me. Be good to yourself." Teary-eyed, I embraced the girl. "You're not to be concerned about me, Mrs. Barnes," she countered. "Five bairns will keep me out of mischief!" I reckoned their widowed father could be a greater challenge.

Mr. Arnold handed every cabin passenger a gift of a dozen packets of vegetable seeds, and Mr. Perry came forward to give each of the boys a small canvas bag of wooden bricks, a numeral carved on every brick. He presented each of the ladies with a set of carved wooden napkin rings which, as you know, I have kept for my lifetime.

And thus, my darling granddaughters, the *Abbotsford* carried us for five months across sixteen thousand miles to New South Wales "safely and in the best of health." A life different from anything we had ever known lay before us.

In her eighty-fourth year, shortly after completing this story of her voyage to New South Wales for Nellie and Lilla, Elizabeth King Ellen Barnes fell ill. She died on the 18th of January, 1886. In the pages that follow, Elizabeth's hope that someone might record the events of her colonial life has been realized.

FOUR

Parkside

So he bringeth them unto their desired haven.
— PSALM 107:30

On the bright morning of April 6th, 1841, Elizabeth Barnes stood at the port rail of the *Abbotsford* and looked down on a crowded wharf at Port Jackson. Clattering carts, screaming guards and clanking shackles pierced the cool autumn air as she watched an Overseer snap his knotted rope above the heads of fettered men clad in yellow who struggled to unload the barque. "Move on, ye useless canary bastards!" Elizabeth flinched when the prisoners, shackled at the ankles and chained to one another, shied away from the stinging rope only to have red-coated soldiers prod them back into line with bayonets. What sort of place had she come to?

Into this confusion, proceeding cautiously, came a shiny black carriage pulled by a black matched pair, their clinking harness brasses glistening in the sunshine. A tall coachman in grey livery halted the team and helped from the carriage a woman in an emerald dress and a bonnet and shawl of darker green. He stood protectively beside her whilst she scanned the *Abbotsford*. "Susan!" shouted John over the chaos on the pier. His sister smiled through tears when John lifted George into his arms and descended to the wharf. Holding Thomas and Johnny by the hand, Elizabeth followed.

"My dear, how splendid to see you!" John Barnes held his sister close to him, and her tears dampened his frock coat. "May I introduce Elizabeth and our sons, Thomas, Johnny and George." Elizabeth embraced her sister-in-law, whose letters from Sydney she had often read. Susan Nichols' ringlets were fairer than John's brown hair, yet she thought sister and brother looked alike; they had the same large brown eyes and cheerful countenance. The boys in their sailor suits, who were eager to get close to the black horses, allowed their aunt to hug and kiss them.

Susan Nichols introduced her coachman, Alfred Brown. He bowed, then assisted them all into the carriage and placed the two portmanteaux under his seat. As the coachman slowly turned his team around, Thomas and Johnny were fascinated by all the horses competing with Alfred's team for leeway on the wharf.

Manoeuvring around barrels of rum, bales of fleece and crates of goods, past soldiers, convicts and their Overseers, and up a slope thronged with waiting emigrants proved to be a lengthy and demanding task for Alfred and the horses. Elizabeth was unnerved by the sight of prisoners and guards and the sounds of whips and shackles. How horribly inhumane! She was grateful her children were paying more attention to horses in harnesses than convicts in chains.

When Susan reached for her hand and smiled encouragement, Elizabeth felt herself relax a little. She looked forward to getting to know this friendly woman, much younger than she was yet so self-possessed in this strange land, and to meeting her husband, Robert, and their little sons, Robbie and Francis. Until John had their house ready on the western slopes, she and the boys were to remain with the Nichols family.

"Sydney is a bustling city with paved streets and brick buildings!" Elizabeth exclaimed to Susan. "It's become a busy place," replied her sister-in-law, "and growing very quickly." The team took them to a residential area and came to a halt in front of a large brick bungalow with Parkside lettered on a transom of ruby glass. "Now do take a good look around the house," said Susan, "whilst I fetch the servants to meet you." The boys had their own agenda. "Where did the black horses go, Papa?" asked Thomas. "Can we see where the tall man took them?" Susan pointed out a stable at the back of the property, and John took the three boys off to find Alfred Brown and the horses.

On that April morning, after nearly five months at sea, Elizabeth Barnes stood unsteadily in the Nichols' large drawing room, where a French window opened onto a terrace and a flower-filled back garden. Wistfully, she looked at the Broadwood pianoforte in a corner of the room and wondered if Susan would allow her to practise. The fragrance of overblown roses drifted up from a crystal bowl set on an inlaid table. She stared at the India rug on the polished hardwood floor, the mahogany furniture, red and gold glass lamps and porcelain ornaments. How would she ever supervise her children in this elegant house? The tall clock in the hall chimed eleven as she wandered into the dining room, where the table could seat twelve, into Robert Nichols' leather-furnished library and into the four bedrooms.

Still affected by the motion of the ship, she walked carefully along the broad, covered verandah around three sides of the house and discovered two white birds with yellow crests sitting on a railing. At the rear of the property, in addition to the stable and a small paddock, she saw two small brick buildings connected to the house by a flagstone footpath. Someday, she promised herself, she would have a home like this.

"There you are!" Susan appeared on the verandah and shooed away the white birds. With her were two tall women in the uniforms of cook and maid and a plump young girl in a muslin dress who held the hands of two small boys. "I should like to introduce Alfred's wife, Mrs. Brown, who is our cook, and their daughter, Dinah, who is our housemaid. And this is our nurserymaid, Mary Fleming, who will care for your boys as she does for our Robbie and Francis."

"I do hope we won't cause too much disruption in your routine," said Elizabeth. "I must tell you that Thomas, Johnny and George are active children."

"Just as they should be," said Mrs. Brown. "You come along with me, Mrs. Barnes, out to my kitchen and tell me what you would like me to make for the wee lads' meals." Mrs. Brown's kitchen and the servants' quarters, Elizabeth discovered, were the two small buildings at the end of the flagstone footpath.

When she commented on the location of the kitchen, Cook replied, "Proper houses here are built with kitchens separate, Mrs. Barnes. Keeps cooking smells and heat away from the house itself, like basement kitchens in England. And with windows on all four sides, I can have a bit of a breeze in the hot months. It can be a scorcher here at Christmas, it can." She served Elizabeth a cup of tea and questioned her about the boys' meals. Revived by the tea, Elizabeth left Mrs. Brown to her luncheon preparations and strolled back to the house.

"Alfred's horses have names," announced Johnny, as he and his brother came bounding out of the stable. "They're called Ebony and Trojan." Thomas added, "They look the same, but they're not, really. Trojan has a small white patch of hair on his left hind fetlock. That's at the back of his leg above his hoof, Mamma." Elizabeth smiled at her son, thinking his visit to the stable had been put to good use. "We're going to learn all about horses. Alfred's going to teach us." Alfred Brown, it seemed, had replaced Mr. Perry as tutor.

Warm breezes rustled her maid's uniform as Dinah set tables on the verandah and served the adults a light luncheon of cold roast chicken slices in aspic, cress and cucumbers, fresh rolls and a summer pudding. The Barnes children, seated with their cousins and Mary Fleming at a separate table, were more eager to chase the two resident white birds than to eat the eggy bread, applesauce and ginger snaps that Mrs. Brown had made especially for them. After lunch they romped with the nurserymaid and the Nichols children in the park across the street, where they gave the remains of their eggy bread to magpies and tried to see how many rosellas they could find perched in the gumtrees.

Late in the afternoon, Alfred brought Susan's husband, Robert, home from his office in the city. George Robert Nichols, who seemed to be about John's age, was a handsome man and very tall, well over six feet, with a kindly grace about him. The two couples, seated in cushioned rattan chairs on the verandah, were observed by the two persistent white birds, which were sulphur-crested cockatoos, explained Susan. When Dinah had served them sherry, Robert said, "You must tell us about your voyage." John and Elizabeth looked at each other and chuckled.

"Parts of it we would rather forget," said John, and then spoke of ports of call, vegetation, birds and sea creatures they had seen. Elizabeth talked of the Christmas celebrations and the crossing-the-equator party and surprised John by happily relating the experience of finding Thomas and Johnny partway up a mast. Robert Nichols was an appreciative listener. He had made the return voyage himself as a youth, for he had received his education in England.

Whilst the adults were enjoying their sherry and conversation, Mary Fleming, much to the consternation of Thomas and Johnny, bathed all five children. She supervised their evening meal at a table in the nursery and presented the children, scrubbed and fed, to the adults to say goodnight. The three Barnes boys firmly clutched stuffed horse, lion and bunny. As the nursemaid led them away to bed, Thomas and Johnny looked very disgruntled. Susan commented, "I trust you approve of Mary's care of the boys. She came well recommended by a friend of ours." Elizabeth rushed to reassure her hostess. "I'm very grateful you've arranged for her to care for our children," she said. "When we arrived, I was concerned lest they disturb your lovely home."

"No worries!" said Susan. "And Robert and I thought you might like a rest after the long voyage before you begin the rigours of homesteading." Elizabeth wondered how long it would take Thomas and Johnny, following five months of adventure at sea, to become accustomed to the routines of a nurserymaid.

Alfred, his coachman's hands covered in white gloves, announced dinner. He carried in savoury pumpkin soup, smoked salmon garnished with sour cream, roast beef with Yorkshire pudding, roasted potatoes, baked onions and carrots in a cream sauce, followed by a sherry trifle and a selection of cheeses and sliced apples, plums and pears, all served competently by Dinah. Whilst Elizabeth sat at the long mahogany table, sipping a glass of colonial red wine sparkling in the candlelight, she found it difficult to realize she was on the other side of the world from civilized England.

"I hope," said Susan, as she poured tea, "you will have a good long visit with us. It's been so many years since I've been with my family." John replied slowly, "Unfortunately, I must leave in three days' time, because I've engaged a convict Overseer and his crew to clear our land." His sister's face fell. "Oh, John, I am disappointed you must leave so soon! Very well, I shall enjoy the company of Elizabeth and your boys all the more!"

Attention turned to Robert, whose comments had made it clear he was a patriotic spokesman for New South Wales and a passionate advocate of colonial self-government. John asked him about growing up in the colony.

"My father was Isaac Nichols, Sydney's first Postmaster, and we had a comfortable life. When I returned from school in England, I took my articles with W.H. Moore, Esquire. Many of my Sydney friends, however, received their education from a most excellent convict teacher." Elizabeth could think only of yellow-clad felons chained together and beaten into submission on a wharf. Robert continued, "Early education, even preparation for entrance to British universities, can be provided by ruined clergymen and schoolmasters sentenced to transportation for insignificant offences. Some, particularly Irish Catholics, were transported on false convictions."

"Surely you're not serious!" protested Elizabeth.

"Dear lady, New South Wales is a place founded on many injustices. In a future election I intend to run for the Legislative Council. Not that I promise to cure all the ills of my native land, but I should like to help establish a government in the colony which doesn't depend on the decisions of a Parliament sixteen thousand miles away, nor on the minions it sends to do its bidding."

When she and John were about to retire, Elizabeth asked Robert, "What sort of person was the convict teacher you mentioned?"

"Anthony? He was an earnest Irish cleric and a brilliant man, much younger than my father and quite different from him, but they had both come to the colony in chains and were the best of friends."

"In chains? But you said your father was the first Postmaster in Sydney!"

"So he was, but in 1791 he arrived here as a Third Fleet convict. When Father was emancipated, he became a successful sheep breeder and a publican before he established the Post Office in 1809. He was Principal Superintendent of Convicts in Sydney until 1814. I'm the son of a felon, Elizabeth, native-born and called a Currency Lad. And you settlers from Britain, I should tell you, are known as Sterling Folk!"

That night, tired as she was, Elizabeth could not sleep. She still felt the motion of the *Abbotsford* and wondered when her body would realize it had reached dry land. Finally falling into a restless slumber, she dreamt of an Overseer with a bloody whip guarding convict teachers who instructed her sons as she looked on helplessly.

The next morning John went with Robert to his office and rode on in the carriage to the wharf to arrange transportation of their belongings southwestward to their property. Once he had settled his family at his sister's home, John was to leave by coach on the 180-mile journey to Yass. Weeks would go by whilst an Overseer and convicts felled trees and cut the timber into slabs for the Barneses' first home and farm buildings. When John finished building the house, he would send for Elizabeth and the children. Elizabeth appreciated the strangeness of the tasks which lay ahead of him, for not only must he deal with a convict Overseer but also construct a house from suggestions in a Colonial Office manual.

"You look bereft," said Susan, when she and Elizabeth were strolling arm in arm in the garden after John's departure. "Let's see something of Sydney tomorrow. In the evening the Graingers will be joining us for dinner, and on the following afternoon we'll visit Miss Penelope Anderson, a friend of mine at Balmain who has asked us to call." The mere thought of all that socializing with strangers left Elizabeth feeling quite overwhelmed.

After lunch the next day the two women set out in the carriage drawn by Ebony and Trojan. George Street in central Sydney, Elizabeth observed, was a crowded thoroughfare filled with stores. "A mile and a half of shopping," said Susan. Military officers, confident in their authority over this outpost of the British Empire, strolled in gold-braided magnificence along every footpath. Conversing in doorways in the morning sunshine were government officials and groups of merchants, all looking as if they belonged in London. John would be right at home amongst the storekeepers here, mused Elizabeth.

Improving and extending the streets of Sydney were road workers who, like the convicts on the dock, were chained together and clad in yellow with a black arrow painted up the back. The Canary Gangs, explained Susan, were made up of felons who had tried to escape. At the street corners, hoping for employment, stood clumps of ragged, grey-faced men and women; they were emancipists, Susan told her, prisoners who had qualified for a conditional pardon. Elizabeth recalled Dorcas Dartnell's comment about convicts hardened by transportation and imprisonment and wondered whether she and John would ever want to hire an emancipist.

With what little money she had, Elizabeth bought knitting and sewing supplies. Susan's purchases were much more elaborate, and she was soon relieved of boxes of garments by Alfred. The coachman then drove them to the top of a spacious park, the Domain, where he halted his team and helped the ladies down.

Elizabeth appreciated the stroll out to a viewpoint where they met Alfred spreading a blanket on the grass near a rocky promontory. On a linen cloth he set out their luncheon: small pieces of cold roast chicken, pickles, fresh cheese scones, grapes, raisin cake and a bottle of wine. He returned to his nearby carriage, placed nosebags on Ebony and Trojan, and kept his horses company whilst he watched over the ladies and ate sliced roast beef between thick pieces of crusty bread.

When they were drinking their wine, Susan said, "Down on that outcropping, Mrs. Macquarie, wife of Lachlan Macquarie, a former Governor, used to sit and admire this scene. Legend has it she longed to board a ship and return to Scotland. Over to the left is Farm Cove, where plantings were attempted by the first convicts. The next promontory is Bennelong Point, named for an aboriginal who was taken to England to meet royalty, and beyond it is Sydney Cove, with the new wharves at Semicircular Quay. Look at the narrows, where the two shores seem almost within bridging distance. Beyond the narrows is Balmain, an original land grant given to William Balmain, an Assistant Surgeon with the First Fleet. That's where we'll visit Penelope Anderson tomorrow."

Despite Susan's companionship and the Nichols' generous hospitality, Elizabeth felt strangely adrift. Until she was in her own home, she would not feel settled. As she sat looking out from the viewpoint on that autumn day in 1841, she was fascinated by the huge flotilla of ships in Sydney Harbour. Vessels of varying sizes floated at anchor whilst their longboats plied to and from shore. Other vessels were secured at wharves, their crewmen scrambling over them to make them seaworthy for the next voyage. With gigantic loads on their shoulders, lines of chained convict shore workers laboured to fill the holds, and departing emigrants straggled up the gangplanks.

Elizabeth, curious about Susan's well-trained house servants, asked her sister-in-law how she had managed to acquire them. "Mary Fleming is an assisted immigrant recommended by a friend," explained Susan, "but Alfred, Mrs. Brown and Dinah are Special Convicts. My father-in-law, Isaac Nichols, was one of the Specials, skilled convicts who are valued in the colony. Mrs. Brown has told me Alfred was steward on an estate in Kent, and she and Dinah served in the great house. When Alfred challenged the squire because he had tried to have his way with Dinah, a trumped-up charge of larceny was laid on the three of them. Transportation to New South Wales was a better sentence than incarceration in Coldbath Fields House of Correction."

Elizabeth stared at her sister-in-law. Why should a father face false charges for protecting his daughter? And why should his wife and daughter be falsely labelled criminals, too? When Alfred helped her into the carriage after the picnic, she found it hard to believe this kindly man and his wife and daughter were transported convicts.

At dinner that evening Elizabeth met Hester and Noah Grainger, long-time friends of Susan and Robert. Noah was an accountant in the Surveyor General's office, and Hester was a volunteer at the Female Immigrants' Home. They were both interested in hearing about Elizabeth and John's plans. Later, Hester played the pianoforte and Elizabeth was persuaded to sing several folk songs.

The following afternoon Alfred drove Elizabeth and Susan some distance to the tree-lined streets of Balmain, where he brought the horses to a halt in front of a two-storey brick home. The atmosphere of Balmain—tall brick houses, walled front gardens, paved roads and footpaths, and rows of leafy trees—brought to mind elegant parts of London.

Their hostess was a short, voluptuous woman, much-bejewelled, and elaborately dressed in a gown of cerise silk. She led them through the house to a sunlit conservatory furnished with cushioned settees, a tea table and shiny jardinieres filled with unusual plants. A pretty Irish maid, her abundant copper hair scarcely tamed by a starched cap, set out a selection of delicacies. On the lace-covered tea table were plates of the thinnest crustless sandwiches of minced ham and cucumber slices, pinwheels of even thinner bread swirled with smoked salmon or soft cheese, small luscious scones with strawberry preserves and clotted cream, and tarts and iced cakes so diminutive they were but a fleeting taste. A silver teapot held a tantalizing blend of flavours, and a china basket overflowed with pieces of minty chocolate.

When Susan and Elizabeth complimented Miss Anderson on the refreshments, she replied in confidential tones, "The Duchess of Bedford prefers such refreshments at this time of day. All the current rage in London, you must agree, Mrs. Barnes." Elizabeth merely smiled. Perhaps in Mayfair. Certainly not in Cheapside.

Penelope Anderson lifted her lorgnette to inspect Elizabeth and continued, "I think you are very brave to live in the bush, Mrs. Barnes. Sydney is far enough for me, thank you. As you can see, we have all the creature comforts: servants, shopping, society, and entertainments too numerous to mention. It's such a pity you will not be in Sydney this winter for the regimental balls. The band plays all the latest music for quadrilles and waltzes, and you should see the dress uniforms and the haute couture, scarcely six months behind the London fashions! What will you do for entertainment at Yass?"

"I expect to be too busy with my family and our farm to require entertainment, Miss Anderson." Elizabeth knew she was being churlish, but she was bridling at Penelope Anderson's condescension. Susan shook her fair curls and giggled behind her hand. Penelope took no notice and went on.

"I must tell you, Mrs. Barnes, accommodations on the track to the western slopes will be non-existent or primitive in the extreme. You will encounter long-horned cattle, those dangerous beasts which are allowed to roam freely. Your progress is sure to be blocked by Iron Gangs of vicious convicts, and if your horses go lame, the convicts will bail up your coach and plunder all the passengers. I have heard of conveyances losing their wheels, causing injuries to everyone aboard. I am appalled your husband would allow you to undertake such a journey without him. You say you will have small children with you? You have my deepest sympathy."

Elizabeth held her tongue. Her hostess continued in full voice. "I would never go to the western slopes myself, of course. The climate is simply unbearable: miserably cold, wet winters and blistering hot, fly-ridden summers, completely insupportable, my dear. Many settlers, whole families in fact, have not survived and lie buried in the hills."

Elizabeth chose to ignore Penelope's continuing comments and enjoy the view of the park below and the narrows in the distance. The sun shining on the masts and yards of moored ships cast shadowy lines on the glassy water like spiderwebs over a still pond. Along a shaded footpath in the park, a stalwart young officer strolled arm in arm with a young woman in pink-striped dimity who protected her complexion with a pink parasol. What a civilized scene, thought Elizabeth, such a contrast to the sights at dockside. Her musings were interrupted by Penelope's maid, who offered her a selection of tiny tarts on a silver tray.

"Penelope Anderson always means well," said Susan on their way back to the Nichols' home. "She just exaggerates the negative aspects of any new situation." Elizabeth smiled slightly. "I admit I found her patronizing," she said. "She lives in a beautiful home and appears to be independently wealthy. Why did she leave London for the colony?"

"She was born to a Covent Garden flower-seller who attached herself to the late Captain Anderson and followed him out to New South Wales. The Captain did very well for himself in the notorious Rum Corps. It was common knowledge that Penelope was not his daughter, yet he gave her his name and left her his fortune."

Elizabeth supposed she would become accustomed to forming friendships with people of much different backgrounds from her own. George Robert Nichols, a well-known solicitor in the colony, was a son of the convict who became Sydney's first Postmaster. Penelope Anderson, a member of Sydney society, was a daughter of a camp follower and recipient of an inheritance of dubious origins. One's beginnings, it seemed, did not present any impediment here.

Meanwhile, far to the southwest near Yass, John Barnes had been joined by a penal Overseer with a bloody knotted rope. The nasty man, eager to put his gang of twenty-two convicts to work, appeared the day after John's arrival. The property was not heavily treed, a fact which later became significant, and the gang made easy progress felling trees and sawing them into rough slabs for the house and outbuildings and into rails for fences. The pitiable convicts wore leg irons with long chains connecting each one to the next, and when John tried to speak to one of them, the Overseer told John he was interfering with discipline and warned him off.

No such experiences appeared in John's letters to Elizabeth. He wrote only of matters that he hoped would be of interest and comfort to her.

Near Yass, May 1st, 1841

My Dearest Elizabeth,
I write to inform you of my safe arrival at Yass. The coach trip was uncomfortable but uneventful, and I am no longer worried about your taking the journey with the boys.

The countryside around Yass is, I am sure, all you have ever longed for—endless green hills sweeping in gentle slopes towards a distant horizon and groves of tall trees, unlike any variety in England, silhouetted against the sky. In the woods, the bush it's called here, the thick vegetation is home to interesting creatures. Dingoes (tawny-coloured wild dogs, bigger than a fox but with similar characteristics) can be seen in early evening. They will be a danger to our sheep, and we'll need to have a sheepdog on guard. I have yet to see a kangaroo or wallaby. They are shy animals, according to our neighbours, and one has to watch carefully at dusk to see them at the edge of the bush. There are birds of great variety as well.

We have pines on our property to use for our furniture and both gum and box eucalypts. The gumtrees with their smooth trunks shed their bark in great strips, which can be used as a kind of thatch. The box eucalypts have a heavy bark, and pieces can be removed intact to be used for carrying items of considerable weight, or for building shelters. Boxbark huts, they're called.

Of great help and comfort to me are the Munros, who live on a large farm a mile to the east of us. Thaddeus Munro saw me walking from the village to our property on the day I arrived and came over at once to offer his advice on locating our homestead. A low hill close to the road has a large, level crest to it, wide enough for our house, your garden and some outbuildings. Unfortunately, it is not treed, and plantings will be needed to shade our yard. The one tree on the hill is a magnificent dome-shaped specimen called a kurrajong, and Thaddeus has advised me to place our house in its shade. Whilst the convict crew clears our land, Thaddeus and his son Allan will help me build our homestead. Meanwhile, I am to stay with the Munro family.

I miss you and the boys, but I know Susan and Robert will take good care of you. My prayers are with you all.

I remain your loving husband,

John

Imagining their spacious property and new home, Elizabeth re-read John's letter many times. She longed for the day she would live there.

Several days later she and Susan were sitting on the verandah, admiring the last blooms of tall dahlias in the borders whilst Mary

Fleming played with the children under the Sydney gumtrees in the park opposite. Whilst they waited for an afternoon guest, Elizabeth asked Susan how she and Robert had met.

Susan smiled at the memory. "I was governess to Hester and Noah Grainger's two young sons when Robert came from the solicitor's office one morning to discuss a property transaction. I was sitting on the verandah instructing the boys. Noah Grainger and Robert sat on the verandah, too, and Noah commented that Robert was paying more attention to me than to the property transaction. Robert began to court me soon afterwards."

Susan's guest for tea that afternoon was Mrs. Caroline Chisholm, who eventually arrived, not in a trap or buggy, but mounted on a white horse. Susan and Elizabeth came down from the verandah to welcome her. Mrs. Chisholm dismounted smoothly and looped the reins around the gatepost. She did not wait for an introduction. "Mrs. Barnes? How do you do? I'm Caroline Chisholm." A strong hand came forward to grasp Elizabeth's. "And dear Susan! So good to see you! Are you well?"

"Yes, thank you, Caroline," said Susan. Elizabeth was tentatively stroking Caroline's white horse, which had nuzzled her hand in hopes of a treat. He looked taller and more vigorous than any horses she had seen ridden by ladies in Dorsetshire, yet he seemed docile and friendly.

"Magnificent animal, isn't he? Captain and I go everywhere together. He's very well behaved and can move with great speed if we are in danger." Caroline Chisholm astounded Elizabeth by making the sign of the cross. She swept up onto the verandah and apologized for her tardiness.

Elizabeth watched Caroline casually toss her bonnet and shawl on a chair. A tall, russet-haired woman with grey eyes and a cherubic face yet a no-nonsense manner, Caroline Chisholm was patroness of immigrant girls at Sydney, and Susan was certain she would be able to find Elizabeth and John a girl-of-all-work for their farm. Caroline had asked for the meeting that afternoon.

"Mrs. Barnes, I had hoped to interview your husband as well."

"I'm sorry, Caroline. John has already gone to Yass."

"Then I'll rely on the opinion Robert Nichols has given me." Elizabeth felt affronted for John's sake, but Susan was hiding a smile as Caroline continued. "The girl I have in mind grew up on a farm in Berkshire. Her name is Bess Mason and she's a nineteen-year-old assisted immigrant who's good with children and capable of doing all the usual farm chores. Her employer, a married farmer at Penrith, forced his attentions on her and when she resisted his demands, beat her severely, brought her into Sydney and left her in the street. We are restoring her to health at our shelter and intend to find her safe employment. Can you guarantee a compassionate situation for her on your farm, Mrs. Barnes?"

Wide-eyed, Elizabeth thought of her gentle, conscientious husband and declared firmly, "I can promise you the girl will be safe with us." With a spasm of anxiety, Elizabeth remembered Rachel Gibson on the *Abbotsford* and hoped the girl from Newtownards was being well treated by the widower Garvey at Camden.

"I'm glad to hear it," said Caroline. "You will pay her the usual rate for assisted immigrants, twenty pounds a year, and although she's not officially bound to you, I must insist she be under your care until she comes of age." Whilst Dinah served the ladies afternoon tea, Caroline told them of her mission to ensure the protection of women immigrants in New South Wales.

As their visitor rose to put on her bonnet and shawl, she looked intently at Elizabeth. "Mrs. Barnes, our shelter often comes to the aid of girls who are much better employed in the interior rather than here amongst the temptations of Sydney. I often have girls who need a chaperone on their way to the country. Would you please contact me before you leave for Yass?"

"I should be pleased to do so," replied Elizabeth. She wondered how, on a lengthy coach trip, she would be able to supervise three children, the unknown Bess Mason and Caroline Chisholm's girls as well.

The women walked to the gate to find Mary Fleming and the children admiring Captain. The white horse had lowered his head to sniff inquisitively at the little boys, who giggled when he fanned their hair with his breath. Meanwhile, Caroline greeted Mary Fleming in a genial manner and they chatted about her well-being and employment with the Nichols. Captain's ears pricked forward when Caroline mounted, and the white horse broke into an easy canter when they crossed the park.

"What an interesting woman!" said Elizabeth. "Do you see her often? And why does she cross herself?"

"She has a home out at Windsor, and I haven't seen her for some time. She often travels around the colony, taking her new charges to country employment. Mary Fleming is one of Caroline's, as is the maid who served us tea at Penelope Anderson's home. I'm sure Caroline Chisholm intends to correct, single-handedly, abuses in the treatment of female assisted immigrants in New South Wales. She's a Roman Catholic, probably the first one you've ever known."

Such a strange land, Elizabeth thought. I've just become acquainted with a papist!

On Sundays she rode in the carriage with Robert and Susan and their servants to Saint James Church of England. One of the women servants always stayed behind to care for the children, who were too young to participate in the lengthy services at the impressive sandstone edifice. Elizabeth was surprised to learn that the church, which had been built by convicts, had been designed by a convict architect, Francis Greenway. He had also designed the massive Hyde Park Barracks, located directly across the street. During church services Mary Fleming was permitted to sit in the congregation; the Browns, who were felons, were relegated to the convict section in the right gallery, watched by guards standing at each end.

When Susan went off to her frequent afternoon engagements, Elizabeth practised on the Broadwood pianoforte or sat on the terrace, embroidering, crocheting or knitting and watching the children at play. Surrounding her were flower borders where lazy bees hummed as they ambled from one bloom to another. Gaillardia blossomed richly in wine and gold, and chrysanthemums nodded their great bronze heads above a profusion of marigolds. It's April, mused Elizabeth, and I'm surrounded by the colours of autumn. As she began to doze in the sunshine one soporific afternoon, she had a vision of their farm at Yass and soon dreamt of lush green hills covered in woolly sheep, a kitchen garden green with vegetables, a cow resting in the shade of the kurrajong tree, hens flocking for the feed she scattered, and the First Officer on the *Abbotsford* smiling at her accomplishments.

Near Yass, May 17th, 1841

My Dearest Elizabeth,
Our house takes shape daily. Tomorrow, Allan Munro and I will finish thatching the roof and then we shall lay the floor. Most slab houses here have earthen floors, but I cannot conceive of having dirt under my feet as I sit by my fire, or of your keeping such a place clean. And I have purchased the best glass I could find for your kitchen window, which enjoys a grand view of the hills.

In a previous letter I mentioned the Munro family, our closest neighbours. It was Thaddeus Munro and his son Allan who laid out the house for me and began construction as soon as the convicts had sawn the first slabs. Thaddeus has left his older son Jude to tend their large property whilst he and Allan help me here. I do believe Thaddeus Munro, who is a former Ship's Carpenter, is happier with saw and hammer than with a flock of sheep, although his station is a successful one. You will like Naomi, his wife, a fine woman of many skills, warm in her manner and very motherly. She has kept me well fed.

Of greatest importance to me is your arrival here at our farm. Please ask Robert to book you on a coach leaving Sydney in the second week of June. The trip will be tedious for you and the children, but your arrival will lighten my heart, and I hope to restore you to some degree of comfort. Do write to me as soon as your arrangements have been completed so that I may come to meet you at Yass.

My prayers are with you all.
I remain your loving husband,

John

At the beginning of June, Susan and Robert hosted a farewell party for Elizabeth. Caroline Chisholm attended and was most enthusiastic about Elizabeth's upcoming adventure; Hester and Noah Grainger were warmly encouraging, and Penelope Anderson was vociferously opposed to Elizabeth's living anywhere but Sydney.

Kangaroo and joey

FIVE
Yass

*I love the Lord, because he hath heard my
voice and my supplications.*
— PSALM 116:1

In the third week of June 1841, Elizabeth and her children, accompanied by their girl-of-all-work, Bess Mason, and two of Caroline Chisholm's girls, set out on a coach journey of 180 miles to Yass. They began by heading southwestward towards Camden, where Elizabeth's shipboard friend, Rachel Gibson, was now indentured as a housekeeper. When Bess Mason and the two girls sent by Caroline Chisholm each took charge of one of the children, Elizabeth realized Caroline had planned to ease her journey and was grateful to her.

The only male passenger, a stout, red-faced retired army officer, took it upon himself to be their commentator on the journey. Lieutenant Augustus Love, a garrulous gentleman with a full head of white hair ("At your service, dear lady!"), snorted when they came to fields tilled by convicts who were supervised by rope-wielding guards.

"Those felons are sure to be Irish Catholics. They'll be gibbering in Erse to confound their keepers. I'm an Englishman, raised in County Kildare. Eldest brother has the family's stud. Second brother's an Irish Magistrate. I was for the army. Grand place, Ireland. Finest studs. Marvellous hunting parties, don't you know. Family hosts a hunt every year. Friends and family over from England. Out with the hounds in the morning, horns blaring, dogs howling. Five miles round the walls of our estate and off on a tear across the countryside after a fox, scattering taigs like matchsticks, smashing their miserable potato fields to muck. Great sport!"

Elizabeth shuddered. Great sport, indeed! Aside from a terrified fox, what about the "taigs"? She surmised they were Irish Catholic tenant farmers, and their English landlord's hunt destroyed their supply of food. The officer began to nod off. For the moment she would not have to listen to the arrogance of perversely named Lieutenant Love.

Like the Lieutenant, Elizabeth's three children frequently fell asleep during the long journey; she hoped they would not have memories of heartless Overseers whipping exhausted convicts in irons who struggled to improve the road. "Bone-lazy drongos! Need regular whippings to keep them in shape," said the Lieutenant, roused by the sound of whips cracking. "Iron Gangs are escapees, don't you know. Deserve a good scourging." Elizabeth resolved to stay focussed on the scenery and ignore the officer's comments and the bloodied backs of convicts.

The coach always stopped for a noon meal on the eight-day journey. The driver fed and rested the four-horse team or harnessed up a new team. Nights were spent in whatever lodgings were available. They continued southwestward towards Goulburn, an established inland city with paved streets and brick buildings. At Goulburn Elizabeth handed over Caroline Chisholm's two girls to employers previously interviewed by Caroline at Sydney, and the coach passengers spent that night in a presentable hotel, where warm baths were available. With a team of fresh horses, the coach left Goulburn and rolled westward. When they reached Yass, she said goodbye to Lieutenant Augustus Love, who was continuing on to Wagga Wagga and his "sweet wife." Sweet and long-suffering wife, thought Elizabeth.

Never having been separated from her husband, Elizabeth wept with joy when John helped her from the coach and took her in his arms. Their neighbours had loaned him their wagon and draught horses, nautically named Drake and Nelson, and the Barnes family and Bess set out for the farm in great anticipation.

Five miles from the town, Elizabeth had her first view of their homestead. It was built on a broad rise close to a large tree that John had said was a kurrajong. They drove up a muddy lane to the small dwelling, John eager to show Elizabeth his handiwork: a slab house with a thatch roof made of strips of bark extending over a verandah; a carefully pieced slab floor, which Elizabeth thought must have cost John hours of determined labour; two bedrooms, each with a wide bed covered with pine boughs and Munro sheepskins; and a larger room for cooking and eating. Against a wall of this room stood a slab bench covered with a straw pallet for Bess; their carpet from the cabin on the *Abbotsford*, beaten to cleanliness by Naomi Munro, graced the floor; the rest of the furniture comprised pine chairs and a table, with John's pepper mill in the table's centre, and a new rocking chair, a welcoming gift made by Thaddeus Munro. John was proudest of his stone fireplace, where he lit a fire to heat the boiled dinner prepared by Naomi. Best of all, shaded by the kurrajong tree, was a kitchen window with the view Elizabeth had longed for. Whilst Bess romped with the children across the grassy farmyard, she stood contentedly in John's arms.

Next morning Elizabeth put jumpers on the children and asked Bess to play with them outdoors so that she might clean the house and put away the family's belongings. She waltzed around her new home singing an old folk song, "The Ash Grove," secure in the knowledge that this dwelling, though small and rough, was all theirs. No more living in a flat above a shop. No more keeping the children indoors for their safety. From her kitchen window she saw the winter sun warming gentle green hills. Her eyes filled with tears of happiness.

"I know you'd like a nice plump hen for our dinner today," said Bess. "Mr. Barnes told me he was sure Mrs. Munro would give us one. I'll just take a walk over there with the boys." The tall, comely girl, her thick golden tresses braided around her head, lifted George to her shoulders, gave her hands to Johnny and Thomas, and set off on the mile walk to the Munro farm.

That girl is a wonder, thought Elizabeth. She sang happily as she worked, absorbed in her chores, until Thomas's voice startled her. "Mamma! Mamma! Come and see! We've got a dead chook for you! Mrs. Munro caught it, and Bess chopped its head off with an axe, and it flopped around and fell over, and we had milk and biscuits whilst it bled! We're going to pull its feathers off, and Bess says you're s'posed to clean out its innards and cook it!" Elizabeth stood on the verandah, her stomach churning at the sight of a headless, bloody chicken and her children dancing around a blood-splattered Bess.

When she was growing up in Dorsetshire, she had been unable to watch her mother kill and clean chickens. In Cheapside she had gone to a butcher's stall at the market to purchase a fowl fully dressed and ready for roasting. Her children, it was obvious, had none of her qualms. Bess took pity on Elizabeth, plucked the chicken with the children's help, and removed the innards for her.

On her first Sunday at Yass, Elizabeth met the Munro family of whom John had spoken so highly. Thaddeus Munro was a tall, grey-haired man of few words, Thaddeus the Bold in the New Testament, Elizabeth recalled. His sociable wife, Naomi, was a cheerful, confident woman with lustrous auburn hair pulled back and coiled at the nape of her neck. Their sons, Jude, who was large and dark-haired, and Allan, his muscular, ginger-haired brother, were both shy and blushed easily.

In the Munro wagon on Sunday morning, the Barnes family went with their neighbours to Saint Clement's at Yass, where Naomi was president of the Ladies' Guild and her husband was Churchwarden. Saint Clement's was not a church as such, but a small building rented by the Diocese at the edge of the Yass River. That morning the recessional hymn was one of Elizabeth's favourites: "Let Saints on Earth in Concert Sing with Those Whose Work Is Done." We'll grow old in this place, Elizabeth said to herself, and when our earthly life is over, we'll be buried here under those pine trees.

"You'll stop with us for dinner, surely," said Naomi, as Thaddeus urged his team out of the churchyard and along the road. "It's only roast of mutton, but there's plenty to go round." The meal, more than just roast of mutton, included mint sauce, roasted potatoes, large servings of cabbage and turnips, apple pie with heavy cream, beakers of milk for the children and many cups of tea for the adults.

Whilst the men enjoyed a pipe by the fire, Naomi, Bess and Elizabeth did the washing up in the kitchen at the rear of the house. Afterwards, Naomi took Elizabeth and Bess for a walk around the farmyard to show them her large henhouse with broody nests and a pullet run, and her dairy, which was a cool room down behind the barn. In her kitchen garden, manure from her three cows had been dug in to prepare for spring planting. Up the path and around the verandah were borders planted with primulas and pansies, at present little islands of green in the red-brown earth. In early spring, Naomi explained, daffodils would appear.

"At the weekly market at Yass, I sell my milk, butter, eggs, pullets and some chickens—chooks, they're called here—and in autumn my daffodil bulbs. Thaddeus lets me keep the money for my own use, but we've had two bad droughts since we came here, and the money I've saved kept us from disaster." Overcoming some of her shyness, Elizabeth said, "I wonder when I'll have the time and skills to accomplish what you do. I've never milked a cow nor churned butter. I've never even planted a vegetable or a flower." She had never killed and cleaned a chook either, but she was not about to admit that to Naomi Munro.

"Bess will be a help to you. Until you have a cow and a kitchen garden, I'll send Allan over every day with milk, butter and vegetables." Bless you, thought Elizabeth, and smiled at her.

Thaddeus and John constructed a slab barn on the property and began fencing paddocks whilst Allan and Bess dug a root cellar for Elizabeth and lined it with slabs. The two young people built a box-bark henhouse and brought over a rooster, a dozen chooks and a dozen pullets from Naomi's flock. With the teasing and giggling that went on, it was obvious Allan and Bess enjoyed working together.

"We need a team of draught horses and a wagon," said John one evening. Elizabeth did not agree. "Until we have an income from the farm, surely one horse and a cart would do us," she said. "If we need a team and wagon at any time, we could ask to borrow Thaddeus Munro's. We must get a milch cow soon." Her husband looked fondly at her.

John and Elizabeth both knew how to drive a horse and trap, but they had no experience buying a horse and cart at auction and had never owned a cow. Allan offered to go with John to the next market at Yass, and at the end of the day, they came back along the road looking very pleased with themselves. John drove a cart pulled by a chestnut mare called Amber, and Allan led a lovely young black and white cow, which Elizabeth named Molly.

When she had a moment to herself, Elizabeth sat down to compose a letter to John's sister and brother-in-law.

Near Yass, July 11th, 1841

Dear Susan and Robert,
My first thought is one of gratitude for your gracious hospitality. A more generous welcome to our new country could not have been imagined.

I will not dwell on our journey, except to say we arrived here safely. I assure you that John and I and the boys are well.

Our three-room slab house is snug, well built by John and our neighbour, a former Ship's Carpenter, and his son. From my kitchen window I see green hills which remind me of Dorsetshire. We have a barn and henhouse, a mare, a cart and chooks. We also have a cow which, I admit, I have not yet learned to milk.

Caroline Chisholm's Bess Mason is a blessing. She's a delightful young woman, skilled and hard-working, and the children follow her everywhere. I shall enclose a letter of appreciation to Caroline. Would you kindly forward it to her?

Last Sunday afternoon John harnessed Amber, our mare, to take us for a drive in the cart to the highest point on our neighbours' land so that we might look westward across our property. We have forty acres (a portion of it has been cleared) and we could look down at our homestead on the southern boundary. A creek which crosses our neighbours' land curves around the rise on which our home is built. We could see the canopy of our kurrajong tree, like a great green cloud shading our homestead.

Our next farm projects are the purchase of a small flock of sheep and the preparation of my kitchen garden. John says our sheep will be cross-bred to enable them to cope with the tough grasses and warm summers here. Having been taught how to keep a garden by her mother in Berkshire, Bess is full of ideas about planting and cultivating, whilst I shall have to depend on my notes from the shipboard botanist on the Abbotsford.

And now, my dears, I really must close my ramblings. Please remember me to the Browns, Mary Fleming and everyone I met during my stay.

I remain your loving sister-in-law,

Elizabeth

Bess more than proved her value by keeping the children busy as she went about her chores. She also killed and cleaned chooks for dinner, a task Elizabeth managed to avoid completely.

On a dismal July morning, Allan drove Drake and a sledge with a plough and harrow over to the Barnes farm. Allan ploughed the ground for a kitchen garden and then hitched up the frame harrow to level the soil for planting. Afterwards he drove the draught horse into the yard and set him free from the heavy frame. John and Allan raked over the plot, and Bess let the children help by holding Drake's long reins whilst she walked the horse several times around the yard to cool him out. Once she was satisfied the animal was comfortable enough, she handed pieces of hessian to the three little boys.

"Wipe his legs clean of mud. He'll not want to be carrying that dirt everywhere on those great hairy legs of his." Elizabeth gasped as her children scrambled around and under the draught horse. She retreated to her kitchen.

Whilst she and Bess were enjoying a cup of tea, Elizabeth commented on her patience with the children. The young woman smiled and replied, "I'm the eldest of a family of eight and responsible for the youngest ones. Your three boys are no bother at all. And you'll be wanting to learn to milk, I expect. If you have a moment, I'll show you how." Elizabeth reckoned it would take more than a moment and was avoiding the lesson.

With the fabric and yarn she had bought in Sydney, Elizabeth sewed curtains and knitted jumpers and stockings for the family. In the metal bathtub she washed clothes and dried them in front of the fire. Using the Bible and their wooden bricks from the *Abbotsford*, she taught Thomas and Johnny to write their letters and numerals. The boys still recited the alphabet in nautical terms: "A is for anchor, B is for bowsprit, C is for capstan . . ." At the end of the long days, Elizabeth was exhausted, but she felt secure and settled.

They had Sunday dinners at Winchester, the Munro home. "You need one meal a week prepared for you, Elizabeth," said Naomi. "You have a heavy load, establishing your farm and raising three little ones, and I enjoy cooking for a full table." Elizabeth's children loved the Munro house; its large verandah gave them plenty of space to play ship, the verandah serving as a lookout. Of course, Drake and Nelson had to be visited under Jude's supervision; the elder Munro son was impressed by the boys' knowledge of horses.

"Young Thomas said he'd noticed Drake and Nelson were higher in the withers than the croup and he thought that gave them more pulling power," Jude remarked in astonishment after a Sunday visit to the stable. Elizabeth remembered the hours Alfred Brown had spent teaching Thomas and Johnny about horses.

On the verandah one Sunday afternoon, the boys discovered Jude whittling. "Mr. Perry on the *Abbotsford* could do that," said Thomas. "He made us our bricks. He even put numbers on them. What are you making, Jude?"

"It's a whip handle of myall wood for a stockman friend of mine."

"If I had a knife and some wood, I could do that. You could help me, Jude."

"You'd have to be careful. A whittling knife is especially sharp."

"I'm very good at being careful, aren't I, Johnny?"

Johnny agreed, and said he wanted a knife and some wood, too. The following Sunday, to Elizabeth's dismay, Jude presented the little boys with these and began to teach them how to hold the wood securely and work the knife away from their hands. Several Sundays and many cut fingers later, the children could turn out recognizable shapes. Thomas was often found amusing himself with his whittling. Elizabeth was reminded of watching her father carve buttons as he sat on a stool in his wool draper's shop in Dorsetshire.

Every farmer's wife must know how to milk, Elizabeth kept telling herself, and one rainy afternoon she asked Bess to teach her. Thomas, Johnny and George sat down on the barn floor to watch. Bess showed her how to clean the teats and demonstrated how easy milking was by sending streams of frothy warm liquid noisily into a milking pail. When Elizabeth took her place on the low milking stool, Bess set her mistress's bonneted head against Molly's flank, placed the partly filled pail between her knees, and positioned Elizabeth's fingers around two teats. Molly turned her head, flicked her tail at Elizabeth, and stared at her in disbelief.

Elizabeth gripped hard with both hands and pulled down. Molly raised the hind hoof nearest to her and sent Elizabeth tumbling backwards with a bruised leg whilst the milking pail and its contents went flying across the barn. The children exploded in merriment and rolled about in giggles. Molly, having dealt with the annoyance, resumed the chewing of her cud.

"Out of here, you three!" ordered Bess. "Play on the verandah until we finish this milking!" She rinsed the empty pail, tied the end of Molly's tail to the offending leg, held the cow's head straight on, and crooned softly to her. "Now, once more, Mrs. Barnes," said Bess. "Molly must not get the better of you. Squeeze your fingers from the top of the teat to stretch the udder, one hand at a time. Lower each teat with a steady squeeze. Don't pull!"

Elizabeth recalled the pamplet she and Dorcas Dartnell had read on the *Abbotsford*, which said cows readily dispensed their milk. Bess demonstrated once more, splashing milk into the pail. Elizabeth sat down again, ignored Molly's snuffles of disapproval, and tried to imitate Bess's movements. It was a lengthy effort for the cow and her owner before much milk appeared.

Bess said, "I'll just strip off the last bit for you, Mrs. Barnes." What she stripped off was more than a bit. "That's grand!" declared Bess.

"Tomorrow afternoon you can milk her again." Elizabeth patted Molly, and favouring her sore leg, limped to the house. The following afternoon she busied herself in the kitchen in the hope that Bess would do the milking on her own.

"Come, Mrs. Barnes," said Bess, standing at the door with a clean pail in her hand. "A little practice is all you need." The milking was not much of an improvement, but at Bess's insistence Elizabeth continued to practise each day until, after some weeks, milking Molly became a pleasant late-afternoon interlude.

Elizabeth now realized the farm was burgeoning the way she had dreamed. She and John would establish traditions here, as her parents had done in Dorsetshire. They would have more children, God willing, expand their leasehold, add livestock, and build a large house in this land of space and freedom.

When the boundary fence had been completed, John went with Thaddeus and two of his dogs to buy a small flock of cross-bred merinos at auction. They came back with a flock of ewes and their skittering lambs. Two determined Munro dogs drove the bleating sheep along the muddy road and up into the fold on the Barnes farm. It was then that Patch came into their lives.

"He looks to have the makings of a good sheep herder," said Thaddeus in their farmyard later that day. A young black dog splotched with white, from a litter on the Munro farm, quivered beside him in anticipation. "I'll teach you what he knows and bring my best dogs over to work with him for a bit." Eyeing the boys, who were obviously excited, Thaddeus added, "He's not a pet, you understand. He's a working dog and on duty at all times. He sleeps and eats outside and guards your livestock and property. He is not here for your amusement." Fascinated by the black and white dog, Thomas, Johnny and George did not hear a word the man said.

The appropriately named Patch slept under the kurrajong tree in a large hollow log John had placed there for him, or near the sheepfold behind the house in a similar log. Even whilst seeming to sleep, he was alert, lying on his belly in the log, his nose outside, his ears pricked forward, ready for intruders. He kept the family company on the verandah and played with the boys in the farmyard, but when the children tried to smuggle him into the house, he planted his paws firmly on the threshold and refused to enter. Thaddeus had trained him well. Elizabeth, Bess and the children, sitting on a fence, delighted in watching John practise his commands and signals, and the dog respond with darting raids into a mob of sheep to separate and reorganize them.

Allan and Bess had set straw-filled nesting boxes on shelves at the end of the henhouse. With spring in the offing, one after another of the chooks went broody in her nesting box, and Bess kept an eye on each of them, ignoring the hens' objections when she checked on their eggs. The family was rewarded with the farm's first flock of chicks. Rudy, the rooster, made certain more chicks followed.

In the next two months when the springtime weather became notably warm, the sheep, wheat and Elizabeth's kitchen garden prospered magnificently. Soon Elizabeth and Bess were out early each day, thinning carrots and beets, harvesting peas, green beans and lettuce and lifting early potatoes. Elizabeth watched her children run and play in the warm spring air, "in sunshine and safety," she said to herself with satisfaction.

SIX
The Farm

When my spirit was overwhelmed within me,
then thou knewest my path.

— PSALM 142:3

Talk at the Yass market was of other warm spring seasons and early summers. Thaddeus Munro scanned the brilliant sky with concern. "You'd be well advised to top up your cistern from the creek," he said to Elizabeth. "Don't let your water supply get low. Water your garden thoroughly and mulch it. Your plants have no shade over them and need to be tended with care."

At daylight one morning, he sent Allan over in the wagon heaped with empty barrels from the Yass market. Bess helped Allan scrub the insides of the barrels, rinse them, and fill them with water dipped from the creek. They sealed the barrels and spent the rest of the morning rolling them up under the kurrajong tree, the only shade the yard possessed.

As Christmas approached, the days grew hotter, and swirling winds scooped up the dry earth and tossed it against the house and outbuildings. Elizabeth stood perspiring in her kitchen preparing Christmas puddings with fruit from Naomi's larder. The puddings were to be stored for yuletide in an earthenware crock in Naomi's dairy.

Elizabeth had a new concern: money, or the lack of it. Establishing their home, replacing the items smashed in the storm at sea, and buying tools and livestock had consumed much of their capital. Until they sold their wool and wheat, they had little cash. In addition to their debt to the penal authorities for clearing the land, they owed the annual fees for their property and livestock and they would need to pay Bess. Every evening Elizabeth thanked God for a caring, affectionate husband, three healthy children, a home of her own and the generous Munros. Yet fears haunted her, and she prayed the family would endure on the farm.

Despite her concerns and her increasing discomfort in the heat, for she was with child, Elizabeth set about organizing a Christmas party for all the neighbours. They came from miles around, eager to share the day with the new family in the district. The women unloaded a feast of breads, cold meat pies, cold roast chooks, cakes, tarts and fresh fruit, and the men brought their home-brewed beer for the occasion. Quite unlike the yuletide meal on the *Abbotsford*, it was a picnic rather than a Christmas dinner, although Elizabeth provided ample servings of Christmas pudding with custard. When the evening sky softened from blue to violet, Elizabeth led the singing of the Song of the Angels, "While Shepherds Watch'd Their Flocks by Night," and felt she had never sung the hymn in a more appropriate setting. A deep indigo enveloped the heavens, and stars of the Southern Cross came out to guide the guests on their homeward journey.

Elizabeth paid little attention to Bess's dreamy mood in the following days because Bess was given to romantic notions. Early one evening, as Elizabeth looked for three stray hens to put to roost, she wandered behind the barn with Patch, who thought rounding up chooks was even better sport than herding sheep. In the shadows the dog wagged his tail and gave a friendly *woof!* There on the dry grass, oblivious to her approach, were Bess and Allan, locked in an embrace of unmistakeable passion.

Patch ran up to them and barked in anticipation of being petted. The young couple scrambled to their feet, hurriedly rearranging their clothing. Elizabeth, dismayed by her ignorance of their relationship, gave up all thoughts of stray chooks and headed for the house to consult John. The next day in the kitchen she reminded Bess of their promise to Caroline Chisholm: she and John were to be responsible for her until she came of age.

"I'm ever so grateful for your goodness towards me, Mrs. Barnes," responded a genuinely contrite Bess. "You and Mr. Barnes are the best of employers. It's just that I love Allan, and he loves me, you see. We'll both soon be of age and when we've saved enough for a property of our own, we intend to be married."

Before John could set off for the Munro farm to ascertain whether or not Bess's lover had the same intentions, a blushing Allan appeared on their verandah. "I'm devoted to Bess, I am," he blurted, "and she's agreed to marry me. I know she's in your care and I'd be honoured if you'd consent to our betrothal." John said, "What would your parents say about this betrothal?" Allan was quick to reply, "Oh, my mother and father have approved, but my father told me not to think of marriage until I'm of age and can get my own property."

John asked Bess to come out from the kitchen and, as he and Elizabeth had agreed the previous evening, they gave the pair their blessing. Allan shook hands with them, and Bess hugged them both and then her beloved, who blushed even more. Elizabeth wondered how long it would take the young man to save enough money for a property of his own.

Just as conversations at the market had predicted, January in the valley became exceptionally hot and dry. From a cloudless vault of azure sky, the sun scorched the dusty air every minute of the long days. The creek became a trickle, and the cistern had little water left for the family's use and none for the garden. Elizabeth saved waste water from the kitchen to distribute over her plants. She had harvested carrots and onions and lifted some potatoes to store in the root cellar, but her green vegetables, despite all her efforts, withered away to nothing. As the heat grew more intense, she feared for the children, who were listless, perpetually thirsty and too exhausted with the heat to want to follow Bess. Elizabeth prayed every day for cooler weather and rain and rationed the limited supply of barrel water.

Lighting a fire to cook a meal made the house intolerable and put the roof in danger of fire from sparks. The slab walls had dried and contracted, but John was too worn out from tending sheep to caulk the cracks, which invited rodents and snakes into the dwelling. Most fortunately, Bess was with Elizabeth when the first snake slipped through an opening and slithered across the floor. Before Elizabeth could scream, Bess dispatched the reptile with a cleaver.

Strips of honey-covered paper hanging from the ceiling whined with the doleful din of dying flies, and the stench and the flies made using the dunny unbearable. The dry thatch teemed with insects, which crawled down the walls and in and out of the cracks in the slab floor. Too late Elizabeth realized the advantages of having a smooth dirt floor. The ever-thoughtful Naomi sent over cold meat pies and fresh fruit and loaned them fine netting for their verandah, where they slept and ate, when they slept and ate at all.

In the searing heat, Elizabeth often felt faint, and her increasing heaviness demanded that she rest every afternoon. She had abandoned all efforts to keep her house and family clean. At Saint Clement's parishioners talked of nothing but drought and said the Prayer for Rain at every service. Like any responsible Churchwarden, Thaddeus Munro checked on the water and food supply of each family. Older women of the parish, having experienced many a dry spell, assured Elizabeth that the drought would end, rain would come, and everything would turn green again.

One evening John did not come home when darkness fell. Terrified, thinking he had been injured, Elizabeth sat up waiting throughout the night and at dawn sent Bess to ask Allan to look for him. Not until nightfall did the two men stagger into the yard, their faces thick with dust and streaked with sweat. They had worked for hours helping Patch sort out the Barnes flock, which had escaped the boundary fence in search of grazing and had mingled with a stray mob in the bush.

Hunched over a beaker of hot tea on the verandah, Allan explained. "In the drought some assigned convict herders will let their masters' flocks wander, leaving the animals to find their own grazing and water whilst they look for food and water for themselves. I wonder you didn't have a convict shepherd begging at your door. I'm sure I don't know where that rum lot came from, all full of burrs and insects and God only knows what diseases. Patch was a treat to watch as he sorted out your flock and sent the others packing."

In mid-January Thaddeus Munro told John to set his sheep free from pastures now so overgrazed that the small flock nibbled dust. "They can browse the saltbush and get some moisture that way. You and the dog will have to shepherd them. They'll easily get into difficulty and become food for dingoes, or another stray mob may mix with them in the bush."

Every morning Elizabeth packed John a meal for the day and gave him a bottle of precious creek water, both of which he shared with Patch. They were gone long hours, keeping track of the meandering sheep, rescuing those in trouble, shepherding them home again, both dog and master parched, hungry and exhausted.

One scorching evening John and Thaddeus came to the verandah and sat down in silence. John's tired face was blurred with dirt, his trousers and shirt torn and soiled. He ran his fingers repeatedly through his thinning hair as Thaddeus said to Elizabeth, "Most of your sheep have the scab. Mites and ticks are burrowing into their flesh and destroying their fleece. They all must be shot and their carcasses burned." Elizabeth was incredulous. "Shot . . . and burned?"

"You cannot cure them, and that's that," said Thaddeus solemnly. "The boys and I will be here before daybreak with two of our dogs. The bottom pasture where your pond was would be the best place." Elizabeth and John, sleepless and silent, stayed far apart on the verandah that night. Their savings were spent; they were in debt; their bills were mounting and they had a baby on the way. Their vegetables, chooks and wheat were gone, and now their sheep must be slaughtered. Elizabeth tried not to think of Penelope Anderson's lecture about life on the western slopes. Seized by a pounding headache, she lay awake in the devastating heat and prayed for God's support.

She would never forget the agony of the next day. Darkness still shrouded the farm when the Munro men drove up with rifles, kerosene, pitchforks and shovels, barrels of well water and their two best dogs. Patch jumped into the wagon, innocent of the task that lay ahead. John's face was grey with anguish as he held Elizabeth close to him. "The noise and smell will be frightening for the boys. Take them over to Naomi's."

When the children had wakened and were dressed, Elizabeth gave them each a drink of Molly's decreasing supply of milk. Leaving Bess in charge, she set out in the cart with the boys in the relative cool of early morning for the Munro farm a mile away. There, Naomi did her best to amuse the children whilst their mother sat on the Winchester verandah, numb and unseeing.

On the hot morning wind came the bleating of sheep, the crack of rifle shots, the stench of burning wool and the odour of charred mutton. The puzzled children clutched at Elizabeth, expecting her to explain. Unable to speak, she held them in her arms as the last of the family's food, livelihood and dreams turned to cinders.

The dogs returned first. The boys wanted to pet them and play with them, but the animals paid no attention and threw themselves down in the shade of the verandah. Elizabeth fetched a pan of water, and with their ears and tails drooping, the dogs drank gratefully. Patch stumbled over to Elizabeth, laid his head on her knee and cried. He had driven to their deaths his very reason for being.

Three days later, after she had said evening prayers with the children and settled them down in a corner of the verandah, Elizabeth sat with John in the gathering darkness of another stifling evening. "We can start again with my inheritance," she said. "We can settle our debts, buy another flock of sheep, plant shade trees around the kitchen garden, dig watering ponds in all the pastures, plant vegetables again and wheat . . ."

John shook his head. "I can't." He was close to tears. "I've brought you and the boys to the other side of the world only to prove myself a useless duffer at farming. Our flock got the scab when I let them mix with those strays. And never in my life will I forget the sound and sight and smell when I destroyed our sheep." He sighed heavily. "I'm beaten, Elizabeth." Elizabeth's mind searched desperately for a way to persuade him to hold on to what they had.

Next Sunday morning, having sent Bess and the children to Winchester with the Munros after church, John took Elizabeth for a drive in the cart. In the white glare of the midday sun, Amber slowly climbed the dry, dusty Yass hills. John drove out of the sun into a grove of gumtrees and whilst they sat in silence in the oppressive shade, he took Elizabeth's hand and looked earnestly at her. She avoided his gaze, fanned vaguely at the ubiquitous flies and stared through the dusty air at the small village.

"I've corresponded with Robert Nichols," said John quietly. "He has found a situation for us, and I need your consent to his proposal before I answer his letter." Elizabeth had seen him writing a letter and reading mail from Sydney and wondered why he had not shared these with her as usual. "A recently widowed woman at Concord, west of Sydney, holds the lease of a shop, a flat above it and a small orchard nearby. She will sell us her leases on reasonable terms because she wants to return to England. I'm asking you to agree and to lend me your inheritance. I'm a merchant, not a farmer, and I want to begin again at Concord."

Elizabeth could not believe what she was hearing. Give up her beloved farm after less than a year? For a flat above a shop? Does he not care about the home he built for us? What about our children's future? And fresh air, space and freedom? She knew in her heart her husband did care, but the drought had robbed him of all confidence and left him back where he began. John's troubled brown eyes pleaded with her to understand.

"Yes," she whispered, unable to say more, and burst into sobs. He held her close for a long time, then roused the dozing Amber and drove down into the valley. It was a solemn dinner at the Munro house that afternoon. Naomi and Thaddeus were not surprised by John's decision because over the years they had seen several settlers go under. At least John had other prospects.

"You've always been so enthusiastic about farm life, Elizabeth," said Naomi later on the shady verandah, "but John has never seemed as keen. Perhaps his heart always has been set on a store of his own." Aware of an unspoken concern, Naomi added, "You've no worries about Bess. She's a darling girl and she'll live with us until she and our Allan are married. I'll enjoy her company and I promise you, until those two are wed, I'll be the best of chaperones!" Elizabeth, remembering Bess and Allan behind the barn, smiled and shook her head.

John discharged his debts with part of Elizabeth's inheritance and arranged for Thaddeus to take over his lease on the understanding that the property be transferred to Allan when he came of age. As the sun set in flaming splendour one summer evening, Elizabeth, John and the children presented Bess and Allan with their wedding gift of Molly, Amber and Patch. In the days that followed, Bess spent hours crying over their departure and their generosity. The children rode on Amber every day, stroked Molly, and lay under the kurrajong tree with Patch.

Elizabeth knew God would want her to be grateful because John had found a way out, yet in the late afternoons when she milked Molly, she wept against her warm flank. In the evenings as she sat on the verandah with her arms around Patch, her tears soaked his lovely head. John alone was cheerful and full of resolve.

On a cloudy morning at the end of February, Elizabeth and her family bade farewell to their farm and the Munro family. The men embraced John in an unaccustomed show of affection whilst the women clung to one another in tears. The family boarded the coach at Yass, and when it began its journey across the hills, Elizabeth looked back at Saint Clement's just as the rain came—only a shower, but rain. She knew her confinement was less than a month hence.

SEVEN
West Sydney

He that trusteth in the Lord,
mercy shall compass him about.
— PSALM 32:10

When the Barnes family arrived at Concord, west of Sydney, the village had been settled for almost fifty years. It had been named by Francis Grose, a Commandant of the New South Wales Corps, for a battle in which he had fought during the American Revolutionary War. A notable feature of the village was a prison holding French-speaking rebels captured in an 1837 insurrection in Lower Canada. On taking the children for walks, Elizabeth saw convicts tilling fields, and when she witnessed Overseers whipping them for so much as uttering a word in French, she steered the boys in another direction.

Elizabeth reckoned her labour went well, a little more quickly than she had expected, and she thanked God for an accoucheuse who was scrupulously clean and very encouraging. After six hours of steady travail on the 25th of March, 1842, in a flat above a shop at Concord, Elizabeth Barnes was delivered of another son.

As she had done in London after the birth of each of her children, Elizabeth went to church six weeks later for The Thanksgiving of Women After Childbirth and her Holy Communion. The thanksgiving service ended with a prayer: "Grant, we beseech thee, most merciful Father, that she, through thy help, may both faithfully live, and walk according to thy will . . ." Elizabeth prayed she would be able to "walk according to thy will" with three young boys and a new baby in a cramped flat above a shop.

Concord, New South Wales
June 23rd, 1842

My Dear Naomi,

I write to tell you of our life at Concord and the safe arrival of our fourth child. You knew of my condition, of course, but I could not bring myself to discuss it with you because our situation seemed distressing enough without speaking of another little one to care for. The latest Barnes baby is a vigorous boy, much like Thomas, and we have named him for my brother who was killed in England in the course of his duties as a farm bailiff. Our new William commemorates him.

An orchard which comes with our lease is within walking distance of the village. It consists of an acre or so of fruit trees and a small pasture, not enough for a proper farm. I have taken to walking there with the children to give us some fresh air and exercise. The fruit trees need more attention than they're getting, but I know John would rather devote his energies to his business.

We live in a small flat above a shop where John is occupied as a merchant once more. He sells household goods, a few of which are made here by hand, although most are imported from England.

I manage my four young sons as best I can in the flat. In my low moments I weep for our lost farm and long for Bess's help and your companionship. After the freedom of the farm, Thomas and Johnny are restless in the flat, indeed, sometimes badly behaved, and I was greatly relieved when I could enroll them in school.

I do not tell John my problems. He spends long, happy days downstairs in the shop, his eyes shining as he arranges his shelves and serves his customers.

Please give my regards to your family and Bess, as well as to everyone at Saint Clement's. My thoughts are often with you all.

I remain your grateful friend,

Elizabeth

Fortunately for Elizabeth's well-being, Susan and Robert Nichols invited the Barnes family to spend one Sunday afternoon with them each month. Alfred Brown fetched them in the carriage; Thomas,

Johnny and George got into mischief with their cousins whilst Mary Fleming fussed over baby William, and Mrs. Brown provided generous meals. Susan wanted John and Elizabeth to join her soirées, but Elizabeth begged off, feeling she had neither the clothes nor the spirit to face the Nichols' guests.

The last of Elizabeth's inheritance went towards the first shipment from England of basic household goods for the shop. Coincidentally, this shipment arrived on the *Abbotsford*, which continued to transport some of John's goods on its annual voyage from London. John placed a small advertisement in a Sydney newspaper and was rewarded with a crowd of tinsmiths, weavers, carvers, seamstresses, potters and others who came to display their wares. He and Elizabeth selected a few of them for the quality of their work, much to the satisfaction of customers who had grown used to waiting a year or more for most of their necessities. Sales dramatically increased, and Elizabeth, who kept accounts for the shop, was pleased with the growth in trade. For his best-quality items, John continued to rely on English manufacturers.

One Sunday when the Barnes family was visting Parkside, Susan handed Elizabeth a letter postmarked "Camden," which she opened at once.

July 5th, 1842

Dear Mrs. Barnes,
I write to let you know I am in good health and enjoying myself. I trust you and your family are the same.

All five bairns are thriving and our farm is prospering. I say our farm because I have married Mr. Garvey, the children's father. He is much older than I am and a quiet sort, but he treats me very well.

Although I was not looking to be a wife, Mr. Garvey became fond of me and thought marrying the right thing to do. We expect the birth of our first child shortly.

You are not to worry about me, Mrs. Barnes. I am happy with my life.

*With my special good wishes to you and Mr. Barnes and the boys,
I remain your friend,*

Rachel Garvey

That evening Elizabeth composed a letter of congratulations to Rachel and gave the young Irish girl all the family news. Rachel, only seventeen years old, was now married to a "much older" Mr. Garvey, "a quiet sort," and carrying his child. Elizabeth vowed to include her young friend in her daily prayers.

Elizabeth and John had been considering William's baptism as well as George's, for he had not been baptised in London as Thomas and Johnny had been. The family occasionally attended Saint John's Church at Parramatta, an early church in the colony, founded by an Assistant Colonial Chaplain, the Reverend Samuel Marsden, who had also been a magistrate of draconian reputation. Like Sydney's Saint James Church, the Parramatta church was a place of exclusivity and hierarchy, attended by "respectables," as they were called, where sermons were preached on reputed sins of the lower classes, especially Irish Catholics. Elizabeth, "respectable" though her family was, decided her children would not be baptised in a place that perpetuated prejudice and English snobbery. Until she could find a church that encouraged acceptance of all human beings, she trusted God would watch over George and William.

Elizabeth enjoyed taking care of the shop whilst John tended the orchard, but George was an active little boy and William a demanding baby. It was difficult for her to manage the little ones and see to the customers as well. "We should hire a live-in assistant for the shop, John," she said one evening as she sat doing the accounts. "Yes, I was thinking of doing so," he replied, "and I've consulted Robert Nichols because he often works with the penal administration. On the day after tomorrow, I'm going to interview a man with a conditional pardon whom Robert has recommended highly. He came from Manchester, where he had experience as a shop assistant."

"John! A pardoned convict? Do you really want a person like that living in the back of our shop? You have your family to consider! And what if he's a thief?"

"This man is not a thief. He was convicted of murder."

"Good heavens, John! Is Robert Nichols actually recommending a murderer to us? I find this conversation completely outrageous! Please say no more!" Elizabeth had a throbbing headache all that night. Next day, contrite and affectionate as John was, she refused to speak to him.

On the appointed afternoon, whilst Thomas and Johnny were at school and George and William were having their naps, John climbed the stairs from the shop with a pardoned man who had served his time for murder. "Elizabeth, this is Matthew Neale." Elizabeth beheld a slight, elderly man in a soiled, torn shirt, dirty trousers in tatters and filthy rags around his feet, who had walked for two days from the centre of Sydney and was white-faced with hunger and fatigue. Her two days of revulsion were at once overcome by compassion, and in sympathy she stared at this beaten man, wondering how she could help him.

"Your servant, Madam." His voice was a mere whisper. He would not hurt anyone, she thought. He's a sick man who needs good food and decent clothes. What has he suffered to reduce him to this state? She stood in silence, puzzled by this most unlikely looking criminal.

Remembering the purpose of their meeting, she said, "I'm sure Mr. Barnes has informed you of the requirements of the position." Matthew Neale raised sad eyes to Elizabeth and nodded. "And do you think you could fulfill the responsibilities laid out for you?"

"I have had experience in doing so, Madam."

"Please tell us about your experience." The man paused for several moments, and Elizabeth suspected he was struggling to find suitable words for the first woman he had spoken to in many years. In a barely audible voice he replied, "I was the assistant in a wool draper's shop at Manchester. My employer was a beast of a man who committed an act of such abomination that I stabbed him to death. I was sentenced to transportation and I've served my time, recently as a prison supply clerk. I would like to be a shop assistant again and have a place to live." Unused to speaking about himself and at such length, he bowed his head and fell silent.

"If you will wait downstairs," said Elizabeth, "my husband and I will make a decision and inform you." She watched the pardoned convict shuffle away as if he were still in chains. "What on earth made that gentle soul kill his employer?" she asked John. "His story is a most disturbing one, my dear, and I had thought to keep it from you. Robert Nichols has told me that when Matthew Neale's wife died at Manchester, he was left to care for their sickly son, who was about Thomas's age. One day Matthew heard the child screaming in their rooms at the back of the shop. He went to attend to his son and discovered his employer committing an unspeakable act of perversion upon the child's person. Matthew used his fabric shears to kill the man. The child died whilst Matthew was in prison awaiting trial."

Elizabeth did not know the meaning of "an unspeakable act of perversion upon the child's person," but she understood the protective instincts of a parent and the tragedy of a child's death. "We must hire him at once," she said. "Wait for me whilst I get some bedding for his cot, and we'll tell him together. Then I'll sort through your clothes and find him something to wear and I'll send him to the cobbler tomorrow to order boots. Matthew will take his meals with us, of course." John nodded and smiled fondly at his wife as she bustled off to find sheets, blankets and clothing.

The pardoned convict's first meal with their family, Elizabeth realized, was his return to the ordinary world. He had washed and put on the clean clothes she had given him, a mended muslin shirt and a pair of patched fustian trousers. When he met the children, Thomas asked him why he wasn't wearing boots. "I was a convict for many years, Master Thomas, and I wore out my boots long ago." Thomas was adamant. "Everybody needs boots," he said. Matthew, his eyes moist, smiled at the boy.

Elizabeth's table was laid with an embroidered cloth and matching embroidered napkins rolled into the carved napkin rings she had received from Mr. Perry on the *Abbotsford*. Sliced cold pork pie, chutney, green beans, fresh cheese scones and apple cobbler with heavy cream were set out for the family. She watched Matthew tremble at the sight. Everyone stood around the table and joined hands to sing the Doxology, and Thomas and Johnny, standing on either side of Matthew, clasped his fingers as if they had always done so. When they finished the prayer, the man crossed himself and immediately looked anxious. Johnny observed his behaviour with interest.

"Why did you cross yourself, Matthew? Only a Vicar does that." The man took a deep breath. He's hoping, reckoned Elizabeth, that he won't put an end to his employment with his next words. "I'm a Catholic, Master Johnny," he said, "and I always cross myself when I pray." Johnny seemed perplexed. "Oh," he said. "That seems a lot of extra bother." The man chuckled and patted the child on the head.

Matthew worked six days a week in the shop and each night tidied the place and swept it before he went to sleep on his cot in the storage room. On days when John worked in the orchard, or set off in a hired wagon to collect a shipment at Port Jackson, he left Matthew in charge. The man took his meals with the family, and no further mention was made of his crosses or his religion.

Thus it happened that Matthew Neale, murderer, transportee, pardoned convict and a papist, became part of the Barnes family. Elizabeth immediately forgot he was a murderer and set about helping him with his new life. Despite his appearance, he was scarcely older than she was, and in time he was restored to health under her care.

Early in 1844, continued success with his store made it easy for John to find a shopkeeper to purchase his leases, which enabled him to move to much larger premises in George Street at Sydney. Elizabeth cried quietly to herself at leaving their orchard, even though it had not amounted to much, because it represented the farm she still longed for.

John was full of enthusiasm for his new location in the capital city. His store had a wide frontage on the busy street and large display windows on either side of the door. Inside were counters on three sides, a central display table, and a door at the back leading to a large storeroom and three small rooms: John's office and

Matthew's bedroom and sitting room. Matthew thrived in the new setting. He helped John organize the store and willingly accepted his employer's cast-offs when John began consulting Robert Nichols' tailor and wearing suits befitting a city merchant.

John and Elizabeth were able to buy a small property seven miles west of the centre of Sydney in the new residential area of Ashfield. Still sparsely inhabited, Ashfield had been claimed in 1817 by a merchant, Joseph Underwood, who had named the area for his birthplace in Suffolk. The Barnes home, not quite as grand as that of Susan and Robert Nichols, was similar in design, complete with a separate kitchen and a stable for a horse and buggy. John's success had liberated Elizabeth, she hoped forever, from the confines of a flat. She hummed with contentment as she set John's pepper mill on the dining room table and hung their English watercolours on either side of the drawing room fireplace at Shaftesbury, which Elizabeth had named in honour of her Dorsetshire birthplace.

In need of transportation to and from his store, John sought the advice of Alfred Brown, the Nichols' coachman, and bought a well-trained mare and family buggy at auction in Sydney. Thomas and Johnny, who had fond memories of Amber on the farm, were thrilled and asked what their mare would be called. "She's already named," their father said. "She's called Stella."

"We think she should be called Star," said Johnny, "like Thomas's toy horse, because she has the same white mark on her forehead." Their father replied, "She *is* called Star. That's what Stella means in Latin." "That's good," said Johnny.

Once she was settled at Ashfield, Elizabeth persuaded John that if she were to continue helping in the store, they would need household help. She wrote to her old acquaintance, Hester Grainger, who was sure to know about girls seeking work. Hester replied immediately, inviting her to an employment office in downtown Sydney. There she welcomed her visitor warmly. "Elizabeth Barnes! How grand to see you again! Do sit down. Caroline and Captain are on their way westward, escorting a wagon filled with recently arrived girls, or 'new chums,' as Caroline calls them. What may I do to assist you?"

When Hester learned Elizabeth was looking for a cook-housekeeper, she said, "I believe we have someone here who can help you at once. She's a Scot from a fishing village in Fifeshire, and I must say she's older than most of our girls, past forty, I believe, and a Roman Catholic. She was rejected at dockside by her prospective employers, who had expected an attractive young Protestant girl." She rang for her assistant and asked her to tell Marion Rowley to appear for an interview.

Elizabeth had in mind another Bess Mason for her home, but the woman who appeared before her was much different from Bess. Short, square, with chapped hands and a weather-beaten face, she stood with her arms folded beneath her ample bosom. Her plain countenance was redeemed by large dark-brown eyes and a profusion of nut-brown hair curling around her face and falling in a single plait down her back.

Without being introduced, Marion Rowley stated her terms. "I do good, plain cooking, Madam, and your house and linen will be scrubbed proper. I'll dig your garden and tend to your stable. A cot in the kitchen will do me. I'll have one evening off for confession and every Sunday morning for Mass. At all other times, I'm at your service for twenty pounds a year."

Quite taken aback, Elizabeth stared at the woman. Marion Rowley had presented all the requisites and more, and with another baby due to arrive soon, perhaps her offer should be accepted. As well, the woman was Elizabeth's age, old enough not to be found with a neighbour's son in a compromising position. "Your terms are acceptable, Marion. I should like you to start today." As Elizabeth waited for Marion Rowley to gather her belongings, Hester Grainger served her a cup of tea and said that she and Noah would look forward to seeing them again at Susan's soirées.

On the 14th of May, 1844, at Ashfield, Elizabeth gave birth to Edward, her fifth son. Her confinement was an easy one, but the infant was not as vigorous as her other babies, a factor of her age, her accoucheuse said. Nevertheless, Edward was healthy enough and a contented baby. He looked like Elizabeth but developed his father's brown eyes. She was touched by John's gift on the arrival of their son, a gift he had long wanted to give her, the return of her inheritance.

"And, my dear, you must consult a dressmaker for a new gown as soon as you feel up to it. We have friends here at Sydney, and it's time we became part of a social circle. The gown is a belated present for the birth of William." Warmed by his thoughtfulness, Elizabeth gave him a lengthy embrace.

Despite Marion Rowley's insistence on a high standard of deportment, the older boys enjoyed her company. Thomas and Johnny could often be found in her kitchen, chatting to her about their childish concerns because she listened sympathetically and never admonished them as their parents did. They declared she was the very best cook, especially when she treated them to Scottish tea pancakes or demerara shortbread. Marion knew of their enthusiasm for Stella and got them to help muck out the stable and groom the mare. She showed them how to harness up and when the boys were on their best behaviour, rewarded them with driving lessons around Ashfield.

Their one objection was to Marion's menu every Friday at evening tea. "We're having fresh fish again!" groaned Thomas. "No one eats fresh fish! Only papists and convicts make a meal of fresh fish. That's what everybody at school says." The boy refused to lift his fork to his fried whiting.

"Thomas, you are rude!" his father said sternly. "You obviously don't appreciate the good food prepared for you. Leave the table at once and stay in your bed until morning, at which time you will apologize to Marion. Go!" At evening tea the next Friday, Thomas quietly ate his baked cod.

On mild winter days Marion took care of William and Edward so that Elizabeth might enjoy an hour of fresh air on Ashfield Common. One Saturday afternoon she sat on a bench at the edge of a small field, watching Thomas and Johnny attempt to teach George how to play football properly. The little fellow's legs were showing signs of tiring, as was the patience of his mentors. Two older boys arrived on the Common and quickly made a foursome with Thomas and Johnny, leaving George to retreat unhappily to his mother. As he did so, a pretty woman, somewhat younger than Elizabeth, came to share the bench, bringing with her a little girl, who smiled at George.

"I'm Esme Arnold," said the woman, extending her hand to Elizabeth, "and this is Leah. Those two playing football are Jeremiah and Simon." Elizabeth had a distant memory: the First Officer on the *Abbotsford* had told her his wife and three children lived at Ashfield, and she wondered whether there could be a connection.

"I'm very pleased to meet you. I'm Elizabeth Barnes, and this is George. My two football players are Thomas and Johnny. And may I please enquire whether your husband is First Officer on the *Abbotsford*?"

From that time forward, the Barnes family regarded Esme and her three children as their closest friends. With her husband spending most of his life at sea, Esme was grateful for the company of Elizabeth and her family. Watching over each other's offspring on the Common, exchanging knitting and crocheting patterns, recipes and confidences, the two women became part of one another's lives. Jeremiah and Simon were each a year older than Thomas and Johnny and attended Burwood Church of England School; Thomas and Johnny soon joined them there.

Esme, who had been born at Sydney, was the only child of a retired master mariner, Captain Buchanan. He was a jolly elf of a man who lived with Esme and his grandchildren and told the Barnes children to call him Grandpapa. He taught the boys card games and draughts and dominoes and introduced them to chess.

Although she felt at home at Ashfield, Elizabeth often thought about their farm at Yass. She corresponded regularly with Naomi Munro, who gave her all the news of the valley and the people at Saint Clement's. Elizabeth had warm recollections of a small building always crowded to its walls with worshippers. She couldn't bring herself to take her family to the forbidding Saint James Church at Sydney, yet she missed attending worship services. She confided as much to Esme.

"Come and join Saint Andrew's Scots Presbyterian congregation, why don't you? You'll not have all the pageantry you're probably used to, but the Gospel will offer the same comfort. Do say you'll come with us!" Esme's invitation worked, and the Barnes family became part of the Scots Presbyterian congregation.

One afternoon as she sat knitting a vest for baby Edward, Elizabeth realized that with moving into Shaftesbury and giving birth to her son, she had neglected Matthew Neale. She sent a note to the store with John, asking Matthew to come to dinner the following Sunday. She sent Marion in the buggy to fetch him.

"Matthew! Matthew!" said Johnny, as he and Thomas rushed out to greet the man. "Do you know how to play chess? Grandpapa Buchanan is teaching us, and we're really good at it!" Whilst he admired baby Edward, Matthew chuckled at Johnny's confidence. "I do indeed know how to play chess. Perhaps later on you'll give me a match." The two boys scrambled to stand on either side of Matthew at the table and hold his hands for the Doxology. When Matthew crossed himself afterwards, Elizabeth caught Marion looking at him.

Proud of their chess strategies, Thomas and Johnny competed to see who was the better player and begged Matthew to continue playing after Marion had served her tea pancakes later that afternoon. Elizabeth asked Marion to drive Matthew back to the store and when they climbed into the buggy, she noticed her housekeeper give Matthew a plate of the remaining pancakes covered with a linen towel.

During a Sunday afternoon visit to Parkside, Robert Nichols said, "You'll shortly receive an invitation to a wedding because I've given your address to the bride-to-be. A solicitor at Parramatta, Gideon Leonard, who is a good friend of mine, is betrothed to Judith Dartnell, one of your shipboard companions. The wedding will be held in Saint James Church, and the wedding breakfast will take place in the reception rooms at the new Government House. We'd enjoy taking you with us in the carriage, wouldn't we, Susan?"

Susan looked at Elizabeth and smiled. "Of course, Robert," she said, and she reached for her sister-in-law's hand. Elizabeth's mind went back to that first night on the *Abbotsford* and Dorcas Dartnell's stated intention to have her daughters "meet people of quality." Gideon Leonard, Solicitor, seemed eminently suitable.

Patch

EIGHT
Surry Hills

And the Lord shall help them, and deliver them.
— PSALM 37:40

Early on a summer afternoon in 1845, Robert, Susan, John and Elizabeth attended the wedding of Judith Dartnell and Gideon Leonard, a grand affair with five bridesmaids. Groomsman Robert Nichols was elegant in cream breeches and a gold brocaded waistcoat under his burgundy tailcoat. Chloe Dartnell, as the eldest, led the bridesmaids, her sister Esther and three other girls, all charmingly dressed in an array of colours.

The bride, she of "Tyger! Tyger! burning bright" at the crossing-the-equator party on the *Abbotsford*, was a statuesque beauty in an elegant, low-cut dress of ivory satin with a lace bertha collar and lace-flounced sleeves. The dress was patterned after the one worn by Queen Victoria at her marriage to Prince Albert, and Elizabeth decided the dress was more flattering to the tall Judith than to the diminutive monarch. During the signing of the register, the congregation sang "Through All the Changing Scenes of Life," and whilst the lovely melody lilted through the congregation, Elizabeth mused that Saint James Church had some vitality in it for once.

The new Government House was set on a height of land overlooking Bennelong Point. To reach the entrance, government officials and their privileged guests drove through wrought-iron gates and around a sweep drive past recently planted gardens, destined to become an impressive botanical display in the years to come.

Wearing a new satin gown in the Wedgwood blue of the pottery John imported from England, Elizabeth was greeted in the receiving line by the mother of the bride, Dorcas Dartnell. "My dear Elizabeth! How pleasant to see a familiar face! I would love to have a long talk with you. After the wedding breakfast we'll find a corner for ourselves."

A sextet of musicians from the regiment struck up the bridal waltz, and in an afternoon of quadrilles, waltzes and a new dance, the polka, Elizabeth was partnered by John, Hiram Dartnell and Robert Nichols until she managed to escape the whirling warmth of the dance floor to sit quietly with Dorcas. They found a comfortable settee in a sunlit withdrawing room overlooking the harbour.

"What a relief to be able to speak with someone I know," sighed Dorcas. "I know Gideon has political ambitions, and I realize the wedding is an opportunity for him to invite all the right people. Not that Hiram and I couldn't provide all this, you understand."

"Your dairy farm must be a prosperous venture," said Elizabeth, remembering their many shipboard conversations about establishing their farms. "Very prosperous, I'm pleased to say. We have a dairyman now and three milkmaids, all pardoned convicts. I enjoy helping with the milking, which has been an easy chore from the beginning, I'm sure you'll agree."

Elizabeth recalled the swift kick in the leg from Molly and said nothing about her own experience. "Hiram takes care of our customers and does the accounting," continued Dorcas. "He's discovered he doesn't like cows." Whilst Elizabeth wondered how one could be a dairy farmer yet not like cows, Dorcas said, "I was surprised to learn John is now a merchant here at Sydney. On the ship you spoke so enthusiastically about leasing farmland at Yass. What made you come to the city?"

Elizabeth knew she would have difficulty explaining to this successful farmer on the coastal plain the perils of farming on the western slopes. "A severe drought destroyed our crops, our sheep got the scab, and we had to give up our lease. I was greatly saddened by the circumstances, but as you know, John had been a merchant in London and he's been able to re-establish himself." Dorcas said she could appreciate the anguish in giving up one's land.

"I'm pleased to be able to see Chloe and Esther, too," said Elizabeth. She noticed that all four Dartnell women were much more ruddy-complexioned than she was; the parasols and gloves they had favoured on the *Abbotsford* must have been abandoned.

"Esther is keeping company with a Curate. Not as good a match as Judith's, of course, but he's a pleasant man and they enjoy each other's company. Chloe is my despair, such a shy girl and not one to show herself to best advantage."

Elizabeth knew that the fate of a daughter in this frontier place could be a serious concern. Men in the colony outnumbered women four to one, but to find a man worthy of being a husband was often a problem. Elizabeth had heard many parents express their worries about daughters pursued by unsavoury suitors.

Elizabeth and Dorcas ended their companionable afternoon by promising to write to one another. The sun was setting when an open landau came up the drive to take the bridal couple to their honeymoon at a beach cottage. The guests assembled to watch them set off on their life together.

In the late spring of 1845, when she began to recognize the symptoms of her mother's experience in middle age, Elizabeth knew she was going through the change. Although she would never admit it to anyone, at four and forty years of age she was quite weary of caring for five young boys and grateful she would have no more children. Light-headed and queasy, she had to summon the energy to assist in the store and when she was at home, she slept through the afternoons.

As Elizabeth wandered around Esme's garden helping to gather summer flowers one February morning in 1846, she reached across a border to pick some daisies. She stopped and stood very still. Her hands went to her abdomen and with dizzying comprehension, she felt familiar movements. Pale with her new-found knowledge, she stumbled to a garden bench. Esme hovered over her. "Dearest Elizabeth, whatever is the matter? Are you ill?"

"No, Esme, I am going to have a baby." A bewildered Esme sat down. "But you told me you were going through the change!" Elizabeth smiled. "Not for a while yet!" They both began to giggle. Esme, pleased at her friend's condition, felt the baby's movements and declared, "A girl! I'm sure of it!"

When he was apprised of the news, John strutted like a peacock, especially after Elizabeth told him of Esme's prediction. The accoucheuse came to examine Elizabeth and prescribed simple, nourishing meals, fresh air, gentle exercise and plenty of rest in view of Elizabeth's age and the newborn frailty of her previous child. Marion took on a special air of importance in the house, made the meals her mistress most enjoyed, and insisted she do no chores. The housekeeper put little Edward in the pram and took William by the hand as she accompanied Elizabeth on daily walks. She hushed the older boys so that the house might be quiet for their mother.

Monthly visits to Parkside remained a highlight for John and Elizabeth and their older sons. The boys played with their cousins; Susan and Elizabeth went for walks or sat talking and embroidering, whilst Robert and John discussed politics. Seated in a corner of the verandah on fine days, or otherwise in front of a fire in the library, the men discussed concerns that were political in origin, but personal to both of them. The conservatives in the colony, mostly farmers, had petitioned Parliament at Westminster for the resumption of convict transportation. When penal transportation to New South Wales had ceased in 1840, the flow of free labour had come to an end. Convicts had since served out their time and been emancipated. The Browns, for example, had served a sentence of seven years and were now emancipists and paid employees of the Nichols' household.

George Robert Nichols, son of a transportee, was an abolitionist. He was opposed to transportation on personal grounds, but he was also concerned about the political process. If responsible government were to be a reality in New South Wales, the colony had to have a free population that was eligible to vote. Robert was looking to be nominated by the democrats in the next Legislative Council elections.

He knew he could count on the support of John Barnes. As a merchant, John was opposed to the resumption of convict transportation for economic reasons. His business depended on paid workers who were able to buy his goods. John Barnes became an abolitionist, a member of the democratic party and a supporter of his brother-in-law's electoral ambitions.

On their visit to the Nichols' home in April, John and Elizabeth found the household ready to receive them as usual, except for Susan. Elizabeth was dismayed to discover her sister-in-law in bed, for Susan was always so full of energy. "Why didn't you send us a message? We would have delayed our visit until you're up and around again!" she exclaimed. "Then, my dear Elizabeth, I wouldn't have seen you for many months, because I must stay in bed until my confinement."

Throughout that autumn Elizabeth went to call on Susan as often as her health would permit. Susan was thrilled that Elizabeth was also expecting. Their visits became briefer because neither woman had the strength for long conversations. "Won't it be wonderful for our new babies to grow up together!" said Susan.

Before daylight one morning at the end of June, John set off in the buggy to fetch the accoucheuse. Elizabeth's labour was slower and more painful than she had ever experienced, and almost twenty-four hours went by before she began, in complete exhaustion, to push her baby towards the sunrise of the 30th of June, 1846. As the winter sun lit up the bedroom, a tiny infant squalled lustily, suckled vigorously and squalled even more. Elizabeth and John Barnes had a healthy daughter. They named her Elizabeth Mary Maria for her mother and her two grandmothers, and they called her Beth.

Pampered as she was by Marion Rowley and John, Elizabeth enjoyed her bedrest following Beth's birth and lay cozily amongst the pillows, offering thankful prayers to God for enabling her to have a daughter. When Beth was three months old, she was taken to Parkside to meet the Nichols family. Elizabeth found a wan-looking Susan lying in bed, eager to hold her niece in her arms.

On the warm afternoon of the 12th of November, 1846, Elizabeth was rocking Beth to sleep in her cradle on the verandah when a familiar black carriage came slowly into Ashfield. Alfred Brown tied Ebony and Trojan to the gatepost at Shaftesbury and walked up the path to the house. The tall man refused the chair Elizabeth offered and spoke quietly.

"Madam, I have sad news. Mrs. Nichols was delivered of a daughter early this morning. The baby... died, and... Mrs. Nichols... passed away before noon." Elizabeth burst into tears, fled to her bedroom, and cried and cried into her pillow. The coachman sank into a chair on the verandah and sobbed. Cruelly vivid in his mind was the sight of his beloved employer slipping away whilst her household, the accoucheuse, the doctor and the Vicar watched helplessly.

Summoned from the store by Alfred Brown, John Barnes came back to his house more distraught than he had ever been in his life. He found his way to Elizabeth and held her in his arms as the two of them wept. Dear, dear Susan had been taken. Why were God's ways so difficult? Why?

Elizabeth and John were accompanied by Thomas, Johnny and George at Susan's funeral at Saint Laurence Church, Redfern, the following day. The church was crowded with mourners who wept at the loss of their generous, delightful friend. Susan was buried by the Reverend Cowper with her baby in her arms. Elizabeth thought her heart would break when she saw George reach for his cousin Francis's hand as the coffin was lowered to its resting place.

Perhaps to help overcome his lingering grief, Robert threw himself into political activities. In the colonial elections of 1848, George Robert Nichols became the new representative of the Northumberland Boroughs and held a grand victory celebration at Parkside, with Elizabeth in charge of the festivities. A Currency Lad, the son of a Third Fleet convict, was now a Member of the Legislative Council of the colony of New South Wales.

The next time the *Abbotsford* docked at Port Jackson, from the hold came John's gift to Elizabeth, commemorating the birth of Beth. Elizabeth was ecstatic when four husky men set a Broadwood pianoforte into a corner of the drawing room. Despite the rigours of the voyage, the Broadwood with its bolted iron frame had arrived intact, its burled walnut finish showing nary a mark. Telling her husband he was the most thoughtful, generous man in the whole world, she happily practised the many selections of music that came with the pianoforte.

The Barnes Store in George Street continued to prosper, but one evening John came home with the news that a bank was to be constructed on the site of the store. Such an occurrence was to be expected because George Street, once a centre of shopping, was rapidly becoming a street of banks and insurance companies.

In April 1849, John moved his business to Surry Hills, the broad ridge of land in south Sydney named by Lieutenant-Colonel Joseph Foveaux of the New South Wales Corps for his home shire of Surrey in England, his spelling notwithstanding. Foveaux, a former Acting Governor of the colony, had been a Commandant of convicts on Norfolk Island, one who prided himself on his precise record of floggings.

Elizabeth was dismayed because John had arranged to move the business out of the city without consulting her. She loved the George Street store in the midst of all the activity of central Sydney. She recalled the first time she had walked along the street, shopping with Susan Nichols on an autumn day in 1841.

"These new Crown Street premises should provide us with a good living for years to come," declared John. Elizabeth could do nothing but agree with him.

Shaftesbury
Ashfield, West Sydney
June 18th, 1851

My Dear Dorcas,
Thank you for your recent letter. I always appreciate receiving news of your family.
May I begin by saying how pleased I am to hear of Chloe's marriage to Amos Winters. They are both earnest people, and I feel they are very well suited. I regret to learn of the destruction of Amos's orange

orchard in a flood; I have heard that the river which flows through the Hawkesbury Plain presents a constant threat of flooding to farmers there. How fortunate that Amos was able to establish himself in a bank once more and be transferred to Parramatta. Please give my enclosed congratulatory message to Chloe and Amos. I'm certain they will be very happy together.

Do give my regards to Esther and her husband. His appointment to a church of his own on the coast is a notable achievement, although I know it is far away from you at Parramatta.

We offer you congratulations on the arrival of your grandchildren. I am sure you enjoy having Judith and Gideon and their twins nearby.

John has moved his business to Crown Street in Surry Hills, where he is doing a good trade. Our children are still at Burwood School, and we are watching them develop individual interests and skills.

Please remember us to all your family, with our special regards to Hiram.

I remain your friend,

Elizabeth

As Christmas of 1852 approached, Elizabeth and John realized Thomas would soon be finished at school. At a Sunday dinner John broached the subject of their eldest son's future. "You'll soon be leaving Burwood, Thomas, and I look forward to having you work in the store with me." Elizabeth watched sixteen-year-old Thomas finish a plateful of Marion's plum duff and take a large swallow of tea before he looked at his father.

"I'm heading west, Papa, beyond Yass, to find a cattle station in need of a jackeroo. I want to be a stockman with my own stock horse and saddle and a kangaroo hide whip with a myall wood handle," he said, grinning. "I'm sorry about the store, but I've never thought of being a merchant."

John had difficulty controlling his distress. "By rights, Thomas, the business is yours to inherit! Instead, you seem to be driven by a passion for horses!" Thomas did not answer his father. A short time later he was on a coach heading for the western slopes. He promised his mother, who was more understanding of his dreams, that he would write often. Meanwhile, John continued to be bewildered by his son's decision.

A year later, Johnny, probably anticipating a discussion of his future, made an announcement at a Sunday dinner. "I've heard the goldfields are proving very productive. As soon as I'm finished at school, I'm heading west to the Turon River diggings to try my luck. I plan to get enough together to buy a property on the western slopes."

John's disappointment at Thomas's decision the previous year was nothing compared with his reaction to Johnny's plans. "You're an able student, Johnny," said John emphatically. "You've a confident manner and you speak well. You should take training in the law and when you are older, enter politics. Working in the diggings is a waste of your time and ability!"

Until Johnny completed his schooling that year, Elizabeth had to listen to John lecture his second son on the perils of being an itinerant digger and the need for a worthwhile goal in life. Like Thomas, Johnny did not argue with his father. As soon as he was out of school, however, he boarded a coach travelling in the direction of the Turon diggings. John was gravely concerned, but he knew Johnny well enough to acknowledge his determination.

Two of her boys had gone to make their way in the world, and Elizabeth was grateful she still had four children at home with her. Young George enjoyed helping his father and Matthew in the store on Saturdays, and Elizabeth became hopeful their third son might be the one to take over the business. Their next son, William, was keen on the out-of-doors and declared he planned to spend his life on horseback, like Thomas. Edward, known in the family as Ted, was the most thoughtful of the boys. Having inherited his mother's musical talent, he enjoyed singing in the school choir. His free time was spent in football, cricket and sailing with William and their schoolmates. Young Beth, who was adored by the whole family, was enough like her Aunt Susan to have been her daughter. Her sunny disposition and irrepressible giggle often brought tearful memories to Elizabeth.

On a Sunday afternoon in the spring of 1853, as Elizabeth sat crocheting a lace collar, thirteen-year-old George appeared in front of her. "The Headmaster says I've reached the years of discretion. That means I'm old enough to decide if I want to be a confirmed member of the Church of England. Next term, may I attend Confirmation classes at Burwood?" Elizabeth smiled at "the years of discretion" and set aside her crocheting to pay attention to her very serious son. She was seldom embarrassed, but this was one of those moments.

"Of course you're ready for Confirmation classes, George. However, you must be baptised before you take instruction for Church of England membership," she told him.

"Wasn't I baptised when I was a baby?" he asked.

"No, you weren't, I'm sorry to say, and neither were William, Ted or Beth. I'll talk to your father, and we'll see what we can do to remedy the situation."

Later that evening she said to John, "I've allowed my feelings about church politics to take precedence over having our children baptised. I feel very ashamed because all these years have gone by and I've not done my duty as a Christian parent!"

"Don't be hard on yourself, my dear. I'm just as much to blame."

"Perhaps Mr. Stewart at Saint Andrew's would baptise the children," said Elizabeth. "Let's have a word with him on Sunday."

The Presbyterian minister proved to be an understanding pastor who chuckled at Elizabeth and John's excuses rather than chastising them for neglecting the spiritual well-being of their offspring. "Next week," he said, "I'll ensure they're all properly received into Christ's flock!"

On the 27th of September, 1853, George Robert, age thirteen, William John, age eleven, Edward Prior, age nine, and Elizabeth Mary Maria, age seven, were baptised by the Reverend Mr. Robert Stewart of Saint Andrew's Scots Presbyterian Church at Sydney. The tardiness of the event caused Elizabeth to struggle with feelings of guilt for a long time. George began attending Confirmation classes at Burwood School and was duly confirmed as a member of the Church of England.

Elizabeth still helped Matthew in the store when John went to the docks about a shipment. Not all shipments arrived intact, and the destruction of a crate of valuable English pottery, for example, was a costly disappointment. Maritime insurers, many of them in George Street, were kept busy settling claims.

Moving the business to Crown Street in Surry Hills had been a good decision because Surry Hills was a well-populated area where the residents appreciated the merchandise in the Barnes Store. There came a time, however, when Elizabeth sensed that John had become worried about his business. He was spending long hours at the store and arriving home late for his evening tea. Although something more serious than usual was bothering him, her husband was not the sort to complain.

As they sat by the fire one evening, she said, "You haven't said a word since tea time. Please tell me what's troubling you." John sighed. "We don't have the trade in the store, my dear, that we once had," he said. Elizabeth did not want to admit it, but from the monthly accounts she knew their custom was slowly declining. "Sydney has many retail establishments now," he added, "with more appearing every year. We're facing competition unlike anything we've ever known. I'm thinking of moving our home and business to the outskirts of the city to take advantage of the spreading population."

Elizabeth stared at him. She had not imagined so drastic a solution to their concerns. She was upset at the mention of leaving their Ashfield home, where she could relax on the wide verandah and enjoy a sweeping view of Sydney, or spend enjoyable hours planting and cultivating the borders in her back garden. After Susan's death, she and Esme had grown very close, and how would she manage in an outlying village without her dearest friend nearby? She had disturbing recollections of those lonely days at Concord and she did not answer John.

Lying awake that night, she wondered whether God felt she had been too long in one place and wanted to use her elsewhere. She resolved to encourage her husband to talk about the move. Weeks of distressing discussions followed, but at least she and John were trying to find a solution together. Whilst Elizabeth was concerned lest they move and find themselves in even worse circumstances, John was as determined to move out of the city as he had been to leave the farm. Elizabeth's old headaches returned.

Always a welcome diversion were the letters from their eldest sons. Thomas wrote every fortnight and although he addressed his letters to both parents, he seemed to be explaining life on a cattle station to his mother. Johnny also wrote regularly to his parents, but his letters were written to appeal to his father.

After a year in the goldfields, Johnny wrote to say he was going south to Melbourne to enjoy the entertainments of the city. Unaware of his parents' concerns, Johnny wrote to them about the success of merchants in the capital city of the colony of Victoria. Gold was being mined in Victoria, and miners arriving at Melbourne needed particular items to take to the diggings. Any store that supplied their requirements was heavily patronized, reported Johnny. When he received an interested reply from John, he persuaded his father to travel to Melbourne to see for himself. John did so and came back to tell Elizabeth he was certain they could establish a successful business there.

Elizabeth was grateful for John's new-found enthusiasm, but now his original suggestion of the outskirts of Sydney seemed strangely preferable to distant Melbourne. She knew, however, that John had done as much as he could with his Crown Street store, and the colony of Victoria did seem to offer new opportunities. Albeit with great reluctance, she agreed with John that their best course lay in moving to Melbourne. Elizabeth said endless prayers for Heavenly support and resigned herself to the move. Her life was taking another turn. She must trust in God to guide her along a new path.

Rebecca

TO OWN A FARM

They say there's bread and work for all,
And the sun shines always there—
But I'll not forget old Ireland,
Were it fifty times as fair!

—HELEN SELINA, LADY DUFFERIN, "LAMENT OF THE IRISH EMIGRANT"

Historical records reveal that of the 465,100 souls who sailed during the 1850s from the British Isles to the Australian continent, 231,600 of them were assisted immigrants bound for work in the colonies. Australian colonial governments of that decade, in need of labour after the reduction of convict transportation, chartered former convict ships and offered assisted passages to those hoping for a better life. Steerage compartments that had previously transported convicted felons to penal servitude now carried immigrant workers to colonial employment.

The *Caroline*, a full-rigged ship of 733 tons with a steam engine augmenting her canvas, left Plymouth, England, on July 8th, 1854, for Port Jackson in Sydney Harbour, New South Wales. She carried eight passengers in her cabins, general merchandise in her hold and 258 Irish assisted immigrants in steerage. Fifty-four men, one hundred sixty-nine women, twenty-one girls and fourteen boys were bound for service in the colony as agricultural labourers or house servants. Amongst the farm workers sailing in steerage on the *Caroline* was the second daughter of a farmer and cooper in Dromore, County Tyrone, named Rebecca Nixon.

NINE

The Caroline

The Lord also will be a refuge for the oppressed...
—PSALM 9:9

Rebecca Nixon was a vigorous young woman wearing a dress of grey muslin with an exquisitely crocheted lace collar. The dress, the lace collar and the dainty lace cap that held her thick dark hair in place were of her own making. Stitched to the underside of her lace-trimmed petticoat was a sachet containing her dowry of ten pounds. She carried two drawstring canvas bundles of clothing and other belongings. At the bottom of one she had placed a Holy Bible and *The Book of Common Prayer*, and in the other, wrapped in heavy brown paper, a memento, a piece of turf her father had given her from the stack at the windward side of their stone cottage in Dromore.

As an assisted immigrant, she had paid a shipping agent her one-pound fare, earned in the fields of her father's neighbours, towards the ship's steerage tariff of fifteen pounds. From Londonderry she had travelled in an overcrowded barque southward over the Irish Sea to Plymouth. Not knowing any of the other passengers, seventeen-year-old Rebecca Nixon boarded the *Caroline* and departed for New South Wales.

Rebecca chose a top bed, not that she had any experience in doing so, but she reckoned she would sleep better if she were above the to-ing and fro-ing in the steerage compartment. Of course, she would have to share the narrow bed, and her sleeping companion would be known soon enough. Lord save me, she prayed, from someone who snores in my ear or thrashes the blanket about.

She had been amongst the first steerage passengers aboard, believing that timeliness was always an advantage, and had been directed to a set of steep stairs at the stern of the vessel under the cabins. More like a heavy ladder, the stairs led down to the centre of one side of the steerage compartment reserved for the girls. There in the gloom she found a narrow table and benches in the middle, three double-level beds at right angles to the far side and two double-level beds at right angles to the stairway side. She counted: at two to a bed, there was room for twenty. She noticed they would be able to relieve themselves in a water closet in a corner to the left of the stairs, much more discreet than using the one on deck. Having chosen the top bed opposite the stairway, all the better to get some light and air and see who was coming and going, she hung her bundles on one of the pegs at the head of the bed. Thus Rebecca Nixon claimed her space for the voyage.

Her compartment mates came tumbling down the ladder all at once, giggling nervously. Behind them, carrying two lanterns, was the officer in charge, Mr. Speer, he told them. He was a thin man with a lean, weathered face twisted into a sneer. He ordered the young women to stand around the table. Rebecca quickly counted twenty besides herself. "You three!" he barked, pointing at the three smallest. "You'll be sharing this bed!" He indicated the bed beneath Rebecca's.

One of the three, a saucy little thing with long ginger hair, squealed, "But the agent said for the fare of one pound, we'd be no more than two to a bed. If I'd wanted to sleep more than two to a bed, I'd have never left home!"

"If this isn't good enough for you," snapped Mr. Speer, "get off the ship and go home!" Not a possible option, Rebecca said to herself. "The rest of you, choose a bed and hang your bundles on a peg as this first girl has done. Stand by your beds till I check your names on the manifest. Be quick about it!"

Confusion reigned as the young women sized up each other and claimed their spaces. A slim girl with pale blue eyes and thick black curls touched Rebecca's arm and asked if she might share her bed. "Suit yourself," answered Rebecca and immediately realized she could have been more gracious.

Mr. Speer, who had identified himself as the Steerage Overseer, checked off their names. "What about our boxes?" wailed a girl at the end of the compartment. "Your boxes are already in the hold. You'll be permitted to open them in a month's time. Until then, you'll make do with what's on your back and what's in your bundles." Rebecca had learned this from the shipping agent in Ireland, but it was news to the girl at the end of the room and several others, who joined in the wailing.

"Keep silence! You'll obey Captain's Standing Orders on this ship! No smoking in these quarters. If you fancy a pipe, go up on deck. There'll be no drunkenness and no hanging about the crew's quarters in the fo'c'sle, not that any man would be interested in you lot anyway." Why did he have to be insulting? Rebecca asked herself. "You'll be told when your clothes and bedding are to be washed and dried. You'll be ordered below when it turns dark and you'll be in your beds by ten o'clock. You're not to go on deck at night. Those lanterns are to be lit only at mealtimes. Two mess leaders in this compartment will prepare your rations and check that your bed and the space around it are kept clean and tidy." Not an easy task in this gloom, muttered Rebecca.

"You!" he bellowed at her. "You're in charge of these beds," and he counted off the ones he meant. "You!" he shouted at a girl who stood opposite Rebecca. "You'll take the remainder. This compartment will be inspected at any time on any day." He turned on his heel and disappeared up the ladder.

A clatter of conversations followed, including unflattering comments about Mr. Speer ("He thinks he's still transporting convicts!") and introductions all round. Rebecca learned her bed partner was Alice Foley from County Waterford, and her fellow mess leader, a tall, attractive girl with auburn hair and green eyes, was Hannah Sarah Wallace from County Down. "Just Hannah will do," said the tall girl.

Whistles and clanging, shouts and thumping on the main deck drowned out any further talk, and Rebecca reckoned they would soon be underway. "Come on," she said to Hannah. "We'd better bid farewell to old England." The girls climbed the ladder and stood at the port rail of the *Caroline* whilst her lines were slipped and she was pulled away from Plymouth harbour by steam tugboats. The main deck was filled with steerage passengers: men, women, boys, girls, married couples, small children and babes in arms. Their laughter, sobbing and lilting Irish voices washed across the ship.

Whilst the *Caroline* was guided through the harbour by the tugboats, Rebecca took a good look at the ship. In the centre of the deck a smokestack rose from the steam engine below. The shipping agent had told her the engine would be fired up when sails were furled for lack of winds, or during a severe storm. Near the rails were four hatchways to steerage, two on each side of the deck. They were open in this calm water, but they would be closed in rough seas, and how then would she and the others manage in their small, dark space below? Voyages to New South Wales could now be done in three months, still a lengthy time in confined quarters when she was so fond of the out-of-doors. She decided she would spend as much time as she could on deck.

Rebecca looked across at the cabin class passengers, a family with six children, who sat in canvas chairs on the aft deck, drinking tea and lemonade and enjoying the view. With money enough to afford that kind of passage, what had prompted them to quit the land of their birth, she wondered. Perhaps the husband had been given an important post in the colony. She knew well the reasons many steerage passengers had abandoned their birthplace: thousands of starving and homeless Irish, if they had not been shut up in a workhouse or thrown into prison by the British, were eager for any chance of employment, even on the other side of the world.

She was distracted by giggles and squeals nearby. The small girl with long ginger hair, whose name was Kitty Flynn, and her two bedmates were attempting to get the attention of a trio of stalwart young men. "Ooh! So brawny they are! Did you ever see the like of those shoulders? Able to lift anything, to be sure! I wonder where their quarters are?"

"They came from that hatchway," said one of Kitty's new companions. "That's where the single men and boys are. The married folk and their bairns are along there, and the older women are down that way." Kitty laughed. "What fun!" she said, swishing her skirts. "We'll have to look sharp, girls! There's far too many females on this ship!" Kitty Flynn was one of Rebecca's responsibilities. Was she to be held to account for Kitty's behaviour as well as her bed space?

The Overseer had selected two shy, plain-faced farm boys as mess runners for the girls' compartment. Because female passengers were not allowed near the ship's galley with its Negro male cooks, Bern Rooney and Uel Grady had been ordered to fetch the girls' food for them from the Steerage Steward. At tea time that day, Bern came staggering to their hatchway with two great pails of soup, and Uel struggled with a mammoth jug of tea, a basket of bread and an earthenware jar. Cabin class passengers on the *Caroline* would fare much better. Rebecca had watched the Cabin Steward heading for the dining saloon with trays of meat pies, steaming mashed pumpkin, fragrant cheese scones and a large dish of apple cinnamon cobbler with cream.

The girls' first evening meal consisted of tepid pea soup, lukewarm strong tea with demerara sugar, and pieces of bread with treacle from the earthenware jar. Would the food ever be served hot, and would there be any variety in the weeks to come? Yet, since the blight had first ruined the potatoes nine years before, many Irish families were surviving on nothing but Indian meal, and at least the food on board seemed ample. By the look of the girls hungrily waiting, Rebecca believed many of them were emigrating because they were starving at home.

The young women crowded together on either side of the narrow table. Hannah Wallace, who proved to have a pleasant voice, led them in singing the Doxology. Rebecca was about to serve the soup when she noticed Alice Foley and several others making the sign of the Cross. Lord love me! I'll be sharing my bed with a papist! She had never known a Roman Catholic. She did now.

At lights out on the first night aboard, Rebecca settled her muscular form on the straw pallet beside the slim figure of Alice Foley.

The papist girl from Waterford fell into a quiet sleep, and Rebecca decided she would be no bother as a bedmate. In the bottom bed the three smallest girls giggled as they lay head to foot.

All was well for the first hour, but the large, three-masted *Caroline* had sailed from sheltered Plymouth Harbour into the English Channel, where the seas could be rough at any time. Battling the prevailing westerlies, the Captain tacked towards Land's End, sending his vessel tossing through choppy swells in blustery winds.

"Jesus, Mary and Joseph!" moaned Alice Foley. She sat up and vomited her evening meal over her bedmate. Rebecca came awake protesting whilst Alice groaned and heaved at her a second time. Alice was not alone in her retching; most of the girls were losing their meals. The sour stench of half-digested pea soup and treacle filled the darkness. Rebecca and Hannah, their stomachs blessedly only queasy in the rolling, pitching ship, climbed down and lit lanterns in defiance of Mr. Speer's orders. They tried to persuade seasick girls to get out of their beds and vomit in the water closet. At dawn the two of them went to fetch pails of sea water to rinse their clothes and buckets of sand to clean the compartment deck.

A robust older woman, her competent manner softened by a smile, descended the ladder, carrying a basket with some hard biscuit and a small bunch of leaves. Although the health of all passengers had been checked in Ireland before their passage was accepted, Matron and the Surgeon had also inspected the boatload of Irish when they boarded. Those who had failed this inspection for any reason had been abandoned at the dock and left to fend for themselves in England. Employers in the colony expected fit and healthy workers.

"Listen carefully, girls," said Matron. "You must keep something in your stomachs, lest you injure yourselves with retching. A few leaves of scurvy grass and a hard biscuit will help settle the heaves. Make sure you take the scurvy grass and chew it whenever it's offered to you. Carry a biscuit with you each day and eat a bit of it frequently to keep your stomach settled. Stay up on deck as much as you can. Stand at the rail and look at the horizon to help prevent the retching." Most of the girls were too seasick to pay any attention to her.

Matron told Hannah and Rebecca a bunch of scurvy grass would be delivered from the galley once a week to be shared amongst the girls until the ship reached the Canary Islands, where fruit would be taken aboard. Rebecca had seen sailors with bits of grass in their mouths. Stems and leaves seemed a strange thing to be eating, but after Matron had advised the girls about seasickness, she lectured them on the horrors of scurvy: blotchy skin, bleeding gums and wretched weakness ending in death. Rebecca took Matron's word for it; scurvy grass was the ticket.

"You'll find some will refuse the grass," she said to Hannah and Rebecca, "and I'll rely on you to insist they all take it. The Ship's Surgeon is determined we shall avoid scurvy on this voyage." This might seem a noble aim, but Rebecca had heard a Ship's Surgeon was paid according to each healthy worker he delivered to the colony. Little wonder he took an interest in the welfare of assisted immigrants.

No sooner had the *Caroline* cleared the Channel than winds across the Bay of Biscay sent her rolling heavily. Alice was apologetic, but even in a sound sleep, the poor thing could be taken with the heaves. Never-ending days of seasickness throughout the ship made Rebecca think the whole journey might be as miserable.

"Thanks be to God," she said one morning when she climbed up on deck to find the *Caroline* sailing over calmer waters in soft, warm breezes.

An abbreviated Matins on the following Sunday was performed perfunctorily by the Captain. He had come out on deck to inspect his crew and leave an officer to mumble a few prayers and dismiss everyone quickly. There was no hymn or homily, and Rebecca, who enjoyed a church service, was disappointed to realize a truncated version was all they would get here.

One bright day whilst the *Caroline* sailed slowly southward over calm seas, Hannah Wallace and Rebecca sat side by side on a small box locker in a corner of the deck, sharing an apple from Rebecca's precious supply. She was concentrating on her daily Gospel chapter whilst Hannah knitted the ribbing of a jumper. Rebecca had expected a sailing ship to be a quiet place. Instead, a confusion of nautical sounds came from all sides and aloft: the rudder creaking as they slept, sails snapping, sailors hauling ropes, the boatswain piping his calls and those in charge shouting commands. And bells! As many as eight clanging one after another! Matron had explained watches to them and the number of bells marking the passage of time in each watch. Rebecca appreciated a quiet, orderly life and looked forward to working once more on solid ground at a peaceful farm.

The more than two hundred steerage passengers around them added to the clamour. They sat or stood anywhere on deck and lounged against the rails; both women and men smoked pipes. Some were asleep on coils of rope whilst children romped in all directions, and three men played fiddles for a chorus of sentimental singers. The assisted immigrants had laboured in the fields and houses of Ireland from a very young age, and their voyage to a new homeland was, to be sure, the one chance in their lives for an extended period of leisure. Their quarters were cramped and gloomy, but in good weather the deck of the *Caroline*, though crowded and noisy, was a fine place for good old crack in Irish or English, music of the fife and fiddle, songs and relaxation during the long, warm days. The ship rolled and pitched gently, her tall, square-rigged masts displaying billowing canvas as she headed ever onward into tropical waters.

"Rebecca!" said Hannah. "Look over there! Standing by the rail. There he is again! Isn't he the most handsome man you've ever seen?" Rebecca glanced up from her Bible at a man nearby. She had seen him before. He was very tall, several inches over six feet, well-built and probably more than thirteen stone in weight. She went back to The Gospel according to Saint John; it was easy to imagine young John following in the Master's footsteps. Meanwhile, Hannah's knitting needles clicked rapidly as she further described the tall man.

"He's no mere boy. He's a rugged man with good bones. Look at his fair wavy hair! See how it curls round his neck? Such a flowing moustache! I wonder if it would tickle?"

"Whisht, Hannah! Control yourself! You've been staring at him for two days now. Tend to your knitting, lass!"

"Where do you suppose he's from, and where will he work in the colony, do you think?"

"Lord bless me, Hannah Sarah Wallace, but you do try my patience!" Rebecca closed her Bible and got up. She pushed her way through the crowd to the object of Hannah's curiosity. "Excuse me, sir. My friend would like to know where you're from and where you're going to work in New South Wales."

The man eased himself away from the rail and laughed in a low, rumbling chuckle. He took Rebecca's elbow to guide her through the throng to her seat and sat down on his haunches in front of the two girls.

"My name's David Andrews. I'm from Convoy in County Donegal and I'm bound for the Oxley Estate, somewhere called Wingecarribee." He pronounced the name of the place with exaggerated clarity and chuckled.

"The Oxley Estate!" exclaimed Hannah. "And so are we! I'm Hannah Wallace from County Down and this is my friend Rebecca Nixon from Tyrone. We're glad to make your acquaintance, Mr. Andrews."

"Call me David, please, Hannah." When he smiled, his great blue eyes crinkled at the corners. "Will you be working as house servants, then?"

"Not us," said Rebecca. "We're both field hands. We'll be putting our backs into lifting potatoes. What will you be doing there?"

"They tell me I'm a good man with horses, and I'm to have a team for ploughing and harvesting. We'll be meeting in the fields, then!" he said, sounding pleased. The striking of a bell signalled the hour for the evening meal, and Rebecca and a blushing Hannah excused themselves to get their rations from Bern and Uel.

Mr. Speer had said the young women's quarters would be inspected at any time on any day. Not so. Every morning he came down to their compartment at precisely seven o'clock, arriving just as the girls, some clad only in undergarments, were washing themselves in the two pails of sea water Rebecca and Hannah had fetched. The Overseer opened the hatch, descended the ladder quickly and stood leering in the semi-darkness. Every morning Hannah and Rebecca intercepted him and asked him to wait until all the girls were washed and dressed. His response was to volley curses at the two of them and barge amongst the shrieking girls, letting his hands roam in all directions.

Rebecca was enraged. "He has to be stopped!" she declared to Hannah. "He's lecherous, he is! Sure an' he thinks we're here for his pleasure, like the convict women before us!" She hitched her skirts, stormed up the compartment ladder and went to look for Matron. She found her down near the galley sorting limes she had brought aboard when the ship had stopped for provisions in the Canary Islands. The girls were objecting as much to lime juice as they had to scurvy grass.

"You're not the only mess leader ever to complain about Mr. Speer," said Matron, as they came back up on deck. "I've sailed with the man before, and he makes a practice of tormenting women on every voyage. Some of them, unfortunately, will enjoy that sort of attention, and he knows it." Matron knew this was not the first or the last voyage to leave a girl abandoned on a wharf at Port Jackson, unemployable because of her condition.

"So you're telling me you'll do nothing to stop him?" said Rebecca.

"I'm here to help the Ship's Surgeon attend to the health of passengers and crew, Miss Nixon. I'm not able to discipline inappropriate conduct." Rebecca replied, "Then I shall go to the Captain! Surely he has the power to put an end to such lascivious behaviour!"

"I would strongly recommend you take this matter no further," said Matron. "You seem to be a clever, sensible lass, so you'll understand me when I tell you a record is kept of each assisted immigrant. You don't want to have a reputation as a troublemaker, and I know the Captain is too busy to consider your complaints." Rebecca was concerned. "Some of the girls in our compartment may succumb to Mr. Speer's advances. There'll be no accounting for the consequences if he should seduce them with his lewd antics!"

"You are not responsible for the poor character of those few, Miss Nixon. Protect yourself and the others as best you can and pray we reach Port Jackson without anything unfortunate happening." Rebecca stared at Matron, certain she knew much more than she was saying.

When Matron left her on deck, Rebecca burst into angry tears. She was not a tearful girl by nature, but frustration had overwhelmed her. She was about to descend to her quarters when David Andrews caught up with her. "I saw you talking to Matron, Rebecca. Would you care to tell me what the trouble is?" Trying to stifle her crying, she told him about Mr. Speer and her conversation with Matron.

"You lassies have no chance at all against that slimy sod! We'll not be able to change his behaviour, but we can alter the hour of his inspections a little."

"How?" she asked. "Hannah and I have asked him to wait until the girls are dressed, but he pays no attention!"

David had a ready answer. "Then we'll prevent the man going down that ladder until you're all ready."

"And who are 'we,' may I ask?"

"Me and my mates! Never fear, Rebecca. We'll be on duty early tomorrow. Mr. Speer will not get by us till you say so!"

"He'll have you thrown into the brig, and where will that get you on the Oxley Estate? Don't be foolish, David!"

"I may be foolish, but I've no fear of an Overseer or a brig. As for the Oxley Estate, they need a farmhand who's good with horses and if they don't want me, sure an' other landowners do. I'll have a bunch of the boys ready tomorrow."

Before seven next morning, six farm labourers the size of David Andrews lounged at the closed hatchway leading to the girls' compartment. Mr. Speer, who was considerably smaller than any of these men, swore at them and ordered them to step aside. David Andrews, his arms folded across his broad chest, stepped forward, not aside. "As an officer and a gentleman, you wouldn't want to do an inspection until the young ladies are dressed, would you, sir? We'll just wait a wee while till they're all decently clothed."

"You insolent bastard! Out of my way!" When his words had no effect whatsoever, the officer marched off in a fury. David and his friends resumed their lounging at the hatchway. The Overseer returned the moment Rebecca pushed open the hatch to indicate the quarters were ready for inspection. The Donegal Guards, as David called them, watched over the girls' compartment for the rest of the voyage.

Mr. Speer retaliated by venting his rage on Rebecca and Hannah, hurling curses at them for the slightest discrepancies in their quarters. On his worst days he flew into a temper and had the two of them down on their knees with buckets of sand, scrubbing the compartment deck over and over until their knees bled. Every morning he continued to grope all the girls as much as he could and complained they wore too many clothes.

To his satisfaction, Kitty Flynn and her bedmates simpered flirtatiously whenever he approached them and made no objection to his lewd advances. Rebecca sighed in despair one afternoon when she saw Kitty heading for the fo'c'sle and disappearing into the Overseer's cabin. He is a hypocrite as well as a lecher, Rebecca muttered to herself. "Not that any man would be interested in you lot!" he had told them, obviously excluding his own appetites. When Kitty arrived back in time for tea, the smell of strong drink and the girl's slurred speech made Rebecca furious.

TEN

Port Jackson

*These see the works of the Lord, and his
wonders in the deep.*

—PSALM 107:24

Days of reading and chatting on deck were over. Rebecca and her companions spent tedious hours lying on their beds in the steaming stench of their quarters, marking time by counting the ship's bells. The *Caroline* had entered the doldrums of the equatorial region, where the tropical heat was particularly unbearable for the steerage passengers, coming as they did from the cool climate of Ireland. Moreover, the noise of the steam engine drove everyone to distraction. The engine banged with deafening regularity whilst stokers, stripped to the waist, shovelled dusty coal into the insatiable fire under the boiler. The din and the heat made any attempt at sleep or conversation impossible.

"In the time of pure sail, ships travelled across to Rio to avoid the doldrums and back again to the Cape. Twice across the Atlantic Ocean they went and took five months to reach Port Jackson." Matron was shouting into Rebecca's ear as the two of them stood at the rail, the girl momentarily exchanging her foetid steerage compartment for the roaring deck. "At least the five months were quieter than this!" Rebecca shouted in reply.

A week later when the sails began to fill once more, the steam engine was put to rest. The passengers, their heads still pounding from the din, settled down to the familiar sounds of proceeding under canvas. Conversations on deck were again possible, and one day Rebecca looked up to find Matron standing in front of her, offering her a book. "Good morning, Miss Nixon. I thought you might like a bit of a change from your Bible."

"My daily Bible chapter keeps me headed in the right direction, Matron," she answered stiffly. "Of course," said Matron. "I just wondered if you would be interested in reading about your new country. *Travels in Australia*, by Major Mitchell, one of the Queen's Surveyors, is most informative."

Rebecca did not neglect the Gospels, but in her sheltered corner on deck, she began to read about the strange, distant land that was to become her home. The book described bizarre beasts such as kangaroos, wallabies, dingoes, koalas and snakes, and an alien countryside with unusual flowers, trees and birds. She was briefly homesick for those Sunday afternoons in County Tyrone when she read books of poetry under a hazelnut bush in a dappled green glen whilst a younger brother, fishing pole in hand, searched for salmon in the sparkling stream below. She read Major Mitchell's book aloud to Hannah, and both of them realized there would be more to adjust to than they had thought. What would the Oxley Estate be like? They hoped for something familiar nearby, like a shaded stream and a village with shops and a church.

Matron admired Rebecca's spunk in dealing with Mr. Speer and told her so. David Andrews and his Donegal Guards had a shipboard reputation as determined protectors. Indeed, the steerage compartment of the older women passengers was now similarly protected by the Antrim Guards, and the two groups of men flexed their muscles and glared disdainfully at any crew member who looked to challenge them. The Captain, very aware of the inclinations of his Irish male passengers, had given stern warnings and had threatened to lock up anyone caught fighting; it was scarcely a meaningful threat, however, because a shipload of brawling Irishmen would more than overflow his brig.

The girls came up from their quarters one morning to find the *Caroline* sailing into a great bay. Before them rose an enormous, flat-topped mountain. The ship was soon anchored, and cabin passengers were rowed ashore to explore Cape Town for the day. Steerage passengers got no such liberty. Instead, as they had in the Cape Verde Islands and the Canaries, they had to remain aboard. On more than one voyage the Captain had known assisted immigrants, like convicts before them, try to slip ashore and disappear in the attractive Cape of Africa. Consequently, steerage passengers were closely watched as they took turns standing at the rail, straining to see the activity on the wharves in the distance.

Hannah and Rebecca and other steerage passengers who could read and write spent part of the day writing letters. Whilst she sharpened her pencil with her pocketknife, Rebecca reminded herself that her father was impressed by good handwriting. She would remember to keep her pencil sharp and use the best of her skills from Carraghamulkin School. She and Hannah set themselves up in their corner of the deck and in the warm spring sunshine at Cape Town, began their tasks. Rebecca addressed her letter to James Nixon at Grennin, Dromore, Tyrone.

Aboard the Caroline, Cape Town, Southern Africa
September 6th, 1854

My Dear Father,
I write to you at the first opportunity for we are now at rest in a harbour, which will make my handwriting legible. Here, too, are ships sailing north, and our ship's Matron will place this letter on a vessel headed that way.

Be assured I am in good health and managing well on the voyage, not even feeling any seasickness. We are in our beds at ten every evening and awake by seven. I am with many in steerage, all assisted in our passage.

I have made a good friend of a girl from County Down, Hannah Wallace. She will be working with me in the fields of the Oxley Estate in New South Wales. We are mess leaders together, each of us responsible for a group of girls, their bed space and their meals.

Each person is allotted rations for the week: hard biscuits, pea soup, tea, sugar and treacle every day, then bread, potatoes, carrots, salt pork and plum dough three times a week, and flour and lard twice a week. We have hard biscuits and tea every morning and pea soup, bread, treacle and tea at tea time. The fare is filling, but monotonous.

Our noon dinner is the meal requiring preparation. My friend Hannah and I, as mess leaders, prepare the dinner together, and the girls take turns doing the washing up. They all like pork pie, which we can manage twice a week, and we make plum duff three times a week. With the fresh sea air, the girls have hearty appetites. It is difficult to get the galley to cook the meals the way they should be cooked and by the time the food is delivered to our compartment, it is usually cold. From this port of call we shall have fresh vegetables, pumpkins, onions and such, and some tropical fruit, oranges and bananas, as a treat with our meals.

Despite the presence of sailors and male passengers, you must not fret about my good character. Some reliable lads from Donegal have taken to watching out for us, and we feel quite safe. Amongst them are fishermen from the coast, and along the way they have devised hooks and lines to catch young sharks, which Cook bakes for us and we all share. It makes a nice change from our usual meals.

Please remember me to our neighbours. I send my love to you and William, Alexander, James, Martha, Archibald, Margaret, John and little Isabella. All of you at Grennin are in my prayers each day.

As ever, I am your loving daughter,

Rebecca

She had not written to her father of her difficulties with Mr. Speer, nor had she mentioned her bed partner, a papist. Some things were better left unsaid.

The *Caroline*, fully re-provisioned, set sail and rounded the Cape of Good Hope. The tropical waters of the Indian Ocean gave way to the cold seas of the southern hemisphere, and the swells brought on another siege of seasickness. Hannah's busy knitting needles had created jumpers and woollen shawls for Rebecca and herself, and the two friends bundled up and spent long hours on deck, watching the dolphins and seals playing in the seas surging around the ship.

The vessel was scudding swiftly onward when Matron commented to the Ship's Surgeon that no voyage was ever free from illness. A farm worker had come down with a raging fever, no doubt a result of unsanitary conditions in the crowded steerage quarters. He sweated and tossed in his bed and screamed at his hallucinations. Despite the best efforts of Matron and the Surgeon, he lay dead on the third day. "We're sure to have more steerage passengers down with this," said Matron.

Rebecca thought the man's burial service was indecently brief. Two seamen lifted his shrouded body on a plank to the rail and waited for the order to tip it over. Mr. Speer opened *The Book of Common Prayer* and read some committal phrases from The Burial of the Dead. The corpse, stitched into canvas and weighted with a short length of rusty chain around the ankles, then slid feet-first off the plank and sank in the clear waters. Rebecca doubted the man's family would ever know what had happened to him. Strong winds drove the ship onward.

As Matron had predicted, many in steerage began to complain of sore throats, aching bodies, nausea and fever. Even Mr. Speer took sick and missed several inspections. Rebecca remembered her mother's common sense in keeping her family as free from illness as possible. "You must wash your hands after you use the water closet and again before you eat," she instructed the others. "Wrap up warm and stay on deck in the fresh air."

Kitty Flynn was sceptical. "What good will that do?" she countered. "Hands don't give you a fever, and it's windy on deck!" Rebecca repeated her instructions. "Just wash your hands and stay in the fresh air!" All the girls followed her advice except for Kitty and company, who rolled their eyes and ignored her.

One of the pretty young house servants in the family steerage section was next to die, and her sister succumbed a few hours later. As two seamen lifted their shrouded and weighted bodies and tipped them over the rail, Rebecca was heartsick with grief for their family. A wee girl Rebecca had seen dancing about on deck died three days later, and the following week a year-old baby boy passed away. Papist though they were, the mothers, keening with grief, deserved Rebecca's condolences, and she sat with each woman in turn. The number of children who died would be listed in the Surgeon's records, but he was more interested in the deaths of those who were old enough to work.

The fever throughout the ship gradually diminished, and Rebecca was relieved that no one in her own compartment had become ill. Yet a few nights later she was in a deep sleep when Kitty Flynn's bedmates shook her awake. "Rebecca! Come and help! Kitty's burning up and she's sweating something terrible!" Rebecca roused herself and lit one of the lanterns. The girl was on fire, delirious and dripping perspiration.

"She needs to be cooled down!" said Rebecca. "Take her clothes off and keep the blanket over her. I'll fetch some water." Taking a lantern and a pail with a length of rope tied to it, she climbed the ladder in her nightdress, opened the hatch and stepped out into the dark. Swirling clouds cloaked the moon and turned the rigging and lockers into ominous shadows. As she moved through the blackness, a watchman loomed up in front of her. Her heart beat with frightening speed.

"Oi! What're you up to? Get back down below!" Rebecca stood firm. "Not until I get a pail of water for a girl who's burning up with fever!" He blocked her way. "You're a friend of those Donegal boys! You're a proper nuisance, you are!" After a few seconds he let her pass, probably anticipating what the boys from Donegal would do to him if he did not.

By the time Rebecca had lowered the pail into the sea, hauled it up and carried it back down to the quarters, Kitty Flynn was in the throes of delirium. Her two bedmates had been too shy to remove her clothing, so Rebecca quickly stripped the girl down. She soaked Kitty's dress in the sea water, wrapped it around her hot, slight body, and sponged the girl's face and neck. She put cool compresses of rags under her armpits whilst the two bedmates moaned in a corner.

Hannah woke up and offered to help. "Keep sponging her, please, Hannah, whilst I send the watchman to the galley for a pot of fresh water. We'll have to get her to drink." Up on deck the watchman obstinately refused to get the fresh water for her. Rebecca's mother would have washed her mouth out with soap for the names she called him. She took pleasure in assuring him the boys from Donegal would knock out every tooth in his head. He fetched the water for her.

All night Hannah and Rebecca worked to bring down Kitty's fever. They took turns braving the watchman and fetching more pails of sea water. Before dawn Rebecca looked outside to see if David Andrews were close by. Faithful to the moment, the tall man smiled at her as she pushed open the hatch. "David, get Matron at once, please. Kitty Flynn's in a bad way." David sprinted down to Matron's quarters. Matron came, and the Surgeon, but Kitty died that afternoon. An hour later, to a muttered committal prayer from Mr. Speer, Kitty's body was dropped into the ocean. "You'd be hard-pressed to know," Rebecca said to Hannah, "that he'd ever been acquainted with the girl. Like as not, he gave her the fever."

Hannah stood at the rail with Rebecca, and although Kitty Flynn was a papist, the two of them said the Lord's Prayer for her. Matron assured them she would write of the girl's passing to the people who had raised her, an aunt and uncle in County Clare. Rebecca wondered whether the aunt and uncle would grieve over the demise of their saucy ginger-haired niece.

Less than a month hence, Matron told them, they would be at Port Jackson. She warned them of increasingly heavy weather ahead and said that on their next opportunity to open their boxes in the hold, they should fetch all the warm clothes they had with them. In truth, some of the young women had little more than what they were wearing.

Boredom with the daily routine now infected the ship. Rebecca had read her New Testament as far as Saint Paul's First Epistle to the Corinthians, had finished Major Mitchell's book on Australia, and had chatted with Hannah until they knew each other's lives in great detail. The rest of the girls had become bored much earlier. They complained loudly every day about their mess leaders' meals. Gone were the days when they could be persuaded to take lime juice. They quarrelled constantly, and one night Rebecca's strength was put to the test when she separated two screaming bedmates who were pulling each other's hair out. The Donegal and Antrim Guards, looking for a donnybrook, were now flexing their muscles at each other. The Captain increased his threats of brig and chains.

The *Caroline* was approaching Van Diemen's Land when the winds that had provided a steady passage began to blow something fierce. Towering seas crashed across the deck, the vessel pitched and rolled alarmingly, and passengers were ordered to stay in their compartments. Sails were furled, and stokers went to work firing up the boiler to drive the *Caroline* through the storm.

Bern and Uel brought rations of bread and water to the compartment before the Captain ordered all hatches battened down to prevent the ship from being swamped. Rebecca and the others were now entombed below. Should the *Caroline* founder, they would sink with it. Terrified for their lives, the girls no longer quarrelled or complained. They lay in their beds in the fearsome darkness, Catholic and Protestant clinging to one another, wretched with seasickness and fright.

Alice Foley, having vomited herself dry, lay trembling beside Rebecca. The frightened girl from Waterford fingered her beads and murmured Hail Marys, seeking comfort in the familiar words as she anticipated her hour of death. Rebecca repeated from memory The General Confession in *The Book of Common Prayer* which began, "Almighty and most merciful Father; We have erred and strayed from thy ways like lost sheep..." If Rebecca Nixon were about to meet her Lord, she would have The Confession as the last words on her lips.

Those with appetites consumed the bread and water, and then the whole compartment went hungry and thirsty. Not all who were sick made it as far as the water closet, and waste and vomit soiled the bedding and spilled across the floor. With the hatch battened, buckets of water and sand could not be fetched for the girls to clean themselves, their beds and the deck of their quarters. Trying to maintain her composure in this black, stinking place, Rebecca measured the hours by counting bells whilst she prayed that the relentlessly pounding steam engine could drive the ship out of the storm.

When the hatches came open one blustery day, Rebecca gave hearty thanks to her merciful Heavenly Father and scrambled up on deck with the others to discover the *Caroline*, her canvas billowing, sailing past towering black cliffs. Whilst the ship lay at anchor for re-provisioning and repairs at Port Arthur on the Tasman Peninsula, everyone, even the crew and cabin passengers, stayed aboard because the port, although no longer a penal destination, was still a convict settlement and not deemed a safe place. Hannah and Rebecca organized the girls to scrub the compartment deck and wash their bedding and clothes and hang them out to dry. Chandlers came aboard with supplies and provisions, and the Captain supervised speedy repairs so that the voyage to Port Jackson might be completed on schedule.

The steam engine, chugging noisily against the Australian Current, carried the *Caroline* northeastward to Sydney. On the warm spring morning of October 13th, 1854, the ship carrying 254 field labourers and house servants and eight cabin passengers sailed into the glistening, sheltered waters of Sydney Harbour. The *Caroline*, when snug to a wharf at Port Jackson, was boarded by officials. The Ship's Surgeon, looking pleased with himself, announced that only four workers had died on the voyage.

Under Matron's organization, passengers were examined quickly by the Surgeon and sent to Mr. Speer for their disembarkation document. Wearing his best uniform, he sat at a small table on deck and smiled at each person who approached him. From her place in the queue, Rebecca watched his performance and prayed that when her turn came, she would be able to restrain herself. She presented the Surgeon's slip of paper to Mr. Speer, who filled in her Record of Assisted Immigration. When he asked the last question, his smirk was malicious. "Do you have any complaints with respect to your treatment on board, Miss Nixon?" You'll not catch me that easily, Rebecca said to herself. She looked straight at him and answered, "None." Mr. Speer, still smirking, handed Rebecca her completed document. Matron had told them to keep the Record on their person at all times, lest they be mistaken for former convicts.

ELEVEN

Oxley Estate

When they went from one nation to another...
—PSALM 105:13

Rebecca was to travel some eighty miles south from Sydney to her employment near Berrima. Four men and ten girls from the *Caroline* were destined for the Oxley Estate, but before they left the ship, the girls had to face Mr. Speer once more. "I can't wait to see the last of that nasty man," muttered Rebecca to Hannah. Supervised by the leering Overseer, she and the others, on their knees with sleeves rolled up and skirts hitched, were scrubbing down their steerage quarters a final time. Meanwhile, seamen on the *Caroline* were hauling passengers' boxes out of the hold and onto the deck, ready for loading into wagons the following morning.

At first light on the 14th of October, 1854, after a hurried meal of tea and hard biscuits, Rebecca and Hannah said farewell to compartment mates bound for other employment. "Best of Irish luck to you, Alice," said Rebecca. "You're the first Roman Catholic I've ever known, and a good soul for all that." Slim, curly-haired Alice Foley from County Waterford was to be housemaid to a solicitor's family at Parramatta.

Rebecca and Hannah picked up their canvas bundles and set out through the crowd to find the Oxley Estate wagon. The solid footing beneath them felt strange after the pitching, tossing deck of the ship, and they giggled as they swayed along the jetty. Accompanied by David Andrews and his mates, Rebecca and Hannah and the other eight girls pushed past horses, drays, wagons and buggies crowding the dockside, around bales of wool tottering alarmingly, and past merchants and agents arguing over shipments. Rebecca noticed one well-dressed merchant who was running his fingers through his thinning hair and staring at a crushed crate marked "Wedgwood." An anxious insurance agent was trying to placate him. "That's some grand pottery in smithereens," she said to Hannah.

The Oxley Estate wagon took them in a southwesterly direction across the city of Sydney. Hannah and Rebecca agreed they had never seen so sprawling a place. The Irish villages they had known nestled snug against low hills, and the Irish cities they had seen, Londonderry and Belfast, stood within long-established boundaries. Sydney seemed to be made up of one settlement after another. A confusion of wandering streets eventually gave into a single road, and soon the horses were making their way down a broad track through tall trees that gave shade on the warm journey.

That night they camped in a field, making a meal out of food provided by the driver, whose name was Sean Oliver. Rebecca, Hannah and the other girls slept close together in their shawls in the wagon whilst the men slept on the ground. Sean's two large bay mares grazed nearby.

In the morning Sean drove his horses on towards the town of Camden, meeting other teams on their way to Sydney with loads of wool, hides and wattle bark for tanning. Vivid parrots burst noisily out of trees, and shy kangaroos bounded off through the bush whilst herds of long-horned cattle, roaming freely across the track, shifted uneasily away from the intrusion of the wagons.

"Give us a song, Hannah, to help us pass the time," said Rebecca. A farm boy named Bertie Marshall brought out his concertina, and the sweet voice of Hannah Wallace rendered a poignant ballad about an emigrant lad who had left his lovely Martha, "The Flower of Sweet Strabane." As she listened to the sentimental music and heart-breaking words, Rebecca decided they expressed more truth than poetry.

"Sure an' now we need a lively tune!" said Hannah, and David Andrews suggested "The Wild Rover." With his blue eyes crinkling at the corners, he stood tall at the front of the wagon and to Bertie Marshall's concertina, launched into the refrain of the old song:

"And it's no, nay, never . . . no nay never no more . . ." Flocks of startled lorikeets exploded skyward in a rainbow of colours, and white cockatoos on high branches fanned their yellow crests and screeched in annoyance.

They stopped for a second night, and as they set off the next morning, the trees thinned out and the land began to rise in low hills, the Southern Highland. Cultivated fields and stretches of grazing land lay before them. "We'll arrive at the Estate later today," said Sean. "It's been here since 1816, when John Oxley's superintendent drove five hundred head of cattle over from Bargo. John Oxley has long since gone to his Maker, and now his family owns the property at Wingecarribee River. Not that it's any concern of ours. We all work for Mr. Simpson, the Overseer."

Late in the afternoon, Sean Oliver swung his team off the road and through a wide gate. At the top of a long dirt track was the Overseer's home, a grand place in the eyes of the Irish workers, fronted as it was by a great covered porch, a verandah, said Sean. A large metal cistern sat high on a platform amongst the trees shading the house, and Rebecca could see a barn, open stables and two big sheds. Five small huts that seemed to be made of bark were scattered to one side of the house, and orderly rectangles of paddocks proceeded across the property towards a river.

As Sean's horses pulled into the farmyard, the Overseer and his wife came out to greet their new workers. Mr. Simpson, a Scot, they soon discovered, was a tall, easy-moving man with a sunburned face under a stiff leather hat. His plump wife, her grey hair escaping in wisps from beneath her cotton bonnet, looked to be a pleasant soul. On trestle tables in the yard, the girls helped her lay out a meal of mutton stew, boiled potatoes, Swiss chard and new carrots, followed by apple tart with heavy cream and pots of tea.

Afterwards, Mrs. Simpson took the girls to a newly built boxbark hut. "Now choose your beds and set your boxes between them," she said. "You can rest easy for the remainder of the day. Curfew is at nine. I'll waken you before sunrise and after your breakfast you'll be walking out to the fields to begin your work." With that, she left them.

"You'd scarce know this hut from our steerage quarters, but at least we'll be washing in fresh water," said Rebecca, as she and Hannah stood in the dark, steaming interior. Five beds were spaced along one side and five along the other. In the middle was a narrow table with benches and at the far end, a metal bathtub. "Where's the water closet?" asked Hannah. "It's two chamber pots," replied Rebecca, "but Mrs. Simpson said there's a water closet down the path, a dunny, she called it."

On the ship Rebecca and Hannah had come to know Bella Carroll, Agnes Regan, Mary Sheehan and Rose Barry, who had shared the steerage compartment with them, but the others, Peggy Nugent, Mona Blake, Ida Ryan and Lily Moore, were older and had been in the women's section. They were all field hands except for Rose, who was to be scullery maid in the Overseer's house. Bella, Agnes, Mary and Peggy were Irish-speakers and papists, but all of them would have to get along somehow, despite their differences in Ireland. Well fed and tired from the wagon journey, they all slept soundly until wakened before dawn by Mrs. Simpson.

In the heat of the morning, the rich volcanic soil was warm to Rebecca's touch and heavy on her hoe. The sun had risen over fields of vegetables stretching as far as she could see, marked at intervals by the stooping figures of women. They worked barefoot, although some had brought the clogs they had worn in the cool, damp climate at home. Rebecca was not yet eighteen years of age but already an experienced field hand, sensitive to the feel of the earth, changes in weather and patterns of growth. This was grand farmland, she thought, able to grow almost anything. Whilst her cotton bonnet grew hot on her head, and her neck and arms tingled in the sun, she daydreamed about owning a farm in this fertile countryside.

It was a futile dream, she knew. On the journey from Sydney, Sean Oliver had told them all the property round about had been claimed by Free Settlers or awarded in land grants to those who had served the Queen. John Oxley, a naval officer and Surveyor General, had been given these fields and pastures as a reward for his duty to the monarch. Just like in Ireland, Rebecca mused, as she tilled one row of vegetables after another. Rebecca decided if she could not own a property here, she would lease one. She would save as much as she could of her wages of twenty pounds a year towards that end.

In the meantime she would get to know the others and learn the ways of this new world. The Overseer of the Estate and his wife seemed to be warm-hearted people, and the girls in the hut were friendly enough. She felt quite settled already, especially with Hannah Wallace to keep her company. The Oxley Estate was now her home, and the people working there her new family. Rebecca wondered what God had in store for them all.

The field hands carried their noon meal with them: two pieces of crusty bread filled with slices of mutton and a basket of fruit to share. Breakfast and evening tea were served at trestle tables in the farmyard. In the evenings the girls lingered to chat with David Andrews and his mates, or with stockmen who came in from tending cattle. More teasing and flirting went on than Rebecca thought seemly.

The Overseer saw to it the girls retired to their quarters by nine o'clock. They sweated in the early summer heat in their boxbark hut yet they appreciated having their own beds. This was the first time most of them had ever slept alone. Mrs. Simpson told the girls they were to draw water from the cistern on Saturday nights and take turns in the bathtub to ready themselves for church the next day.

Holy Trinity Church, designed by the noted colonial architect Edmund Blacket, stood in a grove of pines at the edge of the village of Berrima. With Hannah and the others, Rebecca entered through the arched entrance at the side of Holy Trinity that first Sunday morning and took a seat to the right amongst the field hands and house servants in the rear pews. She did not consider herself a girl of romantic sensibilities, but she was enthralled by the golden sandstone walls, curved timber trusses and stone arches framing the chancel and windows of the small church.

Later that day there was time for Rebecca to write again to her father in Ireland.

Oxley Estate
Camden County, New South Wales
October 22nd, 1854

My Dear Father,
I write my first letter to you on my arrival in New South Wales. On this Sunday afternoon I sit by Wingecarribee River near the village of Berrima. Being able to enjoy some shade by the water is a blessing in this warm weather. With me is my friend Hannah Wallace, who works alongside me in the fields and has the bed next to me in our sleeping quarters. We enjoy one another's company and watch out for each other. Today we have a picnic lunch from the farm kitchen with cold roast chicken, hard-boiled eggs, currant scones and a basket of fruit.

When we arrived at the Estate, large fields of root crops awaited us, mostly potatoes and turnips. Here on the other side of the world, it is springtime, and the work of planting, thinning, weeding and tilling lies ahead of us. We are up well before dawn and at our labour by first light.

Berrima is the largest village near the Oxley Estate. It was laid out by one of the Queen's Surveyors, Major Mitchell, whose book on Australia I read on the ship. Berrima is a pleasant place with a great, wide main street winding through it. It has a bank, an inn, the Post Office, some shops and a market.

Near the edge of the village is Holy Trinity Church, where we took our Holy Communion this morning. The Vicar is the Reverend James Hassall, whose family has long been in New South Wales, he said. He is a son of the Reverend Thomas Hassall and a grandson of the Reverend Samuel Marsden, both of them early clergymen in the colony. Be assured that I shall pay attention to the Reverend Hassall's sermons.

You are not to worry about my well-being. The voyage was without incident, and I am now settled into my tasks here. Our accommodation and treatment are satisfactory, and the meals are nourishing.

I send my love and my prayers to you and everyone at Grennin.
As ever, I am your loving daughter,

Rebecca

With the lecherous Mr. Speer in mind, she realized the voyage had not been entirely "without incident," but her family had no need of knowing her difficulties. They had been dismayed enough by her decision to emigrate. Successful though he was with his farming and barrel-making, her father had many bairns around his table, and she had thought it best to be on her way and give him one less mouth to feed.

"The shipping agent in Ireland told me I would have my own team on the Oxley Estate," David Andrews complained to Hannah and Rebecca one evening. On their arrival David had been put to work keeping the barn and stables clean and helping to feed, water and groom horses. "I've not come to the other side of the world just to be a stable boy mucking out stalls! And that young mare and gelding in the home paddock look ready to be broken to harness." Hannah counselled patience. She said, "Sure an' Mr. Simpson has you in mind for them, but he'll want to know how you handle yourself around horses first."

David began to visit the paddock regularly to become acquainted with the two horses, a dark bay mare and a black gelding, each with four white stockings. Whilst he stroked the white noses of the large horses, he crooned to them and slipped them treats, apples and carrots that the farm lad, Bertie, had given him from the kitchen garden. He ran his large hands over the horses' backs and down their legs, appreciating their massive necks and high withers, their well-sprung ribs and heavily muscled thighs. The two animals, comfortable with David, moved easily to nuzzle him for more treats.

Soon David was ordered to take a regular turn driving the mares hauling Sean's wagon. Mr. Simpson watched him harness up and drove out with him on several occasions. "You've a steady hand with a team, Andrews," said Mr. Simpson one day when they were returning from delivering vegetables to the Berrima market. "Have you ever worked young horses into harness?" David was quick to reply. "Many times. My Da' trained horses all round Donegal and had me helping him since I was a nipper. It was hard to keep me in school, I was that keen on horses. That young mare and gelding in the home paddock are a fine-looking pair, Mr. Simpson, and I'd be honoured if I could work with them."

"That was my plan in hiring you, Andrews. Those two were foaled here on the Estate. I've halter-trained them, and if they're broken into harness properly, they should make a good team. I don't need to tell you they're valuable. If their training is not done just right, you'll be off the Estate in short order, and no other Overseer in the Southern Highland will employ you. You'll need to name them. Give them names that can be easily used."

In telling Hannah and Rebecca about his conversation with Mr. Simpson, David said, "I understand the man's concern. Stud fees and good care have been invested in the horses, and if they're rightly broken to harness as a team, they'll be worth more than one hundred pounds to the Estate." The man from Donegal became immersed in his work. Every evening Rebecca and Hannah listened patiently to the pleasures of training Fan and Bob. "I named them after my oldest sister and brother," he said, chuckling, "and the horses are much easier to work with than those two in Donegal!"

David's mates from the ship were Ian Kincade, Hugh Clarke and Bertie Marshall. Ian Kincade of County Down was a saddler and bootmaker, and Hugh Clarke from Donegal was a carpenter. Bertie Marshall, the youngest son of an Antrim farmer, was a big lad without any notable skills, but he had a cheerful disposition and a willingness to work. Mrs. Simpson had him digging her garden and slopping the pigs. His concertina gave everyone great pleasure in the evenings.

As instructed, the girls took turns on Saturday nights in the metal bathtub at the end of the hut. Rebecca had made herself new lace caps, collars and cuffs, and crocheted snoods of various designs to capture Hannah's abundant auburn hair. They set off in the wagon each Sunday morning in polished boots and their best skirts and shirtwaists sponged clean, their collars and cuffs trimmed with freshly laundered lace. All the Protestants, whether Anglicans or Nonconformists, attended Holy Trinity Church of England. ("My strict Presbyterian grandmother must be spinning in her grave!" said Hannah.) Roman Catholics went to Mass at Saint Francis

Xavier, and afterwards everyone enjoyed an afternoon of leisure along the river.

Its banks shaded by willows, poplars and eucalypts, the Wingecarribee River, full and deep, wandered across the verdant countryside of the Southern Highland. One of its great meanders embraced a gently sloping place which the aboriginals called Berrima. In 1830 Surveyor General Major Mitchell had selected the site for settlement and had laid out the town in a grid pattern. The road from Camden to Goulburn curved through Berrima. The Change House was a convenience for coach drivers and horses, whilst the Surveyor General Inn was a resting place for travellers. Sandstone was the building material of choice throughout the village.

At Holy Trinity Church one sunlit morning in summer, the Reverend Hassall announced, "The Lessons today will be read by a new member of our congregation, Mr. John Miller." Mr. Hassall sat down in his chair behind the lectern of Holy Trinity and assumed an attitude of listening. Rebecca watched a well-built man get up from the front pew and walk over to the lectern. He read in a strong voice from the sixth chapter of the First Book of Kings, describing the building of the temple of Solomon. This is something of a change, thought Rebecca. She admired this fine-looking English gentleman with his even features and straight fair hair and his nicely tied cravat. He had no moustache but he had handsome chin-whiskers. I wonder what brought him here?

"Here endeth the First Lesson," said John Miller. Rebecca had been quite oblivious to the building of the temple of Solomon. The congregation was reading alternate verses of Psalm 84 with Mr. Hassall when Hannah poked Rebecca in the ribs. "Let's ask Mr. Miller to join our picnic this afternoon," she whispered. "We don't want him feeling like a stranger amongst us."

"He looks perfectly at home to me," hissed Rebecca, "and he's much too grand for the likes of us. For certain he's old enough to be married with a half-dozen children!" Hannah cheekily replied she would enquire if that were so. Rebecca told her to leave well enough alone. John Miller resumed the lectern to read the Second Lesson.

On successive Sunday mornings John Miller read the Old and New Testament lessons, and Rebecca looked forward to listening to him. Hannah Wallace and David Andrews teased her about her rapt attention to the reader, promising that bachelor Miller, for Hannah had determined his status from the Reverend Hassall, would be asked to join their Sunday picnics.

Some weeks later Rebecca was spreading their afternoon repast on a blanket under the shade of a willow tree when Hannah and David brought John Miller along. The fair-haired man quietly asked if he might share the meal. He placed his offering of a basket of plums on the blanket.

"Good day to you, Mr. Miller. Please join us," said Rebecca, feeling flustered. Hannah giggled at her. Rebecca had never been shy, yet this Englishman sitting next to her on the blanket was stirring a blush in her cheeks. She knew, however, that people such as John Miller paid no attention to people such as her. "Do tell us about yourself, Mr. Miller," said Hannah brightly, whilst they were all sharing the meal. Rebecca glared at her. "Please, call me John," he said.

Rebecca stole a glance at him as he began to speak, thinking what a pleasant voice he had and what soft brown eyes, like dark, liquid honey. She was blushing and hoped no one noticed. John Miller was explaining that he had emigrated to be a farm worker for family friends, the Barlings at Stroud and the Vernons at Larry's Flat. Although he had recently leased farmland from the Oxleys, he confessed he still was not much of a farmer and had not done much to develop the place. Rebecca, who had lived all her life amongst farmers, found this strange. He had come to Berrima, he explained, because the Reverend Hassall needed someone to help him teach prisoners at the gaol. He is a scholarly man, Rebecca decided. She had not met one before, excepting her schoolmasters. He was still a man, however, and like all men, he must be hungry at this time of day. "Do have another piece of chicken, John," she said.

As Hannah and Rebecca lay in the stifling heat of their quarters that night, Hannah said quietly, "John Miller needs to be married."

"No, he doesn't," Rebecca retorted in a whisper. "He's a confirmed bachelor who's devoted to his teaching and his church work. Don't you start matchmaking, Hannah Sarah Wallace! You can put an end to the teasing, too."

To Rebecca's embarrassment on ensuing Sunday afternoons, Hannah and David went off to lead the workers in song, leaving her alone with John Miller. Rebecca kept herself busy with her crocheting whilst John talked. When he discovered how familiar she was with the Bible, their first conversations consisted of scriptural commentaries. These serious discussions continued for several Sundays, until Rebecca felt confident enough to ask John about his family in England.

"My father is a retired surgeon at Poole in Dorsetshire," said John, "and my mother comes from a family of ironmongers at Newbury in Berkshire. On her mother's side, she is related to Nevil Maskelyne, the fifth Astronomer Royal. He was a clergyman interested in the moon, who founded the *Nautical Almanac*, a compendium of astronomical tables and navigational aids known to be of great help to British seafarers. Our family has always been interested in celestial phenomena." Our family, mused Rebecca as she worked on her crocheting, has been interested in getting enough to eat. John continued, "I have three sisters and three brothers, all unmarried. My eldest brother is a surgeon and he has taken over my father's practice. Now then, tell me about your family."

Would the son of a surgeon, a man who spoke of "celestial phenomena," have any interest in the family of a farmer and barrelmaker? Nevertheless, her father had made a brave living for his family at Grennin, and she owed it to him to speak proudly of his achievements. To her pleasure John Miller showed a sincere interest in her description of farm life in Ireland. He is a lovely man, she decided.

Rebecca's first year on the Oxley Estate, from October 1854 to October 1855, went by as she had expected: spring planting, thinning, followed by summer weeding and tilling and autumn harvesting. Fair Irish complexions reddened in the glare of the Austral sun whilst strong Irish muscles strained to bend and lift. In the quiet days of winter, the land was ploughed under and harrowed by David and Sean and their horses. The workers were sent out to collect stones for stone boats hauled behind the two teams and to rake the fields smooth for the next spring planting. The Overseer, who was as patient as his brown mare, had no objection to David's taking the team and wagon for Sunday morning church-going and afternoon excursions. Each night Rebecca and Hannah thanked God for their employment under Mr. Simpson.

In the darkness of the hut one night, Hannah whispered to Rebecca, "David's moustache isn't ticklish. It's soft and cozy!" Rebecca sat bolt upright. "You're not even betrothed and you've gone and let David Andrews kiss you! You're a girl of good character, Hannah Sarah Wallace, and I'll not have that man leading you down the primrose path!" Hannah laughed. "Not down the primrose path!' she said. "Along the riverbank! And I'll tend to my character myself!" The others in the hut giggled appreciatively.

On a warm Sunday afternoon in April of 1856, when gentle breezes along the riverbank were wafting the willows and sending poplar leaves spinning in the sunlight, Rebecca found herself alone once more with John Miller. He's a scholarly man, and I'm just a farm girl, she often cautioned herself, yet he was a kindly and courteous companion. Sitting in the shade with her back against a willow tree, Rebecca was fashioning a lace cap. "Tell me what you want from your life, Rebecca," John said, as he stretched out on a blanket beside her. Such impertinence! thought Rebecca. "If you'll tell me what you want from your life," she replied.

"Gladly." He looked up at her and smiled. "I'm past thirty years of age and feel I should have a wife and family." Rebecca refrained from any reaction to this statement. "My father planned to make a pharmacist out of me so that I might run a dispensary for my eldest brother, William. After I finished at a Blue Coat school, I was sent to apprentice in London and I worked for a chemist there until I read an advertisement for farm workers in New South Wales. I was never able to see myself going back to Poole to live in my eldest brother's shadow, good man that he is. I've served my time in the colony as a farm worker and I've leased some land, but I admit I really emigratted to become a teacher. My plan is to have a school of my own."

He has a sense of adventure and he's ambitious as well, thought Rebecca. She said, "I want a bit of farmland. Around Berrima it would be leased, of course, but that would do me until I could find a property to purchase." John seemed puzzled. "Surely you want to marry and have children!" He had lifted himself up on one elbow to look at her. She wished she would not blush. "Naturally," she said, "but I've not yet been approached by the right man." John Miller sighed and stared at the river through willow leaves whispering softly in the breeze.

The autumn eased uneventfully towards the winter of 1856, with Rebecca and John still enjoying their Sunday afternoon conversations. Then one Sunday morning Mr. Hassall stopped her as she entered the church. "Would it be possible for you to stay for a few moments afterwards, Miss Nixon? I have a piece of work I believe you could help me with."

"Of course, Mr. Hassall." Whatever does he have in mind? She hoped he did not take long because she was looking forward to getting to the river, where Sunday afternoon gatherings were on the wane as the weather grew more chilly. When the service was over, Rebecca waited whilst the Vicar said goodbye to his parishioners at the church door. Returning to the nave, he said, "Come with me, Miss Nixon." To Rebecca's surprise he led her through the nave and chancel and into the sanctuary. Never before had she been farther than the rail in front of it. The panelled altar, ornamented with carving, was covered with a linen cloth, worn very thin.

"You can see our fair linen is much the worse for wear. It was used at Parramatta in Saint John's Church, which was established by my maternal grandfather, the Reverend Samuel Marsden. A new piece of linen has been purchased, but embroidered crosses and a lace border will have to be done, and Mrs. Hassall feels this work might be beyond her skills. John Miller tells me your crocheted lace is exquisite, and I had hoped you would agree to turning your talents to our new fair linen."

John Miller had said her crocheted lace was exquisite! She and John were always so busy talking, whenever did he have time to notice her crocheting? She smiled at the Vicar. "That's a great honour you're giving me, Mr. Hassall. I promise you the best of my skills."

"Splendid! Next Sunday, then. You'll join us for dinner at the vicarage after the service and have the afternoon to work on the linen. The better the day, the better the deed! We'll see you safely back to the Oxley Estate after tea. Splendid! Splendid!"

As she followed Mr. Hassall down the church aisle, she thought of her usual Sunday afternoons with her friends. The crocheting and embroidering would take weeks to complete, and the others from the Estate would go on their winter wagon rides without her. Yet when else could she do the work? The sin of pride! She had been too proud of her crocheting and too quick to get herself into this.

She could only say to Mr. Hassall, "I'll look forward to getting started next Sunday." Turning to leave the church, Rebecca found John Miller waiting for her and smiling. "I can see you're pleased with your new task," he said. They walked out amongst the pine trees and made their way towards the river. How can I tell him I'll be spending all those Sunday afternoons shut up in the vicarage? That night in the hut, as they readied themselves for bed, she satisfied Hannah's curiosity about her conversation with Mr. Hassall. "I'll be missing our Sunday afternoons together. I'm that keen to work on the fair linen, but not by choice would I be spending every Sunday afternoon in the vicarage."

"Listen to you!" laughed Hannah. "You'll be making friends with the Vicar and his wife and forgetting all about the likes of me and the others. Sure an' we'll manage very nicely without you on our winter wagon rides. You'll not have to worry about playing chaperone when I sit with David on the wagon seat under a blanket!"

"Hannah Sarah Wallace! You're my very best friend, and I won't have you teasing me like that! Please say you understand what I've got myself into."

"Ah, lass, I do! There's nothing for it now except to devote yourself to your crocheting at the vicarage. I'm sorry, Rebecca. I'm a terrible tease." Hannah gave Rebecca a hug and added as she got into bed, "John Miller might want to spend his Sunday afternoons at the vicarage, too!" She ducked when Rebecca's pillow came flying towards her.

Rainbow lorikeet

TWELVE

Holy Trinity Church

How amiable are thy tabernacles, O Lord of hosts!
— PSALM 84:1

From Hannah's teasing about John Miller came the truth. Next Sunday after the church service, he walked Rebecca to the vicarage. The newly built house of dressed sandstone, with its bay window facing the river, was set behind a well trimmed lawn bordered with flowers and new shrubbery. John sat opposite her during dinner, and his gaze caused her acute embarrassment. Rebecca said nothing whilst conversations swirled around her. When they had eaten, she helped Mrs. Hassall clear the table and do the washing up before they both put on white cotton gloves and laid out the new linen. The Vicar's wife had laundered the piece of linen three times to shrink it, pressed it dry and smooth, and rolled it in a muslin sheet. Soft-spoken Mrs. Hassall, who had an air of serenity about her, looked to be a pleasant companion for winter afternoons.

"'Tis beautifully fine cloth," commented Rebecca, "more like cambric." She set about hemming the circumference of the cloth to prevent any fraying. Mrs. Hassall sat with her at the dining room table, and the two of them stitched and chatted companionably, putting Rebcca in mind of the days when she sat with her mother in front of a turf fire at Grennin learning to sew, crochet, embroider and knit. She had decided on a small rose motif for the attached crocheted border. When she was ready to do the crochetwork, she could continue without thinking about it because she had often done the rose motif. The embroidered crosses would require more of her attention.

"Time to roll up the linen and set out the evening tea," said Mrs. Hassall. Rebecca thought it had been a grand way to spend a winter's afternoon. In the vicarage drawing room John Miller had sat reading in a chair within sight of the table where Rebecca was working. After tea he helped her onto the seat of the vicarage buggy, tucked a blanket around her, and drove Mr. Hassall's grey mare slowly back to the Oxley Estate.

The matter of embroidered crosses took Rebecca and John up to the altar one Sunday morning after church. The design of the crosses was unusual, somewhat like a flower with four petals—the Canterbury Cross, Mrs. Hassall told her later. Four of the crosses were embroidered near the edges of the fair linen. When she began to sketch the design in her diary, John stood close to her, looking over her shoulder, and when they walked away from the sanctuary, he put her arm through his. Chilled by the cool winter air in the church, Rebecca glanced up at John and felt pleasantly warm.

Many times in the years to come she fondly remembered the winter of 1856. It was not the serene Mrs. Hassall who kept her company on Sunday afternoons, although occasionally the Vicar's wife came into the dining room to encourage her work. John Miller was the one sitting beside her, reading the poetry of William Wordsworth, Robert Browning and Alfred, Lord Tennyson whilst she crocheted and embroidered. In the evening when the moon was rising, he took her back to the Estate in the Reverend Hassall's buggy. Hannah pestered her for details of "another romantic afternoon at the vicarage," as she called it, but Rebecca refused to rise to the teasing. She would admit only to herself how eagerly she anticipated sitting with John and listening to his lovely voice every Sunday afternoon.

The crochetwork and embroidery did indeed take many weeks to complete, yet there came a day when Rebecca had no more work to do. Mrs. Hassall laundered the finished cloth and pressed it dry, ready for its dedication the following Sunday. The Reverend Hassall was effusive in praising Rebecca's artistry to the congregation, which resulted in a sharp poke in the ribs from Hannah and a smile from John when he rose to read the next lesson.

"And now, Rebecca," said Mr. Hassall as she was leaving the church, "you must consider working on a new corporal and credence cloth. Mrs. Hassall says we also have enough linen for two purificators. The weather's improving, and you might want to take these pieces to your picnics with your friends. No doubt they have missed your company." When she agreed to complete the set of altar linens, the Vicar broke into his litany of "Splendid! Splendid!" and told Rebecca his wife would bring her the material next Sunday.

Rebecca could see virtue in the work for its own sake, and the new pieces were small and should be easy to complete. The corporal was the square piece placed over the centre of the fair linen to protect it when the Vicar prepared the Eucharist, and the credence cloth covered the shelf beside the altar where the vessels were placed before a Communion service. The purificators were the size of small handkerchiefs and were used to wipe the chalice. She would crochet narrow borders for the corporal and credence cloth and embroider small Canterbury Crosses at the corners. For fear of scratching the silver chalice, the purificators would be plain, with drawn-thread-work and the finest of her finishing stitches. She must take care to keep everything clean when she went to the picnics.

With John joining her at the first springtime picnic by the river, Rebecca had mixed feelings about being with the crowd from the Estate once more. She and John had become good companions during the winter and she enjoyed his closeness; she would never say so to anyone, but she found it unusually exciting. She sat against a willow tree and began crocheting a border for the corporal. "Holy Trinity will have a handsome set of altar linens, thanks to you," said John. Rebecca no longer blushed when he said things like that. Instead, she smiled at him and told him to tend to his reading.

Her friend Hannah, strangely enough, had taken to crying herself to sleep every night and spending her days in the fields in silence. She refused to confide in anyone, not even Rebecca. The two friends were working side by side on a spring morning, pulling seed potatoes from hessian bags slung around their necks and dropping the potatoes at regular intervals into parallel trenches.

Hannah, known for singing as she worked, was stonily silent and more gloomy than ever.

"For Heaven's sake, lass, tell me what's bothering you! You can't go on like this, heartsick and saying nothing!" said Rebecca.

"David Andrews is leaving!" Hannah fairly shouted at Rebecca. "He's going to Tarago!" Her friend was puzzled.

"Where's Tarago? And why is David going there?"

"Mrs. Simpson says it's south of Goulburn. That's far, far away, Rebecca! Mr. Simpson knows a grazier who's in need of an Overseer and Coachman. David's going there in a fortnight's time, and I'll be left here!" She slumped to the ground and wept. Stepping across the trench, Rebecca knelt beside Hannah and put her arms around her. "David won't want to leave you! He's sure to come back for you."

"He has no thought of me," sobbed Hannah. "All he cares about is leaving Fan and Bob. And all he talks about are the horses he'll have in his charge at Tarago—carriage horses, draught horses, stock horses. He's daft about horses!"

Rebecca helped her friend to her feet and passed her a handkerchief. Hannah was several years older than Rebecca and had often said she yearned for marriage and children. Rebecca could hardly bear to see her so unhappy.

A fortnight went by, and David Andrews left the Oxley Estate for Tarago, but not before the workers held a grand party to say farewell. Mrs. Simpson outdid herself with the meal, and young Bertie, enjoying more beer than was good for him, squeezed his concertina in merry accompaniment to Irish songs. Hannah put on a brave face, yet Rebecca knew her friend's heart was breaking. That night the girl from County Down curled up in bed and sobbed herself to sleep.

In no time the seed potatoes in the trenches came sprouting through the rich soil and spread out in leafy mounds, turning the field into a giant green counterpane. The girls were kept busy hoeing around the plants, roguing weeds and hilling earth over the growing tubers. When they returned to the farmyard one evening in David's wagon, now driven by a raw-boned young Scot from Lanarkshire, Mrs. Simpson hailed Hannah from the verandah.

"From Tarago!" she called out, waving a letter. Hannah snatched the letter and ran to the hut to read its message. Rebecca, more eager to learn the letter's contents than she would say, quickly finished eating with the others and took a scone and a beaker of tea to her friend. Hannah was sitting on her bed in a daze. "He says he's coming back at Christmas to marry me. The old gentleman who owns the station at Tarago is in need of a housekeeper, and David has told him I will take care of the place starting in the New Year. We're to have a suite of rooms in the homestead." Rebecca sat down beside her friend and hugged her. "I knew David would come back for you!"

Hannah took a large bite of scone and a gulp of tea. "The nerve of that David Andrews!" she spluttered. "He's never asked me to marry him. He thinks I'll come all over grateful when he tells me we're to be wed. And who wants to be an old gentleman's housekeeper? I can barely stand to be indoors, much less spend my time scrubbing floors and washing and cooking. Help me write a letter, Rebecca. I'll soon tell the great David Andrews what he can do with his fine ideas!"

Rebecca managed to dissuade her friend from writing the letter she had in mind; getting her to compose a message of acceptance involved hours of argument and finally outright temper on Rebecca's part. She had not planned to be so severe with her friend, but she was certain Hannah and David were meant for each other. In the end it was Mrs. Simpson who made things right. She knew Cartmel station, a large property at Tarago, and Mr. Charlesworth, the grazier, a kindly, considerate gentleman with a spacious homestead. She sat Hannah down for a long talk about the wisdom of accepting an offer of marriage from a good man and making the best of one's opportunities, no matter how one felt about housekeeping.

With Rebecca's help, Hannah wrote the letter that set her life in a new direction. Rebecca crocheted the lace on her friend's wedding veil and worked three doilies in the clover leaf design as a wedding present. David Andrews, his blue eyes crinkling at the sight of Hannah, arrived at the Oxley Estate on Christmas Eve in Mr. Charlesworth's smart buggy drawn by a white carriage horse. The

Reverend Hassall, having read the Banns of Matrimony on the previous three Sundays, married David James Andrews and Hannah Sarah Wallace on Christmas afternoon in Holy Trinity Church. Rebecca and John stood up for them, and Mrs. Hassall set out a grand wedding supper in the vicarage garden, where the Irish workers made a fine show of singing "The Wild Rover" on the bridegroom's behalf. David and Hannah, much to the amusement of David's mates, spent their nuptial night at the vicarage.

The tall, auburn-haired girl from County Down had been Rebecca's bosom companion from the day they had boarded the *Caroline*, and Rebecca already missed her dreadfully. She realized how much comfort the friendship had provided in a strange land. Their parting was full of tearful embraces and good wishes whilst Rebecca doubted she would ever see Hannah again. They promised to write to one another. Happy as she was for David and Hannah Andrews, Rebecca felt lost.

New Year's Day of 1857 was looming empty for Rebecca. To honour the holiday, Mrs. Simpson had promised a special spread of food for a picnic by the river, but Rebecca had decided not to go. She intended to sit under a tree in a field, write to Hannah and catch up on her Bible reading.

When Rebecca had completed her work on the church linens, Mr. Hassall had asked her to join Mrs. Hassall and two ladies from the village in caring for the altar of Holy Trinity Church. She was on duty on New Year's Eve, laying out linens for the Watch Night service, when John appeared out of the darkness of the nave. The glow of candles cast soft shadows over Rebecca as she turned to him.

"Happy New Year, Rebecca," he said quietly. When he kissed her cheek, she was startled witless. She stood very still and took a deep breath to calm herself. "Happy New Year, John." She hid her blushes from him as she set out the Communion vessels. "Would you care to go for a drive with me tomorrow?" John asked. "James said I might borrow the vicarage buggy, and I would like to take you over towards Bowral. Mrs. Hassall has offered to provide a luncheon basket for us."

Why not? She wasn't going to the picnic anyway, and the outing would occupy the day. She could catch up on her Bible reading and write to Hannah some other time. John arrived at the Estate mid-morning, and they set out over the rolling landscape. Rebecca still longed to have a farm in this glorious countryside.

Along the road leading to Bowral, John turned the grey mare down a lengthy track ending at a slab hut shaded by large pines. Behind it was a barn made of slabs and to the left of the track, a small boxbark hut surrounded by lush-looking paddocks that stretched towards a bend in the Wingecarribee River. On the right side of the track were fields left in fallow. "What have we here?" said Rebecca.

"Come and have a look." John helped her down from the buggy, and they walked over to the slab hut. Rebecca pushed open the door to find three rooms, a fireplace, a dirt floor and a few of John's belongings. "A squatter named Nuttle lived here on his own," explained John. "He was a carpenter who died of drink, and I obtained his lease from the Oxleys. It's a property of thirty acres, if you're interested."

Rebecca ignored his last comment and said, "I'll take a look at the barn." Making her way past a large chicken pen and a sturdy henhouse, she entered the barn, where she found a haymow and a large cart that was in better shape than the slab hut. She searched for chicken feed and scattered some in the pen. The kitchen garden was a disgrace, but the fences seemed well built. A heavy brown horse with a white stripe on his nose raised his head in the shade of a tree and ambled across a field towards them. A black and white cow bellowed in frustration from her paddock.

"When was that cow last milked?" asked Rebecca. "The poor thing sounds in agony. Tip out the trough, please, John, and fill it again. That horse needs water and he won't want it stale." John smiled at her and took care of the horse trough as she had instructed. "A little girl who lives in the boxbark hut under the pines usually milks the cow morning and afternoon and collects eggs from the henhouse," he said.

Rebecca picked up a pail and washed her hands and the pail at the pump. She climbed through the paddock fence and began a sing-song call to the cow, "Cow boss! Cow boss! Cow boss!" The cow gave a doleful moan and made no fuss when Rebecca hunkered down beside her to do the milking. John watched in admiration.

"She's a good young cow," she said to John, handing him the pail of frothy warm liquid and climbing back through the fence. "For certain she's not been milked this morning. I'll cool the milk in the river and see if the child's family can make use of it. The flock of hens looks promising—chooks, Mrs. Simpson calls them. I'll collect the eggs before we leave. The horse could do with some hay."

Rebecca washed her hands at the pump and was drying them on her skirt when John reached for her. "Rebecca Nixon, I'm asking you to be my wife. Come and live on this farm with me." She looked up into his lovely brown eyes and smiled. He had taken long enough to find the words. "Yes, John," she murmured. Limp with happiness, she let him kiss her. He pulled her close and kissed her again and again, more urgently each time, until she collected herself and reluctantly pulled away. Quite overcome with pleasure, she said, "We're to be wed very soon, I gather!"

"As soon as we can arrange it! Let's go down our path to the river. We'll have our picnic there." Our path! She lifted the pail of milk and set out arm in arm with him past wilted vegetables, scratching chooks, an ambling horse and a contented cow. Their afternoon by the river was what one might have expected of a newly betrothed couple who were unobserved under a canopy of willows. Although she was a girl of good character, Rebecca found several hours of seclusion with John full of temptation. She was astounded at her sensations, even stronger than those she had been feeling at nighttime. She sighed quietly as the sun sank lower in the summer sky and John said they should be going back. Mrs. Hassall's picnic had scarcely been touched.

Rebecca and John only assumed they were unobserved, but watching them come up the path was a small waif sitting on a paddock fence. The little girl was without bonnet or boots, and her body was draped in a shift many sizes too big and so thin one might have seen through it, had it not been so filthy. The child had an elfin face hidden in a tangle of dirty fair hair.

"Who's that you have with you, Mr. Miller?" John and Rebecca stopped in their tracks. "Rebecca, this is Megan, the lass I was telling you about," said John. "May I introduce Miss Nixon, Megan."

"You're not married! Tch, tch! I'm Megan Mary Mahoney, Miss, and I've been waiting for you both. I thought you'd never stop your kissing." Rebecca blushed, and John looked uncomfortable. "I'm sorry I didn't milk the cow this morning, but Ma took poorly, and I couldn't leave her. Can I have the eggs anyway? I milk Bossy morning and afternoon, and Mr. Miller said I could have the eggs and the pail of milk to take home. Thank you for cooling the milk. Ma is trying to wean the baby. I need the eggs. There's naught else for our tea."

The little girl looked to be about eight years of age, but Rebecca had a feeling she was older. The child slid off the fence, and Rebecca's nose started to twitch. God only knew when Megan had had a bath. "And you live in that hut with your mother and the baby?" asked Rebecca. "I live there with Ma and baby Henrietta. She was named for our Pa. His name was Henry Joseph Patrick Mahoney. He was Mr. Nuttle's hired man."

"And where is your father now?"

"Drowned," said Megan. She skipped up the path ahead of John and Rebecca. "He was too fond of drink and one night he came home and mistook the river for our door. Now Ma doesn't have to have any more babies, and I don't have to get beaten. You didn't tell me about the eggs." She stopped beside the henhouse and scowled at Rebecca.

"For certain you may have them," said Rebecca, "and when you've collected them, we'll talk about milking the cow." Amongst other things under the willows, Rebecca had asked John about caring for the farm until they came to live there. Hens had to be fed, eggs collected, a cow milked, and a horse fed and watered. Megan Mary Mahoney, small though she was, looked to be Heaven-sent.

"Perhaps," said Rebecca to Megan, "you could show me how you milk the cow."

The little girl set down her basket of eggs and bristled. "I'm as good at it as you are! I watched you this morning. I was ever so angry when I saw you walk away with the milk. I didn't know you were cooling it for me."

Megan ran to the barn for another pail, rinsed it at the pump, washed her hands and slipped into the paddock. She gave the cow a lengthy embrace and sat on bony haunches to do the afternoon milking. Rebecca stood by the fence to watch. She was amazed at the strength in the child's hands. The milk went splashing into the pail whilst Megan sang to the cow in a high, sweet voice. How many little waifs like this hadn't Rebecca seen in Ireland? She'd known drunken fathers, mothers exhausted from bearing babies, and their children always hungry, too ill-clothed to go to school, enduring a life of filth and beatings. And sometimes there would be a child like Megan, responsible, full of spunk, determined to survive.

Secure in growing up on her father's farm and in working on the Oxley Estate, Rebecca knew her own life had been a sheltered one. She felt certain the future was about to expand her experiences and test her Christian fortitude.

Megan Mary Mahoney refused any help with the pails of milk and the basket of eggs. She could make three trips across the paddock, she said. The afternoon sun was slanting through the pines when Rebecca and John put out hay for the brown horse—whose name was Ned, the child told them—and climbed into the buggy.

Rebecca smiled up at John. "I'll remember this New Year's Day!" John took up the reins, and the grey mare made her way back along the track to the road. "Do you suppose Megan will follow my instructions for the animals?"

"Better than I would!" said John, chuckling. "Until I came to New South Wales, I had lived in cities all my life. I have only a limited knowledge of farm life, Rebecca. You'll have to be patient with me." Before they reached the road, he brought the mare to a halt in the shade of a eucalypt and took Rebecca in his arms. "Are you happy, my dear?"

"I've never been happier in my life." She kissed him slowly as the grey mare nibbled grass along the fence in the glow of the setting sun. John drove Rebecca back to the Estate, and she went into the Overseer's house to tell Mrs. Simpson her news. Then she settled into her bed to have delicious dreams of John and their farm.

Two days on, she sent her good news to Hannah, now living on Cartmel station at Tarago.

Oxley Estate
Camden County, New South Wales
January 3rd, 1857

My Dearest Hannah,
I trust this letter finds you and David in good health. I miss you, my dearest friend, more especially because I have happy news to share.

John Miller and I are to be married as soon as we can arrange it. You know, Hannah, how much I have longed to have a farm. John has the lease of a thirty-acre property together with a small flock of hens, a lovely cow, and a large horse of indiscriminate breeding, not David's preference, to be sure, but he will do us nicely. We scarcely have a homestead, only a three-room slab hut. The outbuildings and animals are in reasonable shape, but the hut is derelict, just a roof over our heads.

Lest you think I care only for the farm, I assure you my feelings for John are stronger still. We have long been aware of our affection for each other, but as you realize, one does not reveal one's intentions until future plans are in place. John has admitted he is just learning to be a farmer, but he's interested in the property and wants to develop it. I must pause here and give you my heartfelt thanks for bringing him to our picnics by the river. I even forgive you for teasing me.

On my first visit to the property, we met a neighbour's child, a daughter of the former hired hand, a man who drowned. Little Megan is a lass of independent spirit, living in a nearby hut with her widowed mother and a baby. Papists, I'm sure. The family depends on milk and eggs from the farm, but when we move there, new arrangements will have to be made. No family, even papists, can be allowed to go hungry, yet we shall need the eggs and milk ourselves.

My concern at the moment is for my age at marriage. Not until the end of this year will I be one and twenty years, and John and I intend to be married much before that. I know John is two and thirty years of age, but he has never asked me how old I am. Because I am not of the age to marry, I believe my father's permission will be needed, although when he gave me my dowry, he said he expected me to find myself a worthy husband in the colony. The great distance to Ireland will delay his permission, and I must seek a word with Mr. Hassall about my situation.

I do wish you were here, dearest Hannah. My thoughts are often with you and David. Write to me soon. I promise to let you know of our plans.

As ever, I am your loving friend,

Rebecca

"Splendid! Splendid!" said the Reverend Hassall as he greeted Rebecca at the church door on Epiphany Sunday. "You and John must join us at the vicarage after the service, and we shall celebrate at dinner! Mrs. Hassall will be thrilled!"

Rebecca knew the patient Mrs. Hassall never fussed about the number of people her husband brought home for dinner on a Sunday. During the previous winter, when Rebecca had been a regular visitor, she had met strangers at the table each week, travellers usually, gathered up at church by the Reverend Hassall and fed at the vicarage before they went on their way through the Southern Highland. Mrs. Hassall's Sunday dinners seemed to be able to satisfy everyone, and Rebecca was reminded of the miracle of the loaves and fishes.

After dinner she and John walked with James Hassall in his garden, where Rebecca revealed she was not of marriageable age. "A common occurrence, Rebecca, and not one that should concern you," said the Reverend Hassall. "Of course, you must write to your father at once and ask for his permission, but as you live on the other side of the world, such a letter will be merely out of respect for him. I have married many underage brides and I shall be happy to unite you and John in Holy Matrimony as soon as I have called the Banns. You have only to let me know the date of the nuptials."

John spoke up. "I have a confession, too, Rebecca." Her eyes widened. She had the uneasy feeling he was about to tell her he was not a bachelor, but a widower. Did he have children somewhere? This was a common enough situation when the bridegroom was much older than the bride. Rebecca held her breath as John continued in a different vein.

"I am not of a Church of England family," he said. "I was baptised a Calvinist at Margate, Kent, in the Zion Chapel of Lady Huntingdon's Independent Church, and at Poole I belonged to an independent church in Skinner Street. When I came to New South Wales, I could find no such places of worship and so I attended the Church of England. The Reverend Maurice Gray gave me instruction and presented me to the Bishop of Goulburn for Confirmation at the Cathedral Church of Saint Saviour. I was concerned you would not consider me, Rebecca, if you knew of my Nonconformist background."

A Nonconformist! Baptised a Calvinist! John's thoughtful courtship of her, however, and his lease of a farm had assured her consideration. She was not going to tell him so, nor that she would have yearned for his proposal of marriage no matter what his church beginnings. Avoiding any mention of Calvinism, Rebecca wrote in glowing terms about John to her father, no more than her future husband deserved, and requested permission to marry him. She was certain her father would approve of the match because James Nixon was a loving, considerate father and not resentful of the English, as were many of his Irish neighbours. She was sure of her father's blessing.

The next few months were a busy time for Rebecca. She told Mr. Simpson she was his employee on the Oxley Estate until the middle of February, when she would accept Mrs. Hassall's kind invitation to lodge at the vicarage. Rebecca had her trousseau to make, not the traditional collection, but more a wardrobe that could withstand the rigorous activities of farm life. John said she might use her dowry as she wished, and she spent it with care on sewing materials from a shop in Berrima. Mrs. Hassall sat with her on the vicarage verandah as they happily worked on Rebecca's household linens and new clothing, and used the scraps left from their work for rag rugs for the floor of the hut.

Rebecca, who quickly realized a vicarage was always prepared for unexpected guests, helped Mrs. Hassall with laundry and meals. When Rebecca made potato cakes for evening tea, the Reverend Hassall was particularly impressed. "No one can make a potato cake like you, Rebecca," said the Vicar. Rebecca winked at Mrs. Hassall and from then on ensured enough potatoes were boiled at the noon dinner to provide sufficient leftovers for the cakes at evening tea.

One afternoon, when marigolds along the vicarage borders were aglow in the late summer sun, the two women sat sewing and listening to the chatter of lorikeets and the call of magpies. Watching the Vicar's wife embroider a pillow cover, Rebecca said, "I'm beginning to suspect you're skillful enough to have finished the new altar linens yourself." Mrs. Hassall laughed. "John confided his intentions to us, and you were asked to work on the linens so that he might have the opportunity of courting you." Rebecca smiled, admitting to herself that she was secretly pleased with John's subterfuge.

On Sunday afternoons John and Rebecca went to check on the property. Silently asking God's forgiveness for working on His day, Rebecca set about making the hut respectable whilst John dug the kitchen garden for her. For his farm work she had stitched a pair of fustian trousers for him and a substantial cotton shirt. When the Irish workers at the Oxley Estate learned what John and Rebecca were up to, they appeared at the farm every week instead of going to the river and used their skills and energy to help the betrothed couple. As she watched them work on the Lord's Day, Rebecca said prayers for their souls.

John was very appreciative because his helpers were far more accomplished at farm tasks than he was. "I've decided to forget it's Sunday. I am regarding your friends' work as a blessing from the Lord." Rebecca was astounded at his liberality.

Hugh Clarke, the carpenter, thought the Millers needed a verandah and began to build one. His construction was a substantial addition to the hut. He examined the cart and decided to reinforce it, then add a lever to it for a brake and build benches in it—for the Miller children, he said solemnly. Bertie Marshall dug a root cellar and lined it with slabs, assisted by Rose Barry, the scullery maid; they also excavated and lined a dairy in the shade of the barn, and Hugh roofed it over. John decided a new toilet was required, and after he and Bertie had dug the pit, Hugh built the dunny for it. Women from the estate helped Rebecca prepare the kitchen garden and plant autumn vegetables, and Ian Kincade put Ned's harness in good order. All this activity was observed by Megan Mary Mahoney from her perch on a fence.

Rebecca and John felt they could now set a date for their wedding. The Reverend Hassall saw no problem in calling the Banns during Lent, a practice acceptable in the evangelical church of the colony. In the early evening of the 12th of March, 1857, Rebecca Nixon, in her best dress of navy crepe, her boots polished and her hair piled high, entered Holy Trinity Church and proceeded in lace-veiled modesty under the sandstone Gothic arches, through the candlelit nave and chancel to the altar rail.

"I Rebecca, take thee John, to my wedded husband, to have and to hold from this day forward, for better for worse, for richer for poorer, in sickness and in health, to love, cherish, and to obey, till death us do part, according to God's holy ordinance; and thereto I give thee my troth."

Afterwards, in the vicarage garden overflowing with wedding guests, Rebecca longed for the presence of her dearest friend Hannah, who lived too far away to attend. The Irish workers from the Oxley Estate made it a jolly party and wished John and Rebecca Miller a lifetime of happiness and many children to see them into old age.

THIRTEEN
Bowral

Yea, the sparrow hath found an house . . .
— PSALM 84:3

Rebecca knew what to expect on her wedding night. After all, she had been raised on a farm, and in their small stone cottage her parents had produced a large family. What gave her the greatest pleasure on her first night with John were the exquisite sensations aroused by his loving attentions. As a proper young woman, however, she refrained from revealing her pleasure. On their bed of pine boughs and sheepskin, its sheets in disarray, Rebecca snuggled closer to her sleeping husband when she heard the cock crow in the early morning hours.

Sunlight crept into the room, and Rebecca roused herself to tend to the fire for breakfast. Taking a moment to step out on the verandah and stretch lazily in the rose-tinted dawn, she found herself face to face with Megan Mary Mahoney. The waif sat on the verandah rail, a clean milk pail in her hand. "Do you want me to milk Bossy? You're probably tired from last night, and I can do it for you."

"Thank you, Megan. That's very thoughtful. Please let me have the pail of milk when you're finished." The child frowned as she slid off the rail and set off for Bossy's paddock. John came out on the verandah and put his arms around Rebecca. She leaned against him and nestled her head on his shoulder. "Have you decided what we'll do about milk and eggs for the Mahoneys?" he asked. "The eggs are no worry," she answered. "We've plenty of pullets, so we'll take some across and help them set up a run and a henhouse. They need a cow, of course, but I'm not sure they can afford one. We'll take a walk over there today and see what's what."

Rebecca stood in John's arms listening to Megan singing sweetly whilst she milked the cow. When the child was done, she treated Bossy to another embrace and climbed back through the fence to hand over the pail of milk. Rebecca took a generous jugful for her own use and gave the remainder to Megan. The child's small face became a large black scowl, and Rebecca decided it was time she explained the situation. "Mr. Miller and I can't go on supplying your family with milk and eggs, Megan. We'll need them for ourselves and for our children, God willing. Has your family never had a cow and chooks?" The child's defensiveness was palpable. "We can't! Ma's too poorly to tend to them, and Pa said Mr. Nuttle would give us everything we needed!" She folded her arms across her narrow chest. "You'll have to share with us like he did!" The last statement had a plaintive, desperate tone, and Rebecca knew the sooner she and John checked on the Mahoneys, the better. That afternoon they walked to the boxbark hut under the pines, where, in place of a kitchen garden, they found a rubbish heap swarming with flies. A defiant Megan barred the door. "You can't come in! The baby's not suckling, and Ma's not up to visitors! Go away and leave us alone!"

"Please understand, Megan," said John, "I have the lease of this property and an obligation to call on my tenant. We have come to introduce ourselves to your mother." His voice was filled with kindly concern. Little Megan, arms folded, stood firm. John gently lifted the protesting child aside and opened the door of the hut with Rebecca at his heels.

What Rebecca faced was worse than anything she had ever known in Ireland, and she was certain that John, who was holding a handkerchief over his mouth and nose, had never seen the like of it. Gagging in the thick smoke and stench of excrement as she peered through the miasma, Rebecca made out a bare room with nothing but a smouldering fire in a corner, a battered armchair before it and a cot against a wall. God only knew where the family ate or where little Megan slept. A woman lay wrapped in a shawl on the cot, convulsing with coughs and clutching a white-faced infant to her breast. She gasped for breath and struggled to speak.

"Good day to you both. Thank you for the milk. I'm trying to wean the bairn." Her voice was scarcely audible, but she spoke as though she had once known a decent life. A glimpse of the bairn convinced Rebecca the infant was close to death. "You're most welcome, Mrs. Mahoney. May I see the baby?"

"You'll not touch her, begging your pardon. This one's my last hope, you see." The words brought on a paroxysm of coughing. She fought to breathe and said, "I've lost six babies since Megan." Her rasping coughs diminished to quiet wheezing.

"Has the doctor been to see you and the baby, Mrs. Mahoney?" asked John. No answer came from the cot. Not likely, thought Rebecca. She stared at the two beings bundled together in the filthy shawl and reckoned neither was long for this world. The foul atmosphere was about to make Rebecca vomit, and she headed out into the March morning with John close behind her. Both of them wiped their smarting eyes and took deep breaths of fresh autumn air.

"We'll get medical help for your mother and the baby," John said to Megan. She protested: "Don't you go sending for any quack! No telling what he'd do, and Ma and the baby might die!" Despite Megan's protests John did send for the Berrima doctor, who emerged from the hut shaking his head. The following day John fetched the priest from Saint Francis Xavier Roman Catholic Church. The cleric came away from the hut saying that he had baptised the baby and given extreme unction and would be available for a graveside service. For three days Rebecca called at the hut to see if she could make Mrs. Mahoney more comfortable, but her efforts were merely merciful, not restorative. During her third visit Mrs. Mahoney, with the lifeless body of her infant lying at her breast, uttered a wretched sigh and breathed her last.

Megan at once blazed into anger and assaulted Rebecca with vitriolic curses, learned from her father, reckoned Rebecca. She held the raging Megan gently in her arms, remembering her own grief and strangely similar anger when her mother died, although she had not expressed it in such words. Megan's curses gradually subsided into sobs of despair. The two of them stood by the cot, and

Rebecca encouraged the weeping child to say two Hail Marys for the souls of her departed mother and baby sister.

John summoned the doctor again, who certified the baby's death as "cholera infantum" and the mother's as "phthisis pulmonalis." Next morning the Millers placed the bodies of baby Henrietta and Mrs. Mahoney into shrouds Rebecca had made and drove them in the cart to Saint Francis Xavier Church in Berrima. Megan rode with the shrouded bodies, fulminating in a fury at Rebecca and John for causing the deaths of her mother and the baby.

On their way home from the graveyard, Rebecca said, "You'll come and live with us, Megan. I'll be grateful for your help." But the girl would have none of it. "You'll not make me your slavey! I'll live by myself in our hut!" Megan meant what she said. She holed up in the boxbark hut, appearing twice a day to milk the cow and take a little milk and a few eggs. Rebecca had scant hope of caring properly for the child, who was thinner and dirtier than ever.

"We must destroy that boxbark hut, John," said Rebecca. "It's a place of filth and contagion, and I'll not have Megan staying there any longer. We'll put stout ropes around the corner posts and use Ned to collapse the place."

The following morning Rebecca, John and Ned set about their task. John fastened ropes around the posts and secured them to Ned's harness, lifted the reins and shouted, "Giddup!" The heavy horse put his head down, set his shoulders into his collar, stretched the ropes taut, and planted his great rear legs. He drove forward until the posts snapped and the hut exploded in shards of bark. Released from his burden, the horse knew to ease up and come to a halt. Rebecca had reached for Megan and held her tight whilst Ned demolished her home. The small girl kicked and screamed with a violence that taxed all Rebecca's strength. When the hut was flattened, Rebecca let Megan tear herself away, and the child ran sobbing towards the river, her anguish echoing through the trees.

Rebecca had never imagined that caring for Megan Mary Mahoney was going to be easy. The child had done exactly as she had pleased all her life, her mother too ill and her father too drunk to provide any upbringing. On many days, once she had milked Bossy in the morning, Megan disappeared until after dark. Rebecca worried about her whilst John tried to convince his wife the child knew how to take care of herself. Rebecca had made bloomers and two cotton dresses for the little girl and knitted her a jumper, but these were rejected out of hand. Nor would Megan bathe. She slept and ate wrapped in a blanket in a corner of the verandah, refusing to let Rebecca and John near her. She's a real little savage, thought Rebecca, not unsympathetically. She's lost all she's ever known and she's lonely and terrified.

On an April morning after John had left for Berrima to teach at the gaol, Rebecca put the metal bathtub in front of the fire and filled it with warm, soapy water. Having set out a flannel cloth, a towel, new bloomers and a dress, she climbed through the fence and called to Megan, who sat slumped against a tree in Bossy's paddock. The child set off pell-mell across the paddock with Rebecca in hot pursuit.

She caught the shrieking, kicking child and lifted her through the fence and into the hut. One vigorous rip removed the girl's filthy shift, and Rebecca plunged the naked Megan into the tub. Pushing her under the water, she brought her up spluttering and screaming and proceeded to wash her hair. She took a soapy flannel to the small frame of skin and bones and marvelled at the child's strength in battling her every inch of the way. The bath water was a rancid grey, and Rebecca was worn out and soaked from the tussle by the time she helped a howling Megan out of the tub and wrapped her in a towel.

In her new clothes, her golden hair brushed down her back (Rebecca had reluctantly taken scissors to the worst of the tangles), a subdued Megan Mary Mahoney attempted an air of dignified calm. "I've never had a bath, you see," she said, "only a dip in the river before Christmas each year. I think perhaps I could get used to warm water and soap. Thank you for the dress and bloomers. Would you like me to peel the spuds for dinner?" Rebecca laughed at the shining child and gave her a long hug. Megan responded by wrapping thin arms around her. She's a frightened bird, thought Rebecca.

The path ahead for Megan and the Millers was not smooth. The little girl accepted a cot in the kitchen, kept herself clean and learned to plait her hair before bedtime and brush it out in the morning, although she preferred that Rebecca brush it for her. She also continued to milk Bossy and collect eggs. However, any expectation she would do as she was told was merely an expectation, because Megan herself decided on any additional chores. John's understanding extended further than his wife's, whose exasperation surfaced daily. Rebecca prayed each night for patience and endurance.

One afternoon Megan came storming into the hut and set down a quarter-full pail of milk. "Bossy won't give me her milk and she kicks the pail! She tries my patience! She's so unco-operative, I'm exasperated with her!" Rebecca smiled at the child's choice of words. It was time the cow was taken to a bull, for she was drying up. Next day Rebecca walked Bossy to a bull she had seen on the road to Berrima whilst Megan followed behind with a switch to urge the cow onward. They did not stay to watch the proceedings, but entrusted them to the bull's owner. Rebecca paid him only half his fee. He would get the rest when she was certain Bossy was carrying a calf.

Before dawn one morning in April, Rebecca came awake and slipped out of bed to use the chamber pot. She felt so queasy she lay down again. Using the pot could wait until her head stopped spinning. When her dizziness eased, she sat up and immediately vomited at the side of the bed. She realized she could be with child. John rolled over and snored gently whilst Rebecca struggled to clean up the mess.

In the ensuing days Megan eyed her knowingly as Rebecca stuffed crusts of bread into her apron pockets, ready to stave off any nausea. She said nothing to John about her condition because she thought it wise to keep silent until she felt a quickening. Each morning, whilst John slept on unaware, Rebecca nibbled bread crusts. She finally told him about the baby when she lay warm in his arms one winter night at the end of July. He was enthusiastic about his impending fatherhood and, because he viewed with concern Rebecca's continued vigorous approach to her chores, redoubled his efforts to assist her around the farm. Megan forgot all about her reluctance to co-operate and got underfoot in her determination to help.

Each day after the noon dinner, Megan, who had never been to school and could not read, relied on Rebecca to read aloud to her. Rebecca felt the need of a lie-down at that time of day and went to bed with the Bible or a volume of Wordsworth's poetry. Megan liked "I Wandered Lonely as a Cloud" and asked for the poem every afternoon until she had it memorized. Rebecca often fell asleep afterwards, and Megan awakened her later, a cup of tea in her hand.

When spring arrived, Rebecca enjoyed a surge of energy as she organized her kitchen garden and planted seeds. The rooster responded so enthusiastically to the onset of the season that a number of chooks went broody. The tall green crop of hay and the blue-green oats that Rebecca and John had planted now moved in an undulating rhythm in the fresh spring breezes, putting Rebecca in mind of gentle waves on a tropical ocean. Tussocks of lush grasses sprang forth in the paddocks, and pale, pendulous willow boughs shaded the brim-full river. Had she and John held the place freehold, Rebecca would have felt completely fulfilled. As it was, she contented herself with enjoying their burgeoning leasehold property.

The Millers discovered that Megan, a quicker child than most, was strangely reluctant to learn to read, preferring to regard the skill as some sort of magic performed by adults. At breakfast one morning, John said, "I don't see you practising your letters and numerals, Megan." The child scowled. "There will never be a child in my house who can't read and do sums. Tomorrow I'll examine you on the alphabet and numerals to one hundred." Megan glowered at him and demanded Rebecca's help that afternoon. "I'm as quick to learn as those prisoners Mr. Miller teaches at the gaol!" she insisted. "You'll get no argument from me!" said Rebecca. She was knitting a baby shawl and watching the child write the alphabet in a determined hand.

Megan's verbal skills were much advanced, and once she had unlocked the printed code and associated it with the sounds of her own words, she was lured into the intrigue of reading. Arithmetic fascinated her. Rebecca wrote out the multiplication tables for her, and many a morning and afternoon Megan could be found milking Bossy and chanting times tables until she had them mastered.

"How old are you, Megan?" asked Rebecca one summer morning when the two of them were weeding the kitchen garden.

"I don't rightly know, but I'm sure I must be twelve," she replied. Rebecca had a plan. "We must find out when you were born and invite all our friends to a party to celebrate your birthday. I'll make a cake for you, and we'll sing songs and play silly games." Megan gave her a puzzled look.

Rebecca asked John to visit Saint Francis Xavier Church in Berrima to look at baptismal records. Megan had been born when evidence of a child's birth was not on a birth certificate but written on a Certificate of Baptism. Although Saint Francis Xavier was a relatively new church, Rebecca was certain a Roman Catholic congregation had existed at Berrima for some time. If a church had not been available, Megan could have been baptised by a Roman Catholic missionary. The child deserved to be one of Christ's flock, papist though she was.

"I saw your baptismal record today, Megan," John reported at tea time a few days later. "You were born on the 21st of December in 1846. You'll soon be eleven years old!"

"Oh, well," sighed Megan. "*Next* year I'll be twelve."

Rebecca had not anticipated hosting a party quite so soon. She turned one and twenty years of age herself on the 22nd of December. Back in Tyrone her family would have had a coming-of-age celebration for her at Grennin, but here in New South Wales, she would turn her attentions to this little girl who had never had a birthday party.

The pre-Christmas weather was very warm and certain to become even warmer in the weeks to come. She sent John to the Oxley Estate to invite the Irish workers to a birthday picnic. Megan's birthday, complete with a cake, was celebrated on Sunday afternoon, the 20th of December, and featured nostalgic Irish songs and vigorous games of Blind Man's Bluff. In the evening Megan sat under a tree with Bertie Marshall and Rose Barry, who told her stories of their childhoods in Antrim. As she settled into her cot that night, Megan pronounced her party "the best ever."

That Christmas at the Miller farm was spent quietly, with Rebecca summoning enough energy to roast a chook and Megan offering to boil the vegetables for Christmas dinner. From the cool recesses of Rebecca's dairy came a Christmas pudding, which she heated for dessert. Megan was keen on the pudding and ecstatic over the gift Rebecca and John had given her, a kitten from a litter in the Oxley Estate barn. The small tomcat, as independent as his new owner, strutted about the Miller property in all his scruffy glory, his mottled brown fur and brave hiss ready to rise in defence against anything unfamiliar. Megan named him Abner.

"Abner? Wherever did you get that name?" Rebecca asked. "From the Old Testament. Abner protected King Saul." Rebecca was not sure a cat should be named after someone in the Holy Book, but at least the child had been paying attention to John's daily Bible readings.

Rebecca's pains began in the early hours of Sunday, the 3rd of January. At daylight John harnessed Ned to the cart and went to Berrima to fetch the accoucheuse. From observing her mother's experiences, Rebecca was familiar with the stages of childbirth. With great forbearance, for she was a young woman with an impatient nature, she endured a first labour of sixteen hours. Into this world on the evening of January 3rd, 1858, came Mary Jane Miller. She was dark-haired like her mother, bright-eyed and sturdily built, and she squalled lustily. "Thanks be to God," sighed Rebecca when the accoucheuse placed the vigorous infant in her arms.

Megan avoided the baby and spent her days sitting silently under trees in the paddocks whilst Abner paced around her like a sentinel. One afternoon Rebecca discovered Megan, beads in hand, gently rocking Mary Jane in her cradle and repeating over and over, "Hail Mary, full of grace! the Lord is with thee; blessed art thou among women, and blessed is the fruit of thy womb, Jesus. Holy Mary, Mother of God, pray for us sinners, now and at the hour of our death. Amen."

When Rebecca asked why she was saying Hail Marys, Megan replied, "Mary Jane isn't going to be with us for long, and I'm preparing her for Heaven." Rebecca shuddered; Megan had only known babies who had died. Lifting a wriggling Mary Jane from her cradle, Rebecca ushered Megan out to the verandah. She sat the girl in the rocking chair and settled the infant in her arms.

"Megan, I promise you that Mary Jane is going to grow up healthy. I'm depending on you to teach her all you know, except she's not to hear any more Hail Marys. Rock and sing her to sleep now, and then I'll read you the story of Noah and the Ark." Megan moved the rocking chair slowly, trying to accept that the bairn in her arms was going to survive. From that moment on, she became an overly conscientious childminder who took her responsibilities as mentor very seriously.

With caring for the new baby, Rebecca's attention had been distracted from the expectant Bossy until Megan came running into the hut one morning. "Come quick, Rebecca! Bossy's wandering around in a rare state!" Rebecca prayed the animal would have an easy birthing. From watching her mother help with calving, Rebecca knew if Bossy got into difficulty, she didn't have the strength at this time to help her.

"Now is the time for prayers, Megan. Stand there by Bossy's head and pray quietly for her calf." Megan was never more obedient. Rebecca gave thanks to God when a calf slid easily onto the grass of the paddock. Proving herself a good mother, Bossy quickly licked away the afterbirth whilst poor Megan vomited. The calf was a pretty little heifer, which pleased Rebecca because she would have a second supply of milk. She took Megan inside for a bath and clean clothes.

As she was brushing the child's hair, she said, "You must choose a name for our heifer." Megan was confused. "Why do you call her a heifer?" "Because she'll grow up to be a cow like Bossy," explained Rebecca, "and not a bull like her father. It's a heifer we needed, and we're fortunate to have one." She took Megan out to see the still-damp black and white calf standing on wobbly legs. "I'll think of a name for her," said Megan. Next morning she announced, "We'll call her Julia, because Saint Paul thought Julia was important to the early church, and our heifer is important to us." First a cat, now a calf, mused Rebecca, this time from Paul's Epistle to the Romans.

Mary Jane, a good baby who slept and suckled well, was the delight of both her parents. For her baptism at Holy Trinity, her mother made a cambric christening dress for her, trimmed with crocheted lace, and the Reverend James Hassall welcomed Mary Jane into God's family: "We receive this child, Mary Jane, into the congregation of Christ's flock, and do sign her with the sign of the Cross, in token that hereafter she shall not be ashamed to confess the faith of Christ crucified, and manfully to fight under his banner, against sin, the world, and the devil; and to continue Christ's faithful soldier and servant until her life's end. Amen." The Reverend Hassall and Mary Jane's parents had no idea how prophetic those words were. Six weeks after the birth of Mary Jane, who had been named for John's mother and his maternal grandmother, Jane Maskelyne, the Reverend Hassall conducted the service of The Thanksgiving of Women After Childbirth for Rebecca and gave her Holy Communion.

When Megan was rocking the baby to sleep one afternoon, Rebecca took the opportunity to write to her father with her happy news.

Near Bowral,
Camden County, New South Wales
March 5th, 1858

My Dear Father,
I write to thank you for your blessing on my union with John Miller and to tell you of the safe arrival of a granddaughter. Our wee Mary Jane was born on the 3rd of January, and everyone says she favours me in appearance. She has been baptised in Holy Trinity Church at Berrima. Mary Jane is a good bairn, solemn, observant and, I must say, possessed of a mind of her own.

Less than two miles beyond our property is the hamlet of Bowral, a settlement on the vast Oxley Estate, the leaseholder of our farm. The family home of the Oxleys at Bowral is a very grand place. The

Reverend James Hassall of Holy Trinity Church conducts Sunday afternoon services there for local worshippers. John and I support him and attend each Sunday.

John is keen on having a school of his own, but a location at Bowral will have to be arranged. Most of the children hereabouts have never attended school and are without any skills in reading or arithmetic. John is determined our Mary Jane will have a school to attend.

Please give my warmest regards to everyone at Grennin. You are all in my prayers every day.

As ever, I am your loving daughter,

Rebecca

Each day in the Miller household began with Family Prayer. John read the Collect for the day and a Bible reading from one of the Proper Lessons in *The Book of Common Prayer*, and Rebecca and Megan joined him in saying the Lord's Prayer. The brief early morning service of worship was to take place every morning throughout their lives.

Rebecca acquired a stall on Saturdays in Berrima marketplace where she sold butter, eggs and pullets. She had in mind that Megan would take care of the baby whilst she dealt with customers, but Megan, although she enjoyed caring for Mary Jane, was more interested in how much money she could make at the stall. Anyone who tried to bargain with Megan Mary Mahoney was in for a challenge.

During the next two years, Rebecca gave birth to another daughter and a son. Emily Elizabeth was born on the 4th of June, 1859, and the Miller heir, John James, known as J.J., arrived on the 9th of November, 1860. Emily was fair-haired, quiet and thoughtful like her father. J.J. was an active child, confident and adventuresome from the beginning of his life. Like Mary Jane before them, Emily and J.J. wore the crochet-trimmed christening dress when they were baptised in Holy Trinity Church at Berrima by the Reverend James Hassall.

Had she not had Megan's help, Rebecca would have been hard-pressed to care for the babies and do her farm chores as well. Rebecca doubted John would ever have her enthusiasm for farming. Although he was faithful in his daily chores and always willing to help, she knew his heart was elsewhere. One evening, having watched John spend the day struggling with a sickle in the oat field, she said, "You need to go to Bowral and find a location for that school you've always wanted, and I've decided we need a hired man. I can pay his wages from my market money, and you can devote yourself to your teaching." John laughed and kissed her. Rebecca hadn't meant to be amusing, but at least her husband appreciated her decisions.

When the workers at the Oxley Estate learned of Rebecca's need, Bertie Marshall walked over to the Miller farm with Rose Barry, his betrothed. "We've an arrangement with Mr. and Mrs. Simpson," said Bertie. "We can be at your service on Saturday and Sunday afternoons. How would that suit you, Rebecca?"

"Very well," said Rebecca. If truth be told, she had not been sure where she would find full-time wages of twenty pounds a year for a hired man. Yet she was certain she could afford to pay Bertie and Rose for two half-days of work every week. There was still the matter of their souls in jeopardy when they worked on Sunday afternoons, but she would let them settle that with their Maker.

The hamlet of Bowral, where John wanted to establish his school, was taking on the look of a proper village. The Oxleys had employed a man named Adam Windsor to clear a road starting from the settlement at Bong Bong and continuing on through Bowral. At the mid-point of the hamlet, he cleared another road at right angles. The Oxleys had given Adam Windsor permission to build himself a hut on the northeast corner.

When John approached the Oxleys about establishing a school in Bowral, he was well received, but they were not about to provide him with a school building. He decided to seek the advice of Adam Windsor, who seemed to know the place better than anyone. "I'm going to build a slab hut on that corner," said the man, "and I could add a boxbark skillion to it for your pupils. Would that do you?"

"Indeed, it would," said John. When he learned that Adam Windsor was living rough beside the roads he was clearing, he invited him for a meal at the Miller farm, and the man said he would be pleased to accept on the following Sunday. John drove home, eager to tell Rebecca about his acquaintance with Adam and their arrangements for the school.

Rebecca was basting a chook that Sunday when she was interrupted by Megan. "Rebecca! Come quick! There's a big black man coming down our track!" Abner, his fur on end, hissed from a paddock fence. John walked out to greet their visitor. "The man doesn't seem to be one of the sable folk," said Megan, "but why is he so dark, Rebecca?"

Adam was the first Negro they had met. Although there were Negro cooks on the *Caroline*, Rebecca had not seen any of them. She knew about Negroes who were taken from darkest Africa to America as slaves and about black savages in the South Seas who had threatened Mr. Hassall's grandparents. Where had Adam Windsor come from? And how had he acquired his names, one so Biblical and the other so English? For certain, those were not his childhood names in his native land. She offered her hand to him as Megan scrambled up on the fence to perch beside the hissing Abner.

When John's school was established in the skillion at the crossroads hut, Adam Windsor was quick to chide any child who showed up late for class. John often invited the man to Sunday dinners, and he became a devoted friend of the Millers. Rebecca and John never did learn about the man's names or place of origin, nor did it matter.

A letter from England, written to John by his sister Elizabeth, arrived before Christmas with the sad news of their father's death at Poole in Dorsetshire on August 30th, 1861. William Miller Sr. had been attended by his surgeon son, William, who had been helpless to prevent the ultimate consequences of old age.

John's school at Bowral prospered, for the small building was always full of young scholars. He charged a fee of twopence a week, and most parents were able to pay him. All his pupils, who ranged in age from four years to twelve, had to be taught their letters and numerals, even the oldest ones. In the second year, he took little Mary Jane to school, where she proved to be an apt pupil.

On July 29th, 1862, less than a year after the death of her husband, John's mother died at Poole. John's brother William wrote to say that he and his sisters Mary Jane and Elizabeth had tended to their mother through a lengthy illness and watched her succumb to phthisis pulmonalis one warm summer's afternoon. "The doctor wrote 'phthisis pulmonalis' on the death certificate of Megan's mother," remarked Rebecca. Surely her mother-in-law, whose elegant letters to John she had read, had not suffered like that in her final days? John was greatly affected by his mother's death. He spoke about her interest in educating her children and her lifelong studies in astronomy. Listening to him, Rebecca wished she could have known Margaret Mary Maskelyne Miller.

Holy Bible

FOURTEEN

Murrumburrah

O give thanks to the Lord, for he is good . . .
— PSALM 107:1

In 1855 Elizabeth and John Barnes again supported their brother-in-law Robert in a political campaign at Sydney. Sixty-eight years after founding the colony, the British Parliament at Westminster granted New South Wales responsible government and thereby empowered the colony to govern itself. The Colonial Council soon called an election to choose an Assembly. George Robert Nichols won his old Council seat and became a Member of the first Legislative Assembly of New South Wales. On formation of the first Cabinet, he was appointed Auditor-General and later, Secretary for Lands and Works.

"In three months' time, I shall be establishing a store at Melbourne," John Barnes announced to his family at Christmas dinner in 1855. "The prospective purchaser of our Crown Street business wants to keep you on as his assistant, Matthew. We'll take you with us to Melbourne, of course, Marion." Elizabeth had agreed to these plans, but, understandably, the news upset the others. George, William and Ted looked most unhappy, and Beth fled from the table in tears at the thought of leaving her school friends. At the sideboard stood Marion Rowley, stonily silent, her arms folded under her ample bosom. Matthew Neale, in puzzling contrast, was beaming as he rose to his feet.

"I won't be staying at the Crown Street store," he said, "and Miss Rowley won't be going to Melbourne." He smiled at the startled faces around the table. "We're getting married!" Pink-faced with happiness, he sat down. Marion Rowley's eyes softened as she spoke.

"Aye. I've enjoyed working for you all these years, but you'll not be taking me to Melbourne. Mr. Neale and I have long had an understanding. When we heard the two of you talking of moving, we took our saved wages and my inheritance from Fifeshire and bought a confectioner's shop and a cottage out at the beach. We're to be married within two months."

Elizabeth sat open-mouthed. She suddenly thought of Bess Mason's romance with Allan Munro on the farm. Marion and Matthew had "long had an understanding." But when had they ever had a chance to meet, except at Sunday dinners? They scarcely knew each other! Ah . . . those buggy rides, when Marion fetched Matthew from the store! She shook her head, wondering how she could be so ignorant about the romantic attachments of her employees.

When the nuptial day arrived, Elizabeth arranged Marion's nut-brown hair in long loose curls beneath her veil. The bride's stony expression, Elizabeth observed, had been replaced by a self-conscious smile and shining eyes.

That day the Barnes family attended a Roman Catholic church for the first time and were fascinated by the Latin liturgy and sumptuous vestments. With Beth serving as Marion's bridal attendant and George as Matthew's groomsman, John escorted Marion down the aisle and proposed a gracious toast to the bride at the wedding breakfast in Shaftesbury. In the afternoon the Barnes family saw the happy couple off on a coach taking them to a new life together.

All four children regarded Sydney as their home and protested going to Melbourne. "I would like to stay at Burwood," said eleven-year-old Ted. "I could board there and come to Melbourne at the holidays." Ted was such a quiet lad, never one to make a fuss, but one look at him convinced his parents he knew his own mind in this matter. Ted's older brother, William, declared he would stay with him. Beth wanted to stay in Sydney, too, but her parents thought she was too young to be left in boarding school and insisted she accompany them to Melbourne.

Elizabeth sympathized with the children and found herself weeping quietly in private as she packed up the household belongings.

Leaving the Ashfield house was as painful as leaving the farm. After settling William and Ted in boarding school, she said a lengthy and tearful farewell to her best friend, Esme Arnold, boarded a coach with John and Beth, and set off on the long road to Melbourne to start once again.

The wide, paved streets of Melbourne, some of them two miles in length, were lined with fine stone buildings. Gold had been discovered in the new colony of Victoria in 1851, and much of the construction in Melbourne's business district had been financed by successful gold miners. By the time the Barnes family arrived, Melbourne was an expanding city. Along one of the main thoroughfares, John found a good location for his store. In an effort to overcome her homesickness for Ashfield, Elizabeth set to work helping her husband stock the new premises, and she was encouraged when the Barnes Store quickly flourished. One day a chance meeting on the street briefly reunited Elizabeth with Caroline Chisholm, who had been arranging for the construction of shelters along the routes to the Victoria goldfields.

In September 1857, the Barnes family received a heart-wrenching letter from Francis Nichols. He conveyed the sad news of his father's death from dropsy. Elizabeth and John mourned the passing of George Robert Nichols, a hospitable, generous friend and a tireless advocate for colonial self-government.

On the 14th of July, 1858, Elizabeth and John celebrated their silver wedding anniversary. As she dressed for the occasion, Elizabeth realized the twenty-five years had had their effects. She thought her figure was still good, but her braided hair was going grey. John, ten years younger, was as fresh-faced as ever, although he fussed about his rapidly thinning hair. At their anniversary party they exchanged gifts that had been purchased, they discovered, at the same jeweller's in the city. John presented Elizabeth with a gold cross on a fine chain. Her gift to John was a gold ring set with a jasper-flecked bloodstone. In the presence of their family and friends, they pledged to wear these always as tokens of their everlasting regard for each other.

By the end of their third year at Melbourne, Elizabeth was again feeling that sense of security so essential to her. John was happy in his store, and she enjoyed their new home, although she felt it would never have the charm of their place at Ashfield. Life had fallen into a pattern once more, and whilst she still missed her Ashfield home and Esme Arnold, she acknowledged that the move to Melbourne had brought them prosperity.

Elizabeth often daydreamed about the day when John retired and they could move to a small property on the western slopes of New South Wales. She would have a friendly cow, a shaded kitchen garden and a flock of chooks. She wished she could feel more sanguine about killing chooks for dinner. She would love to have a dog like Patch, but one did not keep a sheepdog without sheep, and the memory of that experience was too painful.

One early autumn afternoon Elizabeth sat at her dining room table, happily answering a letter from a nephew on the western slopes.

Shaftesbury
Melbourne, Victoria
March 7th, 1859

My Dear Harry,
May I say how much I appreciate your correspondence. Since the death of my dear brother James two years ago, I thought I had lost touch with your family. Your recent letter has restored our connection.

John and I and your cousins are all in good health. We enjoy our home in Melbourne and entertain as often as we can, musical gatherings and card parties mostly. I often think of those days long ago in Dorsetshire when Mother played for the family, and we sang great old songs around the pianoforte.

Your cousin Thomas is a happy stockman who rides the western slopes north of Wagga Wagga. He sends us letters full of details about his stock horse, Star, and his adventures mustering cattle. His brother Johnny, after some years in the goldfields, is now in Sydney, apprenticing as a cabinetmaker. George is our assistant here in the store, and William has gone to work for a grazier. Ted and Beth continue at school.

Do write again of your life at Yass, a place of many memories for me. I remain your loving aunt,

Elizabeth

As she addressed the envelope, she thought of Thomas and wondered why they had not heard from him as usual. He always wrote once a fortnight.

Summer still smothered the dusty western slopes, refusing to let autumn slide softly onto the hills. Thomas Barnes would spend the next few days riding in the scorching sun through dry gullies and rocky back hollows to flush out strays. It had been an uneventful muster, except for O'Brien and his dogs. O'Brien said they were a dingo cross-breed called Hall's heelers. Useless dogs, Thomas thought, horse-chasers and just plain stupid, as likely to nip at the heels of stock horses as at cattle. Surely a better cattle dog could be bred. So far he had been successful in keeping his distance from the dogs and O'Brien.

With any luck two more days should see the last of the strays brought in and then the cattle would be driven for two days to Anchor Point yards near Wagga Wagga, which were owned by the grazier Thomas worked for, Captain Hawser. Thomas was looking forward to a beer, a decent meal and a bath. He would enjoy a bed, too, heavenly compared to the rough, dusty ground he slept on during a muster.

After breakfast he and the other stockmen headed for the higher slopes, leaving young jackeroos to mind the mustered long-horned cattle down on the flat. He hoped O'Brien would ride in the opposite direction, but the man with his fool dogs chose to ride with him. As the hollows became more numerous, Thomas managed to separate himself from O'Brien and once again enjoyed the solitude of the work. The uneven ground and heavy thickets made for tough going, but with a well-placed whip and Star's determination, he dug out the strays and drove them down to join the others.

He was working his way up a narrow gully when he spotted a bull in a dense thicket. Bulls, Thomas was well aware, feared neither horse nor man, and a whip was nothing more than an annoyance. The wild-eyed look of this one, baleful enough to frighten Lucifer himself, told Thomas trouble lay ahead. Hollering and snapping his whip, he rode Star around the thicket whilst the bull, hooves planted in the rocky slope, continued to glare. Thomas circled again, searching for a larger opening so that he could drive harder, growing impatient with this bad-tempered animal. At last Thomas found the opening he wanted. He galloped in tight behind the beast. The bull spun around and faced him straight on. Too late Thomas realized his mistake. The clear path behind him was the bull's route to freedom. The bull lowered his head and charged horse and rider. Cursing his carelessness, Thomas hauled back on the reins to lift Star clear of the bull's ravaging horns. Echoing down the gully came the ringing yelps of O'Brien's Hall's heelers. One dog threw itself at the hindquarters of the bull, driving him forward harder and faster. The other dog rushed at Star from behind and snapped at his heels. In a mad entanglement of dogs, bull and horse, the bull spun around and plunged a horn into Star. The horse reared and collapsed, his rider trapped beneath him. Blood poured from a great hole in Star's breast. Thomas lay screaming, his leg crushed by the weight of his horse. With his blood gushing, Star fought to regain his footing. The muster Overseer, with a rifle across his back, came leaping down the slope to drag Thomas clear of the frantic horse. A shot from the Overseer's rifle put an end to Star's misery. O'Brien's dogs, yelping after the bull, disappeared up the gully.

Thomas thrashed in agony as the Overseer, with the help of O'Brien, got a blanket under him. When the men struggled to sling him out of the thicket and onto a wagon, he screamed in torment. He writhed in and out of consciousness until his body gave way to the mercy of oblivion in the torture of the two-day journey to Wagga Wagga.

"We haven't heard from Thomas in three weeks, John," said Elizabeth one evening. "I know he's on a muster this time of year, but he writes faithfully every fortnight, no matter where he is." John tried to reassure her. "Perhaps he's far back in the bush, my dear. I'm certain he'll post us a letter as soon as he can."

Yet days passed and they waited in vain to hear from Thomas. Then, on a cloudy Melbourne morning, they received a letter from a hospital in Kincaid Street at Wagga Wagga. The brief message was signed "Alan B. Morgan, M.D."

Elizabeth and John boarded the next coach heading for the northeast. They rode in silence, Elizabeth clutching John's arm and praying their son would survive his injuries. Once more, she knew she could depend only on God's mercy. When they arrived at the hospital, Matron advised them Thomas was sleeping, lulled by laudanum to ease his pain. He lay motionless, his left cheek and arm covered in bandages, his left leg stretched by weights at the end of the bed. Elizabeth sat at his side and wept. John stood opposite her, stroking their son's hair.

The Chief Surgeon, Mr. Morgan, appeared at the foot of the bed and offered his sympathies. "I can say I've done my best for him. He has cuts, bruises and broken bones, but the only grievous injury is to the left side of his pelvis. I can straighten his leg bones with splints and traction. I cannot repair his hip. He will remain here until his fractures knit."

"Will he walk again?" It was John who asked the question. Elizabeth was sobbing, holding Thomas's hand and praying for God's help. The Surgeon chose his words with care. "Whether he will ever sit up properly again, much less walk, will depend entirely upon God's providence and your son's determination. He seems to be a healthy, clean-living young man, and his legs are very strong. Perhaps he'll be able to move somehow. We must be patient in awaiting the outcome."

On their way back in the coach from that wrenching first visit to Thomas, John said, "It's time we left Melbourne. Thomas will need country air if he is to get well, and I know you've always wanted to go back to the western slopes. A small town with prospects would be right, where George and I can have a store. Not a farm, Elizabeth. I can't bear the thought of sheep."

The remainder of the year 1859 became a blur in Elizabeth's memory. At regular intervals she and John took a coach to the hospital at Wagga Wagga, but for weeks Thomas was scarcely aware of their presence because of the opiate given to him. It was many months before Mr. Morgan set him free from traction and told John and Elizabeth they could take him home.

Home was now a rambling house on a property at Murrumburrah, almost forty miles north of Yass on the western slopes. Murrumburrah was without a large general store, and John had been certain he and George could establish a successful business there. Elizabeth had packed up their belongings once more, boarded a coach at Melbourne, and had started life again in a different setting, but this time not an unfamiliar one.

At the beginning of January 1860, John and Elizabeth set out from Murrumburrah for Wagga Wagga to fetch Thomas home. Their buggy was of no use because Thomas could not sit up. Instead, they had piled their wagon with straw pallets, pillows and blankets to ease Thomas's discomfort on the lengthy journey. The young man carried from his hospital bed on a litter was a pale reflection of the son they had known. Their sturdy little boy who had become a vigorous outdoorsman was now a haggard patient wincing with pain and blinking in the unfamiliar sunlight. John and George had built a high cover of metal hoops and canvas for the wagon, and under its shade his parents tried to make Thomas's thin body comfortable. His mother rode with him as John drove slowly northeastward for eighty-five miles over the rough roads. The stoicism of her son on the long, painful journey left Elizabeth tearful with sympathy and admiration.

In the hot, dry air of Murrumburrah, the attentions of his family seemed to revive the young man's spirits. John and George screened in a portion of the verandah, where Thomas lay dozing on a cot most of each day, often clutching the myall wood handle of his prized whip of kangaroo hide. His mother prepared soft, nourishing food for him that he could manage to eat whilst half reclining, and she saw his cheeks regain their colour and his eyes brighten. Elizabeth said many prayers to her Heavenly Father for her son's continued recovery.

One day Thomas told the family he had decided how he could sit up, but he would require their help. "I'll need a crutch, Papa, and a stool of my own with a back on it to support me. A soft cushion, too, please, Mamma." The crutch, stool and cushion were quickly made. John and George gently lifted Thomas from his bed and at his instructions carefully placed his right hip on the cushion on the stool. He leaned back, supported on his left side by the crutch. Sweating with exertion and pain, he grinned at the family.

In no time George had made Thomas another crutch so that he might get around the house. After many months he was able to manage with only one crutch. When he was tired, he hitched himself onto his stool in the kitchen and amused himself with his whittling. On the sitting room mantelpiece one winter afternoon, Elizabeth found a newly carved wooden horse with a white star painted on its forehead. She held Star close to her and wept.

"I'll never ride again," said Thomas one morning, his face stoic. "Since I'm not to be a stockman, I'll be a merchant, if you'll have me, Papa." On Albury Street at Murrumburrah, John built the T. & G. Barnes Store, named for his merchant sons, Thomas, now age twenty-four, and George, age twenty. Sadness filled Elizabeth's heart as she watched Thomas make his way around the store with his crutch, but he never complained. He took to resting his good hip on a corner of the central table. Balanced by the crutch, he whittled whilst chatting to the customers. Never again did he mention being a stockman.

Thomas found he liked meeting people in the store, hearing about their requirements and supplying items they needed. He was quick to learn from George, now a capable merchant. The T. & G. Barnes Store at Murrumburrah soon became a prosperous enterprise.

At the horse races on New Years's Day in 1861, Thomas stood leaning on his crutch, assessing mounts whose owners were challenging each other for district prizes. He had decided if he could not ride, his father would. The family was waiting for the auction at the end of the races, hoping to buy a suitable mount for John.

"You need a fine saddle horse, Papa, one with some Thoroughbred breeding," said Thomas. "I'll find one for you." John was not much of a connoisseur of horseflesh, but Thomas knew what to look for. He came towards them leading a good-looking mare named Ariel.

"I like her conformation," said Thomas, stroking the mare's neck and withers. "Her gait is easy, she collects herself well, and her stamina is good. She handled the point-to-point with little effort. Her saddle has been well used, but it fits her nicely." John had driven a number of horses, but he had not ridden much since days on the farm at Yass and seemed hesitant. "I'll teach you to ride, Papa," said Thomas with a grin.

On subsequent Sunday afternoons out on a distant field, John soon discovered his son was a demanding taskmaster. Balanced by his crutch, Thomas rested on his good hip on a cushion on the front seat of the buggy. He was determined to make an accomplished rider out of his father by sternly insisting he get the best out of the mare. "Sit tall!" ordered Thomas. "Hands easy. Knees tight." John came home exhausted from these lessons, whilst Thomas and Ariel looked as if they had enjoyed themselves. Elizabeth, in honour of John's fiftieth birthday, surprised her husband by arranging for her sons to obtain a new saddle and bridle for Ariel.

One morning Elizabeth was sitting in the sunshine on her verandah, having left her usual chores to mend a skirt she had carelessly torn. She had been stitching for several minutes when she glanced up and into the dark eyes of a man who was standing at the foot of the steps. He was of average height and seemed young, but she could not really tell because he was Chinese. He wore a brimless hat, more like a black bowl inverted over his head, and his black hair was braided into a long tail which swung in the morning breeze. He had a clean, angular face, its planes shadowed in the slant of the morning sun.

In the rising warmth of the day, Elizabeth thought his loose cotton clothes looked comfortable. Whilst he stood in front of her with his arms folded across his chest (she remembered Marion Rowley in a similar stance), he kept his hands inside the wide sleeves of his black jacket, which was fastened with loops around carved wooden toggles. His wide black trousers were draped over black slippers.

Elizabeth assumed his possessions were in the two baskets roped to either end of a long smooth pole lying on the ground behind him. The man moved closer and bowed deeply.

"Missy Barn?" he asked. She decided he meant "Mrs. Barnes" and nodded. He straightened, his hands still in his sleeves. "Chung Yip!" he said proudly and bowed again. Elizabeth reckoned "How do you do?" would be the appropriate response. He was the first Celestial she had ever met. She had seen a few of them in the Melbourne store, and John and the boys had mentioned Chinese miners who stopped at the Murrumburrah store for supplies on their way to the goldfield at Lambing Flat, some twenty miles to the north.

"You need gardener and cook," said Chung Yip. It was a statement, not a question. "I grow good vegetable and do good cooking." He bowed again. "I start today." Elizabeth was taken aback. "Heavens, no!" she said. "I'm sorry, but I very much enjoy working in my garden and I do my own cooking. You'd best be on your way to Lambing Flat!"

"Chung Yip not go to Lambing Flat!" he said decisively, although "Lambing Flat" was difficult for him to say. "That be bad place! Too many Chinese!" Elizabeth thought he pronounced it "Chinee." "Big trouble come there! I stay here! Mista Barn very important man in town. His house need gardener and cook. I go make dinner now."

Elizabeth rose up in protest, but Chung Yip had pulled a large white apron out of his belongings, hefted the pole with its two baskets across his shoulders, and headed for the back of the house. Elizabeth tossed her mending aside and followed him. In truth, she followed a horrid noise, because Chung Yip had set down his pole, seized a hatchet, and was shouting in Chinese at the squawking chook he was chasing. He caught the hapless hen and dispatched her with a flourish. His hands, freed from the wide sleeves now rolled up to his elbows, flew amongst the feathers as he sat on an upturned pail and plucked the chook clean in his aproned lap. Elizabeth watched him and thought perhaps she should accept Chung Yip's offer. He looked up and asked, "You got prums for prum sauce?" Elizabeth fetched plums from the larder.

John and the children arrived home for their noon meal and stood around the table to sing the Doxology. Elizabeth said nothing of their new cook and sat down with them. To her family's surprise, Chung Yip marched in bearing Elizabeth's soup tureen, from which he ceremoniously removed the lid and ladled out servings of broth flavoured with chives and swirls of egg. He presented a platter with pieces of roast chook smothered in plum sauce, together with bowls of chard, pea pods and rice. When everyone had had more than enough, he brought in large helpings of treacle pudding and poured cups of tea.

"What an excellent meal!" said John. "Quite the best dinner I've had in a long time!" Elizabeth's children added a chorus of compliments. Chung Yip beamed and bowed low. "You get good food now," he said, smiling at the family. Elizabeth stared at them all and shook her head.

Their self-appointed cook took over Elizabeth's kitchen. Each morning, after he had cleared away the breakfast things, he appeared before his Missy, bowed formally and asked for menus for dinner and tea, which he earnestly followed. Elizabeth realized he had been well trained somewhere. She was not allowed to interfere with his cooking, but she was permitted to assist in the garden, spending many pleasant hours with Chung Yip tending to vegetables as she had with Bess Mason at Yass. He left the flower borders to her care, except for his occasional knowing comments as to where various plants must be situated in order to "grow happy." John and George built a boxbark skillion for Chung against the barn, where he settled in contentment.

The crowds of Celestials heading northward to the goldfield at Lambing Flat became hordes, and if they stopped at the store for necessities, John and the boys summoned their cook to act as interpreter. Chung Yip's prediction of trouble at Lambing Flat proved correct. Chinese miners straggled back through Murrumburrah after a violent roll-up at the goldfield, when white diggers attacked the miners they called "barbarians" and drove them out. Many former Chinese miners settled in the western districts, clustered in small groups in country towns.

Meanwhile, Chung Yip had firmly attached himself to the Barnes household. He was to serve the family for the rest of his life.

Elizabeth's gold cross and chain

FIFTEEN

Cootamundry

Draw nigh unto my soul, and redeem it: deliver me, because of mine enemies.

—PSALM 69:1

At the end of each day, Thomas and George came home from the T. & G. Barnes Store with all the latest news. No event in the District escaped their attention. "There's to be a new town established on the road from Yass to Wagga Wagga on Mutta Muttama Creek at the site of John Hurley's horse paddock," George told his parents one winter evening in 1861. "A surveyor named Adams has been drawing up plans for the Secretary for Lands."

Although Elizabeth was not familiar with John Hurley's horse paddock, she was aware that the grazier had pastured stock in the area since the 1840s. His Cootomondra Run, as he called it, was the first and largest property in the District, comprising almost fifty thousand acres.

"You'll recognize the location, Mamma," said Thomas. "It's in that broad low valley southwest of here. The town is to have a fine, wide main street, and George knows where it will be. The settlers there will need a store, Papa, and a hotel as a meeting place and rest stop for travellers. George could ride down with you—it's about twenty-five miles or so—and select a good location for a store and hotel before the town plans are published."

Elizabeth could see what was coming. "I'm not moving again, John. Talk to the surveyor if you wish, but you'll have to attend to any business in this new town on your own." Her husband nodded. "I understand, my dear. However, if the opportunity presents itself, I owe it to all of us to investigate the possibilities."

The trip to Hurley's horse paddock was made, and a location for a new enterprise selected. John soon constructed the first two buildings in the settlement: a hotel he called the Albion, the Roman name for ancient Britain, and the Barnes Store. The Secretary for Lands confirmed the townsite on the 9th of August, 1861, and the *Government Gazette* listed the new town as Cootamundry. By the time the first ninety-six town lots were auctioned off at Gundagai on June 27th and 28th, 1862, the Albion Hotel and Barnes Store were doing a good trade.

Elizabeth loved the western slopes, but she missed the proximity of women friends. Her new friend, Annie Mackay, a bride who had recently arrived from Scotland, lived miles away at Wallendbeen. The women Elizabeth had met in various places over the years had become correspondents whom she cherished. Amongst them was Esme Arnold, now living in Margate, Kent.

Shaftesbury, Murrumburrah,
New South Wales
August 1st, 1862

My Dearest Esme,
I write in answer to your solicitous letter enquiring about Thomas's progress. Your correspondence is always a comfort to me.

I know you find it difficult to accept that Jeremiah's vigorous chum was so badly injured. However, I assure you he now moves around very well with his crutch and never refers to the accident. He works in our T. & G. Barnes Store here alongside George, who has been appointed Murrumburrah's Postmaster.

John and I continue in good health. I keep the accounts, as usual, for the store and also for our hotel and store in the new town of Cootamundry. I have never seen John happier. He knows so much about selling household goods, I am sure the settlers in Lachlan District are impressed by the available choices.

Johnny is working for Alex Moore and Co. in Sydney, after years of prospecting in goldfields at Turon, Ophir, Abercrombie and Tambaroora and completing his apprenticeship as a cabinetmaker. He has married

Miss Jane Marshall, a lass from Yorkshire whom he met at Sydney. You will be interested to know they were married in Saint Andrew's Scots Presbyterian Church. William, as he always said he would, is spending his life on horseback. He has become an Inspector of Conditional Purchases, a dangerous job, I think, because he has to evict selectors who have not been developing their properties. He was married in July to Miss Janet Brown of Wooloomooloo. Ted is still at Sydney. He writes to us of his football, sailing and cricket and his tenor solos in Saint Mary's Church at Balmain. I now cannot imagine myself without Beth, who is the dearest girl. She arrived here recently from Melbourne, having finished at school. She often seems quite disconcerted by the male world she and I live in.

What I miss most about our life here is not being able to attend church, for there are no churches nearby. The closest is Saint Clement's at Yass, much farther away than a Sunday journey. Our family reads Matins together on Sundays in our home, but that is not the same as being part of a church community. Once a year Bishop Mesac Thomas of Goulburn tours his far-flung Diocese and conducts the service of Holy Communion wherever space is made available.

I understand, dearest Esme, how you must long to be back at Sydney, yet I can appreciate Henry's wanting to retire to Kent because his family ties are there. Our lives are with our husbands, wherever that may be. I feel for your plight. Write to me soon.

With warm thoughts of you, I remain your loving friend,

Elizabeth

In 1862 the Barnes family gathered at Murrumburrah for Christmas. Johnny and his wife, Jane, had made the lengthy journey with Ted from Sydney, and William and his bride, Janet, had also joined Thomas, George and Beth and their parents at Shaftesbury. It was a jolly holiday with picnics, croquet matches, carols around the pianoforte and card games. Much to Elizabeth's joy, Johnny announced on Christmas Eve that he was planning to settle on the western slopes and establish a furniture-making business. His father, who was smoking a pipe in his favourite chair on the verandah, looked at him thoughtfully.

"Not to deny your trade, son, for you know how proud I am of your skills, but would you consider settling out west as publican of the Albion? Since George became Murrumburrah Postmaster, he has had to stay here in town. I want to expand the Coota store and I can't manage that and the hotel on my own. Would you think about it? More people are travelling between Yass and Wagga Wagga than ever before, and the Albion is the only stopping place. It needs a good man in charge. Until you get a property, you and Jane could live at the back of the store next door." On Christmas morning Johnny accepted his father's offer, and Elizabeth was thrilled by the thought of having more of her family nearby.

In 1863 Cootamundry was less than two years old and a primitive settlement. Its main thoroughfare, Parker Street, had been named by John Hurley for the Premier of New South Wales, Sir Henry Watson Parker. Along the edges of Parker Street, logs had been laid end to end to distinguish the road from the flat terrain around it. Next to each other on Parker Street, John Barnes had built his hotel and store, simple, one-storey wooden buildings with front verandahs.

Johnny arrived from Sydney to take over the hotel and with the help of an assistant, John Hanlow, soon also ran the store. The Barnes Store, with its connections to suppliers at Sydney, equipped each house built in the town and met the requirements of many stations in the District.

"John, must you and the boys stock firearms?" Elizabeth asked one evening as she went through an inventory. "Surely they're dangerous and scarcely household goods." Their previous stores had not carried guns. In cities one went to a gunsmith for such a purchase.

"True, my dear," answered John, "but a farmer needs to be able to buy a reliable gun. Remember Thaddeus Munro and his sons bringing their rifles to dispatch our sheep." How could Elizabeth forget? The mere mention brought back the sounds and smells of that fateful day. "And you've heard about Ben Hall's gang of bushrangers," added John. "They will not get the run of my premises!"

She could not argue with that. Thomas and George had told them about the bushranging gang: Ben Hall, John Gilbert, Fred Lowry, John Vane, Mick Burke and Johnnie O'Meally. Young outlaws, they defied any authority and roamed at will, stealing whatever they wanted in broad daylight. They carried guns, rode only the best of stolen horses, and knew the District so well, they hid in the hills with impunity. Worst of all, they had become legendary, even admired by settlers who were emancipated convicts. Such settlers were impressed by the bushrangers' exploits and were suspected of providing the outlaws with food and hideouts.

Ben Hall's gang was often in Elizabeth's thoughts, especially when Thomas and George came home with reports of ambushes and raids. At regular intervals John rode from Murrumburrah to Cootamundry, and although he had a fast mare, Elizabeth worried he would be attacked. It was not John, however, but Thomas who first encountered the bushrangers.

Because there was no bank at Murrumburrah, many customers of the T. & G. Barnes Store left their cash in the store for safekeeping. The arrangement made more sense than one might think, for customers received credit until their crops or livestock produced income. Any money they deposited in the store was put towards their ongoing purchases, and Thomas routinely put customers' remaining cash into his large safe at home. Until the Commercial Bank was built some years later, Thomas Barnes was Murrumburrah's banker.

One quiet morning Thomas was sitting at his accustomed place in the store, balanced on a corner of the central table whilst he worked on a carving. Thundering on horseback through Murrumburrah, brandishing firearms, came Ben Hall's gang. They burst into the store as George slipped out the back to summon help.

"The cash deposits, Barnes! Hand them over!" Thomas didn't move. "You'll get nothing from me." The gang wrenched open the store till and Post Office drawer and took the small amounts they found there, some silver coins and one sovereign. They tossed merchandise from the shelves, up-ended boxes and spilled bulk goods, but found no more money. Bellowing oaths, they stole rifles from the back wall and stormed out and onto their horses. By the time George and several men returned to the store, the gang had disappeared into the hills. Thomas remained seated on a corner of the central table.

Underneath him was the table leg he had whittled hollow, which safely held the cash deposits.

Ben Hall's gang continued to plague Cootamundra District. The bushrangers stole liquor and money from hotels, raided homesteaders' property for food and horses, and ambushed riders and coaches along the roads. The rule of law was slow in coming to the western slopes.

Elizabeth realized she fussed over Thomas, who went bravely on with his life. Whilst confident at home and in the store, he was a shy man in social situations, and although he often joked at his own expense about being a cripple, his mother knew his handicap made him self-conscious around young women. She was therefore pleased, on arriving at the store one morning, to discover an attractive young woman having a conversation with him. To be honest, the young lady, who was wearing a stylish riding costume and carrying a smart leather crop, was doing all the talking; Thomas was staring at the floor. Elizabeth introduced herself and the two women chatted pleasantly at some length. Thus began a friendship which included Isabella Stinson's presence at many Sunday dinners at Shaftesbury.

Isabella was an exceptional horsewoman who rode like the wind on a gelding of Thoroughbred ancestry. He was a strong, active animal, much beyond the capabilities of most women riders. When Isabella visited their home, Elizabeth noticed she did her best to charm Thomas, but he was more interested in her horse.

Bushrangers were notorious horse thieves, and Isabella Stinson's mount would naturally arouse their envy. Out riding one day, she was ambushed by three members of Hall's gang. The thieves charged out of the bush on horseback, aimed their revolvers at her, and ordered her to dismount. Isabella ignored their guns and assessed their horses. Her gelding could show them, she decided. She put her heels to him and raced down the road, blinding the outlaws with dust and stones. The story of her experience became a local legend.

The store at Cootamundry was close to a new junction from which roads led in all directions to other settlements. It stocked items the gang needed to maintain their rough existence, and because of its location, the bandits could approach the store from one direction and choose amongst several others to escape. The single constable on duty was hardly a match for them. None of this was reassuring, as events were to prove.

On Tuesday, the 21st of April, 1863, John Hanlow, the assistant at the Cootamundry store, raced along the twenty-five dusty miles to Murrumburrah. At the Barnes house he threw himself off his mount and collapsed on the verandah. Thomas and George tended to his lathered horse as the man struggled to catch his breath. "Ben Hall and his gang! At the Coota store today. Four of 'em. They stole about a hundred pounds' worth of goods. They had a packhorse."

"Take it easy, mate!" said John. "Was anyone hurt?" Elizabeth shuddered at the thought of bushrangers shooting at Johnny in the Cootamundry store. She had enough worries about William and his Inspector's job. "They waved guns about, but they didn't shoot at anybody. They were after supplies and clothes—lanterns, blankets, shirts—and some of the stuff they took, they dropped in the street—hats and such. You know Mrs. Hinkley, the seamstress? She walked across Parker Street in the middle of the robbery. She saw John Gilbert loading up two bolts of cloth she had come to buy and said, 'You young scamp! Give me those!' He did, and she carried the bolts into the store and bought them from me! Mrs. Hinkley and some other people helped me gather up things the scoundrels left behind."

"Could you recognize any of the gang?"

"Aye. Everybody knows John Gilbert. He comes from Upper Canada and speaks with a funny Canadian accent. Some say he's the real leader of the gang, but folks forever talk about Ben Hall. He's the oldest, I think. He's soft-spoken and handsome, but quite lame. Fred Lowry was there, more of a follower than anything else, in my opinion. It's Johnnie O'Meally you wouldn't want to meet, a black-haired, red-faced menace! They called each other by name and worked through the store like a well-seasoned crew. They headed south at a great rate. Even the packhorse was going apace. O'Meally was out in front, riding like a madman."

John and Elizabeth knew the hundred pounds' worth of goods had gone forever. Prosperous as their Coota store was, they could not afford many robberies like that. Elizabeth fed John Hanlow a good meal, and he spent the night with them. Next morning she saw her husband and his assistant off on the ride back to Cootamundry.

They would break their journey halfway along at Wallendbeen station, where the Mackays lived at Rose Cottage. Alexander Mackay, an experienced station Overseer, was a Scot from Ross-shire and a God-fearing man. His bride, Annie, whom he had brought out from Scotland, had become a great friend of Elizabeth. She reminded Elizabeth of a young Esme Arnold, and Annie and Elizabeth, although differing greatly in age, developed a similar companionship. Elizabeth thought Rose Cottage was a lovely place with its hardwood floors, grand pianoforte and welcoming hosts. John and the boys always called there for a meal on their way from one store to the other.

A few weeks after the robbery, John told Elizabeth of a strange experience. He had been alone in the Murrumburrah store, arranging new stock on the shelves, when Ben Hall limped in. John described the bushranger as a good-looking fellow in his late twenties, whose appearance was marred by a twisted leg, the result of an improperly set broken bone. Everyone knew that Hall was a son of Irish convict parents and as resentful of authority as they were. He had become even more embittered since his wife had taken up with a policeman.

"I'll sell this to you, Barnes," he had said, offering John a lump of metal. "It's pure silver. Give me a hundred pounds." John was furious. "Out of here, you villain! I'll not buy any of your ill-gotten gains!" Ben Hall smiled and set the lump on the counter. "Keep it. It'll cover my account in your store." He limped out into the street, climbed on his horse and disappeared.

"Such arrogance!" said John to Elizabeth later. "That thief wandered nonchalantly into a store his gang raided!" John handed her the lump of silver. "How would Ben Hall have come by this?" she asked. "His gang bailed up a Royal Mail coach a while ago," he said.

"Besides the mail, they took money and valuables from passengers. This seems to be silver chains and pocket watches melted down." Elizabeth put the lump of silver on John's desk, as if it were a paperweight. She was disturbed to learn that Ben Hall and his henchmen continued their lawless activities unchallenged, but she had also heard enough from John and the boys to know that the District's few policemen did not stand much of a chance against experienced outlaws like Hall's gang.

On the 16th of May at six o'clock in the morning, Johnny was awakened in his quarters behind the Cootamundry store by a furious pounding on the front door. When he threw the latch, he faced the revolvers of Gilbert, O'Meally and Lowry. Whilst Gilbert held a gun on Johnny, Lowry and O'Meally loaded the store's entire stock of blankets onto two packhorses. Before they left, Gilbert emptied a tin of lamp oil on the floor and threw down a lighted match.

Gilbert laughed as Hanlow frantically quenched the flames. The bushranger put his gun to Johnny's head. "And don't try to follow us!" Hanlow managed to put out the fire whilst Johnny grabbed a rifle off the back wall and loaded it. From the street he shot at the escaping gang, but they galloped towards the hills unharmed.

Elizabeth and John were not aware of this robbery until later that day when Hanlow once again arrived exhausted at their house at Murrumburrah. Elizabeth watched her angry husband stride around the kitchen. "They're thieves and vandals, and no one can stop them! Some people even admire their villainy! At least Johnny took a shot at them!"

SIXTEEN
Wallendbeen

Let the wicked be no more. Bless thou the Lord, O my soul.
— PSALM 104:35

In the cool winter months of 1863, whilst she sat playing cards with her family in the evenings or reading by the fire, Elizabeth felt snug and secure in her Murrumburrah home. John described to her his ideas for a two-storey addition to the store at Cootamundry, and she spent happy hours sketching plans for him.

Because the District was free from further raids by Ben Hall's gang that winter, Elizabeth worried less about Johnny in the Coota store or her husband on the road. John, now a confident rider, told Elizabeth that Ariel seemed to enjoy the journey to and from Cootamundry, especially those stretches where he gave the mare her head and she broke into a canter. He was careful to pace the journey so as not to tire her.

On the 29th of August, 1863, Johnny Barnes sent Hanlow to fetch John to Cootamundry because rumour had it Ben Hall's gang was planning a third robbery of the Coota store. Hanlow stayed overnight with them, and Elizabeth fed her husband and his assistant a good breakfast before they set out the next day.

It was a clear morning, full of promise. The men were riding into the valley in the warmth of a spring day, with the hills coming alive with new growth. Wattles grew in profusion in this part of the countryside, their yellow blossoms scenting the breezes with a honey perfume. Eucalypts were fragrant with new blue-grey leaves, and bottlebrushes were vibrant in shades of red. "Be careful," Elizabeth said as they were leaving. "Those men are armed and very determined."

"They may have robbed the Coota store twice, my dear," said her husband as he embraced her, "but they won't take anything from us this time!" He mounted Ariel and added, "Hanlow will keep in touch with you. And I've just remembered my pepper mill. Would you please be so good as to fetch it for me?"

Elizabeth brought him the pepper mill, and John put it into the carryall on his back. He and his assistant headed their mounts southwestward at a fast walk. They would ride steadily until they reached Wallendbeen station, about twelve miles distant, where they could rest their horses at Rose Cottage. A quick meal from Annie Mackay would see them on their way to Cootamundry.

The dirt road sloped to the west between the hills until Rose Cottage could be seen in a clearing as the road veered towards Coota. Hanlow and John became aware something was amiss when they saw two horses, one without a saddle, only a rug and surcingle, near the doorway of a hut a short distance ahead. "That looks suspicious," said Hanlow. "I'll wager someone is after a saddle."

They moved on smartly towards Wallendbeen station. Within moments, two men left the hut and galloped up to cut them off. Hanlow recognized the unkempt black hair and unshaven ruddy face of Johnnie O'Meally. His henchman, barefoot and riding without a saddle, was big John Vane, a suspected horse thief.

O'Meally brandished his revolver at Hanlow. "I know who you are, you stupid bastard! Bail up!" Then the bushranger turned his gun on John. "You bail up, too! That looks like a good mare! Get off her! I want her—and that saddle and bridle!" John did not move.

"You heard me!" O'Meally bellowed. "Off that mare! And if you stir, I'll put daylight through you!" John put his heels to Ariel. The mare shot past O'Meally and raced for Rose Cottage. Johnnie O'Meally swung around and fired at John. He missed. Meanwhile, Vane held his gun to Hanlow's head, ordered him off his horse, and echoed O'Meally's threat: he'd put daylight through him if he stirred.

Ariel had almost reached the Mackay homestead. Within sight was the farmyard gate, always left open. Today it was latched shut. John urged Ariel to take the gate, but she judged the height better than he and refused to jump. John spun away and raced the mare across the Mackay property. O'Meally, close behind him, cocked his revolver again and sent a shot through the brim of John's hat.

O'Meally's third bullet bounced off John's metal powder horn in the carryall on his back. Another shot cut across his pepper mill and almost tossed him off Ariel. The next shot tore through his heart. The body of John Barnes fell head-first down a gully and slammed against a tree stump.

O'Meally spurred his horse after the frantic Ariel and caught her. He dragged her back along the road, where an unarmed Alexander Mackay blocked his way. The bushranger dismounted and aimed his revolver at Mackay. "Open your storeroom! My mate needs some gear!" With O'Meally's gun at his head, Alexander Mackay opened his storage shed. The outlaw snatched up a coat and a pair of large boots for Vane. Having sent Hanlow sprawling in the dust, Vane rode up and abandoned his horse with the rug and surcingle. Grabbing the coat and boots, he mounted O'Meally's horse.

O'Meally leapt onto Ariel and taunted Mackay. "Do you still have good horses? I once stole a racehorse of yours, called Chance!" The bushranger glanced over at the limp body of John Barnes. "I'm sorry for him. It was his own fault. He should have stood and he wouldn't have been shot." O'Meally dug his heels into Ariel, and the two bushrangers raced away and disappeared up a narrow track into the hills. John Barnes lay motionless in the sunlight. His life-blood spilled across the rough ground.

Elizabeth worked her embroidery of a tray cloth as she sat on the verandah whilst Chung Yip prepared the Sunday meal for the family. After eating dinner with their mother, Thomas, George and Beth went off to visit friends, leaving Elizabeth to finish her embroidery and enjoy a doze on the verandah in the pleasant warmth of a spring afternoon.

She woke to the sound of a wagon coming along the road. Alexander Mackay was driving and Annie sat beside him. Elizabeth did not think anything was amiss until she saw John Hanlow riding behind the wagon. She stumbled down the verandah steps. Annie Mackay was weeping when her husband helped her down from the wagon seat. Hanlow moaned apologies and lowered the wagon gate. He dragged John's body forward on a sheet of boxbark and pulled back the covering of stained linen. Elizabeth gave an anguished scream and threw herself on John's body. She put her head on his blood-soaked chest and cried out in pain, her husband's blood on her clothes, on her face. Annie Mackay lifted her away and helped her into the house and to bed. Elizabeth sobbed and sobbed herself to exhaustion.

She would not remember much of the next few days. Thoughts of Johnnie O'Meally consumed her. He had murdered her beloved husband. He had ridden off like a madman on their lovely Ariel and escaped unscathed. She wept and wept bitter tears, and her heart raged with revenge.

The day after the murder, the Inquest began at Rose Cottage. The boys attended, but Elizabeth and Beth remained at home. Chung Yip grieved with them; in the night they heard him wailing in his hut. During the day he hovered over Elizabeth and Beth, urging them to eat his egg custards and drink his green tea.

John's funeral was held at Saint Clement's Church at Yass, the nearest church and consecrated burial ground. Elizabeth travelled the long journey in their buggy, followed by their hooded wagon with John's body in a coffin made by Thomas, Johnny and George. Chung Yip, moaning softly and muttering in Chinese, sat cross-legged in the wagon beside his dead master.

Elizabeth would remember climbing down from the buggy in the churchyard at Yass and falling into Naomi Munro's arms. Naomi helped her into the newly completed church, filled with John's friends and customers from Yass, Cootamundry and Murrumburrah. Distance had not prevented them from leaving their own concerns to pay their last respects to Elizabeth's conscientious, compassionate husband. The spring sunlight was shining through the sanctuary window of the fine new church as mourners stood for the opening hymn, "Let Saints on Earth in Concert Sing with Those Whose Work Is Done."

It was one of Elizabeth's favourite hymns, but she could not sing. She knew she should pray for the doomed soul of O'Meally, now condemned to eternal damnation. Instead, she stood staring at John's coffin, stunned by her loss. She was devoid of any meditation whatsoever.

The Vicar, who had recently arrived in the parish, solemnly read the Bible passages and prayers. At the close of the service, Beth and Thomas walked with their mother down the aisle of the church behind John's pall-draped coffin, borne by three of his sons, Johnny, George and William, and their Yass neighbours, Thaddeus, Jude and Allan Munro. Young Ted was far away in Sydney and could not reach Yass in time for his father's funeral. The congregation sang the Nunc Dimittis hymn, "The Song of Simeon": "Lord, let thy servant now depart into thy promis'd rest / Since my expecting eyes have been with thy salvation blest."

John Barnes was buried beneath the pines in the graveyard at Yass. Elizabeth's tears fell on the handful of soft spring earth as it slipped through her fingers onto her husband's coffin. Naomi Munro and Beth held tight to her whilst her sons shovelled damp sod into their father's grave.

After the funeral the mourners crowded into Winchester, the Munro home. The fine old house with its large verandah and shaded yard was full of memories for Elizabeth. The Ladies' Guild of Saint Clement's had cooked and baked copious quantities of food, which covered the dining room table Elizabeth knew so well. Through her anguish she tried to compose herself to greet so many faithful friends and receive their condolences. Her brightest moment of the day was the pleasure of seeing Bess and Allan Munro, surrounded by four grown children, two fair-haired sons and two daughters with ginger curls. The Munros were of great comfort to Elizabeth and her family, who spent the night at Winchester before returning to Murrumburrah.

The murder of John Barnes was the first committed by Ben Hall's gang and resulted in widespread concern. Never before had these bushrangers killed to get what they wanted. Settlers throughout the western districts, even those who were former convicts, no longer regarded the gang as admirable renegades. O'Meally was a killer, and other gang members might follow his example.

Elizabeth's youngest son, Ted, wrote a long letter from Sydney, couching his own grief in words of comfort to his mother. He enclosed an article, written in Lachlan District and printed in the *Sydney Morning Herald* of September 7th, 1863, which gave a full account of the Inquest.

The MURDER of MR. BARNES of MURRUMBURRAH

On Monday, the 31st ultimo, an Inquest was held on the body of Mr. Barnes, at the station of Mr. Alexander Mackay, Wallendbeen, before the Coroner of the District, Mr. Robert Falder.

James Brown, being duly sworn, stated: I am in the employ of Mr. Mackay; I am a bullock-driver and live at Wallendbeen. Yesterday morning, about half-past 11, two men came to my hut, which is situated a little off the road leading from Murrumburrah to Cootamundry, and told my wife to get them something to eat, which she did. On my arrival they demanded my hat, which I gave them, seeing they were armed with revolvers; they then demanded my boots, but they would not fit them; they tried on two pair—they were both too small; one of them was going to cut them when the other said, "Oh, never mind, we'll get plenty at Mackay's." At this time two men on horseback passed a short distance off, and they said, "We'll go and stop them and get a saddle." They then left my hut in pursuit of the two men, having only taken my hat. I noticed when they came that they had two horses, but only one saddle—one horse having only a rug and surcingle on; I did not see them overtake the men; soon after they were out of my sight, I heard the report of firearms; I heard the report, as near as I can remember, about five or six times; I saw two men, one galloping after the other and firing; I did not go up to the station till sent for by Mr. Mackay; on my arrival I saw Mr. Barnes, storekeeper of Murrumburrah, being carried on a sheet of bark by four men; he appeared to be quite dead; I did not see the bushrangers after they were in pursuit of the man . . .

The *Sydney Morning Herald* article continued with the testimonies of John Hanlow and Alexander Mackay. The report concluded with the summary statement of the Inquest: "The deceased died from the effect of a gunshot wound, August 30th, 1863, at Wallendbeen. The jury found a verdict of wilful murder against John O'Meally." The writer added, "The determination of the bushrangers and this murder have caused a great sensation here, Mr. Barnes being greatly respected in the District."

If she had been a man, Elizabeth said to herself, she would have ranged the slopes searching for O'Meally, yet she did not counsel her sons to do such a thing. The western districts now had mounted police for that purpose, skilled riders, well armed, accompanied by aboriginal trackers familiar with the territory. Within an hour and a half of John's death, three policemen and an aboriginal tracker had set out to find his killer. Each day Elizabeth prayed the mounted police would ambush O'Meally and end his life the way the bushranger had ended John's. Her prayers always closed with guilt-ridden pleas for forgiveness. "Vengeance is mine, I will repay, saith the Lord," she tried to remind herself.

That spring Ben Hall's gang, seemingly emboldened by the murder, continued to roam freely across the western slopes. The bushrangers raided Bathurst and Canowindra in October, and later that month at Dunn's Plains they attacked the property of Magistrate Keightley. One of the gang, Mick Burke, was killed on Keightley's station. Several weeks later John Vane surrendered to the mounted police.

Elizabeth's mind was a turmoil of guilt and self-recrimination. Why had she not gone to live at Cootamundry, so that John might have been spared the ride from Murrumburrah? In the first instance, what had made her enter that shipping agent's office in London more than twenty-four years ago? How ridiculously eager and naive she had been in insisting her family emigrate to a place inhabited by criminals! Since she arrived in the colony, had she not been sympathetic to the plight of convicts and emancipists? Had she not, unlike many English settlers, been tolerant and accepting of Irish Catholics? And because of her, an Irish Catholic criminal had murdered her husband. She wept in anguish.

A marauding gang, even a murderous one, was not about to curtail the usual activities of the District. On the third weekend in November, the Campbell family of Goimbla station held their annual Summer Ball. The Campbells' invitations were prized; the dancing and games, songs and recitations, food and horse races were famous throughout the area. Guests were invited to Goimbla from every direction, and three-day gatherings of two hundred were not uncommon. Such a group was enjoying the start of the Campbells' festivities on a Thursday evening. Elizabeth was in mourning and did not attend, but she had persuaded her children to accept their invitations. None of them had been out in society since John's death, and their mother thought the Campbells' party would do them good.

Shortly before midnight, when the party was at its height, one of the guests smelled smoke. The barn and stables were engulfed in flames. Cows bellowed; horses screamed in terror. The men rushed to rescue them and pull buggies and wagons away from the fire. They tossed buckets of water from the creek at the blaze in a futile attempt to save the stables and barn. Ben Hall's gang, taking advantage of the confusion, slipped back into the farmyard. Having set the fires, they planned to capture the best of the fleeing horses.

With the male guests occupied with the blaze, some of the gang could raid the Campbells' house and steal money and jewellery from the women. Through a window, in the flickering light of the flames, Mrs. Campbell spied one of the bushrangers heading for her front door. She stepped boldly to the threshold, a loaded revolver in her hand. Behind her was Isabella Stinson. Johnnie O'Meally pointed his gun at Mrs. Campbell. "Out of my way, woman!" Mrs. Campbell stood in her doorway and aimed her revolver. "You'll not be entering my house!" O'Meally stopped and swore at her. "Take one more step," said Mrs. Campbell, "and I'll end your miserable life!" Johnnie O'Meally rushed at her. She fired. He fell dead on her verandah.

Two days later Elizabeth heard the story from a shaken Isabella Stinson. Elizabeth thanked God for Mrs. Campbell and then was filled with remorse for exulting in someone's death, even Johnnie O'Meally's. Elizabeth had spent weeks in an all-consuming rage. Her mind had burned, not only with a desire for O'Meally's death, but also with frustration over her husband's decisions at Wallendbeen. Ariel was a fast mare and John rode her well. If John had headed straight for Cootamundry, Ariel could have outrun the bushranger's horse, she was sure. Trying to take the Mackay gate had doomed her husband. The more Elizabeth thought about the tragic consequences of John's actions, the more furious she became. She sat on the verandah and wept tears of grief and anger. Beth came and put her arms around her, desperate to comfort her.

By Christmas of 1863, Elizabeth felt a great weariness. She was one and sixty years old and in good enough health, but she had little interest in going on. For some reason she began to think of England. She slept very little and when she did, she dreamt of days long gone. She was in Dorsetshire with her parents and brothers and sisters, or in Cheapside with John and their babies. Her dreams always ended on the Thames with her clutching the port rail of the *Abbotsford*.

Elizabeth's children, suffering their own grief, did their best to console their mother. On Christmas night Elizabeth sat with Johnny and his wife, Jane, on the verandah in the fading light of a solemn day. It had not been a yuletide celebration like any Christmas past. Johnny held his mother's hand. "You've not seen our new property just east of Cootamundry at Jindalee. We're planning to have horses and milch cows down on the Flat, once a boxbark hut is built for a hired man and a barn constructed. I remember how much you enjoyed milking a cow, Mamma. We'll have a dog, too. Come and live at Cootamundry with us!"

Elizabeth smiled, thinking of Bess Mason teaching her to milk. What she recalled was not the initial kick in the leg from Molly, but the warmth of the cow's flank and the frothy milk filling the pail. She realized it was the first time she had smiled since John's death. She thought of their lovely Patch and wondered what sort of dog Johnny and Jane would have. Elizabeth promised to consider their kind offer.

Early in January, she began to pack her belongings. Two faded English watercolours from either side of the fireplace went into a box with her set of napkin rings from the *Abbotsford*. She opened a trunk filled with embroidered cloths and crocheted pieces, her work in quiet moments in many places: Cheapside, the *Abbotsford*, Parkside, the farm, Concord, Ashfield, Melbourne, the hospital at Wagga Wagga, and here at Murrumburrah. Elizabeth looked at her handiwork piece by piece, mementoes of her married life, and her tears spilled over them.

Very carefully, she wrapped up John's pepper mill and powder horn, both scarred with bullet marks from that tragic day. In a square of white paper, she sealed his anniversary ring, its bloodstone cracked from his fall to death. George and Johnny and two of their friends loaded her Broadwood pianoforte into the wagon.

Saying goodbye to Chung Yip was much more difficult than she had anticipated. She was in tears. Chung stood on the verandah, his hands inside his wide sleeves, and bowed before her. He straightened and said, "I take care of family."

Grateful for the love surrounding her, she climbed onto the wagon to sit between Johnny and his wife. Silently praying to God for His comfort, Elizabeth King Ellen Barnes set off for Cootamundry.

SEVENTEEN

Pejar

When I said, My foot slippeth; thy mercy,
O Lord, held me up.
— PSALM 94:18

On her way to the marketplace at Berrima one Saturday in late spring of 1862, Rebecca Miller passed by the Court House and stopped as usual to look at the posted notices. One of them drew her particular attention. She sent Megan and the children on ahead and took time to read the notice closely. It stated that the Crown Lands Acts of 1861 allowed Conditional Purchases of 40 to 320 acres of land for one pound per acre. Selectors of such land were required to deposit one-quarter of the price. The notice also advised purchasers that they had to live on their selected land for three years whilst making improvements equal to one pound for each acre. Information regarding available properties could be obtained from the Land Registry Office.

Rebecca helped Megan set up the stall and went to enquire about available properties. She had a bit of money put aside—enough, she reckoned, to make a deposit on a farm of their own. A clerk in the Land Registry Office spread maps before her and pointed out the properties for sale. Rebecca had scant knowledge of the geography of New South Wales, and the only farmlands she knew were in the Southern Highland. Unaware that many of the properties up for selection had been abandoned for good reason, she took note of a few locations and their prices and told the clerk she would return. That evening she planned to discuss her discoveries with John, but she realized his mind was on a concern of his own.

Once the children were asleep, he said, "I don't think my school will be in existence much longer. I'll be a farmer again, Rebecca, whether I want to be or not."

"But you're very successful with your teaching!"

"That may be true, my dear, but James Hassall has told me sufficient funds have now been subscribed to build a Church of England school at Bowral. The foundation stone, you'll remember, was laid by Bishop Barker last year. My pupils would likely choose to be enrolled there."

"You could teach at the new school, surely!"

"I have the education and experience, but I have no teaching certificate, and a church school hires only certified teachers."

"Could you not apply for certification?"

"The colony has no certification service. Until it does, all teachers in denominational schools come certified from Britain." John looked so disappointed at the eventual closure of his school, Rebecca decided not to mention buying a farm.

Yet the very next morning John found his wife spreading his maps across the table. When he wanted to know what she was doing, Rebecca told him about Conditional Purchases and showed him her list of properties from the Registry Office.

"I thought you felt settled on this farm, but it would seem you're still keen on owning a property," John said to her.

"Indeed I am, and I'm sure we can afford a deposit on as much as forty acres out west. I'm looking to buy a property with a homestead on it, and along the Pejar Road there's one available for selection. It has forty acres and a house of four rooms with fitted wooden floors." John was well aware of Rebecca's aversion to the dirt floors of their hut. "Let me have a look at the map," he said. "Pejar looks to be a little more than twenty miles southwest of Goulburn; it's at the junction of Pejar Creek and the Wollondilli. The lease on this farm will expire soon, and if you want to take a chance on moving to Pejar, I'll go to the Registry Office tomorrow and put a deposit on the property you've selected."

"I'm grateful, John, but remember you'd be signing yourself up for three years of naught but farming. The Registry clerk warned me that Inspectors check regularly on Conditional Purchase selectors to make sure they're developing their properties and not working elsewhere. You'd not be permitted employment as a teacher in those first three years."

"I promise you I'll put my best efforts into the property, my dear. I confess I'm very disappointed at having to give up my school, and I feel the need to go somewhere else and start anew."

Rebecca, who was sympathetic to her husband's plight, did not tell him how thrilled she was at the prospect of owning a farm. That night she fell asleep with visions of her very own fields of golden grain and herds of sleek cattle grazing in lush paddocks. Best of all, the farm at Pejar would be only a few miles away from Cartmel station at Tarago and her bosom friend, Hannah Andrews.

With a sad heart John Miller said farewell to his pupils in Adam Windsor's boxbark skillion at Bowral. He assured them the new Church of England school would be ready for them next term. As it turned out, the first enrollment at Saint Jude's School, which had been designed by one of the Oxleys, did not occur until November of 1863. Residents at Bowral eventually completed a building that was used as both church and school.

At Christmas 1862, Rebecca invited Adam Windsor to share dinner with them. When the late afternoon sun of Christmas Day began to slant through the pines, the whole family walked with Adam along the track, bade a final farewell to him, and saw him off down the road to Bowral. Next day the Millers loaded up the cart with their three children, Megan, and an out-of-sorts Abner in a basket with a lid on it. Bertie Marshall had helped John set up a canvas hood over the cart, essential protection from the summer sun. They tied Bossy and Julia behind and harnessed up Ned to haul everything slowly southwestward for more than forty miles to Pejar. Because Bertie and Rose Marshall, married and with a baby on the way, were to take over the Miller's hut and assume the lease of the thirty acres, Rebecca felt she was leaving the farm in good hands. Her present concern was for the child she was carrying, due very soon; she could only pray she would not give birth on the journey.

The Lord was with her, and the Millers arrived uneventfully at the Pejar Road on a hot day at the beginning of January. Parched, exhausted and in need of a decent place to sleep, they located the advertised house of four rooms. It proved to be a ramshackle dwelling with its wooden floors and roof in need of substantial repair. The property, which had not been farmed in several years, sloped towards Pejar Creek in a landscape of dry, undulating fields. Rebecca immediately knew that what she had chosen was far and away from the rich farmland of Berrima District.

Hannah and David Andrews, eager to renew their friendship with the Millers, invited them to dinner on their first Sunday in the district. On Cartmel station they met the grazier of the large property, Mr. Charlesworth, a bright and hospitable gentleman despite being frail and confined to a pushchair. Rebecca found Hannah looking much thinner and older, her thick auburn hair prematurely streaked with grey. Sunday afternoon visits to Cartmel soon became a regular outing for Rebecca and her family. Hannah and David Andrews always enjoyed the Miller children, for they had none of their own.

On her arrival at Pejar, Rebecca struggled in the stifling January weather to get the homestead organized before her confinement. In need of an accoucheuse, she sent John to the hotel, the only commercial building in the hamlet of Pejar, to ask for assistance. Hotels, she was aware, often served as infirmaries for sick and injured farmers and travellers, and she was sure the innkeeper would know of someone who could help in childbirth.

A capable woman named Mrs. Siggs and her friend Sarah McLaughlin responded to Rebecca's need and assisted with the delivery of a second Miller son on the 11th of January, 1863. He was given the name William. Unlike his sturdy brother J.J., their new son was a lanky bairn. His eyes, much different from the brown eyes of the other Miller children, were a startling grey and became more steely as he grew older. William was baptised by Bishop Mesac Thomas in the Cathedral Church of Saint Saviour at Goulburn, the seat of Argyle County, three and twenty miles away from Pejar. John attended a service at the Cathedral Church once a month, and Rebecca and the children accompanied him on Easter Day and at Christmas.

As for the Miller farm on the Pejar Road, when Rebecca tried to establish her kitchen garden, she admitted she had made a serious mistake in selecting the property. John, who had done some reading in geology, told her their farmland was composed of metamorphic shale. Whatever the geology, Rebecca found the ground impossible to cultivate, and she worked diligently in her kitchen garden to ensure a supply of vegetables for her growing family. Even generous quantities of manure could not make up for the dry, hard soil. She was concerned about her cows, for they had little to graze on, and she shared Ned's hay with them. It took John weeks to dig a root cellar and a new pit for a dunny.

Rebecca reminded herself she had longed for a farm of her own. She had selected this property, had brought her husband and children to this place of doubtful promise, and what could she do now except buckle down and work with John to develop it as best they could? Her prideful ignorance had put them into this situation. Nothing but hard work would enable them to deal with it.

When John broke a plough trying to cultivate a field, Rebecca concluded their forty acres were good for nothing but sheep. Rebecca knew something about sheep, but John knew very little. At Grennin in Tyrone, her father had kept a small flock of hardy sheep with mottled black faces and shaggy coats, and Rebecca had helped her mother card and spin their rough wool. But what kind of sheep would thrive here?

A settler aong the Pejar Road, a friendly Welsh bachelor named Trevor Jones, proved to be their saviour. "Get yourselves some crossbred merinos at a Goulburn auction," he advised. "You'll want a sheep as good for fat lambs as fleece. My dogs and I will come with you, if you like, to see you back home with a decent flock." With Trevor's help John soon acquired a flock of cross-bred sheep at the Goulburn market.

Trevor Jones, who was an emancipated convict ("I was transported for stealing a sheep!"), gave Rebecca and John the use of Rex, a majestic-looking sheepdog, all black except for a white ruff around his neck. Managed expertly by Rex, the flock roamed the forty acres and provided the family with mutton and a small income from the sale of fleece and fat lambs. Rebecca did not know how they would have managed without Trevor's help in lambing and shearing.

On the 26th of April, 1864, Mrs. Siggs and her friend assisted with the delivery of another Miller baby, a bright-eyed daughter, whom John called Margaret Mary Maskelyne. Their son William had the name of John's father and brother, and Margaret was named for John's mother. Although the names William and Margaret were also names from her family in Tyrone, Rebecca resolved that next time, should God bless her with another child, *she* would choose the bairn's name.

All five children were watched over by Megan Mary Mahoney, who, in addition to her childminding duties, knitted a succession of baby outfits, stockings and jumpers. She had never been interested in crocheting and her sewing skills were minimal, although Rebecca had done her best to teach her, but she was clever with her knitting. Megan was strict with the Miller children. "Cleanliness is next to Godliness," she would tell them, or "A soft voice turneth away wrath." "The devil finds work for idle hands," she would say when she caught them larking. Her pithy maxims were frequent.

According to Megan, J.J. was the most difficult child to supervise. "That J.J. is so independent!" she complained to Rebecca. "He does whatever strikes his fancy." Rebecca gave Megan a knowing look, remembering what the girl herself was like when she first came to live with them.

John's days were spent restoring the homestead and repairing boundary and paddock fences. With the help of Trevor Jones, he constructed a barn and dairy, which more than satisfied the Inspector of Conditional Purchases on his yearly visits. On one occasion the man said he was surprised they were able to do so much with the place. Yet, after almost three years on the Pejar Road, Rebecca felt discouraged for the first time in her life. Not one to avoid hard work, she nevertheless realized all the effort in the world would not improve this farm. Proud as she was to be a property owner, she knew this would never be a prosperous enterprise, never provide the family with an increase in income. John had done all he could to develop the place and now occupied the better part of each day tutoring J.J., Emily and Mary Jane.

The children adored their father and studied willingly with him, but Rebecca thought they really needed to be in school with other children. No school existed in the hamlet of Pejar, which comprised just twenty souls, nor was there one in the scattered settlement of Tarago. Any school in the city of Goulburn, three and twenty miles away, was beyond consideration.

As she sat on the verandah with her crocheting in her lap one spring afternoon, Rebecca looked out along the desolate Pejar Road. She recalled cool spring seasons in County Tyrone when the gorse splashed golden blossoms across the emerald hills above Dromore, and buttercups and bluebells peeped out beneath cascades of white mayflowers in the hedgerows. In a corner of the Grennin farmyard, plump hens and their babies picked at new shoots of rambling chickweed under the purple shade of a spreading copper beech. At Berrima in Camden County, springtime was warm and lush. Willows trailed pale branches in the overflowing Wingecarribee River; fresh eucalypt leaves perfumed the bush, and green paddocks sprang forth with rich tussock-grasses. In contrast, new growth came reluctantly to Pejar in Argyle County, and the heat of summer dried the sparse vegetation only too quickly.

At that moment Rebecca decided her family would stay no longer on the Pejar Road. They would sell the farm and move to a town where John might establish a school and the children could be educated with others their age. John was astonished at her decision, for he knew very well how much farming meant to her. "You've always wanted to own a farm, my dear. Could you ever be happy living in a house in town?" Rebecca was resolute. "I'll make the best of it, I'm sure. The children need a school and so do you. One day I'll have a farm again, but for the present I'll make do with a kitchen garden, a cow and some chooks." John had an idea of his own. "In a Goulburn newspaper I read of a new National School

Service and I've been thinking of applying for certification," he said. "The Public Schools Act comes into effect next year, and teachers are being recruited for government schools. But if I become a certified teacher, I could be sent to teach anywhere in the colony. Would you be prepared for that possibility?" Rebecca considered this for scarcely a moment. Wherever he was sent, she would gladly go with him; anywhere would be better than Pejar. John set out next day for Goulburn to apply to the National School Service.

Soon Rebecca had good news to share.

Pejar Road
Argyle County, New South Wales
October 1st, 1865

My Dearest Hannah,
John bears this message to you along with my tardy acknowledgement of your latest letter with your grand news. I congratulate you and David on your inheritance of Cartmel. You will be very successful with the property, I know.

I, too, have news. On the basis of his education and previous teaching experience, John has been certified by the National School Service. He is to have charge of the new school at Tarago! When I read his letter of assignment, I could scarcely believe our good fortune. Your friendship has often restored my good humour, and now I shall be living close to you.

Moving to Tarago means I must learn to live in town. John can't manage both a farm and a school, and with my five little ones, I can't be farming on my own. Whenever I come to call on you on Cartmel station, I know I shall feel connected to country life.

A stock and station agent has listed our property, and we arrive at Tarago at the end of the month. I take the liberty of asking, dearest Hannah, if we might stop with you briefly on Cartmel until we find a place to live?

With heartfelt eagerness to be with you again,
I am, as ever, your loving friend,

Rebecca

A buyer was not easily found for the Miller farm on the Pejar Road. John's improvements to the property had equalled the original purchase price, but Rebecca knew they would never reclaim the money. After some considerable time she and John were resigned to abandoning the place when along came a friend of Trevor Jones, a Welsh shepherd with a poke from the goldfields. The shepherd told the agent he would give the Millers what they had paid for the property and a sum for the sheep as well. John and Rebecca accepted the offer, loaded up the cart with their belongings, five children and Megan, and set off for Tarago.

Ewe with lambs

EIGHTEEN
Saint Paul's Parish

*Behold, that thus shall the man be blessed
that feareth the Lord.*
— PSALM 128:4

In the early summer of 1865, Rebecca and Hannah continued to catch up on one another's lives, although they made no mention of Hannah's childlessness. Rebecca was aware her friend had been with child several times, but had not been able to carry a baby to term. Those experiences had obviously taken their toll, for her friend looked much older than her two and thirty years, yet Hannah, dearest Hannah, was still a cheerful spirit, affectionate and fun-loving.

As they sat talking one afternoon on the broad verandah of Cartmel homestead, Rebecca was knitting a cap for her expected baby whilst Hannah was crocheting a tea cosy. "Last year, shortly before Mr. C passed away," said Hannah, "he asked David to take him in the buggy to a solicitor at Goulburn. He made a new will, leaving Cartmel to David, for neither in Lancashire nor the colony did he have any heirs.

"David found the soil here on Cartmel too sandy for his liking, so he first planted a crop of rye and ploughed it in. He's been successful alternating rye with wheat and oats. He's never been fond of sheep, but we have a mob of five hundred because they survive well here and provide us with mutton and an income from fat lambs and fleeces. We couldn't do without Caleb, our shepherd, and Laurie, our farmhand, both emancipated convicts. David has his horses, and I have my cow and chooks and my kitchen garden. We have all we ever wanted."

Except children, thought Rebecca. Little Margaret Miller had toddled away from the shade of a tree where Megan was singing to the children and had climbed the verandah steps and onto Hannah's lap. The two women got up to prepare the evening tea, and Hannah walked out to the kitchen with Margaret on her hip.

Rebecca and the Miller children were not the only ones who enjoyed Hannah's company. Megan Mary Mahoney truly adored her. Rebecca realized how strong the attachment was when, shortly after they arrived in Cartmel homestead, she heard Megan ask Hannah to teach her to crochet. "Rebecca's the expert there!" Hannah said. "Sure an' she'd be willing to get you started." Megan persevered. "I'd rather have you teach me, if you would, please." Hannah had winked at Rebecca and had shown Megan how to chain-stitch. The girl's first piece of work was a snood for Hannah's profusion of greying hair.

The evening tea that day consisted of potato cakes, eggs, ham and boiled greens. Rebecca lifted potatoes left over from the noon dinner out of a pot at the back of the kitchen range and worked up potato cakes whilst Hannah saw to the eggs, ham and greens. The sweet was to be currant square and custard, with beakers of milk for the children and cups of tea for the adults.

"This puts me in mind of the two of us preparing food for the girls on the *Caroline*," said Rebecca. Hannah laughed at the memory. "It was pure Irish luck you were there to show me what to do, or we'd all have been half-starved! Do you remember Bern Rooney and Uel Grady, the lads who fetched meals that were too tepid to enjoy, no matter our careful preparation? Bern Rooney, I must tell you, is jack-of-all-trades here at the Tarago hotel. He says Uel Grady made his fortune in Turon goldfield and lives a swank life at Melbourne."

During the brief sojourn in Cartmel homestead, before she set up house, Rebecca had her sixth child. The baby, born on the 22nd of November, 1865, was a dark-haired, solemn infant whom Rebecca called Sarah, her dearest friend's second name. Rebecca was concerned about Hannah's reaction to her giving birth to another child, but Hannah was delighted to have the infant in her home. Rebecca's eyes filled with tears as she watched the childless Hannah rocking Sarah's cradle and soothing the baby to sleep with lullabies.

On Boxing Day she wrote to her father about their new home and the latest family member.

Tarago
Argyle County, New South Wales
December 26th, 1865

My Dear Father,
On this very warm day I write to you from the verandah of our new home at Tarago. The shady eucalypts around the house are rustling in the breezes, and a flock of green and yellow chattering budgerigars has just flown across the property. This afternoon John has taken the children for a ramble to the creek.

Tarago is located in a picturesque setting, a mile and a half southwest of Lake Bathurst. The soil hereabouts is sandy, sprinkled with fine rocky bits which John has identified as hornblendic granite. The growing conditions here are better than at Pejar, but I still cultivate carefully to ensure a good crop of vegetables.

I take pleasure in telling you of a new granddaughter, Sarah. She is a quiet, dark-haired baby, born on November 22nd and settling into the family very well. As William and Margaret were, she will be baptised by the Bishop in the Cathedral Church of Saint Saviour at Goulburn.

The house we bought is on an acre of property at the edge of the village. Our dwelling is of brick with a wood verandah and five rooms with fitted wooden floors. It was a shell of a place when we bought it, the previous owner having abandoned it and returned to England. With the help of our old friend David Andrews, who has a sheep station close by, John did the finishing. We are pleased with the results.

Our acre of ground is enough for a cow, a flock of hens and my kitchen garden. We gave our older cow to our neighbour at Pejar and will sell our heavy horse at auction. We need a light draught horse for our life here in the village, one that John can ride as well.

John is Master at the new school here, which J.J., Emily and Mary Jane attend. At home I have Willie, Margaret, baby Sarah and our helper, Megan, to keep me company. We thank God we are all in good health and trust this letter finds you the same.

With my love and good wishes to everyone at Grennin,
I am, as ever, your loving daughter,

Rebecca

Rebecca's father, who always wrote to her twice each year, did not answer this letter. Rebecca was puzzled about the lack of a reply until the day John came home from Tarago Post Office with a black-edged envelope postmarked "Tyrone." She burst into tears without seeing the letter inside. John opened the envelope and read a brief note from Rebecca's eldest sister, Martha, with the news of their father's passing. He had collapsed in a field and died in his bed later that day. Rebecca, who had been away from Grennin for more than eleven years, wept in John's arms that night with grief and homesickness. Beside her pillow, wrapped in brown paper, was her piece of turf from her father's cottage in Tyrone.

The village of Tarago, comprising church, hotel and Post Office, had a newly constructed schoolhouse. This simple one-room brick building had slate writing boards on the front and back walls, three windows with shelves underneath on each side wall, and a covered porch at the entrance. One dunny for girls and another for boys stood at the rear of a fenced schoolyard. Children who lived too far away to walk to school left their horses in a small paddock in one corner of the yard. John Miller was once again a schoolmaster, now with twenty pupils ages four to twelve. Three of them were his own children.

"We have some very naughty boys in our school," declared eight-year-old Mary Jane at tea one evening. "Papa has to be ever so firm with them. He's much more fierce than he is at home. And some of the big pupils don't even know how to spell or recite their multiplication tables! I'm already a good speller and I can do problems in multiplication." John shook his head, and Rebecca gave her eldest child a sharp look. "You've had the advantage of your father's teaching for several years, Mary Jane, and we'd expect you to be good at spelling and multiplication." Mary Jane gave a great huff and asked for another helping of sponge cake with custard.

<hr />

The matter of a replacement for Ned was more of a concern for David Andrews than for Rebecca and John. The Irishman, well-known in the district as a great man for horseflesh, was keen on finding them a suitable horse. He had an Irish Draught stallion named Callan at stud on Cartmel. The handsome chestnut was both a saddle horse and light draught horse, easy to ride as well as to hitch to a buggy or farm cart. The stallion's progeny of various breedings were found throughout Argyle County.

At a Sunday dinner in Cartmel homestead, David said to John, "I'd like to take you along towards Goulburn next Saturday morning. A few miles down the road, a woman with a Thoroughbred mare bred her to Callan. The woman can no longer ride and she would like to sell the foal, now a good-looking young mare. I broke the mare to saddle and harness myself, and I've a notion she'd be a good mount for you and a good horse to drive."

And that's how the Miller family acquired Kate. Rebecca knew how to harness up and drive and found the mare easy to manage. Kate was pastured behind the house in a grassy paddock with Julia the cow, who paid her no attention. John built a shelter for the animals at the side of the property and told the children to keep their distance from the mare until she was used to them. But J.J., with brother Willie at his heels, quickly disobeyed his father's instructions and made friends with Kate.

Also in the paddock was a heifer calf, which Megan had named Eunice. From the Bible, Rebecca was sure, but she couldn't recall the reference. "The New Testament," said Megan. "Eunice was Saint Timothy's mother, a woman of 'unfeigned faith,' according to Paul the Apostle in his Second Epistle to Timothy." Rebecca wondered if a cow should be named for Saint Timothy's mother, but once again there was no faulting Megan's knowledge of the Bible.

Once a month Rebecca and John left their children in the care of Hannah and David and drove to Goulburn to purchase baking supplies and knitting, crocheting and sewing materials. Taking lodgings overnight along the way, they arrived at Goulburn in time to make their purchases and have their noon dinner with the Lord Bishop of Goulburn, the Right Reverend Mesac Thomas, and his wife. The episcopal couple lived at Bishop's Palace, scarcely a palace, but a substantial home near the Cathedral Church. The Bishop and Mrs. Thomas had met John and Rebecca on a visit to Saint Paul's Church of England at Tarago. His Lordship was impressed with John, "a layman well grounded in the tenets of his faith," he had been heard to say.

On one Sunday each month, Bishop Mesac Thomas sent a Curate out to minister to the Tarago faithful. "I'd like to open Saint Paul's Church every Sunday," said the Bishop one Saturday afternoon as he finished a second helping of his wife's queen of puddings. "Would you consider conducting services there when I can't spare a Curate?" John put his napkin to his mouth and swallowed. "I'd be honoured to do so, your Lordship, but I'm not qualified." "We'll soon fix that!" said the Bishop. "A little preparation on your part, and you'll have a licence as a Church of England Lay Reader. What do you say?" John quickly agreed, and Rebecca felt pleased for him. Seemingly unconcerned about John's Nonconformist background, the Bishop was offering her husband a distinguished position in the Church of England.

"As a Lay Reader," said the Bishop, "you will not be permitted to administer the sacraments of Baptism, Holy Matrimony or the Eucharist. Your responsibility will be to read the offices of the church: Morning Prayer, the Litany, Compline and Evensong. You'll also see to burial of the dead, instruct the young ones in their Catechism, and celebrate all church Festivals and Saints' Days. You'll read my regular homilies to the congregation and base your own homilies on Proper Lessons and Psalms in *The Book of Common Prayer*. You'll also counsel parishioners as the need arises. It's a heavy load in addition to your schoolteaching but I believe you're the man our Heavenly Father needs in Saint Paul's Parish. I'm certain your good wife here understands the importance of your service to the Lord."

Before Rebecca could reply, the Bishop's wife said in her cultured English tones, "How nice for you both. How very nice." It was not the word Rebecca would have used for the responsibilities the Bishop had just described. She was reckoning how time-consuming her husband's Lay Reader duties would be. As she sat at the Bishop's dinner table, she silently asked God to help her be supportive of John's new-found vocation. Her husband had little enough time with his family, occupied as he was with his schoolwork every evening.

During the next three months, John spent every spare moment preparing to be licensed as a Lay Reader: reading, memorizing, rehearsing, and praying that he would be a worthy disciple of Christ. For her husband's installation at the Cathedral Church of Saint Saviour, Rebecca made him a full-length black cassock and a flowing white surplice to wear over it. She edged the neckline and sleeves of the surplice with crocheted lace and stitched a new cambric shirt for him and a matching cravat. His short cope of black stuff material she would make later. He purchased his broad-brimmed black hat on a trip to Goulburn.

In cassock and surplice John processed after the Dean and clergy down the aisle of the Cathedral Church on Sunday morning, the 23rd of September in the Year of Our Lord 1866, and knelt before his Bishop. In a solemn service, similar to the Ordering of Deacons, he was examined for installation as Lay Reader in the Diocese of Goulburn.

The question involving his family came towards the end of the Bishop's examination: "Will you apply all your diligence to frame and fashion your own life, and the life of your family, according to the Doctrine of Christ; and to make both yourself and them, as much as in you lieth, wholesome examples of the flock of Christ?" John replied, "I will do so, the Lord being my helper." Rebecca glanced at Megan and the six children ranged along the pew. Only when she heard the

Bishop's question did it occur to Rebecca that she and the bairns were part of John's ministry. Dear Lord, she prayed, may thy saving Grace make us all "wholesome examples of the flock of Christ."

Around John's neck the Bishop placed a silken cord from which hung a wooden cross. He presented him with his licence, which John framed and hung in the vestry of Saint Paul's Church at Tarago. After school and on Saturdays, he could be found counselling parishioners or conducting burial services. Unless a Curate arrived from Goulburn to administer Holy Communion, he devoted every Sunday morning to Morning Prayer at Saint Paul's and many Sunday afternoons to visitations on horseback. His family missed his company, but Rebecca admitted to herself she had never known her husband to be happier.

When John, Mary Jane, Emily and J.J. were at school, Rebecca took the younger children and Megan along to Cartmel homestead, where Hannah sang with the children and Rebecca sewed, knitted or crocheted. When the weather was warm, they took a blanket and a picnic lunch out to the creek on the western boundary of Cartmel station. Megan watched over Willie as he launched bits of bark into the water whilst little Margaret and baby Sarah played on the blanket. It put Hannah and Rebecca in mind of their Sunday afternoons along the Wingecarribee River.

On arriving at the creek one day, Rebecca and Hannah found their access to the creek cut off by a new fence that extended as far as they could see. The new selector west of the station had blocked Cartmel's access to water. When David Andrews learned what had been done, he was furious. It took David, Caleb and Laurie many days to remove several miles of fencing.

"John," said Rebecca several days later, "Hannah told me David has received a letter from the owner of the property to the west of their station, putting the boundary of Cartmel in dispute. Would you please see what you can do to help?" John replied, "I'll have a word with David on Sunday." As he and David Andrews took a stroll after dinner in Cartmel homestead, John said, "You seem preoccupied. I'd be willing to share your concerns." David reached into a pocket, took out a cream-coloured envelope and handed it to John. The brief letter inside was scribed in elegant copperplate on creamy watermarked bond, which probably cost one pence a sheet.

<u>Hampshire Gallery of Photography</u>
Goulburn

October 9th, 1867

To the Owner of Cartmel Station:
I am aware that you are responsible for removal of my boundary fence at the eastern edge of my property. Such removal constitutes an act of vandalism.

Should you not replace said fencing within a month of today's date, you are hereby warned that legal proceedings will be taken against you.

Yours truly,
Algernon Hamilton, Esq.

"Could you put your hand on the title to Cartmel station?" asked John. "Surely the boundaries of your property are described there."

"Aye, and there's a map with the title as well. When it comes to creeks, any fool knows boundaries run down the middle of them!"

"Obviously, Mr. Hamilton is not aware of that. Would it help if I arranged an appointment, say next Saturday afternoon, so that we might confer with him?"

"Confer? I'll not confer with any Algernon Hamilton! My Da' was tenant in Donegal to an arrogant English bastard, begging your pardon, John, and when I left Ireland, I vowed never again to touch the forelock to any Englishman. The boundary of my property is in the middle of the creek, and that's that!"

"Then if you'll trust me with the matter, I'll go into Goulburn on your behalf and see if I can get this settled. I'll need the title and map with me."

"I'd be much obliged, John."

On the following Saturday in Goulburn, John located the Hampshire Gallery of Photography. He stepped inside the shop to discover the monocled proprietor, a portly young man with slicked hair, reclining in an overstuffed chair. His head rested on an elaborate antimacassar, and his hands held a cup of tea. No clients were to be seen. "Yes?" said the photographer. He did not move from his position of ease, nor did his monocle twitch.

"My name is John Miller. I am the Church of England Lay Reader at Tarago and I represent Mr. David Andrews on Cartmel station," said John. The man startled John by dropping his cup with a clatter and leaping to his feet. "Then you jeopardize your character by representing trash!" he boomed, and his monocle fell to the end of its ribbon. "That creek supplies my property with water and it must be fenced off!"

John took the Cartmel title and map from his pocket to teach a lesson on sharing the limited water resources of Argyle County. Algernon Hamilton proved to be a difficult pupil. "I see no reason whatsoever to share my water, particularly with an Irishman! When Irish peasants are allowed to own land, trouble can always be expected. Doesn't he know Englishmen are rightful masters everywhere in the world? I'll sue him for the cost of my fence! I'll sue that Irish peasant off his property!" bellowed Algernon Hamilton, his monocle swinging wildly.

John moved in close to his bulky, recalcitrant pupil and spoke like the schoolmaster he was. "Let me give you some very good advice, Mr. Hamilton. That Irish peasant, as you call him, has the law on his side. The western boundary of his station runs to the middle of that creek. Any attempt at trespassing on his land and cutting off his water supply again will result in removal of the obstruction, followed by legal action against you. Enjoy your property, sir, and don't let the sin of greed ruin the pleasure of owning it." The Englishman spluttered in frustration. John stepped out of the shop and softly closed the door behind him.

Next Sunday at dinner, Hannah served her currant square with custard, one of John Miller's favourite desserts. When Megan had herded the children away after the meal, John, to Hannah and David's delight, reported on his interview with the photographer, although he omitted any reference to Irish peasants. "Let me know if you have any more difficulty with the self-important Algernon Hamilton," said John. "I'll gladly represent you."

In the warm summer weather, Hannah and Rebecca and the children looked forward to their picnics by the creek. One afternoon the women watched a portly rider, whom they recognized from John's description, riding an overfed horse towards the other side of the water. In her thickest Irish brogue Hannah, cheeky as ever, shouted, "G'day to you, sir! Do give your lovely horse a drink from this creek we share!" Algernon Hamilton, Esquire, muttered something unintelligible and turned his thirsty horse away from the water. They never saw him again. Word went round he had sold his property west of Cartmel and bought a row of houses at Goulburn.

NINETEEN
Tarago School

Commit thy way unto the Lord; trust also in him . . .
— PSALM 37:5

On the 10th of November, 1867, Rebecca gave birth to her seventh child, a daughter, whom she named Eliza, in deference to John's sister in Essex, Elizabeth, with whom John corresponded. Eliza was smaller than any of Rebecca's previous babies, but she was bright-eyed and sociable. "Such a wee lamb!" said Megan. The girl tied the usual linen sling across her chest where she carried each new infant, leaving her hands free for the next oldest children. Baby Eliza snuggled happily against Megan's slight bosom.

Every weekday morning Rebecca stood with Margaret, Sarah, Eliza and Megan on the verandah to see the four eldest Miller children off to school. Mary Jane and Emily walked together in front, Mary Jane so bossy in their conversation, Rebecca knew, and Emily so amenable. Behind them were J.J. and Willie, darting back and forth in search of items of interest at the roadsides. Willie, who was as tall as his older brother, had become J.J.'s constant companion in adventures.

Their father had walked to school more than an hour earlier to pour lime down the dunnies, empty the horse trough and fill it with clean water, place slates on the shared desks, return copybooks and write arithmetic assignments on the blackboards. On the arrival of his pupils, John began the school day by opening *The Book of Common Prayer* and reading the Collect for Grace, which began, "O Lord, our heavenly Father, Almighty and everlasting God, who hast safely brought us to the beginning of this day . . ." The Collect was followed by a Bible reading and a class recitation of the

Lord's Prayer. During the mornings John alternated between teaching older pupils at the back of the room and little ones at the front. When the older children had finished their assignments and corrections, they were expected to help the younger pupils with phonics and number drills and hear their oral reading.

In good weather all the pupils accompanied their schoolmaster on afternoon rambles to study biology, geology and botany. In his second year of teaching at Tarago, when his pupils had acquired some reading skills, John devoted two afternoons each week to history and geography, although not of New South Wales. Transportation of convicts, habits of aboriginals, even explorations by Queen's Surveyors were not in the curriculum. Instead, those afternoons were filled with British history and geography as pupils read aloud from textbooks, recited dates, places and events, copied maps or re-enacted historical events, such as the signing of the Magna Carta.

At regular intervals, or on afternoons when the weather turned particularly inclement, lessons in art, recitation and music were laid on. All pupils, even the youngest ones, were expected to draw effectively, recite poems clearly, and sing on key. John, pitch pipe in hand, made good use of his tenor voice as he taught folk songs and familiar hymns to his class on those afternoons.

Whilst John sat marking assignments in the evenings, Rebecca heard their children's recitations of multiplication tables, historical dates, spelling lessons, poems and lists of monarchs. The Miller children often interrupted their evening memory work with tales of Tarago School, much to John and Rebecca's amusement.

In early February 1868, shortly after the summer holidays, one of the schoolboys showed up with a fever and dry cough. The boy's fever diminished, but his coughing grew worse, and soon he was vomiting. Several other pupils, including Mary Jane and Emily, developed fevers and coughs. Rebecca kept the girls at home, and John closed the school. He and Rebecca had recognized the signs of whooping cough. Sure enough, a week after they became ill, Mary Jane and Emily were gasping in long screeching breaths, coughing with an eerie cawing sound and vomiting. J.J. and Willie were next to have fevers and dry coughs. Then Megan, who had escaped the disease in childhood because of her isolation from other families, developed the same symptoms.

Rebecca prepared to nurse the children as her mother had done when whooping cough struck at Grennin. She aired out the house and fed the sick children nourishing food which could be swallowed easily: chicken broth, mashed boiled vegetables and stewed fruits. She gave them rags to cover their mouths when they coughed and washed everything they touched twice over. John helped her with the washing and tended the children at night, when the coughing and vomiting were much worse. The crisis point of whooping cough, Rebecca knew, came at the end of the fourth week of the disease. Rebecca feared for the younger ones, who had less strength to deal with the malady. As she nursed one child after another through endless days, she prayed that baby Eliza would be spared and she kept her away from the others.

In the fifth week, Mary Jane and Emily showed signs of being on the mend. Rebecca still had her hands full with J.J., Willie and Megan, and then Margaret and Sarah became feverish. Poor wee bairns. They were too young to understand what was happening to them and cried continually, which only made their whooping worse and more frightening.

At the beginning of March, the baby developed a fever. Rebecca handed over the care of the older children to Hannah, who arrived every day to see to the house and the cooking. Eliza's little body was racked with spasms of coughing and vomiting. Rebecca kept her at the breast, hoping to get some nourishment into her. She counted the days and prayed that God in Heaven would help her infant past the four-week crisis point. With Rebecca's twenty-four-hour nursing, Eliza, although weak and listless, stayed alive. Rebecca and John could only continue to pray for her.

Then, on the 19th of March, 1868, as she lay in Rebecca's arms, baby Eliza Miller, convulsing with choking coughs, reached the end of her short life in this world. John Miller and two men from his church, Henry Phelps and Donald McDonald, signed Eliza's death certificate. The local undertaker, James Woodward, made a little casket and dug a grave for her, and John and Rebecca buried Eliza two days later in Tarago Cemetery. In the absence of a clergyman, Lay Reader John Miller read the service of Burial for his four-month-old daughter.

Rebecca took months to recover from that summer. Her other children and Megan eventually regained their health, although Sarah continued coughing for weeks, and Megan was always to have a tendency to bronchial troubles. Rebecca believed all of them would at least have lifelong protection from whooping cough. Megan, as much as Rebecca, was distraught at the death of baby Eliza, her wee lamb. The young woman's mind returned to her early existence in the smoky one-room hut under the pines near Bowral, and she was plagued by nightmares of babies dying.

No child in John's school escaped the disease, and in addition to burying his baby daughter, the schoolmaster conducted burial services for two of his youngest pupils. He reopened the school six weeks after he had closed it and began to set his classroom routine to rights again. Rebecca's mourning lasted much longer, as it surely does for all mothers.

One afternoon in the late autumn of 1868, after the Miller family had enjoyed their usual Sunday dinner in Cartmel homestead, David Andrews said, "It's time the young ones learned to ride. Come with me, and I'll introduce you to Gwyn." Mary Jane, Emily, J.J., Willie and their father followed David outside whilst Megan minded Margaret, now four years of age, and Sarah, almost two and a half. Rebecca and Hannah got busy with the washing up. In the home paddock Gwyn stretched his neck over the fence and whinnied softly at his visitors.

"I haven't seen this one before," said John. "Is he new to Cartmel?"

"Aye, he is," David answered, as he saddled up Gwyn. "He's a pony of Welsh breeding. I bought him at a Goulburn auction. He's a gentle animal, well-broken and accustomed to children, and I thought I'd use him to teach the young ones to ride." David was much too generous, John protested, but the man from Donegal brooked no argument. "Call it payment for seeing to that boundary problem for me." David then pleased Mary Jane by asking her to mount the pony first.

"Gwyn is a funny name for a pony," said J.J., now almost seven and a half.

"It means white in Welsh," responded David, "although there's a hint of grey on his croup." Whilst David showed Mary Jane how to hold the reins, the little boy slipped around to the rear of the pony to check for grey. Each child in turn mounted Gwyn and was led by David three times around the paddock. The pretty pony stepped carefully over the tussocks and moved steadily and smoothly, proving he had done this many times in his life.

"I want to go round again!" declared five-year-old Willie when his ride came to an end. "And so you shall, next Sunday!" said David, chuckling. "I'll expect you to remember how to mount and hold the reins properly. Now, let me quarter an apple, and you can each give Gwyn a treat."

For the next year David Andrews worked with Mary Jane, Emily, J.J. and Willie each Sunday, one of them on Gwyn whilst the other children stood with David in the centre of the paddock and listened to him—"Up straight! Grip with your knees!"—and took their turns trying to follow his instructions. Their riding lessons were preceded by instruction in grooming and saddling up and were followed by cooling Gwyn out, brushing him down and tending to the tack.

John and Rebecca were impressed with the progress of their children and pondered how they might repay their friend for the hours he spent teaching them. David would not hear of any recompense. "They're good bairns, quick to learn, and there's naught else I'd rather be doing on a Sunday afternoon. Your J.J. has a special sureness around the pony, and all four will be good riders, but the one who'll be a splendid horseman is young Willie. By the age of six, he has steady hands and a good seat and he moves easily with the pony. Mark my words, he has the bearing of a cavalry officer!"

Rebecca had taken to spending weekday afternoons in her rocking chair on the verandah with the plumply mature Abner asleep in his favourite corner. The autumn sun, warming her hands as she crocheted herself a lace cap, made her feel contented. She planned to wear the cap at the christening of the new baby, tempting Providence, perhaps, for the child had not yet been born. Very soon, she hoped. She dozed in the sunshine, longing for the baby's arrival. Although more than a year had passed since the death of Eliza, grief still lay heavily on her heart. She hoped a new bairn would ease the pain.

The setting sun was slowly draping a rosy shawl over the mountains, and eucalypts were beginning to whisper in the late afternoon breezes when Rebecca rose unsteadily from her rocking chair. When she made her way into the kitchen to start the evening tea, a series of strong cramps assured her the baby was indeed on its way.

A baby girl, good-natured and quick to smile, arrived on the 11th of April, 1869. Rebecca offered thanks to her Heavenly Father when she was delivered of another daughter. She named her Jessie, simply because she liked the name. Megan Mary Mahoney tucked Jessie into a sling across her chest and seemed more settled than she had been since the death of Eliza.

"The children need some music in their lives," said John as he and Rebecca lay talking in bed one night. "When we're at Goulburn on Saturday, we'll look for a second-hand harmonium."

"Who's going to teach them to play it?" asked Rebecca. "I'll learn to play it myself and then instruct the children," said John. He kissed Rebecca on the cheek and fell asleep. Rebecca smiled as she lay beside him. He'll master that instrument with the same perseverance he shows in so many other aspects of his life, she mused.

Early every Saturday morning, before he began other duties, John sat with his older children as they learned to play the harmonium. Mary Jane tackled her practising vigorously whilst Emily approached it artistically. Although J.J. enjoyed singing, he had little patience for learning an instrument. Willie was the one for the harmonium. His small hands quickly mastered the keys as he read the notes on the staves in front of him. Little Margaret sat watching how it was done, and Sarah swayed to the rhythms, no matter how tentative the performance. Baby Jessie slept in her cradle through it all. Rebecca gave thanks to God for her devoted husband and his caring ways with the children.

One day as Megan and Rebecca were taking turns with the butter churn, Megan remarked, "Mary Jane and Emily are old enough to learn how to milk."

"Indeed, they are," agreed Rebecca. "I well remember how you milked Bossy at their age." Thereafter, each afternoon when they arrived home from school, the two girls washed their hands and went out to the paddock to try to imitate Megan's sure touch with Julia, Eunice and the new Lois, named for Saint Timothy's grandmother. Megan did most of the milking, of course. Before long J.J. begged to be allowed to try. Megan reported he had the knack, young though he was, and when his hands had grown some, he would be an expert milker.

Megan and Rebecca often sat together talking and doing their handiwork, especially during the winter months. Whilst Jessie slept in her cradle and Sarah played with a rag doll at their feet, they enjoyed the warmth of the kitchen range.

Megan still consulted Hannah Andrews about her crocheting, which amused both Rebecca and her friend.

"You know you'll always be welcome to live with us, Megan," said Rebecca, "but you must be wanting a home and children of your own." It was the winter of 1870, and Megan was three and twenty years of age. This was not the first time Rebecca had broached the subject.

"I've told you I'll not be marrying. I'll never forget the misery of my Ma's life. It's little wonder I've no interest in having a husband. I know you and Hannah are married to good men, but it would be my luck to be courted by a drunken layabout. I'll be staying here as long as you have bairns I can care for. When they're all in school, I'll be off to a convent boarding school at Sydney to offer my services as Matron to the young ones. You're not to concern yourself on my account, Rebecca. I'm certain where I'm headed."

Rebecca was not certain a convent boarding school existed at Sydney, but she knew there was no point in further discussion on this topic with Megan Mary Mahoney.

Because John's success in securing the boundary of Cartmel had been made known throughout Tarago District by David Andrews, the schoolmaster now had a reputation as an advisor. People who needed help caught up with him on his way home at the end of the day or spoke to him after church on Sundays. Many residents of Tarago could neither read nor write, and John's correspondence on their behalf included not only matters of legal importance, but also family letters about births, deaths and weddings, messages to friends and offers of marriage. Often a distant sweetheart replied in astonished acceptance to a swain's proposal that had been elegantly worded by John Miller. Some who required his assistance approached Rebecca first with their problems. Like John, Rebecca regarded each person seriously, realizing how much courage it took to admit their illiteracy or their need for counsel.

In the winter of 1871, Rebecca was delivered of another boy. He was a large baby and caused her some difficulty in birthing him. He was tall, as Willie had been, and for certain a handsome charmer, even as a baby. John was responsible for naming their third son, who arrived on the 10th of June. "Compton South?" asked Rebecca. "Where did that name come from?" The subject of their conversation was sleeping contentedly in his father's arms. "It's the name of my cousin, a son of Uncle Richard Miller. It's quite common for members of the same family to share a name. The world now has two Compton South Millers, one on each side of the globe." Rebecca truly liked the name Compton even if she thought John's explanation was daft.

In the spring of that year, one morning when she and Megan were planting seeds in the kitchen garden, Rebecca looked up to see a familiar face blushing above her. She had glimpsed the man at church occasionally, but when the service was over, he had always departed in haste before she could speak to him. Cap in hand, he said, "G'day to you, Missus."

"G'day to you, Bern." She rose from her knees and offered her hand to the large, shy man she had first met on the *Caroline*. Megan was left to finish planting seeds whilst Rebecca led Bern Rooney up to the verandah. "I'm that glad to see you, Bern," said Rebecca. "It's been many a year since we sailed to the colony together. Hannah Andrews told me you work here at the hotel. To what do I owe the honour of your call?"

Although Rebecca had shown him to one of the wicker chairs on the verandah, the man remained standing. "It's Ginny's father, Missus!" He sounded frightened for such a big man. "Please, Bern, call me Rebecca, and do sit down." Bern perched on the edge of the chair and went on turning his cap. Most men wore stiff leather hats for shade, but Bern's cap seemed to be the same one he had worn on the *Caroline*. His ears were beet-red from the sun and embarrassment.

"Tell me what's bothering you about Ginny's father," said Rebecca in a kindly tone. The long silence that followed made Rebecca think she would never learn what had brought Bern Rooney to her home. Suddenly her visitor found his tongue. "Her father found out Ginny's in the family way, and if I marry her, sure an' he'll murder me!" he blurted.

"Who is Ginny and who is her father?"

"Ginny is the skivvy at the hotel and my intended, and her father is Blue Calhoun, the blacksmith."

"And why should Mr. Calhoun threaten to kill you if you marry his daughter?"

"Her people are papists in Kildare and mine are Protestants in Antrim." The old Irish troubles, mused Rebecca, here on the other side of the world. "Her father beat Ginny something terrible when he found out about the baby. He disowned her and threw her out of the house. I must take care of her!"

"How old is Ginny, and is she willing to marry you, Bern?"

"Willing? Of course she's willing to marry me, or she wouldn't have let me near her!" The big man offered this explanation in all sincerity. "She'll soon be of age!" His tone was defensive.

"I'll ask Mr. Miller to persuade her father to let you and Ginny be married."

"You'll do no such thing! Calhoun's a brute, and I won't have Mr. Miller put in harm's way!"

"Then what can we do to help?"

"Could you find us somewhere to go?" he asked plaintively. "The two of us know naught but Tarago! Ginny and I need a place where her father can't find us." Large tears dropped onto his well-worn trousers. "I'll . . . I'll be leaving now." Bern Rooney rushed from the verandah and headed down the road to the village.

That evening Rebecca explained Bern's problem to her husband. "He's right about Calhoun," said John. "I've seen that man at his forge. He's a massive brute with a great mane of ginger hair. He's destroyed the hotel bar several times in drunken fights. He boasts of being transported to Norfolk Island for killing a man in Dublin. Bern Rooney has reason to fear for his own safety and the girl's. Let me give this some thought." When Rebecca heard John say that, she knew a solution would be forthcoming.

John came up with a plan to save Bern and Ginny and their expected baby from the wrath of Blue Calhoun by sending them northeastward to Berrima. There the couple could find employment at the Surveyor General Inn, have their baby delivered by Rebecca's former accoucheuse, and if Ginny were willing to convert, they could be married by the Reverend James Hassall at Holy Trinity Church. All this John arranged through letters to Berrima.

Getting the couple there was another matter. The Cobb Coach heading north stopped in front of the Tarago hotel, within sight of Blue Calhoun's smithy. John decided to gather up Bern and Ginny and their meagre possessions from the back of the hotel in the early hours of an appointed day and drive them out to a bend in the road a mile beyond Tarago to await the coach. He reminded them of the names of the people they were to contact at Berrima and gave them letters of introduction.

When he heard coach horses pounding in the distance, John swung his hooded cart across the road and stood up with one hand in the air, a shiny coin between his thumb and forefinger. The driver, spewing curses, pulled his team to a halt. John begged his indulgence in letting a man and his wife have passage. The coach driver's eyes glinted like the half a crown John held before him. When John tossed the coin into the driver's eager hand, Bern Rooney and Ginny Calhoun, "man and wife," climbed into the coach and departed for Berrima.

Blue Calhoun was in a rage at his daughter's disappearance, but it took him a fortnight to reckon John Miller had had something to do with it. The blacksmith, very drunk, burst into Tarago School one afternoon as John was gathering up copybooks to go home. The large Irishman grabbed the schoolmaster by the lapels and shook him. John was grateful all the pupils had left for the day.

Calhoun slammed John against the blackboard and bellowed, "What've you done with my Ginny?" Recoiling from the stench of the man, John said, "Your daughter left of her own accord, Mr. Calhoun. She's on her way southwestward towards Melbourne. She and Bern Rooney intend settling in Tasmania." Calhoun seized John by the throat, swore at him and sent him sprawling. Then, spitting a stream of oaths, the blacksmith stormed out of the school. John picked himself up, straightened his clothing, and thanked the Lord for protecting him from serious injury at the hands of a drunken ex-convict. He murmured, "I must tell the Tarago innkeeper that Bern and Ginny are settling in Tasmania."

Rebecca was puzzled by John's confessions when they knelt together that night to say their prayers. "I confess, Dear Lord, very belatedly, I admit, to bribing a Cobb Coach driver to ensure the protection of a man, woman and unborn child. I was also untruthful with the coach driver about their marital status, and I deceived the woman's father and the Tarago innkeeper as to their destination. My prevarications were merely to enable the family to escape to safety. I beg thy forgiveness, Lord. Amen."

Rebecca listened with interest to her husband's prayers every night. Although she often missed the references, as she did on this occasion, she was fascinated and even amused by his familiarity with the Almighty. Rebecca thought of her Lord as a benevolent fatherly figure; John seemed to be good friends with his Lord.

Early in 1873, in her eighth year at Tarago, Rebecca's early morning queasiness told her she was carrying another child. A boy, she hoped, who could provide Compton with companionship. J.J. and Willie were such good friends, and Compton, too, needed to grow up with a brother close to his age.

Rebecca eventually told Hannah she was with child. Hannah blushed and said she herself was four months along with a baby. Rebecca had suspected as much, but because her friend had lost several babies, Rebecca had not wanted to question her. Hannah was now forty years of age, not a worry if one had had previous children, but age could be a problem in Hannah's case. Rebecca arranged for Mrs. McLaughlin, her accoucheuse, to examine Hannah and call on her regularly. Mrs. McLaughlin did so and summoned the doctor from Goulburn. The doctor ordered Hannah into bed and told her to remain there until the child was born. Megan Mary Mahoney was thrilled to learn of Hannah's condition, but, like Rebecca, she worried about her.

Several days later, when Megan was helping harvest vegetables for the root cellar, Rebecca said to her, "I wonder if you'd consider going to Cartmel to look after Hannah and the homestead? I can easily care for the youngest ones, and the older girls can share your usual chores. I'm certain David and Hannah would appreciate your help." As Rebecca had expected, Megan immediately abandoned the harvesting and ran to the house to get herself clean and organized for Cartmel. That afternoon Rebecca drove Megan and her few belongings to the Andrews' homestead. David and Hannah greeted their helper warmly, and Rebecca left her tackling a load of washing.

Hannah Andrews obeyed doctor's orders and stayed in bed, and Rebecca drove out to Cartmel to visit her as often as she could. Each time she saw Hannah, she thought her friend looked less robust. David Andrews, known for wandering the district in search of horses to buy, train and sell, now sat by his wife's bed most of each day. Knowing her suffering in losing previous babies, he fussed over her and was often in tears whilst she slept.

On a Sunday afternoon in May, with Rebecca at her bedside, Hannah complained of sharp pains. The baby wasn't due for almost another month, but Rebecca immediately sent David for the accoucheuse. Hannah, weakened by months in bed, had little strength to push her baby into the world. The accoucheuse said the baby was large and its early arrival timely for the mother. She sent David to Goulburn to fetch the doctor. Rebecca assured her dearest friend she would not leave her bedside.

Just when Rebecca, faint with exhaustion and anxiety herself, thought Hannah had reached the end of her endurance, the doctor delivered her of a large, vigorous son. The accoucheuse sponged the baby clean and wrapped him in flannel before taking him away to the arms of his father. Hannah, who looked scarcely alive, was bleeding profusely. Rebecca held fast to her friend's hand and prayed aloud as the doctor struggled to save his patient. He remained with Hannah for another twenty-four hours before he felt he could leave her in the care of the accoucheuse and return to Goulburn. Rebecca stayed at her friend's bedside, dozing in a chair.

Hannah slept fitfully and called out for her baby. Each time she wakened, Rebecca fed her chicken broth Megan had made for her. Propped on pillows, Hannah began to suckle her son on breasts tender and swollen with milk. The baby, named Robert Samuel for his two grandfathers in Ireland, showed her no mercy and fed enthusiastically.

Megan had never shown much interest in cooking, but with her beloved Hannah in need of nourishing meals, she prevailed upon Rebecca for instruction. At caring for the baby she was an expert, bathing him and changing his nappies, washing his clothes and singing to him in his cradle.

Meanwhile, Rebecca's baby was not expected until August. She felt as healthy as ever. Many times she thanked her Heavenly Father for sparing dearest Hannah in childbirth.

"Isn't he beautiful, Rebecca?" said Hannah one bright afternoon whilst her hungry son satisfied himself. Rebecca sat at her bedside, knitting a shawl for her own baby. "He resembles David, don't you think, although I do believe his eyes and hair will be like mine." Robert Samuel was indeed a beautiful baby, thought Rebecca, but what a toll he had taken of his mother. Hannah was hollow-eyed and grey-faced, and when at last she was permitted to leave her bed and sit in an invalid's pushchair, Rebecca wondered whether her friend would ever have the strength to walk again.

At the beginning of July 1873, John came home with a letter from the National School Service. Rebecca read it before she served the evening tea and learned her husband had been transferred to North Goulburn Public School as of the first of August. "I'll need to prepare Tarago School for my successor," said John. "I'm sure you can pack up things here by the end of the month. I must speak to David about another horse to harness up with Kate because we have a much bigger load to move this time."

Rebecca sighed. Surely her baby would not arrive before they moved. Dear Lord, she prayed, let me not be delivered until we are settled at North Goulburn.

John and Elizabeth Barnes, c.1850s

John Miller, c.1870s   *Rebecca Miller, c.1870s*

Christ Church, Cootamundra, 1878

J & E. Barnes Store, Cootamundra, 1881

Margaret Miller, BA, 1886

Mayflower Tennis Club, 1889. Nellie and Lilla standing on the right

Sketch by Nellie Barnes, 1888

Mayor J.J. Miller and his sister, Mayoress Miss M.J. Miller, 1892

Littledale homestead, 1891

Susie Ellen "Nellie" Barnes and William Miller, 1894

Christ Church parade, 1st Australian Horse, 1898. Alick Miller, Trooper, seated left; William Miller, Lieutenant Commanding, seated centre

Edward Prior Barnes,
c. 1890s

Susannah Maria Gordon Barnes Miller, date unknown

Miller sons: Compton, William, J.J., Alick, Nevil, May 29th, 1900

Nellie, William (reading a book) and Susannah with children, 1901. Above from left: Frida and Goog. Below from left: Bertha, Cora, Bill, Bon and Florence

J.J. and Susannah Miller, 1910

William and Bill Miller, choristers, Saint Saviour's Church, 1910

Susannah

**FROM LOVE
TO LOVE**

*Believe me, if all those endearing young charms,
Which I gaze on so fondly today, were to change by
   tomorrow,
And fleet in my arms, like fairy gifts fading away,
Thou would'st still be adored, as this moment thou art.
Let thy loveliness fade as it will. And around the dear ruin
Each wish of my heart would entwine itself verdantly still.*
— THOMAS MOORE, "BELIEVE ME, IF ALL
THOSE ENDEARING YOUNG CHARMS"

In the English autumn of 1870, Edward Prior Barnes, a merchant from Cootamundra, New South Wales, arrived in London. The youngest son of John and Elizabeth Barnes, Edward was a man of six and twenty years, above average in height and slightly built. He had a quiet demeanour and a notable singing voice. Edward, born at Ashfield, West Sydney, now lived at Cootamundra and had been sent to England by Thomas, John and George, his older brothers, who had all been born in London. In the mother country Edward would meet English relatives and family friends and also arrange the export of British goods to the Barnes stores at Murrumburrah and Cootamundra. A firm of London solicitors was to be the agent for his transactions.

The solicitors' clerk, Mr. John Gordon, observed the colonial merchant in his dealings with the firm and invited him to his home in Paddington for Sunday dinner. There Edward met Susannah Gordon. More dinners with the Gordons led to Edward's inclusion in their Christmas and New Year's festivities, where the colonist enjoyed himself so much he twice postponed his return to New South Wales.

TWENTY

The Commissary

I will go in the strength of the Lord God . . .
—PSALM 71:16

Susannah Maria Gordon, a young woman of cheerful nature and abundant energy, was an exceptionally talented pianist and an accomplished church organist and choirmistress. She was also the capable cook and congenial hostess for her widowed father, who was the solicitors' clerk at a London legal firm.

One Sunday afternoon in the autumn of 1870, the eighteen-year-old was impressed by the colonial merchant her father had invited to dinner, and the couple soon discovered a common bond: Edward Barnes had a clear tenor voice, and Susannah Gordon could accompany him beautifully at the pianoforte. Over the next few months no one who saw them together at the Broadwood in the drawing room of the Gordon home could have been surprised to learn that the colonial merchant and the daughter of John Gordon had fallen in love. Before he returned to New South Wales, Edward Barnes received a promise of marriage from Susannah Gordon.

Letters of affection followed, posted to and from New South Wales, and when Susannah came of age, plans were made for her to join her beloved in the colony. Susannah Gordon boarded the good ship *Commissary* in London at the end of August 1873, her passage to Sydney Harbour arranged by Edward Barnes. She was shown to a small cabin by a seaman who carried her two portmanteaux, one with her changes of clothing for the voyage and the other with her wedding finery and trousseau. Down in the hold were her Broadwood pianoforte and a trunk filled with books, files of recipes and collections of music both sacred and secular. Single women in cabin class customarily travelled with a relative, but Susannah was unaccompanied and required a chaperone. The shipping agency had asked the Captain's wife to take on this role. "I have watched over many girls on this ship, my dear," said Millicent, a robust woman in middle age, on the night before they sailed. "I know my responsibility, and you have only to relax and enjoy yourself. My husband is the finest of master mariners and he will have us at Sydney in no time."

"In no time" was Millicent's description of a voyage of three months that followed a route recently made possible by the 1869 completion of the Suez Canal. It was a comparatively comfortable passage to the Australian continent, much more so than previously, because once past the blustery winds and choppy seas of the English Channel and Bay of Biscay, the *Commissary*, a ship of 899 tons out of Aberdeen, sailed smoothly through the Mediterranean, Isthmus of Suez, Red Sea and thence southeastward. The ship's route to New South Wales was far away from the raging waters of the Roaring Forties that emigrants had faced on the original passage through the southern hemisphere.

The *Commissary* was a substantial ship, and Susannah's stomach held steady even on those days when the vessel tossed and pitched. All the while Millicent fussed over Susannah. One of the unattached male passengers, who proudly told everyone of his insurance agency at Sydney whilst passing around calling cards, became enamoured of the young woman. At this point Millicent's chaperoning grew even more intense.

"I really would like to talk to the three gentlemen who are graziers on the western slopes, where I'm going to live," said Susannah. By listening to them at mealtimes, she had been able to learn their particulars: Captain Seymour Hawser owned a cattle station near Wagga Wagga; Mr. Jude Munro ran a sheep station at Yass; Mr. Malbon Lynch had a property close to Cootamundra, where Edward's store was located. Susannah believed conversations with these gentlemen would give her an opportunity to learn something of her new home.

Millicent, however, disapproved of any such association. "You can overhear them whilst you are taking your meals in the dining saloon, my dear." Susannah understood she was merely to listen, not ask questions, and she chafed at the restriction. Instead, she had to content herself with talking to the other women whilst Millicent, sitting beside Susannah, watched and chaperoned. For a young woman who had been in charge of her father's household and been his hostess on many occasions, this three-month voyage was becoming frustrating. Only thoughts of dear Edward waiting for her at Sydney kept Susannah's spirits up.

Millicent, a former schoolmistress, insisted on occupying Susannah's every free moment with improvement of her mind. "The colony is a rough-and-ready place," declared Millicent, "and one must make time for civilized pursuits." To ensure a good start, she provided Susannah with volumes of Shakespeare to read and discuss with her chaperone.

The voyage continued in this fashion until the evening Millicent succumbed to dyspepsia (she occasionally ate too heartily, Susannah had noticed) and took to her cabin. After breakfast the following day, the amorous insurance agent from Sydney tracked Susannah to a deck chair in a corner, where she was deep into her reading.

"Ah, the lovely Miss Gordon! There is no need for you to be alone on this long voyage. We shall retire to the dining saloon, where you may have my company over a glass of wine!" Amongst her father's many friends, Susannah had never met anyone like this odious man. She shuddered at the thought of being trapped in the dining saloon with him. She slammed shut her volume of Shakespeare's sonnets.

"Enjoy your own company, sir. I am retiring to my cabin." Whilst doing so, she was trailed by the obnoxious passenger and resorted to locking the door in his face. A rude and drastic action, she realized, but the man was distressingly persistent. Confined to her cabin was not the way she had planned to spend any portion of this voyage, but until Millicent came to her rescue, she would remain behind a locked door and venture out only for meals.

The enforced solitude gave her too much time to ponder the objections of her family to her emigration. What was she thinking, they had asked anxiously, going off across the world to marry a man she had known only briefly? New South Wales was full of criminals and ruffians, they said. Susannah had ignored their arguments. Her beloved father had passed away suddenly, and she saw no future in taking the role of a single woman dependent on relatives until she found herself a husband. Moreover, she had pledged herself to Edward and would be his wife, no matter where he lived. Her resolve had been firm. Alone in her cabin, shadows of doubt crossed her mind. Praying to her Heavenly Father for strength, she reminded herself of her initial certainty.

Millicent recovered three days later, and Susannah was much more appreciative of her attentions. The occasional ports of call provided them with diversions, and at each one she and her chaperone set off, Millicent firmly clutching her arm, to see the sights and stroll through exotic markets.

They were accompanied by Fergus, a burly Scots seaman appointed as their bodyguard. Fergus seemed to enjoy the opportunity to forgo his usual duties and escort the Captain's wife and a young female passenger. From Barbary apes at Gibraltar to bright fishing boats at Malta, from gleaming white cottages on the Aegean islands to camels in Egypt, Susannah gathered memories to share with her future children and grandchildren. A favourite story was to be "Fergus and the Cutpurse."

In a crowded market in the Indies, a pathetic native in rags stumbled against Susannah, snatched her purse and took off, their bodyguard after him. Fergus caught the thief by the scruff of the neck and returned him to Susannah. When the big Scotsman pulled her purse out from beneath the beggar's rags, Susannah opened it and handed the terrified native a few coins. Fergus gave the man a good shaking and released him into the mob of beggars now surging around them for money. The hefty Scot bellowed and the beggars backed away. Seizing each lady by the arm, Fergus hustled them out of the market. "Don't look at me like that, Fergus," said Susannah.

"The man was starving!" A glowering Fergus shook his head and steered the ladies towards the ship.

The *Commissary* sailed amongst the islands of the East Indies and southward beyond the Great Barrier Reef until she reached Brisbane, where some of the passengers disembarked. The ship glided onward until, on the 19th of November, 1873, she reached the protected waters of Sydney's splendid harbour and the dock at Balmain. As it turned out, Susannah felt pleased with the voyage. She had discovered she was a good sailor, had enjoyed herself on the ship—aside from her aversion to the odious passenger—and had memories of fascinating scenes along the way. And now she looked forward to a new adventure.

First came a cursory examination by the Ship's Surgeon to ascertain the passengers' good health, followed by an inspection of their immigration papers by colonial authorities. Susannah waited somewhat impatiently whilst Fergus supervised the hoisting of her pianoforte and trunk from the hold. She handed him an envelope with a message of thanks and a sovereign. "Och, 'twas a pleasure, lass!" he responded. "And if you'd take my advice, you'd keep a tight grip on your purse." She laughed at him and at the memory.

Millicent embraced her and wished her Godspeed and a married life of happiness. As she returned Millicent's embrace, Susannah was strangely teary-eyed. She tried to compose herself when she looked down from the deck of the *Commissary*; there on the quay stood the man she had sailed across the world to marry. Edward Barnes, accompanied by his sister and his best friend, waited with a hired carriage. Susannah walked off the ship and into Edward's arms.

"My darling Susannah!" His embrace and tender kiss took her back to those delicious moments in the privacy of her father's vestibule in Paddington. "How brave of you to have endured such a voyage on your own." He introduced her to his sister, Beth, and his friend, Charles Metcalfe. "Are you feeling quite well, darling? We can postpone the wedding, if you wish." Susannah was quick to reply. "Edward, love, I didn't travel all that way to wait to be married. You told me arrangements would be made at a church."

Before Susannah and Edward could be married, however, certain requirements had to be met. Susannah left her belongings at a Sydney hotel, where she would share a room with Beth Barnes. Her future sister-in-law, just five years older, proved to be a most pleasant companion. The group sought the offices of the Registrar of Marriages, where Susannah's age and immigrant status had to be reviewed before a marriage licence could be granted. Calling the Banns in a church on three successive Sundays was not possible; instead, Edward purchased a Licence to Marry. Next came an interview with the Vicar of the church Edward had attended.

Finally, on the 28th of November, 1873, Susannah donned her wedding finery and together with Edward, Beth and Charles, climbed into a hired carriage to be driven up to Saint Mary's Church, Balmain. Less than a month before her twenty-second birthday, Susannah Maria Gordon, with Beth Barnes and Charles Metcalfe as witnesses, gave her troth to Edward Prior Barnes in a marriage ceremony conducted by the Reverend Henry Langley.

"Thank you, Heavenly Father, for Millicent and Fergus," she silently prayed as she knelt before the altar. "Thank you, too, for Millicent's husband, the Captain. He safely brought me here to become Edward's wife."

After a wedding supper in the hotel at Balmain, the newlyweds stayed overnight, where passions kindled in those private moments in Paddington subsided into shyness. Edward was more hesitant than Susannah had expected, given his original ardour and his impassioned letters during almost two years of separation. If she were eager, would he think her a wanton? She had longed to be his wife in every way. She sighed and snuggled against him, and they fell asleep. Suffice it to say, a shimmering summer dawn over Sydney Harbour awakened them to a romantic interlude.

The foursome set out that morning for Cootamundra. They travelled southwestward by train to Goulburn and thence westward by four-horse coach to their destination, a journey of almost 250 miles. Susannah's Broadwood pianoforte and trunk of books, recipes and music followed on the train and then on a hired hooded wagon.

The views from the train and coach, unlike anything Susannah had seen anywhere, amazed her. What a vast, raw land! Strange vegetation surrounded her and even stranger wildlife appeared across the miles and miles of sparsely inhabited landscape. Their progress disturbed wallabies, kangaroos and great flocks of chattering birds. "So many colourful birds!" Susannah exclaimed. "The small brilliant parrots are rainbow lorikeets," said Beth. "When I was a child in West Sydney, a flock of them lived on Ashfield Common. The noisy little green and yellow ones are budgerigars, and the grey cockatoos with the silly antics when they fly are rose-breasted galahs."

On the train and coach Edward held lengthy conversations with Charles Metcalfe about the development of Cootamundra. The two men seemed to be familiar with everyone in town and many people in the District. Had Susannah been aware that Cootamundra was a small settlement, scarcely eleven years old, she would not have been surprised at their knowledge. She talked with Beth, who identified members of the Barnes family for her and told her stories about them, including the circumstances of a debilitating accident suffered by Thomas, her eldest brother, and the tragic details of the murder of their father by a bushranger.

"Then is Cootamundra a dangerous place?" Susannah asked with concern. Beth reassured her. "Not as dangerous as some parts of London, I dare say! You've no worries, Susannah. Bushrangers were hunted down years ago, and Coota is a law-abiding town." Susannah had to take Beth's word for it. She was beginning to realize how ignorant she was of her destination.

When they eventually reached Cootamundra, the place was both more and less than Susannah had expected. The broad expanse of uninhabited town land astounded her; a shallow valley stretched for miles and miles beyond the townsite to low hills along the horizon. The town's unpaved main street, Beth told her, was wide enough to allow the turning of a wagon drawn by eight oxen. Unpaved cross streets were laid out, and a few houses appeared here and there. Edward had described the spaciousness of the place. Her first impression was one of immense emptiness.

The town of Cootamundra now consisted of six small frame buildings: the Barneses' Cootmundra Store on the main street, the Albion Hotel next door, Simpson's Store a short distance away, the Farmers' Arms with its pub and sleeping rooms, a police station and a blacksmith's shop. About 250 people lived in the town and surrounding District, which extended beyond the hills for twelve miles in every direction. Susannah was about to become a resident of a new country town on the western slopes of New South Wales.

Edward's brother, John, was at the Albion Hotel to meet their coach and take the four of them in his buggy to his home. A grand family celebration awaited them, and tired as Susannah was, she put a smile on her face, accepted the family's warm welcome, and became the centre of attention at a party.

They had arrived at the start of Christmas preparations and Susannah, whose yuletides in London had included many rehearsals of her church choir, asked her husband why they were not attending the local Church of England. "Cootamundra has no Church of England, nor church of any denomination," said Edward, who had told her to call him Ted, as his family did, "but a church is to be built. Bishop Mesac Thomas of Goulburn appointed me Bishop's Churchwarden on his last visitation and declared his intention of securing property rights for a church at Cootamundra when he visits again next year." Next *year?* wondered Susannah. "And I suppose you will volunteer my services as church organist?" she teased. Ted admitted he was going to mention her talents to the Bishop.

Ted took her to see the Cootamundra Store, and whilst Susannah stood on the verandah in the glare of the summer sun, he talked business with John Hanlow, his assistant. As she gazed across the dusty expanse of Parker Street, she realized that not only did Cootamundra have no church, but also no school, no bank, no paved streets, no newspaper and no public transportation. London, she mused, with its hundreds of thousands of inhabitants and all these things and more, was very far away in a much different world.

After a great round of Christmas parties with Ted's extended family, during which her accomplishments at the pianoforte were appropriately lauded, Susannah began to feel quite at ease with her Barnes relations. She had a friend in Beth Barnes, who, unfortunately, lived out at Murrumburrah, as did two other sisters-in-law, Isabella and Agnes, the wives of Thomas and George Barnes. A fourth sister-in-law, Jane, the wife of John Barnes, lived quite close. At Christmas gatherings Susannah met all Jane's friends, including Letitia Lynch, the wife of a grazier who had been on the *Commissary*.

Susannah could scarcely now have any thoughts of being lonely. Despite the friendships she was making, however, her mind often went back to the great city where she had spent all her life. She thought of the numerous entertainments in London: museums, art galleries, theatres and great churches, the parks and boating trips. Sometimes in private moments she was misty-eyed with longing. I must look forward, not backward, she reminded herself. My life is here with Ted, and all my pining for London will get me nowhere.

They were soon settled in Clapham Cottage, a house in Cooper Street built by John Barnes. It had a very generous dining room and a spacious kitchen at the back. The Cootamundra Store provided their necessities and furnishings and could order additional items for them from Sydney.

Susannah had not given any thought to the climate she would face at Cootamundra, which turned out to be vastly different from anything she had experienced in England. She had arrived in summer when the valley was searingly hot. Dust storms obscured the sun and relentless winds swirled dust over everything. Without a doubt, the flies were the worst, swarming and buzzing, attacking her kitchen incessantly. Mr. Jobson, the local builder, had installed screens on all the doors and windows and screened the verandahs to offer some protection. Susannah learned to tolerate the heat; she would never get used to the dust and flies.

She must stop fretting, she told herself. She should be grateful for so much in her life. She had many new friends, a lovely home with a peach tree in the garden, a flock of chickens and a kitchen garden to care for, and an affectionate, generous husband who had a large, friendly family. She had learned to harness up their mare,

Missy, and drive the buggy. Her sister-in-law Jane had shown her how to kill and clean her chickens (chooks, they were called) and had taught her, albeit with some difficulty, how to milk Clara, her black and white cow. Best of all, she was expecting a child.

"I've received a letter from the Bishop," announced Ted one evening whilst Susannah sat hemming nappies for her baby. "He expects to be at Coota in a fortnight on his annual visitation." Mesac Thomas, Lord Bishop of Goulburn, and his wife duly arrived. The Bishop, a commanding Englishman who managed a large colonial Diocese, ministered only once a year to his scattered flock on his annual visitations, holding services of Holy Communion wherever a location was offered to him. At Cootamundra in 1874, His Lordship celebrated the Eucharist at the Albion Hotel. The next day he travelled in his coach to the Lands Office at Gundagai to secure property rights for a church and vicarage to be built at the corner of Bourke and Thompson Streets at Cootamundra. He said he was about to appoint a Lay Reader to get a parish started.

"Because you're Bishop's Churchwarden," Susannah said to Ted, "I do believe we should invite the Bishop and his wife to dinner whilst they're here." Truth to tell, Susannah was rather keen to be a hostess again. The Bishop's wife proved to be a most gracious English lady, and His Lordship was an amusing gentleman, fond of telling stories about his adventures on visitations.

In the cooler autumn weather Susannah wrapped herself in a shawl and drove Missy to John and Jane's home once a week. There she sat before a fire, sewing for her expected baby and chatting with Jane and their mother-in-law, Elizabeth. Kindly, white-haired Elizabeth Barnes talked of her many years in the colony: her farm life at Yass, the flat above a shop at Concord, the success of their store in George Street at Sydney, her beloved home at Ashfield, the stores at Surry Hills and Melbourne, Thomas's accident and their move to Murrumburrah. Never did Elizabeth's conversations end without a tearful reference to her husband's murder at Wallendbeen. Susannah's heart was touched by her mother-in-law's stories and her continuing grief.

"It will be several years before we have a proper stone church on the site in Thompson Street," Ted remarked one evening whilst he sat smoking his pipe. If we ever have a church at all, Susannah said to herself. "When a Lay Reader is appointed," Ted went on, "we'll need a place of worship. I've found a property to purchase on a height of land beyond the reservoir, with enough level ground for a slab church and space for horses and wagons. As Bishop's Churchwarden at Cootamundra, I feel I should set an example by donating the land to the parish." Susannah did not enquire as to the sum her husband had spent on the property. She realized Ted was a generous man in all aspects of his life and had faith a parish would be established.

In July of 1874, Ted received a letter from the Bishop saying a Lay Reader had been appointed. He and his family would be arriving at Cootamundra in August. His Lordship added that he expected his Churchwarden to arrange accommodations for them.

The concept of a "slab church" intrigued Susannah, and she was curious to see what would be built on the hill beyond the reservoir.

Organ keys

TWENTY-ONE

North Goulburn

Delight thyself also in the Lord; and he shall give thee the desires of thine heart.

—PSALM 37:4

Moving to North Goulbourn, leaving behind her house at Tarago and her friend Hannah Andrews, had caused Rebecca Miller deep feelings of loss. She had created the family's first real home in her eight years at Tarago, had given birth to four children, and had buried one of them in Tarago Cemetery. Besides leaving her home, she felt she was abandoning her dearest friend, who was still trying to recover from the birth of her first child. She knew David Andrews would continue to hover over Hannah, making every effort to encourage her to health, and Megan Mary Mahoney would expertly tend to baby Robert Samuel and carefully prepare recipes to tempt Hannah's appetite. Rebecca had come to the painful realization that dearest Hannah, her vigorous and spirited friend, was now an invalid.

"Rebecca," said John one evening in July of 1874, "the Bishop will be calling on us this Sunday afternoon." The Right Reverend Mesac Thomas was usually accompanied by his wife on his visits to the Millers. Rebecca had come to enjoy her acquaintance with Mrs. Thomas, a refined English lady, much revered in the Diocese and an amiable guest at all times.

"How nice. How very nice," Mrs. Thomas invariably pronounced when baby Alick made himself at home around her skirts or in her lap whilst Mary Jane and Emily supervised the younger Miller children who romped in and out of the house. On those afternoons Rebecca wished for the strict presence of Megan Mary Mahoney and an acre of property for her growing family.

"The Bishop's wife won't be with him this time," said John. "His Lordship wants to speak to both of us on a church matter." Rebecca frowned. "What in Heaven's name does he have in mind that might concern me?" she asked. "A piece of your scripture cake would appeal to him, I think. You know how much he likes something sweet." Rebecca suspected John was aware of the Bishop's intentions, even though he feigned ignorance.

For almost a year the Millers had lived at North Goulburn, where on August 18th, 1873, their fourth son, Alexander Archibald, had been born. Named for two of Rebecca's brothers and known as Alick, he had recently learned to walk and was developing into a tall, sturdy child with curly dark hair and an adventuresome spirit. Rebecca had only Compton and Alick to care for each day because J.J., Willie, Margaret, Sarah and Jessie went off to school with their father whilst Mary Jane and Emily attended the grammar school. When they were all at home, the place was more crowded and chaotic than Rebecca would have liked. She often thought of Grennin in Tyrone, just a small stone cottage with a sleeping loft for the children under the thatch, but on a farm that had kept them busy and given them room to romp and grow.

John Miller taught at North Goulburn School and on Sundays served at the Cathedral Church of Saint Saviour. On Saturdays he was often busy with church duties, too, for the Bishop made use of John's talents in visiting and counselling parishioners.

Goulburn, located on a large, inland agricultural plain, was a county seat with a population of several thousand. It had a Cathedral Church, a Court of Assizes and a three-storey gaol, bustling markets and a rail connection to Sydney, 128 miles to the northeast. Goulburn also boasted a hospital, two newspapers, five banks and ten insurance companies. For the first time in her life, Rebecca was living on the outskirts of a city and she found the adjustment difficult. She had always appreciated country life with space around her and felt uncomfortable in the confines of a house in a street. John shared her love of the outdoors, but he was accustomed to cities, and his busy life as a schoolmaster and Lay Reader gave him little time to be concerned about where he lived.

Bishop Thomas arrived on the appointed Sunday afternoon, enjoyed three pieces of scripture cake and drank three cups of tea. Rebecca waited for him to reveal the purpose of his visit. "I have recently returned from a tour of the western slopes," said the Bishop, as he eyed the remainder of the cake. "Selectors are finding the land suitable for grazing and growing grain, and settlements are springing up to provide them with necessities. Spiritual care is my concern in these new places, and to that end I have been able to secure rights to a property for a church and vicarage at Cootamundra. As sole trustee of the church property, I must now find the right man to serve the parish and build the church." Rebecca looked at her husband. His eyes were shining.

"I propose that you consider the Cootamundra appointment, John," said the Bishop. "You would have to give up your teaching, for one cannot be employed by both church and state, but the stipend promised by your future parishioners will, I believe, equal your present teaching salary. My dear Rebecca, I know you want to live on a farm once more, and land is to be found in abundance around Cootamundra. Please consider my proposal, John, and let me know of your decision next Sunday."

John had come a long way from his Calvinist baptism, thought Rebecca. Dear God, she prayed, whilst her husband sat smiling and stroking his chinwhiskers, please help me find the courage to support John's enthusiasm for this new ministry.

"My lord, where would Cootamundra be?" she asked.

"One hundred twenty miles west of here and a little to the north. It's in a broad, shallow valley between Yass and Wagga Wagga. The low surrounding hills are quite lovely and available for selection."

"What is the town like?"

"Cootamundra has two hotels, two stores, a blacksmith's shop and a police station. The last Cootamundra District census listed a population of two hundred thirty-seven, but that was three years ago. The people who declared themselves adherents of the Church of England numbered one hundred ten at the time of the census, a good congregation for a start. Within the District are settlements which will be part of the parish: Wallendbeen, Binalong, Ironbong, Murrumburrah, Bethungra. They are not any great distance from Cootamundra."

Interesting names, thought Rebecca. They sounded aboriginal. She wondered what His Lordship regarded as "not any great distance." John was listening in fascination to the Bishop.

"You've made no mention of a school, my lord," said Rebecca.

"It will only be a matter of time before one is established. The two brothers who own the Albion Hotel and Cootamundra Store, John and Edward Barnes, assured me a committee would be formed to make application to the colonial Council of Education. The town is growing so rapidly, a schoolroom will be a necessity."

Forming a committee to apply to the Council of Education for a school was a far cry from having one. If John accepted the Bishop's offer and they moved to Cootamundra, their children's schooling would come to an end.

"We have a large family," she said to the Bishop, "and living quarters would have to be found until we select a property and build our home. Accommodation must be scarce in a new area."

"You are not to be concerned, Rebecca. John Barnes is making a boxbark hut available to you, rent-free for a year, on a large property on Jindalee Flat."

My, my, my! A free boxbark hut to accommodate two adults and nine children with another one on the way! The large property, however, sounded like a promising place for her bairns.

In the midst of Rebecca's conversation with the Bishop, Sarah and Jessie came running to her in tears, and Mary Jane and Emily announced their little sisters were not doing as they were told. Willie and J.J. chose this time to launch into a shouting match on the verandah.

"Whisht! Whisht! Such a carry-on!" said their mother. She shooed them all into the yard and made another pot of tea for the

Bishop. He helped himself to one more piece of scripture cake, drank the fresh cup of tea, and took his leave.

John said nothing after the Bishop had gone and the children had calmed down, but Rebecca knew where his mind was. That night, when the children were tucked into bed, John said to her, "I'm sure David Andrews could find us three more horses."

"What do we need with three more horses?"

"A journey of one hundred twenty miles with a full load will require a four-horse team. The route is macadamised most of the way, but I've heard that the last part, from Coolac onward, is a bush track. The horsepower will be needed there. And you'll require transport at Cootamundra whilst I'm away riding Kate on parish duties. When we select our property, we'll have horses ready to work it. I'll let David Andrews know of our needs."

"You've set your mind on this appointment then."

"There's naught else I'd rather do with the rest of my life, my dear. I'm fifty years of age and I've been given the opportunity to establish a parish and build a church. And think of the property you could select! In no time J.J. will be old enough to run a farm with you, and Mary Jane and Emily are already a great help with the little ones. We shall have a large homestead, Rebecca, on acres of land!"

"And how would our children be schooled?"

"I'll teach them until a school is built at Cootamundra. We'll be pioneers on the western slopes of the colony, founders of a church and selectors of a grand property!" He reached for her hand. "Please join me with a willing heart in this great adventure."

Rebecca and her heart had no choice but to be willing. She admired John's courage in facing such a challenge, and the possibility of owning property again was enticing. Nevertheless, she viewed the coming year with some trepidation. Indeed, the prospect of travelling 120 miles to make a home for nine children in a boxbark hut whilst expecting another baby was causing her considerable concern. She needed God's support now more than she ever had.

"You know I'll go willingly with you to Cootamundra, John. When will we be leaving?"

Her husband rose from his chair and leaned over to kiss her on the forehead. "The Bishop would like us there within six weeks."

On their departure the previous year from Tarago, David Andrews had loaned them a handsome gelding to harness up with Kate for the journey to the city. The new horses required for their journey westward needed to be broken to saddle as well as to harness, and David promised the Millers he would find them. He also had harnesses made to hitch four horses to the Miller cart. He located a mare and two geldings to serve their purposes, each one an offspring of Callan and accustomed to being saddled as well as harnessed with other horses. The team's appearance varied from grey to chestnut to bay to black, but all had their sire's conformation. Ruth, Aram and Sol joined Kate in harness. The names of their new horses, Rebecca noted, were straight from the first chapter of Saint Matthew's Gospel.

Before setting out for Cootamundra, the Millers had one last Sunday dinner in Cartmel homestead at Tarago. Saying goodbye to Hannah, David and Megan was the most difficult farewell of Rebecca's life, even worse than leaving her family at Grennin when she was a girl. "Write to me, Rebecca, and tell me about your adventures! Dear, dear Rebecca! Whatever am I going to do without you?" Hannah had risen from her pushchair and stood clinging to her friend of fully twenty years.

Rebecca was unable to answer. She had resolved not to cry, but she put her arms around Hannah and wept. She knew in her heart, as she suspected Hannah did, that they were saying a final farewell. Through her tears she told Hannah she would write to her from the western slopes. Rebecca gave David Andrews a long embrace and then hugged Megan Mary Mahoney, overwhelmed by the warm feelings she had for each of them. David's fair, wavy hair and flowing moustache of days on the *Caroline* had faded to white, and he had a sad, lost look about him as he said goodbye to Rebecca and John and the children. Megan, weeping copiously, held each of the

Miller children close to her. She thanked Rebecca and John many times for their kindnesses to her and promised she would take care of Hannah.

Wattles and eucalypts

TWENTY-TWO

Cootamundra

*Nevertheless, I am continually with thee;
thou hast holden me by my right hand.*

— PSALM 73:23

On a clear, cool day in August 1874, in their hooded cart drawn by four horses, the Millers left North Goulburn for Cootamundra. The weather had been mild and wet, and in the sunshine of an early spring day, the slopes leading west wore a mantle of glistening green. Once they were away from the city, Rebecca asked John to show her how to take up all the reins and discovered she could manage the well-trained horses quite nicely. J.J. and Willie got down to walk with their father and the team, although in truth the boys just wanted to lark along the roadside. Rebecca knew her sons' energies would fade over the distance.

They stopped frequently to rest the horses, stretch their own legs and relieve themselves, and each night they camped in fields where farmers said they could use the available water and graze the team. When they ran out of food towards the end of the trip, Rebecca purchased eggs, bread, fruit and milk from farmers' wives. Julia had been sold the previous year at Tarago, and the family had depended on Eunice and Lois, pastured at the back of their North Goulburn house, to supply the family with milk. On the day the Millers left North Goulburn, they sold the two cows to a neighbour.

On the lengthy journey, one that could stretch to a week, Rebecca's energy was understandably taxed. She relied on her husband to watch out for thirteen-year-old J.J. and eleven-year-old Willie and assigned Mary Jane and Emily the care of Margaret, Sarah, Jessie and Compton whilst she saw to one-year-old Alick. What Rebecca lacked in eagerness for the long trek, John made up for in enthusiasm. Around the campfire every night, he taught the children a new song or recitation, and at the midday break he insisted the older ones write impressions of the adventure in their journals.

As John had said, the road west of Goulburn was paved with a mixture of tar and gravel, and the going was steady. The macadam continued on through the towns of Yass and Jugiong, as far as the hamlet of Coolac. Here, twenty-five miles from Cootamundra, they rested overnight in a farmer's field. Early next morning John turned off the paved road and drove the cart onto a bush track which wandered between grassy slopes shaded by tall groves of eucalypts. The scent of the gumtrees filled the air, and their blue-grey growth wafted overhead whilst kangaroos and wallabies bounded ahead of the horses, and brilliantly coloured birds announced the family's progress along the winding route.

The bush track, which had first looked so interesting, turned out to be miles and miles of boggy ground. They had travelled but a short distance when the team began to plod through long stretches of mud. The cart reached a broad depression, deeply mired, and John, concerned that his horses could easily be trapped in the muddy hollow ahead, brought them to a halt. The cart with its occupants and belongings tipped precariously. "There's nothing for it but to unload," said John. "Even if the horses can get their footing, the cart will surely sink."

J.J. and Willie found leafy branches to set down so that their mother and the other children could get from the cart over to the grassy bank without wading through mud. Rebecca wrapped a shawl securely around little Alick and clambered down with him in her arms. Mary Jane and Emily helped the younger ones off the cart whilst John calmed the horses. J.J. and Willie began to unload boxes, and when the cart was lighter, John urged the team forward. The four horses leaned into their collars, struggled to find their footing in the bog, and strained to haul the cart onward to drier ground. Meanwhile, Rebecca and the children gathered up their belongings and trudged along the bank. They soon discovered the cause of the mire, a shallow creek that drained across the track. Making their way across the creek and continuing along the bank, they met up with John and the team, loaded up the cart, and climbed in.

We have a long way to go on this track, thought Rebecca, and hoped they had passed the worst of it. She was wrong. Several miles farther on they came to another depression and the horses, now wary, refused to continue. John considered the bog ahead of them and sent J.J. to find a long branch to test its depth. They would have to unload once more.

The noonday sun was filtering through the trees when another depression gave them no choice but to unload for a third time. Rebecca decided they would stop for a meal. J.J. and Willie got a fire going for a pot of tea whilst John put nosebags on the horses. From a farmer's wife at Coolac, Rebecca had purchased fresh bread and butter, two roasted chooks and some fruit. Fatigued though she was, she set out blankets on the grassy hillside and organized a picnic meal.

"What a great adventure!" exclaimed a mud-splattered J.J. "We have the pioneering spirit! We're a happy band of pilgrims on our way to a new home in a new land!" John smiled at their eldest son whilst Rebecca gave him a strange look. She hoped to Heaven they would not have to unload a fourth time.

Mercifully, the track became drier as they neared Cootamundra. Four mud-caked, tired horses moved steadily along the track, which opened up in front of them as the low afternoon sun spread through the bush. John drove and Rebecca sat beside him, almost dozing. She had put Alick to sleep in his cradle in the cart, where Margaret, Sarah, Jessie and Compton were curled up asleep on blankets. Mary Jane, Emily, J.J. and Willie sat on the benches along each side, gently teasing each other, mindful of their mother's warning not to waken the little ones. The horses, seeming to know their destination was near, moved more quickly.

In the afternoon sun the muddy route had become a track of reddish brown dust which effectively camouflaged a large, coiled snake lying in their path. The horses pounded onward, oblivious to what lay ahead. The snake came uncoiled in an instant, spiralled into the air and flung itself at the horses. It hurtled towards Kate and flailed through the legs of the horses behind her. All four horses screamed and shied violently. Frenzied by the monster attacking them, they shrieked and bolted.

John clutched in desperation at the reins, trying to control his team plunging in terror down the track. Rebecca, six months along with child, clung to the rail of the cart, petrified she would be thrown to the ground. The children cried and screamed and their father ordered them to lie down. The jouncing and lurching left Rebecca convinced she was going to lose her unborn child. John stood straining at the reins for what seemed like miles until he managed to ease his frantic horses to a halt.

"My dear Rebecca, are you all right?" he asked with concern. She did not tell him she was as terrified as the horses. She declared she was all right. Taking deep breaths, she silently prayed to God she would not miscarry. John climbed down to soothe the team and check their legs and harnesses. He called to J.J. to take the reins whilst he slowly led the lathered animals forward to cool them out.

As she moved into the cart to care for the children, Rebecca remembered a book about Australia she had read on the *Caroline*. Snakes had been described, yet in all these years she had never been bothered by any. She wondered if snakes were more common on the western slopes and shivered at the possibility.

The Miller cart emerged from the bush into a flat valley of tall kangaroo grass and occasional box eucalypts. A rain shower was sliding away over the distant slopes, leaving a sparkling spring evening. Clouds scudded across a canopy of sky so deeply blue Rebecca was momentarily transported back to the deck of the *Caroline* in Cape Town harbour. Splashes of yellow wattle, like gorse on the hills above Dromore, appeared across the hillsides, their honeyed scent drifting through the evening air. The winding track expanded into Cootamundra's wide, unpaved main street, marked by logs lying along the verges.

Rebecca marvelled at the vault of evening sky arching over this broad, shallow valley edged with low hills. Here she would have space around her indeed! Her children would grow to adulthood in this raw town on the western slopes of New South Wales. She smiled at the vista around her, so far and away from the narrow, cobbled streets of Dromore in County Tyrone.

Along the main street, Parker Street it was called, they came to two small wooden structures next to each other, the Barnes Store and the Albion Hotel. John pulled up in front of the hotel, which prompted a robust man with a substantial beard to step down from the verandah. "John Miller? I'm John Barnes. Welcome to Cootamundra! I can see you've had a muddy journey from Coolac!"

He seemed a jovial sort of gentleman, this man who was providing the boxbark hut. He told Rebecca that Jane, his wife, and Elizabeth, his mother, would be pleased to make her acquaintance. As the sun began to set over the western hills, John Barnes mounted his horse and led the Millers a short distance east of Cootamundra to Jindalee Flat. In a level pasture where milch cows had settled for the night, Rebecca got down from the cart with Alick in her arms and walked through the herd of cows to her new home. She entered an old boxbark hut of three rooms with dirt floors.

"Jane has cleaned the place and left you some bread, butter and eggs," said John Barnes. "I've set up some beds for you. Jane will call on you tomorrow to make your acquaintance and see what else you need. Take as much milk from my cows as you need. We'll speak at the hotel, John, whenever you're ready to get to work. And now I'll bid you goodnight." He mounted his horse and, tipping his broad-brimmed leather hat, rode off to his home.

"Where are we to sleep?" asked Willie. "There aren't enough beds!"

"Compton will share with you and J.J. in one of the beds in the larger bedroom," answered his father, "and Margaret, Sarah and Jessie will sleep in the other bed."

"We don't want girls in our room!" protested Willie.

"You'll do as you're told," said John. "Until we have our own homestead, we'll make use of this hut which Mr. Barnes has so generously provided. Your mother will see about a curtain to hang between you and your sisters. Now, come and help tend to the horses."

Rebecca settled Alick into his cradle beside the bed she and John would use in the smallest room as Mary Jane and Emily moaned about sharing a cot in the kitchen. She told her two daughters they were fortunate not to be sharing a narrow bed in a steerage compartment of a ship. It was almost midnight before she and the girls had made up the beds, fed everyone pieces of bread and butter, and tucked the little ones in. When Rebecca finally put her head on her pillow, she fell asleep praying she would not miscarry. She was too worn out to fret about an old three-room boxbark hut with dirt floors.

At daybreak Rebecca was up tending to the fire. Her mind went back to the day after her wedding, when she lit the first of many morning fires in the slab hut near Bowral. Instead of Megan Mary Mahoney, she had Mary Jane, Emily and J.J. eager to milk cows. John took Willie to fetch water from a dam on a nearby creek to make the porridge and a pot of tea. Rebecca meant to ask Jane Barnes if she might have some pullets to start a flock of chooks.

"When you've finished your breakfast, you're to work on a wood pile for your mother," John told J.J. and Willie. "There's plenty of wood lying around the pasture. Use the saw and hatchet on the larger pieces because the fireplace is small. I'll expect to see a goodly supply of fire logs stacked behind the hut and the horses groomed by the time I return."

John proceeded to brush Kate and saddle her up for his journey to town to talk to John Barnes at the Albion Hotel. As Rebecca watched him reach the road and urge Kate to a fast walk, she wondered where he had learned to ride so well. He had a sure seat on the mare, and she responded easily to him.

Rebecca gazed across dew-covered Jindalee Flat shimmering in the morning sunshine, where Aram, Sol and Ruth were cropping lush grasses amongst a herd of contented cows. The peaceful scene soothed her soul. She said a prayer of thanks to her Heavenly Father for her recovery after that terrifying experience in the cart. As she stood absorbed in her thoughts, along the road came a woman Rebecca took to be Jane Barnes. Walking with her was an older lady, her white hair neatly braided and coiled at her ears, and two boys, who immediately went looking for J.J. and Willie.

"Welcome to Cootamundra!" said the younger woman, extending her hand as she approached Rebecca. "I'm Jane Barnes and this is John's mother, Elizabeth. Those two lads of mine are Frederick and Johnny. We've come to see what you need." Jane Barnes seemed a friendly, outgoing woman, who looked younger than Rebecca and whose speech had a clipped lilt to it. Jane, in fact, was delighted at Rebecca's arrival. Her mother-in-law, Elizabeth, seemed quite reserved, less the result of her age, Rebecca thought, and more the product of her life experiences.

Rebecca located her tin of baking supplies, baked a quick batch of currant soda bread on the rack in the fireplace, and brewed a pot of tea for her guests. The three of them, wrapped in shawls, sat outside, soaking up the spring sunshine on the rickety platform that passed for a verandah. Rebecca admired Elizabeth's crocheting of a traditional cloverleaf doily.

By way of introduction Jane Barnes said, "I came out to the colony from Yorkshire with my parents when I was just a lass. I met John at Sydney, for we both lived in Pitt Street. Johnny Barnes he was called then, to distinguish him from his father. Elizabeth has been with us for ten years now, since John's father was murdered at Wallendbeen."

Murdered! Rebecca was dismayed and curious, but she felt this was not the time to ask what had happened to the senior John Barnes. During her visit Jane promised Rebecca a supply of vegetables, a dozen pullets, a dozen chooks and a rooster. She also identified local people who could be relied on for help when John was away on parish duties. "Jim Roberts for choice, I reckon. He lives along that way, not far. He rents hay fields from us and he's a helpful sort. And it would seem you'll need my accoucheuse, Mary Faunt. I'll ask her to call on you." Rebecca felt grateful for all the help Jane was offering.

After his first conversation with John and Edward Barnes, John came home full of enthusiasm. The Barnes brothers had assured him of large, appreciative congregations because Cootamundra District had no church of any denomination.

On the Sunday morning after their arrival, Rebecca and John put their children into the cart and drove to the Albion Hotel for John's first Cootamundra church service. The hotel dining table had been pushed aside, and the chairs had been arranged in rows. Rebecca and the children were given seats at the front, surrounded by worshippers who filled the remaining places, stood along the walls or sat on the dining table. Churchwarden Edward Barnes rose and introduced John Miller, Catechist for Cootamundra. Catechist was a new word to Rebecca.

In cassock and surplice her husband stood before the congregation and began the service of Morning Prayer: "The sacrifices of God are a broken spirit: a broken and a contrite heart, O God, thou wilt not despise. Dearly beloved brethren, the Scripture moveth us in sundry places to acknowledge and confess our manifold sins and wickedness . . ."

Although she had attended his church services at Tarago many times, Rebecca's heart swelled with pride when she heard him open the first worship service at Cootamundra. John and Edward Barnes read the Old and New Testament lessons, and the Catechist read the Gospel and the Bishop's homily he had brought with him, an exhortation to serve the Lord and raise funds for a fine stone church. The voices of the congregation, without any accompaniment, filled the small hotel with "O Worship the King," "Awake, My Soul," and "All People That on Earth Do Dwell." At the close of the service, John Barnes stood up.

"My fellow parishioners," he began in stentorian tones, "I am pleased to announce that plans have been completed for an impressive sandstone church on the designated site at the corner of Bourke and Thompson Streets. Meanwhile, we shall build a temporary slab church on the hill behind the reservoir. The help of the men of the parish will be required to construct it, and I know the ladies, God bless them, will provide the refinements. Mr. Miller will be visiting all of you to determine your commitments to the parish. My brother Edward, the Bishop's Churchwarden, has agreed to be Parish Treasurer. As you leave this morning, you may give him your first monetary contributions towards the stone church." A fine speech, thought Rebecca, if a bit heavy-handed. She intended to contribute her crochetwork to "the refinements" of the slab church on the hill.

As the members of the congregation left, they stopped to talk to Rebecca and her children. Jane Barnes introduced her sister-in-law, Susannah, the bride of Edward Barnes, who looked as if she were about to give birth at any moment. The young woman insisted Rebecca come to her home for tea on Wednesday afternoon. Before Rebecca and her family left the Albion Hotel, she had three more invitations to tea.

Early next morning John rode off on Kate to introduce himself to his far-flung parish. In his notebook was a list of future parishioners who, according to John and Edward Barnes, were eager to meet him, and so they proved to be. He came back eight days later. Trailing on a length of rope behind him was a half-grown, reddish-coloured dog, who lay down at the door of the hut and thumped his tail happily when the Miller children fawned over him and offered him a pan of water.

"I rode as far northeast as Wallendbeen, where I met Alexander and Annie Mackay at Rose Cottage. I took my noon dinner with them. Rose Cottage is a very hospitable home, and Annie Mackay told me to stop there for a meal at any time. The Mackays are Presbyterians, but they're keen to support my ministry. I also met Mr. Irwin Smith and his family. They offered me their house for a monthly church service at Wallendbeen.

"In the afternoon I rode eastward from Wallendbeen to Murrumburrah and met the Allsopps. They'll let me use their hotel for an evening service there once a month. I also visited the Barnes families. Miss Beth Barnes is John and Edward's sister. Their brother, George, and his wife, Agnes, have a Chinese cook, Chung Yip, the first Celestial I've ever spoken with. He insisted on serving me much more food than was good for me. The Thomas Barnes family is also nearby, and Thomas, who gets around easily despite a severely damaged leg, runs the T. & G. Barnes Store and Post Office at Murrumburrah with George. I spent the night with Thomas and Isabella Barnes and headed to Binalong next morning.

"There's naught but a narrow track southeastward from Murrumburrah to Binalong, and it took me until the afternoon to get there. I located Mr. Robert Hudson, who welcomed me warmly and showed me the police barracks. That's to be the place for a morning service at Binalong each month. Farther on at the settlement of Illalong, I stopped with J.S. Futter's family. Mrs. Futter's hospitality made me feel quite at home, and I'm to stop there when I'm in the area.

"The rest of the circuit took me to scattered farms along the slopes, and I went to each one to introduce myself. Then I came to a boxbark hut not on my list. I found an old squatter lying there, close to death. He was alone, poor soul, and I spent the better part of a day and night sitting with him. He was an Irishman, an emancipated convict who had been baptised a Roman Catholic. He seemed to appreciate my ministrations. When he was approaching his hour of death, he asked me to turn his cattle loose and take care of his dog. Whilst I was reading the Commendatory Prayer over him, he quietly left to join his Maker. Next morning I set his cattle free from a paddock and put his body over Kate's back. I rode over to Gundagai to see to his death certificate and his burial. This is his dog, Rusty."

Rebecca fetched a marrow bone for Rusty. What would have become of the man and his dog if John hadn't visited them? Her exhausted husband had fallen into bed, all the while concerned because he had not called on everyone on his list. She realized her husband had wanted to meet all the parishioners, but surely the time he had spent in a boxbark hut with a dying man was an equally acceptable service to the Lord.

TWENTY-THREE
Jindalee Flat

But the salvation of the righteous is of the Lord;
he is their strength in the time of trouble.
— PSALM 37:39

John had told Rebecca he would teach the children until a school was established at Cootamundra. His parish visitations, however, left him no time, and Rebecca could not find it in her heart to fault him. During his brief times at home, he assigned memory work from his collection of books to Mary Jane, Emily, J.J. and Willie as well as passages for reading and summarizing. He outlined assignments in reading, spelling, writing and arithmetic for Margaret, Sarah and Jessie and relied on Mary Jane and Emily to teach them. When John could free himself from parish duties, he heard the older children's recitations, discussed their assigned readings and checked on the progress of the younger ones.

And when she had time, Rebecca caught up on her correspondence.

Jindalee Flat, Near Cootamundra
Harden County
October 27th, 1874

My Dearest Hannah,
I am remiss in not sending another letter after my note to you when we first arrived. Setting up our temporary home here in a hut has taken every moment of my time, at least that's my excuse. Today, Mary Jane and Emily, bless their hearts, take over my chores whilst I write to you.
Jindalee Flat with its graceful eucalypts and wattles is really quite lovely. There is ample space for the children to play and interesting places for them to explore. I must remind myself of these advantages

when they crowd into our three-room hut every evening. After the baby is born, I am resolved that we will select a property and build a large homestead. Dreams of such a place revive my spirits during unbearable times in the hut.

John's parish schedule has been established. He reads Morning Prayer and Evensong every Sunday, whether at Cootamundra and a nearby settlement such as Wallendbeen, or at greater distances. The services are conducted wherever a location is offered, and he is in cassock and surplice at hotels, homesteads, a police barracks, a Court House, a railway contractor's dining tent and boxbark huts. His church services are the first in the District and they attract parishioners of all faiths. Presbyterians, Primitive Methodists, Wesleyans and even papists make themselves at home amongst his Church of England congregations. John never questions their denominations, just tries as best he can to meet their spiritual needs.

Summer is approaching the Cootamundra hills and turning them yellow under a great vault of deep blue sky. I find the dry heat of Harden County more intense than we were used to near the mountains and lakes of Argyle County. The winds blow steadily across the valley and dust rises up in clouds, sweeps along roads into paddocks and across the surrounding slopes. Our hut is in the midst of a cow pasture, and flies are the greatest annoyance of all. Wherever our homestead is to be built, it will be well and truly screened, I can tell you!

I miss you, dearest Hannah, and treasure your correspondence. Please don't apologize for the brevity of your letters. You need to regain your strength.

I send my best regards to you and David and Megan. Do give Robert Samuel a great hug for me. You are all in my prayers every day.

As ever, I am your loving friend,

Rebecca

Although prayerfully grateful she was still carrying a child, Rebecca knew her condition was adding to her general discomfort and robbing her of energy for her chores. John came home from his parish visits parched and exhausted, his clothes thick with sweat and dirt, and Rebecca struggled to wash his linen and send him out clean on the next visitations. Had it not been for a dam, the Millers' supply of water would have been a slight trickle in a disappearing creek.

Trees on the Flat offered some shade, but entering the boxbark hut was like facing a hot oven, and Rebecca took to living outdoors with her family and cooking over a campfire. At night J.J. and Willie took blankets and went to join Rusty and the horses in the pasture whilst the rest of the family slept on the verandah. The familiar pains began mid-afternoon on Sunday, the 15th of November, 1874, and after tea time Rebecca sent J.J. and Willie in the cart to Cootamundra to fetch Mary Faunt, the accoucheuse.

Rebecca felt she could scarcely be delivered of her baby out in the pasture in front of their hut and reluctantly went indoors later in the evening. Whilst Mary Jane and Emily took charge of the family, Mary Faunt delivered Rebecca of a fifth son in the steaming heat of the boxbark hut shortly before midnight. He looked like J.J. as a baby and was just as vigorous. The baby's father would have to wait until the following weekend to meet and name his latest offspring, for John had left early that morning on a six-day visitation to the southwest to conduct church services and call on parishioners around Bethungra.

"A fine baby, indeed! Thank you, my dear," he said on his arrival home. "I apologize for not being here to give you my support. We'll call him Edward Lanfear Miller." The newly named Edward sighed happily in the cradle vacated by Alick, and Rebecca once more gave thanks to God for a healthy infant. "I've always liked the name Edward," she said to John, "but how did you come by Lanfear?"

"Edward Lanfear Miller is the name of another cousin in Hampshire. My Uncle Richard Miller married Harriet Lanfear, and in my boyhood I was acquainted with Aunt Harriet's distinguished family." Rebecca smiled at him. The name Compton South had come from these relatives and now Edward Lanfear.

Up behind the reservoir, the Parish Committee, headed by John Barnes, was making progress. A temporary slab church with a covered porch, rooftop crosses at the front and back, and space for a window on each side was rising on the hilltop property. Once the shell of the building had been completed, an opening celebration was in order.

Most of the village of Cootamundra came to the party, and selectors arrived from miles around, a tribute, Rebecca felt, to the popularity of her husband. Whilst the women set out a potluck feast, the men played cricket and the children frolicked across the pasture. After the meal everyone was keen to take part in Twos and Threes, which was organized by the Barnes family and guaranteed to encourage new friendships. It was scarcely an appropriate church activity, thought Rebecca, but she reckoned the next game, Kiss in the Ring, was even less appropriate. The participants did not share her concerns.

At sunset candles held in place by nails on wooden brackets around the walls lit the small church building, and an overflow audience crowded in. The benches were packed; boxes and blocks of wood served as more seating. Someone had located a harmonium for the accompanist, Susannah, the young wife of Edward Barnes. She proved to be a skilled musician, who could play by ear many of the tunes and read with ease any pieces presented to her. Thirteen-year-old J.J., always helpful, offered to stand beside her to turn the sheet music pages.

Mary Jane, Emily, J.J. and Willie had been practising for days, and their rousing opening song, "Tramp! Tramp! Tramp! The Boys Are Marching," to the vigorous accompaniment of Susannah Barnes on the harmonium, earned sustained applause. Next, eleven-year-old Willie stood alone to recite "Little Jim, the Collier Child," a poem of fifteen stanzas so heartbreaking that many of his listeners were in tears. Mr. Jim Roberts, a farmer in the prime of life, then regaled the audience with "Shem, Ham and Japheth—Now Who was Japheth's Father?" Rebecca had doubts about Jim's interpretation of the story of Noah and his family, but his performance was so well received, he was obliged to produce an encore. Other songs and recitations followed, all much appreciated by the audience.

Speeches followed, the first a humorous commentary by John on his work, a speech that sustained the mood of the evening. Other men got up to toast the success of the parish, including Mr. Robert Cartwright, a selector on Salt Clay Creek, who urged the congregation to support the Parson's stipend. "Mr. Miller and his family cannot live on hare!" He pronounced it "air." Rebecca had already cooked countless hare—rabbit, actually—so numerous were they on Jindalee Flat. The celebration came to an end with the singing of the Doxology and "God Save the Queen." It was to be the first of many such gatherings at Cootamundra in which Rebecca and her family took part.

On Christmas morning in 1874, the family attended the Nativity service in the slab church on the hill and in the afternoon sought the shade of trees on the Flat, where they had a picnic. Rebecca, Mary Jane and Emily took turns crocheting and reading aloud *Sense and Sensibility* by Jane Austen, which had been John's Christmas gift to Rebecca, whilst J.J., Willie and John devised games for the little ones. Baby Edward, oblivious to the happy sounds around him, slept contentedly on a blanket.

Until the Watch Night service on New Year's Eve, John was free from parish duties and took Rebecca and the children in the cart each day to look at properties. On his visitations around the parish, John had learned of several likely locations available for selection and used his brief respite from clerical responsibilities to show them to his family. One warm day he took them southwest beyond a creek and turned the horses up onto a track that wrapped around a rolling, grassy plateau. On the heights were large groves of eucalypts with small pools of water at their roots and at the far reaches of the property, sweeping vistas of the valley. Rebecca felt she was on top of the world.

"We could place our homestead here on this level part overlooking that pond," said John, his eyes shining. "If the pond were enlarged, it would be a reservoir for our livestock. The creek is down there, convenient for our drinking water. We would need to plant shade trees around the homestead, kurrajongs and eucalypts perhaps, because it's a very open location. The boys and I could start by building a slab house for us in that grove of trees."

Rebecca's eyes shone like John's, for in her imagination she saw a spacious house and a farm of her own with acres of crops and grazing lands stretching across this rolling countryside. Instinctively, she reached down for a handful of soil and let it run through her fingers. It was sandier than the soil of Berrima District and more suited to grain than root crops, but it had a good feel to it. She thought rye grass would do well here.

The children were romping across the grasslands playing catch-as-catch-can, except for J.J. and Willie, who had disturbed a mob of kangaroos resting in a grove of willows down by the creek. The shy animals, bigger specimens than the family had ever seen, easily escaped across the slopes. Mammoth tails balanced long leaps as the powerful back legs of the creatures scored the grasslands and sent up clouds of dust. The two boys whooped and hollered through the dusty wake and exhausted themselves in a futile attempt to keep up with the 'roos.

John and Rebecca put a deposit on the property and began planning the development of the property they called Littledale station.

On a January day in 1875, when Rebecca was struggling to get butter churned despite not having a cool dairy, J.J. complained to her of a fever and sore throat. She took a good look at her eldest son and saw that he not only had a fever and raw throat, but also a mouth covered in pink spots. She examined twelve-year-old Willie, who, not wanting to give up his daily horseback riding, was keeping quiet about the same symptoms. Rebecca recognized measles and knew that ahead of her lay weeks of nursing one child after another in a sweltering hut. She wondered at the disease finding its way to this isolated location, but travellers were numerous along the Flat. A gregarious and helpful boy, J.J. roamed on horseback each day with Willie keeping him company. No telling who might have given them the contagious illness.

The less said the better about Rebecca's miserable days and nights of nursing all those children. John was away much of that time, helpful during his brief sojourns at home, then on his way again to tend to another part of his extensive parish. Through it all, Rebecca was grateful that baby Edward was spared the measles.

It was during this time she made a friend for life in Jim Roberts. The good-natured Jim of "Shem, Ham and Japheth" fame at the opening of the slab church came to Rebecca's rescue. On Rebecca's first day on Jindalee Flat, Jane Barnes had spoken of Jim Roberts, who might be of assistance when John was away on parish duties. Rebecca thanked God for Jim, who showed up as soon as J.J. and Willie took ill, for he had wondered why they hadn't called on him as usual. Jim discovered the family had very little water because the boys were too sick to haul it from the dam. He fetched a goodly supply for Rebecca and came every day to do so. Jim, a bachelor capable of caring for himself, caused her great consternation one day when he lit a fire under the copper boiler in the yard, washed linen and clothes for her, and hung them to dry.

"That's women's work!" remonstrated Rebecca. "And you're a woman with enough work already!" Jim retorted. "You care for those bairns and let a handy bloke like me do the rest." He was an energetic man, Jim Roberts, and on the worst days he not only fetched water, but also chopped wood, milked cows, churned butter, cooked food for the family over a campfire and took baby Edward in his arms for walks along the Flat. Meanwhile, Rebecca continued to nurse her feverish, rash-covered children.

"A friend in time of need is a friend indeed," said Rebecca. Jim tipped his leather hat to her and said he would be back the next day.

Elizabeth Barnes called regularly with soups and fresh bread and stayed to comfort fretful youngsters. "Being out in the sun with measles can affect your eyes," she cautioned the children. "You should always be in a shady spot." The older ones understood to stay out of the sunlight, but as soon as the younger children began to feel better, supervising them became difficult. Jim Roberts came to the rescue and herded the bairns under the trees to regale them with stories of bushrangers, Chinese miners, kangaroo hunts and New Year's Day horse races.

The Miller child most seriously afflicted with the measles was young Alick, eighteen months of age, who suffered severely with the fever. Rebecca kept sponging him and feeding him the barley water and soups Elizabeth Barnes provided, but the child cried constantly and rubbed his ears. When his eardrums broke one night and blood and pus poured out, Rebecca realized the worst of his torment was over. She correctly reckoned the disease had damaged his hearing for the rest of his life.

The measles, Rebecca was not surprised to learn, had been brought to Cootamundra District by a family travelling through who had been accompanied along the way by J.J. and Willie. Weeks later, when her children's fevers had gone and their rashes were subsiding, Rebecca gave thanks to her Heavenly Father for the survival of all her bairns. Not every family had been as fortunate, and John Miller conducted the burials of several Cootamundra children.

John apologized many times for not being of more help to her, but as he explained, it was crucial for him to be out in the parish at the start of the campaign to build Christ Church. He needed to visit many outlying properties and settlements to impress parishioners with their Catechist's competence before they could be expected to contribute funds to a central church. Rebecca told John she understood.

At tea one evening J.J. announced, "I know what happened to Frederick's grandfather, John Barnes, Senior. Frederick told me he was murdered!" Rebecca knew the man had been murdered, but she had never taken it upon herself to question Jane or Elizabeth about the circumstances. "Frederick says his grandfather was riding from the Barnes store at Murrumburrah to the one at Cootamundra when he was bailed up by bushrangers at Wallendbeen. He had a new saddle and bridle and a good mare and he wouldn't let the bandits have them. He made a dash for the grounds of Rose Cottage, but the gate was fastened shut. Johnnie O'Meally, one of Ben Hall's gang, took after him and shot him in the back."

"Merciful Heaven! How horrible!" Rebecca's husband and sons rode along that very same road, but bushrangers, she reminded herself, were merely figures of the past, only the stuff of legends. She knew the gangs had been hunted down and Ben Hall had been killed in a police ambush. Indeed, teams of mounted policemen now patrolled Cootamundra District. "Surely the police caught this Johnnie O'Meally!" she said.

"That's the best part! He got away, but almost three months later, the gang raided Goimbla, the Campbells' station. Johnnie O'Meally tried to rob the homestead, and Mrs. Campbell shot him dead on her verandah. Frederick's Aunt Isabella was standing right there when it happened!"

J.J. told the story with all the relish of a fourteen-year-old, and the other Miller children listened wide-eyed to him. Rebecca could only imagine the grief Elizabeth Barnes and her family had experienced at the tragic death of John Barnes. Rebecca considered herself a pioneer in Cootamundra District, but Elizabeth Barnes had been a true pioneer. She had come with her family to the western slopes to establish a home and business and had lost her husband to a murderous bushranger. Rebecca had a new respect for the quiet white-haired woman who had helped her care for the children during the measles.

Jim Roberts continued to come by often, usually for evening tea and a chat. After the meal had been cleared away, he and Rebecca took a pitcher of lemonade and a blanket out under the trees and sat talking of farming, about Rebecca's days at Grennin in Tyrone and Jim's experiences on farms in the colony before he settled at Cootamundra.

"When I was just a lad, I first worked near Camden for a homesteader by the name of Garvey, the most taciturn Irishman I've ever met. He'd go all day without saying a word, and if you asked him something, his answer was never two words where one would do. He would have seemed inhuman but for his softness towards his wife and bairns. He doted on his wife, Rachel, a pretty Irish lass with the clearest grey eyes, many years younger than her husband and the mother of two of his seven children. When I fell ill with pleurisy, she gave me the best of care and saw me right again."

Such a good companion this man is, thought Rebecca, as she sat in the shade with the stalwart farmer through long evenings. They talked the same language, she and Jim, shared the same background, understood each other. Rebecca looked forward to those evenings when Jim came riding along the Flat.

Towards the end of March, Mary Jane and Emily suddenly felt nauseous and feverish, as did Rebecca, who reckoned it must have been something the three of them had eaten. The boxbark hut and its surroundings were difficult to keep clean, and every day she had to combat masses of flies swarming from cow pats in the pasture to the food she prepared. John was home at the time, for which she was grateful.

During the night she and the two girls became feverish, had severe stomach cramps and vomited violently. Their symptoms continued, and the accompanying diarrhoea was a misery. As Rebecca suckled Edward, she worried her ailment would be passed to him. At four and a half months of age, the baby was dependent on the breast, and his nourishment concerned her. She roused herself enough to prepare barley water and chicken broth for him, but he would take nothing but his mother's milk.

Within hours Edward was screaming in agony and pulling up his legs with cramps. His stools became watery, sending Rebecca into a panic. She was a woman who faced any crisis calmly, but her baby's incessant vomiting and sodden nappies frightened her. In a weak state herself, she kept sponging Edward and attempting to get some fluid into his tortured little body. Despite his mother's twenty-four-hour care, the baby was becoming listless, and Rebecca feared the worst.

She and John suddenly realized Edward had not been baptised. They found The Ministration of the Private Baptism of Children in *The Book of Common Prayer*. Baptism by a layman could take place in extreme circumstances. The Miller children gathered around their parents and the baby. John poured a little water on his infant son's head and said, "Edward Lanfear, I baptise thee in the Name of the Father, and of the Son, and of the Holy Ghost. Amen. We receive this Child into the congregation of Christ's flock, and do sign him with the sign of the Cross . . ." John made the sign on Edward's forehead, but he could not continue the prayer because he was in tears. The infant lay lifeless in his arms. On the fourth day of his illness, the first of April, 1875, baby Edward Lanfear Miller departed from this world.

Next day, with J.J. and Willie signing as witnesses, John completed the baby's death certificate and put the tiny corpse into a little casket made by Robert Cartwright, who acted as the town's undertaker. Accompanied by J.J. and Willie, John drove a mile or so west of Cootamundra to the topmost part of the new cemetery. Robert Cartwright dug a small grave, and as John Miller had done for his baby daughter Eliza at Tarago, he read the service of The Burial of the Dead for his infant son Edward.

Rebecca remained in the hut on Jindalee Flat with the other children, too sick herself and too prostrate with grief to see her baby buried. She cried into her pillow until it was soaked and prayed endlessly for God's forgiveness. When baby Eliza had died of whooping cough at Tarago, she felt she had done all she could to nurse her. Edward's death was different because Rebecca truly believed she had caused it. Her vomiting and diarrhoea had been passed to him, and his small body had been unable to prevail. She was consumed by guilt and despair.

One late autumn afternoon J.J. came back from Cootamundra Post Office with a black-edged envelope postmarked "Tarago," addressed in the firm, round hand of Megan Mary Mahoney. It was the first time Megan had corresponded with the Millers at Jindalee. Rebecca sat in her rocking chair and read Megan's brief note. She had written to say Hannah had become much weaker and one afternoon had slipped away in her sleep to join her Maker. She had always had a bad heart, said the attending doctor, who certified dropsy as the cause of death. The rest of Megan's message was filled with expressions of anguish so heart-rending, Rebecca fervently wished she could be at Cartmel to ease the young woman's grief.

Dearest Hannah had been taken to her Heavenly Rest. Her dear, dear friend, so cheerful, so full of fun, insisting John join them at their picnics by the Wingecarribee River, pestering her for details of "another romantic afternoon at the vicarage," weeping in a potato field when David Andrews left for Tarago. Poor David! He must be devastated. She would write to him at once and to Megan.

Coming as it did after baby Edward's death, the news of Hannah's passing left Rebecca more desolate than ever, and she wept many times each day, not knowing why she was crying. No matter what John and the children did for her, they could not raise her spirits. Morning and night she prayed to her Heavenly Father for His solace, read her Bible to find verses of comfort, and kept busy, hoping to drive away her enduring grief.

Susannah Barnes, on learning of the death of baby Edward, immediately showed up at the hut. Cheerful soul that she was, Susannah proved to be a great consolation. She and baby Nellie made weekly visits to Jindalee Flat, and Rebecca began to look forward to chatting about fundraising for the church and her plans for farming on Littledale station.

With winter approaching, the building of a slab house on Littledale became a priority for John Miller. His nine children and his wife in her grief-stricken state could not be expected to stay in a boxbark hut much longer. He began taking J.J. and Willie up to the property and putting them to work sawing slabs. John Barnes, who had apprenticed as a cabinetmaker, came to help, and the two men and the boys built three bedrooms and a kitchen sitting room with a fireplace. The slab house, located at the rear of an area reserved for a kitchen garden, was a sturdily constructed dwelling with wooden floors and a verandah. From his early experiences on farms in the colony, John Miller knew to search for the stringybark eucalyptus for building because the wood resisted attacks by white ants, ravagers of many wooden structures.

Rebecca spent that winter slowly recovering and gathering her strength. She hemmed sheets, stitched pillow slips and made other items for the new house, keeping herself busy and her mind occupied. She took time to call on Jim Roberts and Jane and Elizabeth Barnes to thank them for their generous friendship and present them with gifts: a knitted jumper for Jim and lace collars and cuffs for Jane and Elizabeth. She told them how much their companionship and help meant to her.

On the August day when the family left the boxbark hut, Susannah Barnes came to help with the clearing out. The older children lifted boxes into the cart, and the Millers set off to move six miles southwest of Cootamundra to their new home on Littledale station.

Slab church, 1875

TWENTY-FOUR

Christ Church

*Lo, children are an heritage of the Lord; and the
fruit of the womb is his reward.*

—PSALM 127:3

At the conclusion of that first Cootamundra church service in the Albion Hotel in August of 1874, Susannah Barnes had introduced herself to Rebecca Miller and invited her to tea. Susannah, a Londoner, and Rebecca, fifteen years older and as Irish as the day she was born, chatted like two friends who had not seen each other for a long time. Both were with child, Susannah further along than Rebecca, and they sewed for their babies as they talked.

Susannah had remarked, "I scarcely think the boxbark hut my brother-in-law provided for you is suitable housing, but Ted has told me every available dwelling around Coota is occupied."

"'Tis no matter," responded Rebecca. "We're grateful for the free lodging, and we'll have our own property and homestead soon enough." When Rebecca described her husband's schedule of ministry throughout the parish, however, Susannah wondered when the Millers would ever find time to select a property, much less build a homestead.

On September 5th, 1874, at Clapham Cottage, Susannah and Ted's first child was born. She was a big baby, and Susannah had to endure a long labour. Dark-haired and with her father's brown eyes, she was named Susie Ellen. Susie was a diminutive of Susannah, and Ellen was the maiden surname of Ted's mother. Despite the careful appellation, their eldest child was forever known as Nellie.

As Susannah had expected, when the slab church on the hill behind the reservoir was ready for an opening celebration, Lay

Reader John Miller asked her to provide the musical accompaniment. "We've obtained a harmonium," he said. Susannah had never played a harmonium, but she did not say so. "Please anticipate a variety of musical selections. My older children have been practising 'Tramp! Tramp! Tramp! The Boys Are Marching.'" An American Civil War song, Susannah recalled, one she had in her own collection, but surely not appropriate for a church opening!

On the day before the celebration, she and baby Nellie had gone with Ted to see the new slab church on the hill. Wooden crosses were attached to the front and rear of the roof, but the building bore no resemblance to any church Susannah had ever seen. Constructed of rough-sawn timber, the rectangular structure was without glass in its windows or pews for a congregation.

"We'll need seating for the opening," said Susannah. "Boxes, perhaps. I have some remnants of light-coloured calico to cover the windows and keep out the flies." The Lord knows, she said to herself, we have to start somewhere.

The promised harmonium stood at the front of the room. She sat down on a tottering bench before a battered instrument, rescued from storage in some barn, she reckoned, and after a little tentative practice, managed to produce recognizable music. Next day, what a celebration! People arrived from miles around, played sports and games and ate a hearty potluck supper. Afterwards, in the glow of candlelight, Susannah played the harmonium in accompaniment to singers of varying abilities. Tucked into a basket, baby Nellie slept contentedly through it all.

On a January day Susannah received a note from her good friend Rebecca Miller, warning of measles in the family and suggesting that Susannah and baby Nellie not come calling until Rebecca's children had recovered. Susannah felt helpless in not going to her friend's assistance, but Nellie was too young to be exposed to the disease. Indeed, the whole town became afflicted with measles that summer, resulting in the deaths of several children. Susannah, like all women, was fully aware of the risks in having and rearing a child. Assuming a woman and her baby survived the birth, there was no guarantee the child would live beyond its first birthday. Diarrhoea, influenza and accidents were the primary causes of children's deaths, and epidemics such as measles threatened the lives of many children as well as adults who had not had the disease.

In April Susannah resumed her weekly visits, offering Rebecca as much comfort and companionship as she could after the death of baby Edward. As Susannah watched Nellie smiling at faces around her and eager to creep and explore, her heart went out to Rebecca. On these visits Susannah had tried to divert Rebecca with conversations about fundraising activities for the parish. Susannah admired her friend's crochetwork on altar linens in the slab church, which prompted Rebecca to put aside her grief for a moment and tell Susannah how she and John Miller had met in Holy Trinity Church at Berrima. Rebecca looked forward to having a farm of her own, and Susannah encouraged her to talk about her plans in hopes of cheering her.

Everyone knew Rebecca Miller bore a heavy load with her husband away so much on parish duties. The Lay Reader's wife was never heard to complain, but Susannah was certain that caring for nine children in a boxbark hut, free lodging though it was, must be adding to her friend's despair. She reckoned Rebecca needed a property of her own very soon if her state of mind were to improve.

An ongoing topic of conversation at Coota in 1875 was the pressing need for a school. John Barnes served on the local committee, as did Ted and Lay Reader John Miller, storekeeper James Simpson, and Coota's first bank manager, Herbert Elder. Dealing with the colonial Council of Education proved tedious, and Cootamundra School looked to be far off. At this rate, muttered Susannah, our Nellie will be ready for school and we will not have one. School meetings took place around Susannah's dining room table, and she always baked a little something—cherry pound cake, apple turnovers, cinnamon rolls or peach tart—to see the men through their deliberations.

After months of negotiation, the Cootamundra school committee received a letter from the Council of Education at Sydney approving construction of a school and the hiring of a teacher. Ted and John

Barnes were to remain on the local School Board, but the School Inspector had removed Lay Reader John Miller because of his church connection. "How ridiculous!" Susannah said to Rebecca as the two of them took turns churning butter outside the hut on Jindalee Flat. "John is a valuable member of the School Board. He's a former schoolmaster with more experience in educating children than the rest of the men together!" Rebecca did not argue. "'Tis true," she said, "but John reminded me this is a state school, and he represents the church." Susannah replied by churning more vigorously.

The rights to the church property at Bourke and Thompson Streets, claimed by Bishop Mesac Thomas, remained rights on paper until the property was purchased at the Lands Office. One evening Ted, who was Parish Treasurer, announced to Susannah, "The donations I've received have amounted to a tidy sum. Five families have contributed fifty pounds each and many others have offered as much as they can." The balance of the cost of the property, Susannah knew, would come out of Ted's pocket, yet her husband was confident the parishioners would make good the loan. Early one spring morning he rode off on the thirty-five-mile journey to the Lands Office at Gundagai to buy the property on which the Cootamundra Church of England would be built. He came back five days later with the property deed and building permits for a parish hall, church and vicarage. Construction of the buildings would take place when more funds were raised.

After a service in the slab church one Sunday morning, Rebecca Miller greeted Susannah with further news about their new property six miles to the southwest, Littledale, they would call it. The sooner the Millers moved there, the better, thought Susannah, for Rebecca Miller had suffered far too long in that boxbark hut on Jindalee Flat. John Miller did not strike Susannah as much of a farmer, but she knew Rebecca had grown up on a farm in Ireland. The eldest Miller son, J.J., was interested in farming and could help his mother when John was occupied with parish duties.

A stone church at Bourke and Thompson Streets still seemed years away. The congregation held a meeting and decided that the available funds would be spent on construction of a parish hall on the site. When they eventually built the church, the two buildings were to be connected. They called their parish hall the Church of England Schoolroom because it also served that purpose until Cootamundra School was constructed. Made of corrugated iron, the schoolroom was hot and sultry in summer and bone-chilling cold in winter, but as one of the largest halls available at the time, it was quickly booked for celebrations and community activities. Susannah knew she would be volunteering many an evening at the schoolroom pianoforte, accompanying singers, musicians and dancers.

On the 21st of April, 1876, Susannah gave birth to a second daughter, whom they named Lilla Maria. The name Lilla was a diminutive of Elizabeth and Maria was Susannah's other name. Nellie and her little sister could keep each other company just as Susannah and her sister, Lizzie, had done in England. Lilla Maria, like many second children, was an easy baby.

In 1877 two men of substance in the town, Thomas Campbell Brown and Fred Pinkstone, took responsibility for publishing a weekly newspaper, which made a significant difference to life in Cootamundra. Although the town continued to be listed in the *Government Gazette* as Cootamundry, the name Cootamundra had been in common use since the establishment of the Post Office in 1864. The town's weekly publication, the *Cootamundra Herald*, was confirmation of the name. Susannah found the *Herald* of great interest. No doubt it was a far cry from *The Times* of London, but it served a valuable purpose in bringing matters of importance to the attention of those residents who could read.

Susannah had become accustomed to Ted's frequent evening meetings at Clapham Cottage. One morning, after she had fed her chooks and tried to harvest vegetables from her kitchen garden whilst keeping an eye on Nellie and Lilla, she put the girls down for a nap and began to roll pastry for apple turnovers. "What is your meeting tonight?" she asked Ted at his evening tea. "Businesses are appearing hither and yon at Coota, and more and more people are taking up residence," he replied, "but we have no town plan in place. Until we're granted incorporation and can elect a council, we need a committee to oversee the town's development."

Around the Clapham Cottage dining room table that evening, over Susannah's apple turnovers with warm custard, a group of original settlers proposed having an election for a Vigilance Committee to monitor the town's progress until incorporation was achieved and a council elected. Their proposal was presented at a public meeting on May 10th, 1877, in the Church of England Schoolroom, where John and Ted Barnes were chosen as two of the founding members of the Cootamundra Vigilance Committee.

John Barnes had succeeded his father as owner of the Albion Hotel and in 1871 had made Ted his partner in the Cootamundra Store next door. Although John Barnes was seven years Ted's senior, Susannah thought the two brothers worked well together. They had similar goals, developing their businesses and supporting their church, but John was also interested in politics and intended to seek public office. She knew Ted drew his satisfaction from continued community service.

The changing face of Cootamundra was prompting more commercial activity, giving credence to plans of the Vigilance Committee to make the town a focal point of the large surrounding agricultural area. At a family dinner John Barnes broached an idea he had had for some time. "Father planned to build a two-storey addition to the Coota store, and Mother has shown me sketches she did for him back in '63. What say we get to work on it, Ted? We have enough trade now to justify better premises."

"True enough," said his brother. "What about the Albion? Is Mrs. Angove still interested in buying the hotel?"

"She is, and I reckon funds from the sale would finance the new store."

"Then let's draw up plans and see what other members of the Vigilance Committee have to say."

Mrs. Mary Angove of Gulong bought the Albion Hotel from John Barnes and received approval from the Vigilance Committee to build a two-storey hotel of twenty rooms. Along the street

John and Ted had a site prepared for a two-storey addition to their store, which was also approved by the committee. Parker Street was showing evidence of the "mushroom growth" reported in the *Cootamundra Herald*.

Whilst the Vigilance Committee watched over Cootamundra's "mushroom growth," the Free Settlers' Association was proposing changes to the Lands Act. John and Ted were eligible for membership in the association because in 1841 their father had landed in New South Wales as a Free Settler. At an August meeting Ted Barnes was elected first president of the Cootamundra Free Settlers' Association, which proceeded to address the numerous regulations governing the distribution and use of Crown lands. Of his many community involvements, Susannah knew her husband was proudest of his role in the Free Settlers' Association in overseeing the development of Cootamundra District.

In August 1877, Bishop Mesac Thomas and Mrs. Thomas arrived by coach from Goulburn for the Bishop's annual visitation and services of Holy Communion. On this occasion, much to Susannah's satisfaction, His Lordship also laid the cornerstone of Christ Church of England. As usual, she was pleased to arrange an evening for the Bishop and his wife. The Millers were included, together with John and Jane Barnes and other leading members of the congregation. Susannah served her queen of puddings at dinner that Sunday.

"How nice. How very nice," said Mrs. Thomas. "It is one of the Bishop's favourites."

As the summer approached, Susannah could scarcely get Ted's attention on any matter because his mind was on organizing a celebration for the completion of the Cootamundra railway line. The coach journey from Goulburn was about to become a thing of the past because the railway line had been extended from Goulburn to Coota. On the afternoon of November 1st, 1877, a great crowd of people from the town and District, including Susannah and her children, gathered at the new Cootamundra Railway Station for the opening of the Cootamundra Line of the Great Southern Railway. Nellie and Lilla, too young to appreciate the historical significance of the occasion, were very excited to see Papa amongst the important men on the platform when the first train arrived.

In February 1878, Susannah and Ted's third child was born. Susannah had been startled to learn she was expecting this baby and whilst suckling Lilla and watching over Nellie, had not felt she was with child. Born rapidly and prematurely one summer's morning, Eva was named by Lay Reader John Miller in an emergency baptism. A frail, tiny baby who scarcely suckled at all, she was much too quiet and grew very slowly. Susannah spent hours holding her at the breast, trying to encourage her to take nourishment. Nellie and Lilla, meanwhile, were active little children, full of merriment and interested in everything.

Almost a year after the Bishop laid the cornerstone, Thomas Jobson and his builders completed the construction of Christ Church of England. The Dedication of the stone church was to take place in July, and Ted, the Bishop's Churchwarden, was gloomy about the prospect of dismal weather. "The good Lord never promised a perfect world," Susannah reminded her somewhat nervous husband as she stitched his new cravat.

The sandstone building, which included a vestibule, bell tower, vestry and sacristy, also boasted an altar, lectern, harmonium, pews and chandeliers with six candles in each for evening services. More funds, however, would be required for a baptismal font, organ, pulpit and bell. Because the Bishop would be in attendance, John Miller was schooling candidates in their Catechism prior to their Confirmation. No matter the inclement winter weather, everyone was ready for a celebration.

Susannah's choir was in fine voice, or so everyone attested. Determined to establish a high quality of music at the first service in the new church, she had conducted more than enough practices. The battered harmonium sprang to life under her touch as the choir, resplendent in new surplices, processed down the aisle to the stirring music of "All People That on Earth Do Dwell." Ted's tenor solo, the graceful melody "Jesu, Where'er Thy People Meet," with its lyrics by William Cowper, was superb, Susannah told him, admitting her opinion could be biased.

Later that day Susannah and Ted gave a dinner party for the Bishop and his wife, John and Rebecca Miller and visiting clergy. On that stormy winter's night, Susannah served a hearty roast beef dinner, followed by sherry trifle, a plate of cheeses and enough wine to put a usually staid group of clergy in the mood for charades. Susannah drew the Bishop as her partner. The resulting charade, with Susannah balanced precariously on a chair in lieu of a balcony and Mesac Thomas kneeling at her feet in supplication, inspired onlookers' suggestions verging on the improper until they were identified as Juliet and Romeo.

Because the cost of building the church, two thousand pounds in all, had yet to be paid off and some interior fitments were still needed, years of fundraising lay ahead of Christ Church congregation. To begin, Susannah had in mind a fête, like those at her church in London. Jane Barnes had something similar in mind and after the Dedication, she suggested to Susannah that they spend a morning together discussing plans. They met at Susannah's dining room table and began their task by making a list of all the women in the parish.

"We must include Mrs. Matthews, the wife of the new Churchwarden, on our committee," said Jane. "She'll be keen to be part of the team." They made notes about the women's recognized talents and planned to approach each of them for donations of sewing, knitting, baking, preserves or fancy-work. Susannah's bottled peaches, Jane's fruit cakes, Letitia Lynch's knitted layettes and Rebecca Miller's crocheted lace would seem to be promising items.

"William Miller," said Susannah, "has suggested performances by his Sunday School choir, donations to be solicited. His goal for his Sunday School pupils is a baptismal font. We'll need to provide space for them to perform."

"Right," said Jane, "and Rebecca has told me that J.J. intends to appeal for unwanted household treasures, knick-knacks, samplers and such, and auction them to raise funds for a pulpit. He's such a persuasive young man, his Auction of Treasures looks to be a promising feature. We'll have a tea corner, of course, and games for the little ones. J.J. also wants a raffle. What do you think?"

"I think that sounds like gambling!"

"J.J. says the proceeds would go to a church organ and he was certain the Lord would approve." Susannah considered the ancient harmonium she was playing, and a raffle was included.

"Let's schedule the bazaar during the September Race Meeting," suggested Jane. "Race-goers from across the countryside flock to Cootamundra that week. Punters will crowd into the schoolroom each evening after the races, eager to spend their winnings. The church will benefit handsomely."

Christ Church Bazaar, with Jane Barnes as convenor, was advertised for Race Week, which turned out to be an excellent decision because the annual event could be counted on to contribute three hundred pounds to the church coffers. Amongst many other duties, Susannah and Jane canvassed all businesses in town for prizes for the raffle, the highlight of every evening. When Mrs. Angove built the Assembly Hall the following year, the bazaar, taking advantage of the much larger premises, was henceforth held there during Race Week.

At the beginning of November, Ted thought that Susannah, having given her energies for several months to the church bazaar as well as the choir and her household responsibilities, was much in need of a change of scene. "Come with me to Sydney on my annual buying trip. The journey is much more convenient now that we have a direct rail line. Perhaps one of your friends could care for Nellie and Lilla whilst we take Eva with us." Despite Susannah's tender ministrations, their baby had not thrived and was still a wee mite lying quietly in her mother's arms or in the perambulator. Ted, Susannah and Eva left for Sydney on the Great Southern Railway in the third week of November.

Susannah was looking forward to a holiday free from duties. Rebecca Miller, dear soul that she was, had suggested that Nellie and Lilla come to stay at Littledale, and the small girls were excited about the prospect of staying at a farm. Her good friend Jane Barnes, one of several parishioners who had taken Susannah's place at the Christ Church organ during her confinements, had offered to serve as organist and choirmistress in her absence. With Eva in her pram, Susannah and Ted strolled along the streets of Sydney in the summer sunshine, looking at shops and meeting with suppliers about stock for their store.

In their second week at Sydney, Eva developed diarrhoea. After a fortnight of Susannah's desperate care and a doctor's daily attendance, the child died in her mother's arms on the 11th of December, 1878. Ted and Susannah returned to Cootamundra on the train with Eva's shrouded body in a tiny casket. Baby Eva's graveside service in the Church of England section of Cootamundra Cemetery was conducted by the Reverend Cocks of Murrumburrah.

Susannah had consulted a Sydney dressmaker who kept a supply of black dresses for ladies in mourning. For the next year she appeared in public only in the unrelieved black of a woman who mourned.

Bewildered and upset by the loss of their baby sister, Nellie and Lilla begged their mother for an explanation. Hiding her own grief, Susannah tried to console them by telling them about Eva in Heaven with Jesus. Christmas preparations at Clapham Cottage occupied Susannah, as did choir practices at Christ Church. She was grateful to young William Miller, the Sunday School Superintendent, who arranged his first Nativity pageant and included Nellie and Lilla as angels.

TWENTY-FIVE

Littledale

Mark the perfect man, and behold the upright:
for the end of that man is peace.

—PSALM 37:37

By Christmas of 1875, Littledale was on its way to becoming the property Rebecca Miller had always dreamed of owning. Her kitchen garden was flourishing, and her four young milch cows from the Barnes dairy herd, Daisy, Dapple, Dolly and Duchess (Megan Mary Mahoney not being available for Biblical namings), provided ample milk, cream and butter for Rebecca's large family whilst her flock of chooks gave them eggs, meat and feathers for pillows.

Cows had to be milked and butter churned, chooks fed and eggs collected. Horses needed feeding and grooming, and their shelter required a daily mucking out. The kitchen garden demanded planting, weeding and cultivating, and vegetables had to be gathered for meals or the root cellar. Rebecca's children were well-occupied and happy helping on the farm.

J.J. was the man about the place when his father was abroad in the parish, and Rebecca was pleased that her fifteen-year-old son had her instincts for farming and an appreciation of working in harmony with the soil and the seasons. Horses responded well to J.J., and he quickly developed the knack of ploughing a straight furrow and driving four-in-hand. As she watched him work with a team, Rebecca was reminded of David Andrews training Fan and Bob on the Oxley Estate.

Without roads crossing its breadth, without fences marking its limits, the Littledale selection stretched across the slopes in undulating splendour. Lovely groves of eucalypts and widespread pastures beckoned those who appreciated life in the open. The lush kangaroo grass grew very tall, prompting J.J. to challenge the local legend by riding his horse into the middle of it and trying to tie the grass over the pommel of his saddle. Making themselves at home on the Littledale grasslands were wild horses, kangaroos and a scattered herd of long-horned cattle from the original station in the District, John Hurley's Cootomondra Run. The Cootamundra wattle, a tree of pleasant proportions, could be found in all parts of the property, and the fragrance of its yellow blossoms sweetly scented the clear air of springtime. Rebecca often walked with the young ones up the track to the topmost pasture and, whilst her children played around her, sat crocheting or knitting and gazing over the broad valley below.

Kangaroos, interesting though they were, competed with livestock for grazing and had to be culled. Rebecca did not like having firearms around but said nothing when John purchased rifles for J.J. and Willie. The boys became good shots and the meat was of value, although Rebecca struggled for some time before she learned the rump and tail of young kangaroo were the parts worth cooking. Organized kangaroo hunts, with prizes and all-night celebrations, took place in every settlement, and the boys begged to be allowed to participate. Rebecca and John decided they could take part in the hunts, but all-night celebrations could wait until they were older.

Large snakes were an ongoing concern and a challenge to J.J. and Willie, who had to be quick at sighting and shooting them. To Rebecca's dismay the boys often brought the carcasses back to the house to give the little ones a fright. She learned to appreciate the morning cackle of kookaburras high in the gumtrees; the plain-looking birds swooped down to dispatch many a small snake. She and her family prided themselves on being courageous selectors in a grand, rugged land. With God's support, she often reminded her children, there was nothing they could not manage.

In the late autumn of 1876, Rebecca joyfully realized she was again expecting a baby. Now in her fortieth year, she had been certain she was experiencing symptoms of the change. She thanked

God for giving her one more chance to raise a child. With the death of baby Edward still haunting her, Rebecca's daily prayers for the birth of a healthy infant took on unusual urgency. One pleasant summer's day, the 20th of November, 1876, in the slab house on Littledale station, she was delivered of a handsome baby boy.

"I'd like to call him Nevil Maskelyne," said John, "in honour of the Astronomer Royal in my mother's family." Rebecca agreed it was a fine-sounding name for their new son. The name, however, proved troublesome for the Reverend Donkin, a retired clergyman visiting at Murrumburrah. The aged cleric baptised the baby at the opening of the new little church at Wallendbeen. "Whisht! Whisht!" Rebecca admonished her children when Mr. Donkin, who had adenoidal difficulties, provoked gales of giggles by christening their baby brother "Devil Baskelyne."

On the church property at Bourke and Thompson Streets, the Church of England Schoolroom now took the place of the slab church on the hill. On one of the Bishop's visits to the parish, Lay Reader John Miller had presented Mary Jane, Emily, J.J. and Willie together with other candidates for their Confirmation and First Communion in the schoolroom.

Foundations of the Miller homestead were now in place. On a broad rise overlooking a pond, a large rectangle had taken shape that included a central hall and six spacious rooms: three bedrooms, a sitting room, a large dining room and a kitchen at the back. Young Willie's interest in mathematics made him a keen surveyor of the dimensions as he laid out the area of each proposed room. Finished wooden floors, a broad verandah and a galvanized iron roof with wide overhangs were also planned.

The supports of the verandah and homestead were to be of stringybark eucalypt, and the homestead itself constructed of wattle and daub, or pisé, as it was called, rammed mud and gravel set in a woven wattle frame. The twelve-foot walls, when dry, would receive a coating of mixed linseed oil and whitewash. Rebecca was familiar with the method of construction because in Ireland she had seen many a cottage made of clay and wattles. If stones were scarce and bricks unavailable or too costly, wattle and daub was the serviceable alternative. Two years of work by all except the youngest Millers went into completing Littledale homestead.

Christ Church, situated next to the Church of England Schoolroom, was more than halfway to completion. Thomas Jobson, a local builder, had been busy supervising stonemasons, a rarity at Cootamundra because Christ Church was one of only three stone buildings in the town. Rebecca had ordered a length of linen through the Cootamundra Store for a fair linen, corporal, credence cloth and purificators, and whenever she had a moment to herself, she stitched altar linens for Christ Church. Mary Jane and Emily sat with her to hem the fair linen and once they had mastered the rose motif, helped her with the crocheted border. As she worked on the linens, Rebecca savoured memories of those afternoons in Holy Trinity vicarage at Berrima, twenty-two years in the past.

As the winter of 1878 approached, John and his Churchwardens began planning for the Dedication of Christ Church. On a cold, blustery Friday, the 12th of July, they welcomed Bishop Mesac Thomas, the Officiant at the Dedication of Christ Church of England, Cootamundra, assisted by the Venerable Archdeacon Pownall and the Reverends W. Cocks of Murrumburrah and S.B. Holt of Gundagai. In his sermon the Bishop offered congratulations on the fine stone building and exhorted the congregation to greater efforts towards paying off the costs of construction. After the Dedication, the Order of Confirmation took place, and then the congregation adjourned to the Church of England Schoolroom for a bounty of refreshments. On the following Sunday, Holy Communion and Evensong were conducted by the Reverend W. May of Goulburn, who was fullsome in his praise of the founders of Christ Church. Disappointingly, the church's much-admired six-candle chandeliers provided only dim illumination for Evensong on that winter's night.

Less than four years after leaving North Goulburn, Rebecca had seen her husband achieve his dream of establishing a parish and building a church. She was filled with pride at his achievements. Thus began a time Rebecca would always treasure in her memory.

Sunday services at Christ Church, conducted by John or a visiting clergyman, had a new significance in the atmosphere of a carefully built place of worship. Rebecca and her children sat in front pews on the Epistle side; Susannah Barnes or another volunteer played the harmonium and conducted the choir; and Edward Barnes was soloist and Bishop's Churchwarden.

Rebecca joined in various fundraising projects at Christ Church to reduce the construction debt and provide interior fitments. The annual church bazaar, organized by Jane and Susannah Barnes, included the sale of her crocheted lace and needlework by Mary Jane and Emily. At church fundraisers J.J. never missed a chance to persuade parishioners to donate "treasures" for him to auction. Willie had charge of the Sunday School, and his choir of Sunday School children, including his young sisters, entertained patrons of each fundraiser. Rebecca was proud of her children's involvement in the life of Christ Church.

Up on Littledale station, the Millers had settled into their homestead. The eldest children were busy giving the exterior its coating of linseed oil and whitewash, and J.J. and Willie were also planting kurrajongs and Tasmanian blue gums around the house for shade. Great discussion had gone into alloting the three generous bedrooms, and Rebecca had decided the matter by assigning the largest bedroom to the five girls. Mary Jane insisted on having a bed of her own; Emily willingly slept with Margaret whilst Sarah shared with Jessie. In another bedroom were J.J., Willie, Compton and Alick, with Nevil in his parents' room.

A dining room table and chairs had been high on Rebecca's list of required furniture; not since Tarago had all the family been able to sit together for a meal. John's priority was a pianoforte, a second-hand Broadwood, for the sitting room. More work still needed to be done on the interior of the house: walls whitewashed and draperies installed. Rebecca wanted a wire fence around the homestead because wallabies were inquisitive creatures who liked to sample her kitchen garden and flower beds, and stray Littledale sheep could be even more of a nuisance. John and the boys built a wire fence for her. Rabbits remained an annoyance and a source of food for the family.

A site on Cooper Street in town had a new brick school building with an attached teacher's residence. Amongst the pupils on the rolls of Cootamundra School were Margaret, Sarah and Jessie Miller, who made the six-mile journey to and from school on horseback. Compton and Alick, too young to make the journey, were tutored at home by Mary Jane and Emily.

John was now away weeks at a time in his new ministry northwest of Wagga Wagga around Narrandera, where homesteads were scattered across extensive grazing lands. His church services in the area, like those in Cootamundra District five years earlier, were the first to be held there and attracted worshippers of all faiths. Meanwhile, Rebecca and J.J. were left to manage Littledale; Willie rode to town each day to work in the Bank of New South Wales.

Rebecca reckoned those first days in charge of the daily operation of Littledale were the making of her eldest son. Always keen on farming, J.J. valued his mother's expertise and added innovations of his own. With Willie's help, he built a platform for a cistern behind the homestead and set up a pump for his mother in her kitchen. Off he went to livestock auctions and came back with sheep and cattle as well as young horses to break into harness and sell. Although she thought sheep were silly creatures, Rebecca was impressed by his Littledale mob of cross-bred sheep. Monarch, J.J.'s prize bull, was the first in a succession of such animals he kept at stud, and Rebecca was appreciative of Littledale's increasing numbers of sleek cattle, expertly herded by Rusty, who had proven himself a valuable cattle dog.

J.J.'s horses were carefully trained; he was developing a reputation as a first-class whip, and his skill in driving four-in-hand was known throughout the District. The rye grass he planted was the station's prime crop, its seed another source of income for the station. From early morning until late at night, J.J. could be found working on the farm and making improvements to the place: lambing, shearing, ploughing, planting, harvesting, branding cattle with the Miller Lazy YZ brand, clearing trees, sawing timber and building fences. No task daunted him. The jackaroos he hired were hard-pressed to keep up with his skills and energy. By the age of nineteen, J.J. Miller had established himself as a respected farmer in Cootamundra District.

His lifelong companion, younger brother Willie, had other interests. He was seldom found without a book in his hand or in his pocket and he devoured volumes on every subject, committing significant passages to memory. He sang well and enjoyed playing the pianoforte, sometimes with his little sister Jessie as his partner in duets. Just as J.J. was noted for his ability to drive four-in-hand, Willie was recognized for his expertise in the saddle. David Andrews' assessment of him as a six-year-old horseman on Cartmel station at Tarago had proven correct, for Willie excelled in point-to-point contests and jumping competitions and was always on the lookout for a better mount. He saw to it his younger brothers and sisters learned to be good riders. Watching him teaching the little ones put Rebecca in mind of those lovely afternoons on Cartmel when Willie and the older children had practised riding Gwyn, the Welsh pony.

Down in the town, now that Christ Church was well established and the parish organized, the churchwardens had petitioned Bishop Thomas to appoint an incumbent clergyman. The Reverend Cocks had been dividing his ministry between the churches at Wallendbeen and Cootamundra, and not until the Reverend Holt was appointed in January 1880 did Christ Church have a cleric and his wife who lived in the parish and became part of its busy life.

The Millers had not heard from Megan Mary Mahoney since her news of Hannah's passing, but one summer day a letter arrived from Cartmel. Rebecca sat out under a kurrajong tree behind the homestead and opened the envelope to find a description of Megan's baby daughter, Hannah Rebecca, six months old, a fair-haired beauty and the light of David Andrews' life. Megan went on to explain:

After dearest Hannah's passing, David was beside himself with grief. In truth, we both were, and sought comfort in each other. One thing led to another, and I found myself with child. David was overjoyed and so was I. Mrs. McLaughlin took care of me and my confinement went easily.

The baby has a handsome big brother in Robert Samuel, who is now seven years of age. He has his mother's green eyes and auburn hair and is very caring with the baby. Later this year we expect the arrival of another little one.

With David a Protestant and me a Catholic and neither of us wanting to convert, we will never marry, but we have a great fondness for each other and feel God favours us, sinners though we be.

I send my very best wishes to you and Mr. Miller and your family.
I remain your grateful friend,

Megan Mary Mahoney

Rebecca re-read the letter several times, uncertain of her reaction. She was astounded at Megan's news. The young woman was obviously happy in her state, as was David Andrews, who was twenty years Megan's senior. Should she condemn their living in sin and having children out of wedlock? What would John say? When John read Megan's letter, however, he was much more sanguine. "Good for them!" he said. "They're both deserving of happiness!" Rebecca was not sure she approved of her husband's liberal attitude; nevertheless, taking her cue from him, she wrote a warm letter of congratulations to the couple.

"The Bishop has asked me to leave my ministry at Narrandera and go to Temora," said John to Rebecca later that same day. "It's less than forty miles northwest of here, and I'll be able to get home regularly. There's a pressing need for spiritual comfort in the area."

"Temora's the site of a new goldfield!" said Rebecca. "The living conditions will be appalling! Where does the Bishop think you'll find accommodations?"

"I expect I'll be in a tent like everyone else. My work is cut out for me. The men are of all races, creeds and backgrounds, and my missionary efforts will be the first in that area."

In the spring of 1880, John set out for Temora goldfield. Much as Rebecca appreciated his being home more often, she reckoned his service to the people of Narrandera would have proved much more fruitful than his efforts in a mining camp. Little did she suspect that John's ministry to the gold miners at Temora was to change her life forever.

Early that summer Willie came to his mother with an announcement. "It's almost the fifth anniversary of the Sunday School, and I'm going to organize a celebration!" Rebecca remembered when John had taught the first Sunday School classes in the slab church on the hill, and now their seventeen-year-old son was the enthusiastic Superintendent of the Sunday School at Christ Church. "I've spoken to the Hurleys, and they'll open their grounds to us. We'll arrange for coaches to collect parishioners at the church and take them to the celebration. Jane Barnes says she and Susannah will see to the catering, and you'll help, won't you, Mother? We're going to have a great country party!"

On a Sunday afternoon in early November, coaches carried parish families to the Hurleys' Willows, where sports and games were available for all ages. Participants tucked into roast beef, Yorkshire pudding, roasted potatoes, gravy, chutneys, bowls of vegetables, fruit tarts of all kinds and pots of tea—hardly a meal for a warm day, but consumed with gusto nevertheless. Not only was it a Sunday School celebration, but also a celebration of the thirty-ninth birthday of the Prince of Wales and J.J.'s twentieth birthday. Toasts were proposed to the health of Her Majesty, His Royal Highness and J.J. Miller.

Northwest of Cootamundra at Temora, thousands of miners had poured into a goldfield as they had for the past thirty years into goldfields across the continent. Alluvial mining, the sluicing of auriferous earth to capture fragments of gold, had made a vast cratered wasteland of the region around Temora. The method required a plentiful supply of water, and although gold could be found at Temora, water was limited. Swarms of miners competed for claims, tents, provisions and especially water for themselves and their sluices.

In no time the drinking water became contaminated, and men fell ill. Dysentery was common, and fever began to spread through the camp.

John arrived home in the third week of December, exhausted and plagued by chills despite the warm weather. The family's Christmas celebrations were subdued as Rebecca nursed her sick husband, and the children took turns at his bedside. Dr. Combe came regularly from his residence at Cootamundra to check on John. With the doctor, the Reverend Holt and numerous parishioners calling to see her husband, Rebecca kept her daughters busy baking and serving tea to visitors.

Rebecca's once-vigorous husband continued to be bedridden. In mid-January fever overtook him, and he developed a cough. Rebecca was fearful of pneumonia. Her husband's fever continued, his coughing worsened, and he grew weaker. Dr. Combe's increasingly solemn demeanour did not reassure Rebecca and the children. When John's breathing became shallow and laboured, the family all stayed at his bedside, leaving only to do the most essential farm chores. John seemed quite unaware of his surroundings, but he recognized his wife and children and, weak though he was, had words of love and encouragement for each of them.

On the afternoon of Tuesday, the 8th of February, 1881, he asked to speak alone with the Reverend Holt. That evening, as darkness settled over Littledale station, John Miller, in his fifty-seventh year, quietly breathed his last and went to be with his Lord.

Despite the tragedies in her past, never had Rebecca suffered such grief. Never had she felt so alone. For the sake of her family, she resolved to bear up bravely, and two days later she walked down the aisle with her children to the front pews of Christ Church for John's funeral service. Afterwards, friends and neighbours joined the lengthy funeral procession through the town and up to the grave. The body of John Miller, laid out in a casket made by the Christ Church builder, Thomas Jobson, was buried beside that of baby Edward in the Church of England section of Cootamundra Cemetery.

The man to whom Rebecca had devoted her life in the colony, the man she had admired and followed, who had shared her bed and fathered her children, had been taken to his Eternal Reward.

In February of 1881, in her forty-fifth year, Rebecca Miller was left to care for a station, a homestead and a family of five daughters and five sons, from Mary Jane, age three and twenty, to Nevil, age four. Daily chores on the farm would demand her attention, the children her affection and understanding. Nights were for grieving in her bed, cold and bereft without her beloved husband beside her.

If her family were to remain together and if Littledale were to prosper, Rebecca knew she must be strong and have faith in her Heavenly Father. On the day after John's funeral, she gathered her children around her as she and John had done each morning. This day more than ever, they needed direction and hope for the future. From the Epistle to the Hebrews, she read: "Now the God of peace, that brought again from the dead our Lord Jesus, that great Shepherd of the sheep, through the blood of the everlasting covenant, Make you perfect in every good work to do his will, working in you that which is wellpleasing in his sight, through Jesus Christ; to whom be glory for ever and ever. Amen."

Rebecca Nixon Miller, certain of God's help, thus began the rest of her life's journey.

TWENTY-SIX

Spring and Autumn Shows

*Praise ye the Lord. O give thanks unto the Lord;
for he is good: for his mercy endureth for ever.*
— PSALM 106:1

When the much-anticipated Cootamundra School had opened, Mr. Edward P. Barnes had been elected Chairman of the School Board, which set the fees at nine pence a week for the older classes, six pence a week for the first class and four pence a week for the infant class. By July 1879, sixty pupils attended the brick building across the street from Clapham Cottage. One of those pupils was Nellie Barnes.

On several occasions in 1879, Ted Barnes, as Bishop's Churchwarden, had written to Bishop Mesac Thomas, urging him to appoint a full-time incumbent for Christ Church. Their fine stone church with its active congregation deserved more than part-time care from the Reverend Cocks of Murrumburrah, much as his ministry was appreciated. On more than one occasion, Ted had recommended to His Lordship that Lay Reader John Miller be ordained a Deacon of the Church and appointed incumbent of Christ Church; John Miller had founded the parish and was beloved of its people, an ideal incumbent in Ted and Susannah's estimation. Mesac Thomas had replied in rambling epistles that praised John Miller's worthy attributes, then reiterated an intention to assign the Lay Reader to a mission field, certainly not what Ted and Susannah and other parishioners had been hoping for.

Susannah was again with child, a boy this time, she prayed, although she knew that would be in the hands of the Almighty. After losing Eva, she anticipated this baby with some anxiety. And her sister-in-law Jane had recently lost her infant son. A mother could only pray that a newborn, even if born healthy, would survive.

On the 28th of August, 1879, after an easy confinement, Susannah gave birth to her next child—a small girl, but not at all a delicate infant, a vigorous one, in fact. The baby was easily distracted from suckling, eager to look around and see what was going on, and Susannah struggled to get her settled and feeding properly. They named her Hilda Prior Barnes.

In the new year His Lordship had finally appointed an incumbent to Christ Church, the Reverend S.B. Holt from Gundagai. The Ladies' Guild laid on a Tea Meeting in the schoolroom on the 25th of January, 1880, to welcome the Reverend Holt and his wife and son. The incumbent's arrival had coincided with the departure from Christ Church of Lay Reader John Miller, who had been assigned to missionary duties out at Narrandera.

"How ridiculous, sending John Miller off to be a missionary after all the work he's done establishing our parish!" Susannah had declared. "The Bishop knows John is devoted to spreading the Word of the Lord and he's taken advantage of him!"

"Now, now, my dear," said Ted. "John will be happy in the mission field, and the Reverend Holt and his family are a fine addition to Cootamundra parish. We should invite them to dinner next Sunday." Susannah was concerned for Rebecca, left to manage Littledale with the help of J.J., her eldest son. The station would continue to prosper, she thought, for J.J.'s reputation as a hard-working young farmer was well-known thoughout the District, but Rebecca would bear the responsibility for Littledale in John Miller's absence.

Susannah followed Ted's suggestion and invited the Holts to dinner the following Sunday. She was impressed by their son, Arthur, a bright, personable boy, quite capable of contributing sensibly to the conversation around the table. His mother was an articulate, enthusiastic parson's wife, eager to join the parish women in their efforts on behalf of Christ Church. "I've always admired the women of Cootamundra parish and the talents and energy they devote to church work," said Mrs. Holt. "I thought the performance of your choir at the Dedication revealed a great appreciation of phrasing and harmony, and the reception in the schoolroom afterwards was evidence of careful organization. I look forward to working with you all." Susannah saw to it that Mrs. Holt was immediately made Honorary President of the Ladies' Guild.

With a new baby to care for, Susannah was finding it difficult to supervise Nellie and Lilla. She had them feeding chooks and collecting eggs and was trying to teach them to weed her kitchen garden without pulling up the vegetables. They quickly got into mischief if they were not occupied and would keep still only if she told them a story from her voyage to New South Wales. Even "Fergus and the Cutpurse," however, had its limitations. Susannah decided it was time for pianoforte lessons. With Hilda in a basket next to the Broadwood, she sat with her eldest daughters as they mastered the fingering of scales and simple melodies. Nellie, age six, was a competent pupil, but it was Lilla, almost five, who took eagerly to the piano. Though the performers might be struggling, baby Hilda gurgled happily throughout the instruction. Susannah had the three of them at the pianoforte every afternoon, which gave her time for a sit-down and a cup of tea.

In the spring of 1880, after the Bishop had transferred Lay Reader John Miller from Narrandera to the chaotic goldfields at Temora, Susannah had said with some feeling, "In Heaven's Name, what is the Bishop doing now, sending John Miller into a heathen, disease-ridden mining camp? Everyone knows that many proper settlements of God-fearing people are without spiritual guidance!" Her husband had agreed that the Bishop's decision was open to question.

When John Miller had arrived home with a fever from bad water at the diggings, she and Ted had made weekly calls at Littledale; Susannah always took along a pudding of some sort.

In February of 1881, they joined the family and all who knew Lay Reader John Miller to mourn his untimely passing. At his crowded funeral, attended by mourners of all denominations, Ted sang "How Bright These Glorious Spirits Shine," and Susannah's choir led the Catechist's favourite hymns: the Welsh melody "How Firm a Foundation," the Doxology, "Praise God from whom all blessings flow . . . " and at the close of the funeral service, the Nunc Dimittis hymn, "Lord, let thy servant now depart into thy promis'd rest . . ."

J.J. Miller was later to write of his father:

Mr. Miller was a devout Christian gentleman, considerate of others, thoughtful and obliging, meek and lowly in spirit, most charitable in word and deed, unselfish, faithful to his God and loyal to his country. He sat by the sick bed, he comforted the dying, he consoled those in trouble and affliction. In every way he diligently strove to follow the teachings of his Lord and Master, and like Him, "he went about doing good." Outside his own denomination he made a host of friends. In early days he visited all denominations in their homes, Protestant and Roman Catholic alike, and was beloved of them all. It may well be written of him, "Blessed are the dead which die in the Lord . . . they may rest from their labours; and their works do follow them."

Susannah treasured her copy of this tribute, given to her by its author.

In the week after John Miller's funeral, Bishop Mesac Thomas appeared at Cootamundra, accompanied as usual by Mrs. Thomas. An announcement in the *Cootamundra Herald* of February 12th, 1881, preceded their arrival.

> CHRIST CHURCH VICARAGE—By advertisement readers are informed of the holding of an interesting ceremony to take place on Tuesday next, namely, the laying of the foundation-stone of the Christ Church vicarage by Mrs. Thomas of Goulburn. His Lordship the Bishop of Goulburn is to take part in the ceremony. The site of the vicarage is in Thompson Street, right opposite the Park and within easy distance of the church. We hope to see a large gathering for the ceremony.

"The Bishop's arrival at Cootamundra after John Miller's funeral is disrespectful in the extreme!" declared an incensed Susannah. "Word of John's death had been sent to him, and he surely could have made the effort to rearrange his schedule and arrive here in time!" Ted noticed there was no game of charades following her dinner for the episcopal couple. At least the Bishop's wife was her usual gracious self in offering condolences to Rebecca and the people of Christ Church.

On a warm summer's evening a few days later, Susannah handed Ted a letter addressed to the family. "Your sister Beth writes to tell us she and Harry Ellen are going to be wed," said Susannah. "I must get busy sewing a new outfit for myself and new frocks for the girls. The little ones will be enchanted by a wedding!"

"The lucky man is Uncle James Ellen's son," said Ted, as he read the letter. "Marrying a first cousin is sure to cause much talk and earnest searching through *The Book of Common Prayer* for the Table of Kindred and Affinity!"

Susannah was happy at the news of her sister-in-law's wedding and wrote at once to tell her so. She had warm memories of Beth Barnes as her companion on her original journey from Sydney to Cootamundra. On the 23rd of March, 1881, family and friends witnessed Elizabeth Mary Maria Barnes, age four and thirty, marry her first cousin, Harry James Ellen, in Christ Church, Cootamundra. No "cause or just impediment" could be found to prevent the happy couple from being joined in Holy Matrimony. Nellie and Lilla declared that the bride, Aunt Beth, was the prettiest lady they had ever seen.

The year she turned seven, Nellie Barnes began to keep a journal, her *Nellie Book*. The new baptismal font at Christ Church inspired her first entry, and for many years her "Dear Book" recorded important events in her life and in the lives of those close to her.

April 17th, 1881

Dear Book
The new font is big. It is made of stone. It came from England. It has a brass sign at the bottom. The sign says the Sunday School paid for it. Willie made us put twopence in a box each week for the font. We sang at church fetes for more money. A font costs a lot.

Mr. Holt baptised many babies at the new font. The last baby cried very loudly. That made dear little Hilda cry. Then other babies began to cry. Mr. Holt told everybody to sing Jesus Christ is risen to-day.

Mamma cooked a big Easter dinner. What a lovely day.

Good night Dear Book.

Nellie Barnes

"What's this new association you and John have been discussing?" Susannah asked her husband one evening as he sat smoking his pipe in front of the fire. Her husband removed his pipe and had a spasm of coughing. "John and I agree that in a farming area like Cootamundra, a means to exhibit agricultural and other accomplishments has long been needed. We're looking to establish an association which will have a show twice a year." Susannah immediately thought of the women's contributions to such a show. She would talk to Jane.

The Agricultural, Pastoral, Horticultural & Industrial Association of Cootamundra was formed in June 1881, with John Barnes as its first President. The APH&I Association's immediate goal was to secure an exhibition ground at the edge of town. "If the Showground Committee can get a site arranged, a show in spring will not be far off," Susannah said to Jane over tea and plum cake one morning. "We could have preserves, spring flowers and early vegetables to be judged, with potted plants and baking for sale. We might also raise money for Christ Church at the show. Surely we can think of a way to support the association and reduce the church debt at the same time."

"What would you think of a Christ Church Refreshment Tent?" said Jane. "Fairgoers are sure to be hungry. We could serve a hot meal at noon, mutton stew and dumplings, perhaps, with tea and a selection of fruit tarts. How does that sound?"

"Jolly good! We'll need to gather the ladies," said Susannah. "I'll do that if you'll see to donations of provisions, and then we'll set out a schedule of duties."

The Presbyterian ladies soon joined them and took responsibility for preparing and serving afternoon tea and sweets. Susannah reckoned the ladies' organizations were far ahead of the men's.

That year Ted's efforts were focussed on completing the construction of a new two-storey Cootamundra Store, which was being built to a design planned by his late father. One could enter the emporium from the original store next door or from the street. The brick building was distinctive, with plate glass windows and a second storey that opened onto a covered upper verandah enclosed by decorative ironwork. The roof featured a varied parapet with an arch in the centre and distinctive cement cornices. J & E. BARNES was embellished in relief below the parapet. Customers immediately enjoyed the spacious layout and much larger selection of stock.

Susannah was again awaiting the birth of a child, this time with increasing distress and concern because she was past her due date and felt tired and uncomfortable. As well, energetic two-year-old Hilda was exhausting her. To give her reprieve from their care, her older children, Nellie, age seven, and Lilla, age five, were spending a month on Littledale station with the Millers.

Littledale, November 2nd, 1881
Dear Book,
Littledale is lovely. We lie under a tree and paint pictures. I paint daisies and poppies and Lilla paints a tree.

We go to school too and play the pianoforte. Emily teaches us and some other children in the slab house. Jessie helps us practise.

Willie sits in a rocking chair and he lifts us up on his foot for Ride a Cock Horse to Banbury Cross. Banbury Cross is far away in England Willie says.

J.J. comes in from the fields all dusty. Before we eat J.J. says For these and all thy blessings Lord we thank thee Amen. It is very sad because they have no Papa. He has gone to Heaven to be with Jesus just like baby Eva.

Tomorrow I will write to dear Mamma.
Good night Dear Book.

Nellie Barnes

Nellie wrote this letter to her mother the following day:

Littledale, November 3rd, 1881

My Dear Mamma,
Did you think I was never going to write to you? I am enjoying myself very much and so is Lilla.

Did you like the flowers I sent you by Willie? How is dear little Hilda? Give her 100 kisses for me and give Papa 100 for me too.

I go to school every day and I practise every day. We have such fun here jumping on the straw and playing with the lambs.

I have not done any of my fancy work yet. Thank you for sending me my Nellie Book.

I remain, my dear Mamma, your loving daughter,

Nellie Barnes

Always a kindly Christian soul, Rebecca Miller had made room for Nellie and Lilla in Littledale homestead as soon as she learned Susannah was apprehensive about her impending confinement. Each day Susannah thanked God for the friendship and generosity of the Miller family.

Nellie's letter of November 3rd was delivered to Susannah at Clapham Cottage, along with the girls' paintings, by William Miller on his way to work at the Bank of New South Wales. Susannah found William an interesting young man, more aloof than his older brother J.J., but like all Millers, always willing to join in a project. A talented chorister and musician, he was very good at training the children in his Sunday School choir.

Susannah was fretful, not only about this birth, but also from being house-bound during lovely warm days. Longing to be out and busy with friends and church work, she appreciated Jane's frequent calls. "You'll never guess what I'm to do next week!" said Jane. "I'm to open the new brewery! A bullock is to be roasted for a picnic supper, and the town band is going to play. With such competition I'll scarcely be noticed, I'm sure!" Susannah liked a crowd and a party, and she could only tell Jane to go and enjoy herself.

On the 17th of November, 1881, after a confinement every bit as difficult as she had anticipated, Susannah was delivered of a large baby girl, whom they named Ivy. That was not the name used by the family, however, for Ivy was such a good-natured child, they soon all called her Goog.

On taking baby Goog to Littledale on an outing, Susannah saw the newly established Littledale School where Nellie and Lilla had been taught by Emily Miller when they stayed on the station. A branch of Cootamundra School, Littledale School was set up in the slab house the Millers had first occupied on their property. It gave the Millers, their station hands and nearby farmers a school for their children who were too young to make the six-mile journey to town. In the years to come, Margaret and Sarah Miller, Emily's younger sisters, would succeed her as teachers at the station school.

Susannah and her friends were fully prepared for the first show of the Agricultural, Pastoral, Horticultural & Industrial Association. To their great disappointment the Spring Show did not take place because the Showground Committee could not obtain a site. By the autumn of 1882, however, a show was ready to go, site or no site. Albert Park, on Thompson Street across from the church, was the location of the first Cootamundra show, where the Christ Church Refreshment Tent became a popular attraction.

March 29th, 1882

Dear Book,

The Autumn Show was such fun. Lots of people came. It cost grown-ups a shilling to get in. Children only had to pay sixpence.

J.J. brought his new cattle dog Red to the Show and he won a ribbon. J.J. won ribbons for his rye grass and lucerne too. Mamma showed her lovely flowers and some vegetables and preserves. She won a blue ribbon for her bottled peaches. Aunt Jane won a ribbon for her flowers.

Aunt Jane and dear Mamma were very busy in the Refreshment Tent. Everybody came to eat Mamma's mutton stew. Lilla and I had to take care of Goog and Hilda. Goog is a very good baby but dear little Hilda runs everywhere. Next time maybe I can help dear Mamma in the Refreshment Tent.

Papa sat at a big table and wrote things and counted money. Mamma and Papa were very pleased with the Show.

At night we all went to a concert in the Church Schoolroom. Mamma played the pianoforte and Papa sang.

Good night Dear Book.

Nellie Barnes

At Christ Church of England, the Reverend Holt was now assisted by a new Lay Reader, J.J. Miller, who had been examined by Bishop Mesac Thomas in a church service during his annual visitation. J.J. told Susannah he remembered being in the Cathedral Church at Goulburn at age six when the Bishop had examined his father and presented him with his licence.

In 1883 Emily Miller became the first of the Millers to marry. On the 28th of March at Christ Church of England, Emily married Edward Godfrey Webster, a clerk in the Union Bank. Susannah pitched in to help Rebecca and her daughters prepare a grand wedding breakfast in Littledale homestead.

In April of that year, the Reverend Holt, who had served Christ Church for three years, left the parish to become Archdeacon of the growing Riverina congregations. Susannah and Ted missed the Vicar and his wife and son, for they had worked without ceasing for the good of the parish. Mrs. Holt had Susannah's particular regard because she was a remarkable conversationalist and a most capable organizer.

The Reverend Maurice Gray, a good friend to the late John Miller when the Lay Reader first came to the colony, was installed as the incumbent at Christ Church on April 8th, 1883. He was an engaging sort of man and a stirring preacher who had been trained in the Wesleyan Methodist Church. A writer as well as an accomplished preacher, the Reverend Gray soon became an outspoken contributor to the *Cootamundra Herald*. He also gave public lectures on a variety of topics; his dramatic presentation entitled "Livingstone in Africa" was undoubtedly the most memorable.

By September the Trustees of the Agricultural, Pastoral, Horticultural & Industrial Association, with the help of a government grant, had obtained showground space at the edge of town. It was convenient for exhibitors and fairgoers for it had road and railway access. The APH&I Association completed sheep and cattle pens, fowl coops, a grain shed and fencing all round in time for a Spring Show. The *Cootamundra Herald* later reported that the event attracted five hundred patrons and included judging of sheep, cattle and draught horses. Some of the judging was done by J.J. Miller, whose discerning eye was gaining him a reputation as an all-round stock judge. J.J. also won a prize for his Littledale rye grass seed. The Christ Church Refreshment Tent was a popular meeting place and raised a goodly sum for the church.

December 26th, 1883

Dear Book,
We had a wonderful Christmas! We went to Uncle John and Aunt Jane's and had a very big picnic. Afterwards we opened our presents and played card games. Then dear Mamma went to the pianoforte and we all sang Christmas carols.

Dear Mamma and Papa gave me lots of drawing paper and a box of pastel chalk. I will have to take good care of my pastels because little Hilda has already broken one of them.

I have the loveliest present from Grandmamma Barnes. It is a card with a picture of a little child. There is a poem on the back. Papa helped me read the poem. Here is what it says.

O happy were the days of youth
When all the world seemed full of truth
Tho' Life proved but a gilded dream
It brought us gladness with its gleam!
So in the world of Life so wide
Ever strive to see the sunny side

Then ev'ry semblance of a woe
Shall fade 'ere it hath power to grow!
I am not quite sure what it means but I shall keep it and Papa says I will understand it when I am older.
Good night Dear Book.

Nellie Barnes

On February 29th, 1884, Susannah gave birth to another daughter, Bertha Jane. She was a particularly pretty baby, very fair-skinned and because of her reaction to the strong sun of the western slopes, Susannah's Leap Year daughter was known for her lifetime as Peeler.

Rusty, cattle dog

TWENTY-SEVEN

Miller & Miller

But thou, O Lord, art a shield for me;
my glory, and the lifter up of mine head.
— PSALM 3:3

In the early 1880s, Cootamundra still depended on the Vigilance Committee to maintain orderly progress in the town. The committee kept up a steady correspondence with colonial departments at Sydney about Cootamundra's civic requirements, foremost of which was the necessity for incorporation and local government. On May 20th, 1884, their efforts were rewarded when colonial authorities proclaimed the town of Cootamundra and the 3,010 acres of surrounding District land an incorporated borough.

"John couldn't wait to tell me that he intends to run for Borough Council. I'm to be a political wife, it seems," said Jane one afternoon whilst she and Susannah sat knitting in Clapham Cottage. "And Ted says he's been appointed Returning Officer for the first voting," Susannah responded.

In the elections several Vigilance Committee members, including John Barnes, James Simpson and Fred Pinkstone, were elected to Cootamundra's first Borough Council. The councillors chose John Barnes as Cootamundra's first Mayor. According to Susannah's mother-in-law, Elizabeth, when John Frederick Barnes was a boy in Sydney, his father had suggested a political future to him. Now John's career as a politician had begun, and Jane Barnes became Cootamundra's first Mayoress. In that role she was called on to preside at community events and was teased by Susannah on every occasion.

With incorporation of the town came a Magistrate's Court. John Barnes was not only Mayor, but also a Justice of the Peace, as was

Ted. They and six other respected men in town shared magisterial duties in Cootamundra and District. A rota for the Bench, with the date of each session and the presiding Justice, was regularly published in the *Cootamundra Herald*.

In September a Masonic Lodge, St. John, Number 704 of the Scottish Constitution, joined several other lodges at Cootamundra, and Ted and John became members. First to be initiated into the Masonic Lodge at Cootamundra was Ted Barnes, who had been a member of Southern Counties Mark Lodge at Sydney. John Barnes was installed as first Junior Warden. The thirty members of Lodge St. John celebrated at a banquet in Mrs. Angove's new Albion Hotel.

November 6th, 1884

Dear Book,
The new bell rang at Christ Church today. Papa pulled the rope with Mr. Matthews and Mr. McBeath. They are all churchwardens and they bought the bell for the church. It is in the tall tower on the roof. The bell is to bring people to church on time.

After the bell stopped ringing Mamma started playing a hymn and baby Peeler started crying and I had to take her outside.

In church Lilla takes care of Goog and I take care of Peeler. Little Hilda sits with Mamma whilst she plays the organ. Hilda is very fond of music and it helps keep her settled in church Mamma says.

Good night Dear Book.

Nellie Barnes

As Christmas approached that year, the weather became exceptionally dry and much hotter than Susannah had ever experienced. Bushfires flared up in the countryside, and water supplies throughout Cootamundra District were hoarded against further drought and fire danger. Susannah felt suffocated by the searing heat and the drifting smoke of bushfires, and her children were listless and cranky.

The town was tinder-dry one scorching evening when the wind toppled a kerosene lamp on the second-storey verandah of the Cootamundra Store. Beneath the verandah was an awning, which caught the lamp and burst into flames. Ted and John were working late in the store and narrowly escaped when the awning collapsed and flames shot along the wooden footpath below. People in the street rushed to throw pails of water from the town pump at the blazing footpath. The brick construction of the store saved it. The awning was destroyed and the windows and footpath scorched, but thanks to the prompt action of those nearby, the store's stock was not damaged and the upper verandah remained intact. Susannah and Jane were grateful their husbands were safe.

In 1873, when Susannah had first come to Cootamundra, fewer than 250 people lived in the town and District. The census of 1884 revealed a town population of 1,604 and within a radius of twelve miles, a District population of 930. The Cootamundra Store prospered as settlers built new homes and established new businesses.

Susannah and Ted were particularly pleased with the next Autumn Show, which featured horticultural and industrial exhibits. The Ladies' Committee had decided to add new categories of competition to this show: fancy-work, artists' submissions and every kind of collection. Each category, new and traditional, was well represented. The Showground Committee was making plans for a Spring Show in September, which was to include machinery exhibits and livestock competitions.

The Reverend Maurice Gray of Christ Church, who had become a dear friend of Susannah and Ted and a frequent guest at Clapham Cottage, was transferred to a new Riverina parish by Bishop Mesac Thomas. Ted's letters to the Bishop on behalf of the Christ Church congregation, requesting continuance of the Reverend Gray's Cootamundra appointment, had been met with silence.

In Maurice Gray's place, Bishop Thomas sent the Reverend J. Auchinlech Ross, former Precentor of the Cathedral Church of Saint Saviour at Goulburn. As Precentor, the Reverend Auchinlech Ross had been responsible for music at Saint Saviour's: the cathedral choirs, organists, and the selection and rehearsal of psalms, canticles, anthems and hymns for every service. Former clergy at Cootamundra had left the selection, preparation and performance of music entirely up to volunteer organists, but the new incumbent wanted to be much more involved. The Reverend Auchinlech Ross observed Susannah's choir practices closely and pronounced them satisfactory. A handsome, imposing man, who spoke in cultured tones and sang in an impressive baritone, the new incumbent found himself preaching and carrying out pastoral duties when his heart was in church music.

Susannah had come to look forward to J.J.'s weekly calls at Clapham Cottage. He brought news from Littledale and usually a gift from Rebecca: a basket of fruit from her trees or perhaps a leg of lamb or a joint of beef. He always appeared in time for afternoon tea. "J.J. called here today and told me he'd become a Freemason of Lodge St. John," said Susannah to Ted one evening. Ted took a few puffs on his pipe and smiled. "I've never met such an enthusiastic initiate. J.J. Miller has a prodigious memory and at this rate he'll work his way through all the degrees in no time!"

By the summer of 1885, Susannah and Ted's eldest child, Nellie, had gone as far as she could at Cootamundra School. Unlike most of her classmates, who would leave school to help at home or work in town or on stations in the countryside, Nellie was to be sent to boarding school.

"Choosing a place for our sensitive Nellie has us in a quandary," Susannah confided to her mother-in-law Elizabeth. "I've written for the prospectus of a number of schools, and what they have to say for themselves does not reassure me. Some of them boast of calisthenics at dawn and vigorous sporting competitions, a sort of jolly-hockey-sticks atmosphere, I'd say. Other schools advertise military order and cold baths, 'to quell the female urges,' declares the prospectus of one school. Ted and I have always allowed our girls a large measure of freedom and trusted them to use their good sense. Each school seems to emphasize regimentation and iron discipline."

"Sending Nellie away for five years of calisthenics or cold baths would be cruel indeed," said the child's grandmother. "She's such an artistic soul. You must continue your investigations. I shall hope and pray you find a suitable place for her."

In the end Nellie did not go away to boarding school that year. Whilst Susannah was trying to find an appropriate placement for her, she and Ted decided Nellie could wait another year and be enrolled along with Lilla, assuming Susannah could find a school for the two of them by then. Nellie spent the following year helping at Cootamundra School in the infant class, which included little Hilda.

Although Ted and Susannah dearly loved their five daughters, they felt particularly blessed with the arrival of a son on December 23rd, 1885. A bonnie bairn, he was christened Edward Gordon and called Gordon.

December 26th, 1885

Dear Book,
What a lovely Christmas! We have a dear baby brother. He is named Edward Gordon because Edward is Papa's name and Gordon was dear Mamma's surname before she was married. Gordon is a very active baby, like Hilda.

I have the best Christmas present! It is a set of watercolours and brushes of my own with lots of paper for painting on. I think I would rather paint than anything. I have so many scenes in my head to put on paper.

I have been painting at school for a long time and with Grandmamma Barnes on Saturdays. Dear Mamma especially likes the small watercolour I did of a barn with a thatch roof and skillion. We don't have straw thatch like that here, but I remembered reading about straw thatch roofs in an English storybook.

Lilla has been pestering me to share my paints with her but dear Mamma has told her to use our old paints and wait until she gets her own paints next year.

Good night Dear Book.

Nellie Barnes

The year 1886 arrived with a summer storm that inflicted damage across the town and District. The winds, rain and hail were so fierce that small children had to be kept indoors for their safety. There were flash floods throughout the region, and Muttama Creek overflowed its banks and swamped nearby Cootamundra streets. Raging winds tore away the awning of the Cootamundra Store and lifted the roof off an outbuilding at Clapham Cottage. Poor Della, Susannah's new cow, bellowed in terror for three days, whilst the normally calm Missy thrashed about and, despite wearing a blanket, managed to scrape herself on the side of her stall. Motley, Susannah's tortoiseshell cat, lost all her aplomb and refused to come out from behind the kitchen range. The stormy weather gradually subsided, and Ted hired one of Thomas Jobson's carpenters to build a secure roof over the outbuilding and replace the store's awning.

Then, on the 18th of January, Susannah found herself in the depths of sorrow at the death of her mother-in-law Elizabeth. Susannah realized how emotionally attached she had been to Ted's mother, who passed away in her eighty-fourth year.

"Elizabeth Barnes was such a dear woman," Susannah said to Rebecca one afternoon at Littledale. "I'll miss her dreadfully. She was the best of mothers-in-law, always supportive and encouraging, more like a caring mother to me. She arrived in the colony in 1841 after a voyage of fully five months, can you believe, bringing with her three very young children. After the murder of her husband, she coped so very valiantly with life. Her abiding faith in God and her devotion to her family saw her through, I reckon.

"In her final days she asked to speak to Nellie and Lilla. I took the girls to her bedside, and she presented them with mementoes wrapped in tissue paper. She gave Nellie a gold cross and a bloodstone ring, gifts she and her husband had exchanged on their twenty-fifth wedding anniversary. Lilla received the pepper mill and powder horn John Barnes had with him when he was shot.

"Before her last illness, she gathered enough energy to write about her voyage for the girls. I feel privileged to have known her."

January 22nd, 1886

Dear Book,

I have never felt so sad. Grandmamma Barnes has gone to be with Jesus. I know she was very old and needed her Eternal Rest, but I miss her so much. She painted with us on Saturday afternoons and told us about leaving England many years ago. She has written the story of her voyage for us, but I have been too sad to look at it.

When we went to her bedside to say goodbye, I tried not to cry but I did, and so did Lilla. Grandmamma gave us presents from long ago, which we will keep forever. She gave me a gold ring which belonged to Grandpapa Barnes. It has a bloodstone which was cracked when he fell from his horse after the wicked bushranger shot him. Grandmamma also gave me her beautiful gold cross on a chain to wear always. Lilla has Grandpapa's pepper mill and powder horn which he had with him when he was killed. They are scarred with bullet marks.

We went to Grandmamma's funeral, and dear Mamma's choir sang "Let saints on earth in concert sing with those to glory gone," and the Nunc Dimittis hymn, too. Grandmamma Barnes was buried in Cootamundra Cemetery, but Papa told us Grandpapa Barnes was buried at Yass. At the cemetery dear Mamma put flowers on baby Eva's grave and cried.

I am too sad to write any more.
Good night, Dear Book.

Nellie Barnes

Susannah and Jane were sitting on Jane's verandah on a fine autumn day, knitting and sharing their news. Nellie, Lilla and Hilda were at school, baby Gordon was sleeping in his travelling basket in a corner, whilst Goog and Peeler were playing catch-as-catch-can in the garden.

"J.J. came yesterday to show me the business stationery he's had printed for his new enterprise," reported Susannah. "He's such an enthusiast! He and William are setting up as Stock and Station Agents and they're establishing an office in town. They will auction land, stations, livestock, grain and estates. William has left the Bank of New South Wales to work in the agency and he'll use his experience to assess properties for taxation. Their bookkeeper will be Edward Webster, Emily's husband, who has been with the Union Bank. J.J. is giving Compton and Alick more responsibility for farming at Littledale whilst he expands the Littledale yards for auction purposes and conducts business from the agency office in Parker Street. He has promised to call often at Clapham Cottage, looking for a meal, I expect!" Susannah pulled a sheet of Miller & Miller stationery from her knitting bag to show to Jane.

Susannah had always enjoyed taking her family out to Littledale station, where Rebecca welcomed them warmly and the children never failed to find something interesting to do. "Come out this Saturday, why don't you?" said J.J. one November afternoon. "It's my birthday. I'm turning six and twenty. It's also a belated celebration of Margaret's graduation from Sydney University. We're having a great auction and potluck supper! You're bound to have a grand time!"

Margaret Mary Maskelyne Miller had been the first Cootamundra student to graduate from university when she received her Bachelor of Arts degree earlier that year. Susannah and her family went out to congratulate her and watch J.J. and William display their auctioneering skills. Both men now had Cootamundra District auctioneer's licences, and the Littledale yards had become a popular place to buy and sell livestock. The *Cootamundra Herald* reported that as many as ten thousand sheep had been sold on Littledale station in one month. Susannah took along a large dish of her queen of puddings, and after the auction everyone who had contributed to the potluck supper tucked into the meal and then joined in the evening's entertainment.

November 10th, 1886

Dear Book,
What fun we had at the auction on Littledale! So many sheep! J.J. has two sheepdogs named Flash and Victor, and they were very clever at herding sheep into pens and out again.

In the evening Lilla and I played a duet in honour of Margaret's graduation and another one in honour of J.J.'s birthday. Jessie played a lovely sonata, and Willie read a funny poem he had made up for J.J. and Margaret. Then dear Mamma played, and we all sang. Willie always wants to sing "Tramp! Tramp! Tramp! The Boys Are Marching," but I like "Red Is the Rose by Yonder Garden Grows" and "Believe Me, If All Those Endearing Young Charms," which is J.J.'s favourite.

Dear Mamma plays the pianoforte with such flair. Her chords are so firm, and her arpeggios are always dramatic. I shall never be able to play like that.

The ladies brought all sorts of food for Mrs. Miller's table. We stayed up past midnight, and Lilla and I fell asleep with the little ones in the buggy on the way back.

Whilst I was getting into my nightdress at home, I heard Papa and dear Mamma talking about the boarding school Lilla and I will attend. I couldn't get to sleep after that. When dear Mamma is ready, I know she will tell us where we are going. I shall try not to worry.

Good night, Dear Book.

Nellie Barnes

Nellie's painting of a barn and skillion

TWENTY-EIGHT

Maybanke College

Thou, which has shewed me great and sore troubles, shalt quicken me again . . .

— PSALM 71:20

"Welcome to Maybanke College, Nellie and Lilla. I am Mrs. Wolstenholme, and this is Cicely Hampstead, our Head Girl. She will take you to your room in the sleeping quarters whilst I show your father through the college. Cicely will bring you down later to join us for tea." So began Nellie and Lilla's five years at boarding school.

Mrs. Wolstenholme, a champion of women's rights, had divorced her husband and organized a new life for herself by establishing Maybanke College in her spacious residence on a large property in Dulwich Hill at Marrickville in south central Sydney. The college had come highly recommended by Malbon and Letitia Lynch, good friends at Christ Church, whose daughters had attended Maybanke. They described the school as a warm, caring place with a comfortable atmosphere and a Headmistress who could be relied upon to bring out the best in her students.

Several graduating students who had taken Sydney University entrance examinations had qualified for scholarships, and the school's music and art programmes were notable. Susannah corresponded with Mrs. Wolstenholme and was impressed by her interest in art, music and academic achievement. She was also much relieved to read in the prospectus of Maybanke College that Mrs. Wolstenholme decried "military rigour" and regarded her school as "a united family." As well, baths were warm, and physical activities were netball, croquet, bowls and lawn tennis. Both girls were accepted into Fourth Form at Maybanke.

Although confident she had located a good school for Nellie and Lilla, Susannah wept when they left on the train with Ted for Marrickville. The girls would have each other for company, she reminded herself, but she already felt bereft without them. She would write to them every week and Ted would fetch them home at half-term. Meanwhile, she had Hilda, Goog, Peeler and Gordon to care for and she was expecting again.

Saturdays now were often spent out on Littledale station, where Goog and Peeler loved jumping on the straw as much as Nellie and Lilla had when they were little. Seven-year-old Hilda could be found at the Broadwood in the sitting room, playing simple duets with Jessie Miller, age seventeen, who was very patient with her. When the children tired of these activities, Flash's latest litter of puppies provided amusement.

Susannah frequently sat out under a kurrajong tree in the training paddock with Rebecca on those Saturdays, watching J.J. break in a new team. He had developed a reputation as a four-in-hand competitor and later that year planned to enter his four dark bays in the New Teams Class at the Spring Show.

Maybanke College
January 30th, 1887

Dear Mamma and Papa,
I am very remiss in not answering your letters, dear Mamma. My excuse is that I have been very busy settling in at Maybanke. Please forgive me.

Lilla and I felt so sad when we said goodbye to Papa that first day. Cicely Hampstead, the Head Girl, told us to buck up. All new girls feel blue, she said. She is always so cheerful and breezy. We will get used to her, and she truly is helpful.

We have little time to ourselves because our schedule is full. Breakfast is very early, then Morning Prayer. Mathematics (not my strong suit) is the first class (Geometry problems at the moment), followed by Grammar and Composition (much easier). We break for Morning Tea and then have Literature or History or Geography classes, all quite enjoyable. After Dinner there is Science class (Botany presently, which is interesting), followed by Arts: pianoforte instruction (Lilla's favourite), or school choir, or fancy work, or drawing and painting (which I like best), then Afternoon Tea. We have two hours of games before Evening Tea. Although we must participate in all games, Lilla and I have decided tennis will be our sport and we are getting better at it. In the evening we have two hours of Prep, then Lights Out.

Thank you, dear Mamma, for your weekly news from Clapham Cottage: Papa's many meetings, Hilda's progress on the pianoforte and the funny antics of Goog and Peeler. I'm sure adventuresome little Gordon keeps you busy indeed!

I must tell you we are enjoying Maybanke. The girls are friendly, and our teachers are kindly and encouraging, except for Miss Wightwick ("Miss Wittick, if you please!"). She has no patience with students who do not pronounce her name correctly or share her fiendish passion for Mathematics.

I remain your loving daughter,

Nellie

Maybanke College continued to provide Nellie and her sister Lilla with a protective yet enriching environment for the next five years. Those same years in Susannah's life were to haunt her forever.

Susannah quickly realized that raising an active little boy like Gordon demanded more of her attention than raising all five girls. Her daughters, even busy little Hilda, kept themselves happily amused in the house, or played close by when she worked in the kitchen garden or relaxed on the verandah doing handiwork. Her son, in contrast, climbed before he could walk, and one afternoon, alerted by Goog's cries of distress, Susannah found him creeping the length of the dining room table.

By eleven months Gordon, a tall child, was up on his feet, running circles around the family and learning to open doors. Now he had to be watched by someone every waking moment, for he was soon out of the house, through the gate and off to visit neighbours. Yet vigilance by Susannah, her family and the neighbours ultimately proved in vain, as revealed in the *Cootamundra Herald* on February 26th, 1887.

SAD FATAL ACCIDENT—One of the most horrifying accidents occurred in Cootamundra on Wednesday, the 23rd of February, and the townspeople were fearfully shocked and stricken with grief on account of it. About 11 o'clock it became known that the fourteen-month-old son of Mr. E.P. Barnes was missing. The parents and friends and neighbours exerted themselves in the search for the little fellow; and this search—horrible to relate—resulted in the discovery of the child's body in the cesspit at Mr. Barnes's. The closet being protected in every reasonable way, it is marvellous how the child managed to fall into the pit, but the only means that appeared feasible after examination was through the closet seat. The details will be found in the report of the magisterial inquiry. (Mr. Barnes being the coroner, an inquiry by the Police Magistrate was held.) We cannot find words adequate to express our own feelings towards the bereaved parents, as to no parents in the whole community could such an accident have occurred to cause more intense grief than they must suffer for some time to come. Mrs. Barnes, naturally, was uncontrollable in her agony of mind on learning the sad truth.

The body was interred at an early hour on Thursday morning.

April 18th, 1887

Dear Book,
When dear little Gordon died, Papa wrote to us at once with the horrible news. He said dear Mamma was just distraught. She has always sent us a letter each week, but she did not write to us for more than a month. Perhaps she was just too full of misery to say anything. Lilla and I wrote immediately to express our sympathy and share our grief. Gordon was such a vigorous little boy, eager to run about when he was less than a year old.

At Easter Break, dear Mamma, wearing black once more, made an effort, despite her mourning, to be her usual cheerful self. She sewed black arm bands for us to wear whilst we were at Coota, and Lilla and

I tried to be particularly helpful during our holiday, not wanting to add any concerns to dear Mamma's burdens.

In trying to provide a distraction, Papa took Lilla and me to the Athletic Sports at the Showground on Easter Monday, although the weather was most inclement. I must say the strength and endurance of the contestants deserved admiration. The crowning event of the afternoon was the 120-Yard Dash. Willie Miller easily won the first two heats and competed with twenty other men in the final heat, which he won by eight yards. He was presented with the Easter Cup, an engraved silver goblet valued at ten guineas. We were very proud of him.

And now, back to Mathematics prep. Naughty students that we are, we amuse ourselves with Miss Wightwick's name. She is tall, stringy, with flaming red hair, and we call her "The Wick." To my horror, she caught me sketching "The Wick" in my notebook (a very accurate sketch!) and gave me five demerits. Poor me!

Dear little Gordon, our only brother. Such a cheerful, active wee boy, always eager to learn about everything. What a dreadful end to his short life.

Good night, Dear Book.

Nellie Barnes

The hills around Cootamundra were home to a multitude of sheep which wandered with their shepherds far from farms in the western valleys in search of good grazing. The well-situated Littledale station had become the place to take sheep for auction by Miller & Miller. According to the *Cootamundra Herald*, in just one month eighteen thousand sheep had been mobbed at Littledale yards and seventeen thousand of them had been sold.

In the Barnes family, Ted and John and their sister and brothers were now making arrangements for their father's remains to be removed from Yass to Cootamundra. When John Barnes, Sr. had been shot and killed at Wallendbeen in 1863, the family had taken his body to Yass for burial in the only consecrated ground available. In 1887 the family brought his remains to Cootamundra, interred them next to Elizabeth's in the Church of England section of Cootamundra Cemetery, and commissioned a large monument over both graves. One side of the monument commemorated Elizabeth Barnes; the inscription on the other side read "Erected to the memory of John Barnes who was shot by bushrangers on the 30th of August 1863. Aged 51 years." A tall iron fence surrounded the burial plots.

Three months after Gordon's death, Susannah went into an early labour. Many hours later she was delivered of twin sons. They were stillborn. Her two tiny sons were perfect, but lifeless. Susannah lay huddled in bed, weeping, grief-stricken and inconsolable. Ted, consumed by his own sorrow over Gordon and now two stillborn sons, was greatly worried. The loss of Eva and especially Gordon had left Susannah distraught, but she had gradually rallied. Coming so soon after Gordon's death, this latest tragedy had robbed her of all spirit. She remained curled up in bed, sobbing, refusing to eat, quite unaware of Ted or her other children.

Jane Barnes and Rebecca Miller arrived at Clapham Cottage, Jane to do Susannah's chores and Rebecca to take Hilda, Goog and Peeler out to Littledale. Six weeks went by before Susannah roused herself from her bed, put on her unrelieved black dress and began to take part in life again. To the end of her days, she bore the image of those two perfect baby boys lying lifeless before her.

In the year 1888 a severe drought settled across the western slopes of New South Wales. Total precipitation, as reported in the *Cootamundra Herald*, was twelve and sixty-five hundredths inches. The lack of rain had a serious effect on Littledale station and the Cootamundra Store. When crops and livestock flourished, auctions could sell grain, sheep and cattle in abundance, and farmers had money to spend at stores in Parker Street. The drought of Centenary Year in New South Wales destroyed grain and livestock across the District. Miller & Miller auctions at Littledale were infrequent, and Cootamundra Store customers were few.

Susannah was concerned for Ted. He was a quiet man by nature and not given to complaining, but his solemn discussions with his brother revealed how worried they were about the business. Ted's health was another problem. He was four and forty years of age, but looked much older. For many years he had been prone to chest ailments, and Susannah was certain his incessant pipe smoking had worsened his condition. His breathing was laboured, and he had little energy for tending to any commitment.

"We've had an offer on the store," he said on a dry, windy night as they were getting ready for bed. Susannah stopped plaiting her hair and stared at him. "Surely to goodness you're not thinking of going out of business!" she said. Ted nodded. "John and I have been talking of retiring from storekeeping. I have plenty of community interests to occupy my time, and John is thinking of expanding his political endeavours to the colonial legislature. We've both invested our funds prudently, and the amount offered for the store by Newman and his sons is especially generous, particularly in this time of drought. If we continue to be careful with our investments, we should all be able to live comfortably."

Susannah, who had been a storekeeper's wife for almost fourteen years, was not able to sleep that night. Could she manage if Ted were to support his family only on retirement funds? Fergus, the Scots seaman on the *Commissary*, suddenly flashed into her mind, something about keeping a "tight grip" on her purse.

Several months went by before negotiations were completed, and R.A. Newman & Sons from Tumut became the new owners of the Cootamundra Store.

April 27th, 1888

Dear Book,
We had a wonderful Easter Break at Coota this year, but I was eager to get back to Maybanke because I've completed a large oil painting of Sydney Heads which I'm keen to show to our drawing and painting mistress, Miss Quinn.

Miss Quinn and Mrs. Wolstenholme often take us on afternoon excursions to do sketches and write descriptions of scenes around Sydney. We must strive for realism in a finished painting, says Miss Quinn, as proof of our powers of observation. She's a stickler for powers of observation.

When I told Willie Miller we were studying Geology this term, he invited me on a ramble over the hills of Littledale to search for specimens. He has an extensive collection of rocks and minerals and he helped me get started on mine. I have begun to write to him from Maybanke. He is interested in our Maths and Science courses and has sent me some notes for Algebra, a subject I find even more difficult than Geometry.

Literature is a blessing each day, for I can lose myself in the works of great English writers. At the moment we're studying the Eighteenth Century, and I'm enjoying the wit of Jonathan Swift and Alexander Pope and the romantic writings of William Blake.

I really must stop and see if Willie's notes will help me solve some wretched Algebra problems, then I can think about our next excursion with Miss Quinn and Mrs. Wolstenholme.

Good night, Dear Book.

Nellie Barnes

On their return to Maybanke after Easter, Nellie and Lilla launched into new assignments. Nellie was still struggling with Algebra and excelling at Painting, whilst Lilla was becoming an accomplished pianist. Nellie's oil painting of Sydney Heads, those great sandstone cliffs protecting the entrance to the harbour, pleased Miss Quinn. "You are developing your technique, my dear. You have caught the effect of afternoon light on the sandstone and your use of perspective improves with each piece of work. A woodsy scene next, I think, all shadows and hollows. I have a parkland excursion in mind."

Such encouragement! Miss Quinn tended to be a taciturn taskmistress, peering over her pince-nez to scrutinize her students' work and saying, "Hmmm," or "Possible," or "Good Heavens! No!" Any praise from her was highly prized.

Nellie and Lilla had been accompanied on their return to school by their mother and Aunt Jane, for Jane Barnes had decided that the grieving Susannah was much in need of a diversion. Rebecca Miller offered to take care of the younger Barnes girls, leaving Jane and Susannah free to spend a week at Sydney, canvassing long-time suppliers of the Cootamundra Store for donations of prizes for the raffle at the next Christ Church Bazaar.

The raffle had become a major fundraiser for the church, and Susannah and Jane had agreed the raffle winners deserved more exotic rewards. They set out to see what could be donated to the cause. By the end of the week, they had collected boxes of goods: men's silver cuff links and shirt studs, silk cravats, stickpins, fine leather gloves, silver belt buckles and ornate pipe racks, ladies' beaded reticules, silver bangles, necklaces, scarves, kid gloves, perfumes and silk shawls. These and other items were designed to tempt stockmen and jackeroos who showed up at the bazaar each night during September Race Week. Station hands and local punters could be counted on to gamble their race winnings in hopes of acquiring a luxurious item for themselves or their ladies.

Susannah and Jane realized the devil was in the details of the raffle. Popular though it was, it was still gambling in aid of a church. The punters paid a shilling each to be one of five competitors in a raffle. Each competitor had three throws of a dice box containing three dice, the prize going to the gambler with the highest total. Raffles went on all evening, and such was the excitement generated that raffle subscriptions were a reliable source of funds in providing Christ Church fitments and reducing the church debt.

"We must make a decision about the raffle soon, Jane," said Susannah one afternoon on their return to Coota. "We've had complaints from parishioners over the years about throwing dice to raise money for the church. No one ever complains about the raffle itself, just how it's conducted! The raffle was J.J.'s idea. I'm going to ask him for suggestions."

At Susannah's table at lunchtime, J.J. laughed when he heard her concern, but admitted the opinion of churchgoers had to be considered. "Discard the dice box and try a lottery bag with numbered discs," he said. "Have five discs drawn in turn by each contestant, with the highest total in each contest determining the winner." He added, "I'd be the first to tell you that using a lottery bag rather than a dice box is merely a distinction without a difference!" From then on, a lottery bag provided excitement, exotic prizes and funds for Christ Church, and no further complaints were heard.

At the fortnight Winter Break, Nellie and Lilla found their mother still affected by grief over her stillborn boys. Their Papa seemed unsettled as well. The girls asked to spend a few days on Littledale, and when arrangements were made, they happily escaped to the sheep and cattle station with all its amusements. J.J. had a new bull, which he called Monarch the Second. His original bull, Monarch, had been carted off to the slaughterhouse. Nellie was saddened by that news but impressed by the replacement. One afternoon she sat on a fence and sketched the second king of the Littledale cattle herd.

During the Christmas Term at Maybanke, outdoor pursuits became emphasized, with more time for games, beach walks, explorations and boating excursions in Sydney Harbour to picnic sites, where journal-writing and sketching were expected. As she sat looking out over Sydney Harbour, Nellie often thought of dear Mamma and Mrs. Miller sailing into the harbour and her Grandmamma Barnes arriving in 1841 with three small children after five months at sea. What a welcome sight the harbour must have been!

Nellie and Lilla were devoting any free moment at school to lawn tennis, serving and volleying for hours in an effort to improve their strokes. Challenging team members to stronger and more accurate shots was Mrs. Wolstenholme herself, who was enthusiastic about encouraging her tennis players.

At Coota, meanwhile, Jane and Susannah Barnes set about organizing a parish flower show in the Church of England Schoolroom. Jane grew flowers in abundance, as did Susannah, and Rebecca Miller cultivated an attractive array of blooms around Littledale homestead. Jane and Susannah agreed on an admission charge for the show, with an additional charge if patrons wished to fill out a flower judging sheet. Flower Show funds would be another contribution towards paying off Christ Church debt. The ladies recruited William Miller and his Sunday School choir to provide appropriate music, donations from the audience always appreciated.

Now finishing their second year at Maybanke College, Nellie and Lilla looked forward to year-end Prize Day. Dear Mamma and Papa had written to say they would both attend. The girls were pleased to see dear Mamma no longer in unrelieved black, but in a dress of deep plum edged with lavender and a black hat trimmed with lavender tulle. They thought that Papa, although wearing a new buff-coloured summer suit and broad-brimmed straw hat, looked very wan and tired.

The prize-giving was held in Mrs. Wolstenholme's spacious garden in the shade of acacias. The ceremony was full of music and colour: flowers in glorious bloom, faculty and guests in their finery, students in summer frocks. Following Mrs. Wolstenholme's words of welcome, the school choir, including Nellie and Lilla, performed two folk songs: "Flow Gently, Sweet Afton!" and "The Ash Grove," once a favourite of Grandmamma Elizabeth Barnes. Next came a speech by the Head Girl, not a breezy type like last year's Cicely Hampstead, but a solemn girl who paid great tribute to the faculty. A star in Mathematics, she praised the teaching of Miss Wightwick, who would not have been Nellie's first choice. At the interlude Lilla played for the assembly, accompanied on the violin by another Fifth Form student. The girls had chosen a Schubert sonata. Susannah, Ted and Nellie were quite overcome with pride.

On a table on the platform, book prizes wrapped in tissue paper stood waiting. Mrs. Wolstenholme announced a variety of categories: an award for every classroom subject, as well as for sports and good conduct. Nellie sat quietly, not daring to expect she would be judged best at anything. Of course, her artistic talents were known, but she was aware that Miss Quinn taught other students who were even more talented. Mrs. Wolstenholme introduced the prizewinners in each Form, and the garden rustled with the unwrapping of tissue paper.

Nellie was certain all prizes had been awarded to the Fifth Form when she heard her name called. She made her way across the lawn to the platform to receive her award. Like other winners, she returned to her seat beside her parents for hugs and congratulations and proceeded to open her book prize. The volume, its cover embellished in gold leaf, was *The Poetical Works of Alexander Pope*. A congratulatory card was tucked into the back of the book; on one side of the card was a portrait of Mrs. Wolstenholme and on the other was written, "With love, from M.S. Wolstenholme." The inscription inside the book read:

MAYBANKE COLLEGE

Awarded to

Nellie Barnes

Form 5 Special Prize

for

Good Conduct in House and School

Christmas, 1888

M. S. Wolstenholme

The writer Alexander Pope was one of her favourite poets. Mrs. Wolstenholme, who taught Nellie's class in Literature, would have known that. A prize for good conduct? Nellie had simply behaved every day as she always had, notwithstanding that regrettable lapse in drawing "The Wick." She graciously acknowledged the prize and congratulations, but resolved to work harder at her painting. The Head Girl, as expected, won the Higher Sixth Form prize in Mathematics.

Prize Day ended with the choir leading the assembly in the Doxology and "God Save the Queen." After luncheon with their parents, the girls, who were packed and ready to go home, left to enjoy the summer holiday.

TWENTY-NINE

Clapham Cottage

In the multitude of my thoughts within me,
thy comforts delight my soul.

—PSALM 94:19

The girls' summer holiday began with Christmas celebrations at Clapham Cottage, where Nellie, Lilla and their sisters were responsible for decorating the house. Hilda, Goog and Peeler fashioned red and green paper chains to hang over doorways and twine around railings. In lieu of the aromatic pine boughs in Susannah's London home, Nellie and Lilla placed sprigs of eucalypt on the mantelpieces and arranged bouquets of flowers in the dining room and drawing room. The best fun, despite the hot summer weather, was roasting popcorn at the kitchen range, where a covered pan snapped with exploding kernels. The girls took a big bowl of popcorn, drizzled with melted butter and sprinkled with salt, out to share on the back verandah.

Their mother inevitably appeared and said, "You're popping that corn to string decorations, not to eat!" If the sisters timed things right, they could eat at least one bowl of buttered popcorn before dear Mamma caught them. Even Goog and Peeler helped to string popcorn, although the thread sometimes got tangled and an errant needle often drew blood. "Look!" said Goog. "My fingers are making pink popcorn!" Nellie and Lilla shrieked at her, and Mamma told them to be patient with the little ones.

Susannah had done much of the kitchen preparation before Ted went to Sydney to collect Nellie and Lilla. Two kinds of shortbread, one with castor and the other with demerara sugar, were stored away, as were light and dark Christmas cakes, Christmas puddings, jars of mincemeat for tarts, and tightly wrapped packages of marzipan and candied fruits for Christmas breads.

A goose from Littledale was hanging in a shed, causing the venerable Motley to pace about, sniffing in anticipation. Equally agitated was Jet, once Motley's fluffy black kitten Susannah had not wanted to give away and now a hefty male with masses of black fur. He and Motley almost went spare when the fowl was plucked and its innards removed.

December was windy and hot in Cootamundra, but Susannah had had enough of picnics at Christmas. This year they would have a traditional English yuletide. The dining table was extended to its limit two days before Christmas and fully set. Then the largest bed sheet, suspended on surrounding chairs, had been draped over it. Susannah was taking no chances their careful work would become dusty or disturbed.

On the morning of Christmas Eve, whilst she rolled pastry for mince tarts, she put Nellie and Lilla to work kneading bread dough for loaves that would be filled with marzipan and candied fruit. Early on Christmas Day, Susannah stuffed the goose, telling Nellie and Lilla the vegetables were their responsibility. The two girls enjoyed the breeze on the back verandah, surrounded by vegetables and pots.

"How many more potatoes, Mamma?" asked Nellie, bored stiff with peeling. "Don't stop peeling, love! We won't stint for Uncle John and Aunt Jane and your cousins! Lilla, it's time you were done with the carrots and cabbage. Hilda, you can pare these apples for the sauce. Mind your fingers with the knife. My dear Goog, stop running around and take this list. Sit here at the kitchen table where I can keep an eye on you whilst you write a place card for each guest. Peeler, sit with her and watch how it's done."

The goose, filled with onion stuffing, was trussed, larded and placed in the oven. Susannah chased the girls into the house to dress for the eleven o'clock service at church. She called to Ted, who had stayed well away from the kitchen, setting out garden furniture and arranging hoops for a game of croquet after dinner.

Susannah was of the opinion her church music at Christmas was never as polished as her presentation at Easter. The music of the Nativity was glorious, but her choristers were distracted by Christmas festivities and summer heat and were not easy to direct. She was the only one who seemed to notice, however, aside from the Reverend Auchinlech Ross, who frowned at any carelessly performed passage. On Christmas Day the Christ Church congregation joined in the music with gusto, overwhelming her choir on "Hark! the Herald Angels Sing," "Christians Awake, Salute the Happy Morn," "Brightest and Best of the Sons of the Morning," and the familiar Wesleyan hymn "Come, Thou Long-expected Jesus." For the choir anthem Susannah had chosen "Lo! He Comes with Clouds Descending." Its sweet eighteenth-century music, with the triple repetition of the penultimate line in each stanza, was an inspired choice, she said to herself. This year she had rehearsed her choir in a new piece of Christmas music to be sung softly whilst parishioners received their Holy Communion. The carol, an English translation of "Stille Nacht! Heilige Nacht!," was one she had brought with her from London. She thought the Austrian melody and harmonies were particularly beautiful.

After the service the family exchanged Christmas greetings with the Reverend Auchinlech Ross, who declared the Christmas music "most enthusiastic," and the gentle rendering of "Silent Night!" during the Eucharist "worth polishing for next year." The two Barnes families made their way to Cooper Street and Clapham Cottage, where Susannah basted the goose, set vegetables on the range to boil, and put beef stock in a pan over to the side to simmer for gravy. Meanwhile, Ted poured wine for the adults and small glasses of peach cordial for the children. He helped Susannah lift the goose from the roasting pan onto a platter. He carried it to the table for carving whilst Susannah poured off grease from the pan to cool and save for rubbing on chests when congestions hit in the wintertime. Ted's chest had often been the recipient of goose grease poulticed with a piece of flannel when his cough was worse than usual.

Susannah's English Christmas dinner was a great success. John Barnes drew the wishbone and won the pull with his brother. The adults had second helpings of goose, which was reduced to a rack. Brandy flamed satisfactorily over the Christmas puddings as Susannah bore them to the table, and those with ample appetites finished off their meal with mince tarts, Christmas cake and shortbread.

Nellie and Lilla were put in charge of the children in the garden whilst Ted and John smoked their pipes on the verandah and talked politics, and Susannah and Jane did the washing up. The summer sun lingered in golden splendour over the Cootamundra hills as everyone exchanged gifts and began a spirited croquet match on the lawn. Jane Barnes, a great competitor, took the croquet prize, which was a box of writing paper, and Peeler won ribbons for her hair because she was the youngest in the match. Susannah served Christmas cakes and marzipan fruit breads with evening tea before Jane and John and their family set off for home.

In the Christmas break Nellie and Lilla were full of stories about Maybanke and eager to see friends in town and spend time on Littledale station. Nellie wanted to ask for Willie Miller's help with a Botany assignment, whilst Lilla was keen on having Jessie Miller play the pianoforte with her.

Nellie and Willie spent several afternoons rambling over Littledale station, identifying flowers. Willie was partial to showy blooms like the *Banksias* and *Eschscholtzia californica*, the California poppy, whilst Nellie preferred to look for delicate blossoms such as *Lysiana subfalcata*, a mistletoe parasite in the acacias, or *Oxalis corniculata*, the yellow wood sorrel. At Maybanke she planned to do watercolour illustrations of her botanical collection. Meanwhile, Lilla practised with Jessie on the Broadwood in the sitting room. Those days ended with Nellie and Lilla joining the Millers for Rebecca's renowned suppers.

February 26th, 1889

Dear Book,
The weather is so hot, I don't feel like doing Prep.

Today I had my appointment with Mrs. Wolstenholme to finalize the subjects I will present in the University Entrance Examinations in two years' time. She knows what a trial Mathematics is for me and suggested I prepare Arithmetic instead. I said that sounded weak and childish, but she told me I must attempt some sort of Mathematical subject, and Arithmetic would be perfectly acceptable. I have dropped Algebra and Geometry entirely (Lilla says that I have "pinched The Wick!") and will report to Mrs. Wolstenholme's office twice a week for tutoring in Arithmetic. Speed and accuracy drills will lead to success in problem-solving, she says. My other examination subjects will be Geology, English, Botany and Geography. With all the time I've spent out on Littledale station collecting specimens with Willie, I should find Geology and Botany my easiest subjects.

I need to tell you something, Dear Book, something I haven't told anyone, not even Lilla. One afternoon during the summer holiday, after Willie and I had rambled over the hills at Littledale for several hours, we stopped to rest and admire the view of the valley. To my amazement, Willie took my hand, looked at me with those steely grey eyes of his and told me he was in love with me and one day he hoped I would be his wife! I was quite overcome and spluttered that I was only fourteen years of age and still at school, but he said he would wait for years, if I would give him permission to do so. What could I say? He is so much older than I am, but I have known him forever and feel comfortable with him and his family. I asked him if we could be friends as we've always been until I am ready for marriage and he said of course we could and then gave me a long, gentle kiss! I really don't remember walking back to Littledale homestead that afternoon.

There! I've told you, Dear Book, and since I keep you locked away, no one else will know what's in my heart. I think I love Willie, yet I'm really too young to be sure. Naturally, I'm excited, but I must complete my studies at Maybanke before I can even think of marriage and I'm keen to try university, too.

Lilla will be back soon from pianoforte practice. I'll get busy on some timed multiplication drills.

Good night, Dear Book.

Nellie Barnes

"Come up and see the new house!" said Jane to Susannah and Ted at church one Sunday. "I have a picnic luncheon ready, and afterwards you can have the grand tour!" The new Shaftesbury, built at a view location on their Jindalee property, was a handsome brick residence, still under construction. "John's first retirement project," Jane called it.

"When the house is finished," said John, "I'm going to seek support for nomination as a candidate in the next colonial elections. The Gundagai Constituency will soon be available, and I intend to run for the seat in the Legislative Assembly."

"You'll have my support in your campaign," said his brother. "Tell you what we'll do: you win the election, and I'll organize a grand celebration for you in town!"

"Done!" said John, shaking his hand.

In February 1889, John Frederick Barnes was elected Member of the Legislative Assembly for Gundagai Constituency. The *Herald* reported his return to Cootamundra by train and his brief journey in a Finlay and Corbett's Mail Coach to the Club Hotel, which had a fine balcony. There Ted introduced him in glowing terms, and a welcoming crowd in the street was treated to the stentorian tones of MLA John F. Barnes as he promised to serve the needs of his constituency and the colony. Later, at the new Shaftesbury, Jane hosted a celebratory luncheon for the Barnes families of Murrumburrah and Cootamundra.

At Christ Church, ten years of fundraising at bazaars, refreshment tents and flower shows had had the desired effect of reducing the debt and providing interior fitments, including an organ. Soon a finely crafted, octagonal pulpit made of close-grained cedar and pine from Queensland was installed, and Susannah was busy preparing music for its dedication.

"Ted, I've decided every English church must come equipped with a pulpit, because I can't find any designated music for separately dedicating one. I think I'll look for rousing tunes and hope they create a suitable atmosphere."

Ted puffed on his pipe for a few moments and had a bout of coughing before suggesting, "How about 'Lord of the Worlds Above' for the processional?"

"Just the thing," said Susannah, "and let's have 'Christ, Whose Glory Fills the Skies' and 'Awake, My Soul.' I'll use 'Ye Servants of God' for the recessional. None of them mentions a pulpit, but they're all inspirational."

The pulpit dedication service went well, enhanced by Susannah's choice of music, which the Reverend Auchinlech Ross found most suitable. Fundraising for the pulpit had begun with J.J. Miller's Auction of Treasures at church bazaars, and the Lay Reader was obviously proud of the result. Susannah reckoned he could not wait to try the pulpit himself.

A hospital at Cootamundra was also nearly complete, and Ted and John, members of the original committee and now Life Members of the Hospital Society, were helping to plan the opening ceremonies. John Barnes, MLA, learned that the Governor of New South Wales, His Excellency, Lord Carrington, would be visiting the western slopes at that time and wrote to ask if he would be so kind as to officiate at the hospital opening. The Governor said he would be pleased to do so, and a public holiday in Cootamundra and District was declared on August 29th, 1889, to honour the Governor's visit. That was also the day the Agricultural, Pastoral, Horticultural & Industrial Association opened its Spring Show, and Susannah suggested to her brother-in-law that the Governor might like to tour the showground. The Governor said he would look forward to a showground tour. J.J. Miller reminded his Lodge Brethren that the Governor was Grand Master of Masonic Lodges and should be invited to a meeting of Lodge St. John at Cootamundra. The Governor graciously accepted.

"Poor man!" said Susannah. "He'll be run off his feet all day!"

"No worries," said Ted. "The *Herald* says here that he'll be moving about 'in H.E. Thorne's sociable, drawn by four matched cream ponies,' in case you thought he had to walk anywhere!"

Lord Carrington arrived by train and led a grand procession down Parker Street in the self-same sociable, opened Cootamundra Hospital, ate luncheon and toured the showground where, to the delight of fairgoers, who numbered four thousand that day, he descended from the sociable to meet some of them. He took afternoon tea and later attended a Masonic Lodge meeting and dinner. At dinner he talked Lodge business with the Brethren, who presented him with a commemorative album from their Lodge. The Governor must surely have been impressed with Cootamundra, or so John Barnes declared afterwards to Ted and Susannah.

Susannah's greatest joy that year was knowing she was expecting another baby. The child would be a boy, she was sure, and they would name him Edward John. She gave birth to a son on September 14th, 1889, and the family was ecstatic. His sisters fussed over him, carried him around, and wheeled him out in the perambulator to show him to everyone.

A fortnight before Christmas, Hilda, Goog and Peeler came down with diarrhoea, and in no time baby Edward also fell ill. Susannah summoned Dr. Anderson, who prescribed rest and a liquid diet for the children. Susannah made chicken broth for the girls and suckled the baby day and night. Hilda, Goog and Peeler recovered quickly, but baby Edward, age three and a half months, died on December 27th, 1889, cradled in Susannah's arms.

Susannah summoned a seamstress and whilst having a new mourning dress fitted, stood in silence, her tears streaming. With his parents and five sisters weeping at his graveside, Edward was buried beside the other Barnes babies.

January 6th, 1890

Dear Book,

Such a tragic Christmas. Poor dear Mamma and Papa are very brave.

Lilla and I hardly knew Edward John, for he was born whilst we were at Maybanke. We had scarcely arrived home for Christmas when he fell ill. Poor wee bairn, he struggled so hard, but he was too weak to survive. No one noticed it was Christmastime. We just hovered over the baby.

Dear Mamma and Papa have buried Eva and four baby boys and we can only imagine the extent of their grief.

After baby Edward's burial, we went out to Littledale, where Mrs. Miller had arranged a lovely luncheon for us. Later, Willie and I went for a long walk.

Willie is very kind and attentive, and my feelings for him grow stronger every time we are together. He has been writing to me at Maybanke each fortnight, telling me about Littledale and his family's activities and his work at Miller & Miller. I always share his correspondence with Lilla, and I have had to take her into my confidence because Willie includes many affectionate expressions in his letters. Lilla finds it all very exciting and eagerly awaits his next correspondence!

I must go and sit for a while with Papa and dear Mamma. Lilla and I are doing our best to be of help whilst we are at home.

Good night, Dear Book.

Nellie Barnes

Susannah, consumed by grief, was consoled by her dearest friend and sister-in-law Jane Barnes. Jane knew only too well the depth of pain a mother suffered at the death of a child: she had lost four babies of her own.

"May I offer you a bit of cheerful company in exchange for a slice of your most excellent peach tart?" asked J.J. He had come into Susannah's kitchen, as he did once a week, taking a break from the affairs of Miller & Miller and looking for something to eat.

"Sit down. I can offer you chicken salad with fresh rolls and a slice of tart," said Susannah. "Tell me all the news. I haven't been at church, as you know. I really must rouse myself and get back into things. Each time I lose a baby, it takes me longer to recover." She pulled a handerkerchief from her apron pocket, wiped her eyes and went off to get cold chicken and greens to serve with the butter rolls she had baked that morning.

"You must take your time," said J.J., as he enjoyed the chicken salad. "Everyone knows what you've been through, and you have our sympathy and understanding. Now, sit with me whilst I tell you my plans. First of all, I'm going to run for Borough Council. I believe people in the District need representation on the council, a voice of the rural voters, whose concerns are often overshadowed by problems of the town. I have just filed my nomination papers. Secondly, the Colonial Mutual Livestock Insurance Society has given notice it will be represented at Cootamundra, and Miller & Miller has been accepted as its agent. The Colonial is a fine company, well funded, and we will be able to bring peace of mind to many a grazier by offering reliable insurance protection. Thirdly, Willie and I are part of a group organizing a Cootamundra musical and dramatic society. I'm certain you and Ted will want to be involved." J.J.'s enthusiasm was so infectious, Susannah began to smile in spite of herself.

"I wish you best of luck in the Borough Council elections," she said, "and in your insurance business. As for the musical and dramatic society, I suspect you're depending on Ted's singing and my pianoforte-playing. You've probably hit upon the very thing to restore our spirits. Let us know when we can get started."

"That's grand! Now then, Mother says to invite you all to a potluck supper on Littledale this Saturday. I'm having a hare drive and kangaroo hunt and I could use Ted's help in keeping track of scalps and tails. Afterwards, we'll have a party. Perhaps you could bring along your queen of puddings." Susannah smiled at him and realized she was feeling better than she had in weeks.

She was familiar with hare drives, kangaroo hunts and wild dog shoots—grisly events, but essential for the maintenance of grazing property and protection of livestock, and always followed by a party. Ted would help with the count, which was the measure of a drive's success, shooters receiving a small bounty for each scalp or tail presented. Whilst the men and their horses and dogs went hunting, she and her girls would enjoy the Littledale garden and the company of Rebecca and her daughters.

During the annual polling J.J. Miller was elected to the Borough Council, and Rebecca held a victory celebration for him in Littledale homestead. Down at Miller & Miller, the contract with Colonial Mutual Livestock Insurance Society was proving beneficial to the insurers and their agent as well as to local graziers. Despite J.J.'s enthusiasm for the Cootamundra Musical & Dramatic Society, it was not organized until September, with William Miller elected Treasurer and Ted elected one of the Vice-Presidents. After perusing several scripts, members agreed on an ambitious offering, *Les Cloches de Cornville*, a popular operetta in three acts, as their first production.

The town was still recovering from a calamity in May, a fierce fire that had devastated a building next to the offices of Miller & Miller. The blaze had started in Mangan's Clarendon Store, and Dr. Brown's son, according to the *Cootamundra Herald*, had heroically entered the burning store and removed the supply of gunpowder before it could explode. Furniture and books were rescued from Miller & Miller and their premises survived, but the damaged building next door had to be demolished to contain the fire. Cootamundra was faced with fire losses estimated at seven thousand pounds.

"We've put everything in our office to rights," J.J. announced to Susannah at noon one dreary day. He was tucking into mutton stew and fresh bread. "No harm done at our agency, and insurers have been prompt in covering the losses of the burned premises. The council is responsible for some expenses, of course, but we'll make those up in time. My latest news is that I'm off to Sydney next week to attend an agricultural meeting as Cootamundra's representative. Delegates are meeting in the board room of the Colonial Secretary's Office to discuss agricultural concerns. It promises to be an important conference." When J.J. had finished a second helping of stew, Susannah served him a dish of peach cobbler.

That winter a highlight in Cootamundra was the completion in Cooper Street of the Masonic Hall of Lodge St. John. A service of dedication was held in Christ Church on the 10th of July, and Susannah sought the help of Ted, J.J. and William in choosing the music. The men suggested the titles of three rousing hymns and Susannah added "The Spacious Firmament on High," with its inspirational lyrics by Addison and stirring music by Haydn. In honour of the event, the offertory at the church service, amounting to seven guineas, was given to Cootamundra Hospital.

During a Sunday afternoon visit to Littledale several weeks later, Susannah and Ted learned of the death of Alexander Mackay of Wallendbeen station.

"He was a Scots Presbyterian," said Rebecca, "but his home, Rose Cottage, was always open to John on his travels around the parish."

Ted added, "My parents were great friends of Alexander and Annie Mackay. In fact, Father and John always stopped for a meal at Rose Cottage on their way from Murrumburrah to Coota. It was near Mackay's home that my father was bailed up by Johnnie O'Meally. Mackay was a witness to my father's murder." Alexander Mackay, according to the *Cootamundra Herald*, had been a colonial magistrate for forty years and in the days when New South Wales was a penal colony, had been noted as an employer who gave his convict workers their freedom.

November 25th, 1890

Dear Book,

Such good news! Lilla and I have received a letter from dear Mamma, telling us about our new baby brother! Mamma was delivered of him on the 18th of November, and he is to be christened Lewis Ernest. Mamma says he is a very alert, happy bairn, smiling and kicking his blanket loose just as Hilda did when she was an infant. Mamma says he is off to a good start. Lilla and I said a prayer that Lewis will have a long life. Papa and dear Mamma deserve a son.

We have been rehearsing choir selections for Prize Day, which won't be quite the same this year because Papa and dear Mamma will not be able to attend. Papa has been feeling poorly, and Mamma is still recovering from the birth of Lewis. She has arranged for J.J., who will be in Sydney on business, to attend Prize Day and accompany us on the train back to Coota.

Lilla and I have come to love Maybanke. We are proud of our progress, if I may say so. Lilla's pianoforte accomplishments are outstanding, and I'm now more certain of my painting. (Miss Quinn has frequently been offering words of praise!) Our tennis has gone well this term, with both of us winning more than our share of matches. This week our tennis club, the Mayflowers, had its photograph taken, quite a handsome photo to take home at Christmas.

In less than a month I'll be at Coota and able to see Willie again. Lilla has kept my confidence, but if Willie and I spend as much time together as we've planned, I'm sure tongues will wag. I believe I should confide in dear Mamma.

Now I must get back to memorizing botanical classifications. Truth to tell, I'd rather be painting flowers than classifying them.

Good night, Dear Book.

Nellie Barnes

Clapham Cottage, now home to the Town and Country Women's Club

THIRTY
Musical & Dramatic Society

O spare me, that I may recover strength, before I go hence...
—PSALM 39:13

Christmas in 1890 at Clapham Cottage was a particularly joyous event. Baby Lewis, very protected by his mother, was the centre of attention. Susannah had not fussed over any of her babies as much as Lewis. She had recently turned nine and thirty years of age and whilst recovering from his birth, wondered if this were her last chance to bear a son.

When Nellie and Lilla arrived home from Maybanke, they announced they would be arranging the Christmas picnic. Many of the preparations, they knew, had been completed by Susannah before her confinement. What remained was baking fresh rolls and breads, preparing pastry for peach tarts (Lilla had the lightest touch), roasting chooks and a Littledale joint of beef to be served cold, and laying out salads on the day. The two girls planned their tasks and organized their sisters to help them. Hilda, in charge of decorating the house, immediately gave Goog and Peeler a list of duties. Whilst Susannah rested and suckled the baby, she listened to her five daughters chattering and arguing; she reckoned she could have managed the whole thing herself much more quietly and efficiently. She smiled at Lewis, who was wriggling in her arms, and put him in his pram to go for a walk.

Two days after Christmas, Nellie and Lilla were invited to Littledale station for a week's visit. They were so excited about going, Susannah wondered what the attraction was. Littledale, which now comprised two thousand acres, was always a hospitable place with lots of activity, but she thought her two eldest daughters had outgrown their interest in staying at a farm. She decided to invite Rebecca Miller to Clapham Cottage for lunch.

"Jessie appreciates Lilla's company," said Rebecca. "Mary Jane and Emily have always had each other, and Margaret and Sarah are good companions. Jessie is my youngest girl and she needs a friend with interests like her own. She and Lilla spend hours at our old Broadwood, sharing music and practising. They play duets quite nicely, even to my untrained ear. Your Lilla is a dear soul, and I like having her in the homestead."

"And Nellie?" asked Susannah.

"Ah, Nellie," said Rebecca. "Such a precious lass! Always so kind and helpful. I'll say no more. Sure an' she'll tell you in her own good time."

Susannah was flabbergasted. Whilst she and Rebecca sat crocheting on the verandah after lunch, she could not for the life of her reckon what Nellie would have to tell her. What was her darling Nellie up to at Littledale? When the girls returned to Clapham Cottage, Susannah decided she could not wait any longer to know the truth, and she asked Nellie to come along to the bedroom that afternoon whilst she suckled Lewis.

"Now, my darling, tell me. What is so fascinating on Littledale station? I have a feeling it's not jumping on hay or playing with lambs!" She tried to keep her tone light. Heaven knows she did not want to upset her eldest daughter. Yet, to Susannah's great dismay, Nellie burst into tears. "Oh, Mamma! I've wanted to tell you for so long, but I've never been able to find the right time to talk to you! Willie Miller and I are keeping company. We're not betrothed or anything, but he does want to marry me. I'm still at school, and then there's university, and I want to train as a teacher, and oh, Mamma, I'm so confused!" Susannah put the well-fed Lewis into his cradle and took her sobbing eldest daughter into her arms.

"Now, now, my love. There's no need to be upset. You have lots of time to think this over. William is a mature, responsible man, and I'm sure he's not pressuring you to marry him any time soon. From your eagerness to visit Littledale, I assume you enjoy being with him."

"Oh, yes! And he's always so good to me, helping me with my Geology and Botany assignments. He even tried to teach me Algebra!"

"Brave man!" said Susannah. "Then I suggest you continue to enjoy his company whilst you're home from school, and we'll see what time will bring. Your papa and I are keen that you do well in your studies ahead of anything else."

"Oh, I will, Mamma! You've no worries there! Willie says he's very proud of my accomplishments at Maybanke!"

"And so are we, my darling. Now, put the kettle on to boil, and you and I will have a nice cup of tea." Nellie gave her a hug and went to make the tea.

Nellie and William Miller! He was eleven years older than Nellie, if Susannah reckoned correctly, and certainly capable of supporting a wife and family in a satisfactory manner. Susannah had always found him aloof and in recent years confident to the point of being arrogant, but she knew Ted did not have that impression of him, and obviously neither did Nellie.

Girls tended to marry young in the colony and not always to suitable partners. Susannah did not want her sixteen-year-old to be swept away, even by William Miller. She must trust Nellie's good sense, as always. She tucked a light coverlet over sleepy Lewis and went to have that nice cup of tea with her daughter.

Her conversation with her husband on the verandah later in the evening revealed that Ted had suspected for some time that William Miller had his eye on Nellie. The two men saw each other in town frequently, attended the same meetings and were Lodge brothers. According to Ted, William often spoke fondly of their eldest daughter. "You could have told me!" said Susannah, rather more forcefully than she meant to.

"We've always let our daughters think things through for themselves, my dear, and I, for one, intend to let Nellie decide for herself about marriage. Should she choose William Miller, she will have an admirable man, much more admirable than some local drongos I could name."

"Of course," said Susannah. "I'm the first to admit that marriage choices for both women and men are limited at Cootamundra, and propinquity has led to many a marriage. William Miller is an acceptable suitor from a good family. I'd just like her to complete her education."

"I'm sure she will, my dear." Susannah found his tone condescending. She huffed and went off to bed.

Ted was in better form these days. With his latest projects seeming to rally his spirits, his health had improved. He and John owned a number of properties at Coota, one of them a piece of land along Parker Street, its limits extending as far as Barnes Street. Ted and his brother decided to subdivide the land and offer lots for sale. They were very successful with their venture. Ted's other business interest was the co-operative roller mill at the edge of town, a massive building of corregated iron which housed machinery to produce flour from the ample grain of Cootamundra District. Ted was a shareholder and in 1891 became Chairman of the Board of Directors. The board worked diligently to make the flour mill a thriving enterprise. Their efforts were displayed on June 18th, 1891, when the Cootamundra Farmers' Co-operative Roller Mill, refurbished and "splendidly fitted," said the *Herald*, reopened with a celebration. The newspaper reported that Mrs. E.P. Barnes, wife of the Chairman, "broke the proverbial bottle of wine," and everyone witnessed the production of the first bag of flour, which "was placed before Mrs. Barnes and christened Conqueror Flour." The bag of flour was later auctioned in aid of the hospital.

"I'm pleased for Ted and the shareholders, of course," said Susannah to Jane, who had admired her vigorous swing with the bottle of wine, "but my best bombazine is splattered, and from now on I'm leaving any such opening duties to other ladies."

"Nonsense!" said Jane, teasing her. "You just need some tips from my experience as Mayoress!"

For more than fifteen years Ted had served on the School Board, and Susannah vividly remembered those evenings when he and a group of men had met around her dining room table to make application for the first school at Cootamundra. The school had finally been built, then enlarged, and higher grades added. Susannah's younger children were thus able to take their secondary schooling in town rather than be sent to boarding school. Once again, Ted was Chairman of the Cootamundra School Board, which now had seventeen schools in the town and District under its jurisdiction.

Susannah and Ted were much involved in 1891 in the very active Musical & Dramatic Society and spent several evenings each week at rehearsals. During the winter and spring of 1891, the society produced a series of plays and concerts which showcased the talents of various members. At one of the concerts, William Miller's recitation of a farcical poem he had composed, "My Brother J.J. and His Bull" (best left unquoted here), garnered a standing ovation. John and Ted Barnes, original supporters of Cootamundra Hospital, prevailed upon the society to offer one of the plays as a fundraiser because influenza had struck the town severely that year, and the hospital was overflowing with patients. (A crowd attending a fundraiser was certain to increase the cases of influenza, but no concern was perceived or voiced.) The society's production attracted a large audience and brought in much-needed hospital funds.

Catering to popular demand, musicians and singers prepared another concert where Susannah was chief accompanist and Ted effectively rendered an Irish Riley ballad, "The Banks of Claudy." Another play followed, and before Christmas, the society presented a third extravaganza, "a grand musical entertainment," said the *Cootamundra Herald*, in aid of the Presbyterian Church.

In the pleasant days of early November, baby Lewis Barnes was approaching his first birthday. He was already a busy little toddler, and such a comical mischief, he was nicknamed "Mickey." His antics brought joy to the family in his every waking moment. Susannah was planning a party at Clapham Cottage for the Barnes families of Cootamundra and Jindalee to celebrate Mickey's birthday.

On the 8th of November, Mickey developed a fever, which progressed to influenza. Susannah went to work to cool him down. She suckled him frequently, sat by his cradle at night, and sponged him and soothed him. Dr. Anderson was summoned to examine him and listen to his chest. Sadly, the efforts of Susannah and the doctor were not successful. Lewis Ernest Barnes died in his mother's arms on November 17th, 1891, a day before his first birthday. The family, rather than hosting a party, stood in tears before a small grave in Cootamundra Cemetery. In the weeks that followed, Susannah spent many hours crying quietly to herself. She prayed to her Heavenly Father to help her accept the death of her precious son, but her prayers offered her little solace.

November 27th, 1891

Dear Book,
Papa has written to us with the devasting news of the death of Mickey. We feel so badly for dear Mamma and Papa. Happy little Mickey was the son they have longed for. Lilla and I have written once again to express our sympathies.

Along with the letter Papa enclosed another envelope. He had opened it when it arrived from the university and sent it on to me with a note of congratulations and a promise of new oil paints from him and dear Mamma. In the envelope were the results of my examinations for entrance to the University of Sydney. The certificate said 1,100 students took the Junior Public Examinations in September 1891, and Susie Ellen Barnes achieved the following results:

Geography	*Second Class*
English	*Second Class*
Arithmetic	*Second Class*
Geology	*First Class*
Botany	*Second Class*

The certificate was signed by the Dean of the Faculty of Arts.
   I must say I expected more First Classes, but perhaps I overestimated my ability to compete with so many other candidates. I'm particularly disappointed in my Second Class Botany results. I felt very confident I had achieved a First Class. Thank Heaven I signed up for Arithmetic. Algebra and Geometry would have been disasters.

Our days at Maybanke will soon be over, and Lilla and I will be packing up for the last time. University begins after Christmas, but I am truly exhausted and Mamma and Papa have suggested I take a year for myself before beginning university studies.

I'm eager to show my certificate to Willie. I know he'll be pleased with my Geology result, but what will he say about Botany?

I keep thinking about dear, dear Mamma. She has buried Eva and five sons.

Mickey was such a cheerful, vigorous, beautiful little boy.

Good night, Dear Book.

Nellie Barnes

Two years earlier, the Reverend Auchinlech Ross, having spent four years at Cootamundra, had asked the Bishop to transfer him to another parish. Christ Church of England had thus been without a Vicar since 1889. The Bishop, who knew the parish was in good hands with J.J. Miller as Lay Reader and Ted Barnes as Bishop's Churchwarden and Treasurer, sent interim clergy rather than appointing another incumbent. Those serving longest at Christ Church were the Reverend S.J. Lowdell and the Reverend J.M. Vaughn. Sincere and hard-working as all the interim clergymen were, the arrangements did not lead to a permanent appointment, but nothing could be done until His Lordship decided on a new incumbent. As Christmas approached, Lay Reader J.J. Miller, who was seldom concerned, no matter what the circumstance, became concerned about Christmas Eucharist.

"As you know, we're presently without an interim clergyman," remarked J.J. whilst taking his ease on Susannah's verandah one afternoon. He came frequently to sit and talk with her, and his company helped lift her spirits. "There'll be no Holy Communion at Christmas unless I can find a clergyman to take the service. I could read Matins as usual, of course, but that won't celebrate the Nativity of our Lord."

"Cootamundra has plenty of clergy," said Susannah, pouring him another glass of lemonade, "but not of the Church of England persuasion."

"You've given me an idea! We could have an ecumenical service! Perhaps a Wesleyan Methodist minister or a Presbyterian pastor would come to celebrate the Eucharist with us!"

"You could ask, at least," said Susannah, smiling at his enthusiasm.

At eleven o'clock on Christmas morning, 1891, the congregation of Anglicans, Presbyterians and Wesleyan Methodists that overflowed Christ Church was welcomed by Lay Reader J.J. Miller as well as by a Wesleyan Methodist minister and a Presbyterian pastor. J.J. Miller conducted the service; Methodist Mr. Beale read the lessons, and Presbyterian Mr. Hutchison preached "a mighty good sermon," to quote the Lay Reader. The two clergymen consecrated the bread and wine and administered Holy Communion to the ecumenical congregation.

The year 1891 had been a notable one for Cootamundra District. The weather had been ideal, if one could discount the flash floods which had caused two deaths. The *Cootamundra Herald* reported a total rainfall of twenty-nine and forty-five hundredths inches, and harvests were magnificent.

On a warm day in January, as he sat smoking his pipe on Susannah's verandah, J.J. spoke of his plans regarding the upcoming borough elections. Confident he would be re-elected, he declared his intention to put his name forward as Mayor. "I feel up to the challenge and I do believe I'll have the support of the majority of the council. I turned one and thirty last November. I'm of an age to assume the responsibility, don't you think?" Susannah agreed he was. On the 6th of February, 1892, J.J. Miller, the youngest on the council, was chosen by his fellow councillors as Mayor of Cootamundra, replacing W.H. Matthews, a Churchwarden at Christ Church and his friend.

"You'll need a Mayoress," said Susannah, teasing him. J.J. Miller always managed to find a lady to accompany him to a Masonic or community social event, but he had never seemed to favour any particular companion. "I could suggest several worthy women who would be excellent at the job, but you'd have to marry one of them first!"

"I have already dealt with your concern, dear Susannah," he retorted. "My sister Mary Jane has agreed to take on the duties of

Mayoress. She'll undoubtedly fill the role with grace and efficiency." Susannah had never associated "grace" with the strong-minded Mary Jane Miller, but reckoned her "efficiency" as Mayoress would never be questioned.

Susannah had not heard from her sister-in-law Jane for more than a week. In the past three years Jane had been enduring a female malady of some sort and was often ill. She had never discussed the problem, not even with Susannah, but had carried on despite her questionable health. One morning in late March Susannah was summoned to the Barnes home at Jindalee, where she found her dearest friend lying helpless in bed and only able to smile at her. Dr. Anderson was there and declared he had no remedies to offer. He told John and the children to keep her as comfortable as they could. He promised to come every day with medicine for pain.

Susannah was shocked by her sister-in-law's condition, for Jane had taken part in the recent election celebrations as well as the Autumn Show. Lately, she had been feeling especially poorly, Susannah was aware, but what had ravaged her like this? Jane Barnes continued to fail and then slipped into a coma, afflicted by a growth in her womb. She went to be with her Lord on the 4th of April, 1892.

Susannah was overcome by a devastating emptiness. Jane Barnes had been her friend of the bosom, the one who had shared all her joys and sorrows, her faithful partner in so many activities: family gatherings, church bazaars, flower shows and refreshment tents, and Spring and Autumn Shows of the APH&I Association. None of these events would ever be the same without Jane Barnes. She begged off playing the Christ Church organ at Jane's funeral, certain she would see neither music nor organ stops and keys. Instead, she sat amongst the large congregation of mourners, weeping beside Ted.

April 19th, 1892

Dear Book,
What a sad time. Aunt Jane and Mamma were such good friends. Mamma has been telling me about her arrival at Coota, when Aunt Jane made her feel very welcome and introduced her to all her friends. Dear Mamma says she can't imagine doing church work without Aunt Jane to keep her company.

It feels strange to be at home instead of at Maybanke. Lilla and I must remind ourselves that our school days are over. We often find ourselves talking about our teachers and friends there. We agree Maybanke College was a grand place to go to school.

In the mornings Lilla and I give dear Mamma a hand around the house, and during the afternoons Lilla helps out in the School of Arts Library and I help at Cootamundra School in the infant class. I can't wait for weekends on Littledale. Willie is very sweet, carrying my drawing and painting supplies out to viewpoints where he reads a book whilst I sketch and paint.

I must go and join dear Mamma and Lilla. Papa is off to a Lodge meeting and Lilla is playing some Mozart in hopes of lifting Mamma's spirits.

Good night, Dear Book.

Nellie Barnes

After four years of interim clergy, Christ Church acquired an incumbent, Canon Betts, who, like the Reverend James Hassall of Berrima, was a grandson of the Reverend Samuel Marsden of Parramatta. Canon Betts came from Bombala, in the southeastern part of Goulburn Diocese. The Bishop had sent him to preach and meet parishioners at Cootamundra, where the persuasive powers of the Lay Reader and new Churchwarden, J.J. Miller, and the friendly reaction of the congregation ensured his acceptance of the incumbency. The Reverend Canon James Cloudsley Betts, his wife, Adela, and their two daughters were soon warmly welcomed by the parishioners of Christ Church.

His Worship the Mayor, J.J. Miller, although taking his official duties at the new Town Hall most seriously, was enjoying a new sporting association, a Pony and Galloway Racing Club, which had elected him President. He had established a Galloway stud at Littledale and was keen to race his sturdy horses of Scottish ancestry against those of other owners.

His first major ceremonial duty as Mayor was the sod-turning for a new railway line from Cootamundra to Temora. "I have written to Mr. Lyne, Minister of Public Works, and he has agreed to officiate," J.J. told Susannah. "His visit will coincide with the first Galloway races, to which he has been invited. The ultimate race of the afternoon will be the Railway Handicap." Susannah thought that J.J. was particularly pleased with himself, especially when the railway sod-turning ceremony on August 3rd, 1892, attracted a crowd of three thousand.

Of even greater consequence to the people of Cootamundra at this time were the provision of a new water supply and construction of a gas works. The Stock Dam, Cootamundra's reservoir on Muttama Creek, was never a reliable source of clean water, and most residents depended on cisterns or underground storage tanks. In 1888 the *Cootamundra Herald* had reported a calling of tenders by the Borough Council. By 1892 a steam pumping station was ready to deliver thirty thousand gallons of water a day from Hurley's Springs to standpipes at Cootamundra.

"I have invited Lord Jersey on a three-day visit to open the pumping station and tour the gas works," J.J. told Susannah.

"The Governor of the colony? Heavens! And has he ageed to come?"

"Indeed, he has! It may be chilly weather when he arrives, and I'll need a mayoral cloak for the greeting and procession. I'm having one tailored in mauve and yellow, Lord Jersey's colours."

"Mauve and yellow! Really?"

Lord Jersey duly arrived at 11:00 a.m. on August 31st and was met at the train station by a colourfully clad Mayor J.J. Miller. Driven by J.J. himself in an open landau pulled by his dark bays, the

Governor led a lengthy procession that extended down Wallendoon Street. He then participated in two days of events and relaxed on the third day at the September Race Meeting, where, thanks to the Mayor's influence, the feature race was the Jersey Handicap. When J.J. came to Clapham Cottage the following week, he could scarcely eat for telling Susannah of the success of the Governor's visit.

Susannah had not taken part in any events attended by His Excellency, nor had she assisted at Christ Church Bazaar, held at the same time as the September Race Meeting. She was still in despair over the death of Jane Barnes. She was also hoarding her strength towards the birth of another child six weeks hence. She prayed the Lord would give her another son. However, a vigorous daughter, Elfrida Mary Barnes, a happy baby, arrived at Clapham Cottage on the 10th of October, 1892. They called her Frida.

The new gas works was now ready to provide service to Cootamundra. The first gas, made on October 27th, 1892, initially provided light, reported the *Herald*, to twenty-nine street lamps and the Church of England Schoolroom. Susannah made sure Clapham Cottage was amongst the first residences at Coota to be lit by gas lamps.

As he walked around the garden one November evening with Frida in his arms, Ted remarked, "Canon Betts tells me he is eager to organize a fundraising event before Christmas."

"What does he have in mind at this time of year?" said Susannah, who was relaxing in a wicker garden chair. "Something which can be put together quickly, I hope, before we're all preparing for yuletide."

"In introducing him around town one day, I took him to the showground, and he's proposing that we use the site for a moonlight picnic with fireworks and a musical concert, admissions in aid of Christ Church. What do you think?"

"I'm impressed! I must see what I can do about organizing a picnic and preparing some musical selections."

"Perhaps his wife, Adela, could be of assistance. She has a lovely singing voice and she enjoys working with the ladies of the church."

"Yes, I'll ask both of them to call. The showground location will require some lively music. I'll go through my collection before they come." Ted smiled at his wife, who for months had not shown any interest in church or community events, so deeply had she mourned the death of Jane Barnes. Perhaps the cheerful Adela Betts could help restore her interest in the world around her.

Under a full moon on a November night, after the ladies had provided a sumptuous picnic, fireworks lit up the sky over the showground. Christ Church choir became a glee club and amused the audience with several music-hall songs. Various soloists stepped forward to entertain the crowd, amongst them Letitia Lynch, who gave a delightfully coquettish rendition of a folk song, and William Miller, who created a hush in the audience with a sentimental ballad. The evening concluded with enthusiastic community singing. Whilst the crowd lustily cheered all the performers, Ted Barnes counted the proceeds of the evening. In all aspects Canon James Cloudsley Betts' Showground Concert had been a resounding success.

THIRTY-ONE
Wilga

*Do good, O Lord, unto those that be good,
and to them that are upright in their hearts.*
— PSALM 125:4

At the Watch Night service in Christ Church on New Year's Eve, 1892, Susannah's thoughts were on Nellie. Her eldest daughter should be preparing to enroll at Sydney University. Instead, she was more interested than ever in William Miller. She spent every weekend on Littledale and came home full of stories about Willie.

January 2nd, 1893

Dear Book,
Such news! After the District horse races on New Year's Day, we went to Littledale for a picnic supper. It was a clear, balmy evening, and instead of joining everyone at the pianoforte later, Willie and I walked to the top of the property and sat looking out over the valley.

Willie took me in his arms and said he thought it was time we were married. My emotions regarding him have been so strong lately, I knew I was ready for his proposal. Very romantically, he got down on one knee and asked if I would be his wife. When I said "Yes!" Willie kissed me and placed the sweetest ring on my finger, and we lay on the grass and . . . I'm sure you get the idea, Dear Book!

Willie came to speak to Papa and Mamma this evening. Papa welcomed him into the family most heartily. He and Papa are Lodge brothers and know each other well. Mamma was more reserved. When she came to say good-night, she told me she wanted to talk to me tomorrow. Surely she doesn't think I'm too young for marriage! Last September I turned eighteen years of age!

Good night, Dear Book.

Nellie Barnes

Next day, after the breakfast things were cleared away, Susannah suggested to Lilla that she take Hilda, Goog and Peeler with her on errands to the Post Office, Cohen's Trade Palace and the School of Arts Library. Lilla set off with three enthusiastic companions whilst Susannah made a pitcher of lemonade and asked Nellie to sit with her on the back verandah.

"Nellie, my love," she said, "are you certain you want to marry William Miller? Not that he isn't an appropriate choice, but you've qualified for university and you've often spoken of becoming a teacher. Perhaps you should at least try a year at university before you become a married woman. I had hoped you would follow in the footsteps of William's sister, Margaret, and graduate from Sydney University."

Nellie and Susannah had always been close, and it pained Nellie to argue with her mother, but she gathered her resolve and said, "I love Willie, and he loves me! And he has waited for me since I was fourteen. If I go away to university, will Willie think I no longer care for him? Maybe he will even find someone else!" Nellie wept as she tried to explain this to dear Mamma. Susannah gave her a great hug and promised she would say no more. The couple were not planning to marry until the following year. Susannah would wait to see what that year would bring. Nellie was hoping the long engagement would give her time to talk to her mother and reassure her.

In 1893 talk of federation spread throughout the Australian colonies. Far away in Britain, investors who had provided financial backing for colonial businesses for more than one hundred years were alarmed by such plans; an Australian federation, if achieved, would likely have an effect on the established trade with Britain.

The unknown economic consequences of a united Australia made British investors cautious about putting more money into colonial enterprises.

As a result, banks failed. Across Cootamundra District prices for grain fell, and to make the situation more grim, bushfires, brought on by drought, raged across the region. His Worship J.J. Miller, Mayor for a second time, was facing a far different term from the one he had previously enjoyed. The boom of the past two years had faded, and an economic depression had settled over Cootamundra. Even the ebullient J.J. was hard-pressed to rally the town to greater efforts.

"What we need is worldwide recognition of our products," he said to Susannah one warm day as he spooned out a second helping of her lemon pudding for himself. "I've read about the Chicago World's Fair in the *Sydney Morning Herald* and I've sent away for entry information. They're advertising for exhibits from around the world. We'll have local farmers submit their products in competition and we'll ship winning samples to the fair."

"A fair in Chicago?" said Susannah. "It's a grand idea, although I fear there is more to restoring prosperity to Coota than exhibiting our products at a fair in America." J.J. agreed. "Yes, I realize that, dear Susannah, but the town needs something to aim for, something to boost our spirits, and exhibiting at the Chicago World's Fair may attract investors from many countries." He is not a man to be deterred, mused Susannah.

Word went out in the town and District that samples were to be brought to the Town Hall for judging. Before long, the best entries were sent by rail to Sydney and, together with selected products from around the colony, were placed on a steamship sailing for America.

The Mayor's sister, Mary Jane Miller, was again discharging her duties as Mayoress, and very effectively, too. Never one to waste a spare moment, Mary Jane took on an additional project for her church. "I do believe Canon Betts is quite overwhelmed by your sister's energy," said Susannah to J.J. one summer afternoon. "At the Ladies' Guild meeting this week, Mary Jane announced she intends to begin a campaign to move our original slab church from Church Hill across to South Cootamundra. She believes a Mission Church needs to be established there. Canon Betts sat open-mouthed!

"Mary Jane went on to say she had taken a survey of the number of parishioners in the area who would be interested in attending a nearby church. She presented a list of their names to Canon Betts. What could he say but offer assurances that he would discuss her proposal with the Church Committee and the Bishop?"

J.J. chuckled and said, "Mary Jane has already approached me regarding the piece of land she has in mind for the new location of the slab church. It seems I'm to buy the property and donate it to the parish. Then I'm to recruit volunteers to dismantle the building and reconstruct it at South Cootamundra. She's impatient to receive approval from the Church Committee and the Bishop."

"Mary Jane has always been such a faithful and energetic church worker," said Susannah. "Canon Betts recognizes her strengths, I'm sure. His congregations are overflowing Christ Church every Sunday, and he may agree with Mary Jane that it's time we expanded. As Lay Reader, you'll probably find yourself ministering to a Mission congregation."

Such was the case when Mary Jane Miller's proposal received approval, and her brother provided the property. The slab building on the hill beyond the reservoir was dismantled and rebuilt as the Church of England Mission Church at South Cootamundra. Canon Betts conducted services there on Sunday afternoons twice a month, leaving Lay Reader J.J. Miller in charge of the other worship services. Mary Jane attended the Mission and soon had a Ladies' Guild organized.

Like many small towns across New South Wales, Cootamundra had established a School of Arts under the sponsorship of the Borough Council. The intent was to provide a recreational and cultural centre for the community. When Susannah had attended the opening ceremonies with Ted, who was a founder of the School of Arts, she recalled the advice of the Captain's wife on the *Commissary* about finding "time for civilized pursuits" in "a rough-and-ready place."

Unlike similar schools, the Cootamundra School of Arts admitted women to full membership. Now in its fourth year of operation, the school sponsored guest speakers and debates and provided smoking and card rooms (for men only, gambling forbidden), a library, and in August of 1893, a tennis court. Margaret, Sarah and Jessie Miller became notable tennis players and organizers of ladies' tournaments. In October of that year, after a majority vote in favour, members of the School of Arts installed a billiard table for use by both men and women, at separate times, of course. Not everyone approved of ladies engaging in this pastime.

Mayor J.J. Miller, the Borough Council and those individuals who had submitted entries awaited results from the Chicago World's Fair. When word eventually arrived, Cootamundra residents were much heartened by the news. Conqueror Flour fom the Co-operative Roller Mill had received "a first order of merit," reported the *Cootamundra Herald*, and wool submitted by James Gibb and his son had received an award for excellence. Such world recognition, however, did not rescue the town from its sinking economy.

The drought of 1893 in the western districts continued to worsen the effects of the economic depression. Fires were destroying ripened fields of grain, searing pastures, burning fences and threatening livestock. Miller & Miller auctions, which had once sold sheep and cattle in the thousands, now sold them in the hundreds; many farmers abandoned their properties and sent their livestock to be butchered.

The ladies at Christ Church knew many Cootamundra families whose breadwinners were now unemployed. Susannah became an organizer of the Benevolent Society, which arranged weekly deliveries of baskets of food to the destitute. In crowded homes, families who depended on income from boarders or from washing taken in by an already overworked mother were astounded to find a basket at their door full of fresh vegetables and fruit. For the rest of her life at Cootamundra, Susannah watched out for the poor and offered them a helping hand.

"Not another meeting of the roller mill directors!" said Susannah one spring evening as Ted finished his tea and reached for his coat. "The situation has not improved, my dear," said Ted. "No matter that our Conqueror Flour won an award of merit at a world's fair or that we produced exceptionally good quality flour this year, we still must find ways to get our product sold. Unless bakers and housewives buy more of our flour, we'll continue to operate at a loss. That can't go on forever." He was right, Susannah knew, and she sympathized with him and his fellow directors who had worked so hard to develop the co-operative.

A decision had to be made to prevent a total loss of shareholders' investments. When Mr. J.F. Stratton from the colony of Victoria came forward and offered to buy the flour mill, directors of the co-operative accepted. On the 23rd of December, 1893, the co-operative mill became Stratton's Flour Mill.

At New Year's Nellie and William announced that their wedding would take place on April 11th. Susannah had long ago resigned herself to the marriage of her eldest daughter, now age nineteen, to William Miller, age thirty. Susannah regretted that Nellie had not taken up her university placement, but the desire to be married was a strong urge in a young woman. She reminded herself of her own determination to sail across the world to marry Edward Barnes. Nellie was obviously in love with William, who had proved an attentive bridegroom-to-be. Yet Susannah was still astounded that he had first stated his intentions to Nellie when she was fourteen years of age! Susannah knew that suitable spouses were in short supply in a small town, but William Miller had certainly staked his claim early.

Whatever her misgivings, Susannah set out to support her eldest daughter in a round of prenuptial events organized by friends and relatives. In the midst of it all, she contacted a photographer, Mr. G.H. Nichols, and arranged to have a portrait taken of Nellie and William. On April 11th, 1894, the *Cootamundra Herald* sent a reporter to record the events of the nuptial day in an article which was published six days later.

Pretty Wedding

One of the prettiest and most interesting weddings seen here for some time was celebrated in Christ Church on Wednesday, the contracting parties being Mr. W. Miller, of Littledale, and Miss Nellie Barnes, eldest daughter of Mr. E.P. Barnes, JP, of this town.

The day was as bright and perfect as any could wish for. the time for the ceremony was 3:30 p.m. and at 3 o'clock there was not even standing room in the church, which had been prettily decorated by the many girl friends of the bride, she being a universal favourite. The bridal party walked beneath a bower of greenery and choice white flowers; and on the communion table was a very pretty bell, artistically worked with white flowers and ferns.

Mr. J.J. Miller, ex-Mayor and brother of the bridegroom, acted in the capacity of best man, and Mr. E. Barnes, cousin of the bride, was groomsman.

The bride looked very pretty in a white brochet silk, with long square train and the usual adornment of wreath and veil. She also carried a beautiful bouquet.

There were six bridesmaids in attendance. Miss Lilla Barnes, sister of the bride, and Miss Miller were alike dressed in pink nun's veiling, trimmed with a paler shade of corded silk, black velvet hats relieved with pink, and black kid gloves with pink-stitched backs.

Next came the Misses Hilda and Ivy Barnes in very pretty costumes of pale green liberty silk and big white swansdown hats, the contrast being very pretty. Last, but by no means least, came the two mites, Peeler Barnes and Rosie Webster in cream and buttercup. Each bridesmaid carried pretty bouquets.

On entering the church, the choir, assisted by members of other churches, and under the conductorship of Mr. W.W. Barnard, sang the Bridal Hymn . . . Mr. Barnard also played Mendelsohn's Wedding March at the conclusion of the service as the party wended its way through the church amid showers of rice and petals of white flowers. . . . An adjournment was then made to the home of the bride, where the relatives and immediate friends joined in the wedding breakfast.

Mr. and Mrs. W. Miller left by the evening mail for Sydney, via Mossvale, Kiama, and Campbelltown. The station was thronged with their friends, all wishing them a pleasant journey; and amid showers of rice, flowers and old boots, not forgetting the "ticket" on the door, the train steamed off, the juveniles singing the picnic song of "The Jolly Miller and His Maid."

The remainder of the young folks were afterwards entertained by the parents, when music, cards and dancing were indulged in until the small hours of the morning, all expressing themselves satisfied that they had indeed spent a very happy evening. The bride received a number of very useful and valuable presents.

We forgot to mention that Canon Betts was responsible for tying the silken knot of lifelong affection.

We heartily join their friends in wishing young Mr. and Mrs. Miller the fullest measure of happiness and prosperity.

Friends and family knew that one of the "mites" in the wedding party, Rosie Webster, was the eight-year-old daughter of Emily and Edward Webster, bookkeeper at Miller & Miller. Readers of the wedding description assumed that the "ticket" on the door of the train compartment announced "Just Married!"

When Nellie and William returned from their Sydney honeymoon, their new home in Hurley Street awaited them. The town lot had been an engagement gift to Nellie from her future brother-in-law, J.J. Miller. The newlyweds named their two-storey house of pleasing proportions Wilga, after the white-flowered, drought-resistant shrub of the same name. Clapham Cottage on Cooper Street was just a short walk away from Wilga.

Susannah, who had been much too busy with wedding preparations to help organize an Autumn Show, was somewhat relieved when it was cancelled. The Show Committee of the APH&I Association had decided that economic conditions in the town and District did not lend themselves to an exhibition of farmers' accomplishments. In September, however, when the Spring Show was also rejected by the APH&I Association, Susannah not only felt some sort of community event was necessary to mark the season, but also knew the Christ Church treasury relied on proceeds from the refreshment tent at biannual shows.

She consulted Canon and Mrs. Betts, who agreed a fundraising social gathering in the Church of England Schoolroom might be a satisfactory substitute. The event in aid of Christ Church cost adults one shilling and children sixpence. A tea corner, indoor games, readings and recitations both amusing and dramatic, and songs to the accompaniment of Susannah on the pianoforte raised funds for the church and brightened an otherwise grey day in spring.

J.J. Miller was often called upon by show associations across the southern districts to assess sheep, cattle and horses at their exhibitions because he had acquired a reputation as a knowledgeable all-round stock judge. In September 1894, when, much to his disappointment and that of other participants, the Cootamundra APH&I Association cancelled the Spring Show, J.J., like Susannah, became determined to offer an alternative. Thus he set about organizing a stock sale and stallion parade at the showground. With J.J. and William as the auctioneers, the firm of Miller & Miller sponsored a successful sale and an interesting parade of stallions of all breeds.

Greatly missing her sister-in-law, Susannah faced the organization of the November flower show in aid of Christ Church with some hesitation. At a Sunday dinner in Littledale homestead, her good friend Rebecca Miller suggested that she and her daughters take on the flower show. Susannah fell upon the offer with gratitude. Listening to their conversation, J.J. said, "With the current dry conditions, the Fire Brigade could put money to good use for more equipment. We could have a concert after the flower show, charge admission for both, and help the Fire Brigade as well as Christ Church with our efforts." Leaving flower show arrangements to

Rebecca and her daughters, Susannah recruited volunteer participants for the concert, and both events were successful fundraisers.

The hot, dry weather at the start of 1895 was similar to that at the beginning of the previous year. The lack of rainfall was a constant worry to residents of Cootamundra because even Hurley's Springs, a reliable source of water, was failing in its output. In March the Borough Council began restricting hours of flow.

Susannah was concerned about Nellie, who was expecting her first child. She was suffering severely from nausea and feeling especially miserable in the hot weather. Nellie had taken to walking along from Wilga to Clapham Cottage every morning to enjoy a cool drink and a chat with her mother.

Although Cootamundra residents could walk to all destinations in town, bicycles had begun to appear at Coota, frequently frightening horses and pedestrians. Mailmen no longer walked their routes, according to the *Herald*, but rode bicycles, as did telegraph messengers and delivery boys. Most people going any distance still rode or drove horses, but occasionally Susannah had seen men cycling to and from work. One morning, whilst Susannah and Nellie were relaxing on the verandah, a well-dressed gentleman came wheeling around the corner and parked his bicycle at Susannah's gate.

"You've given up on shank's pony," said Susannah when J.J. Miller doffed his hat, settled himself comfortably in a wicker chair, and accepted an offer of lemonade and gingersnaps. "Not entirely," said J.J., "but I am planning to join the new League of Wheelmen. You've no doubt read in the *Herald* that when we are touring, we'll wear navy caps, indigo jackets and knickers and navy stockings." Susannah smiled. "Sounds very smart," she said, "and when will ladies be able to join your cycling tours?"

"The League is for gentlemen only," said J.J., "although I believe cycling practices for ladies will soon be available in Albert Park." Susannah felt that she was beyond learning to ride a bicycle, but she expected her daughters to want cycling lessons in the park. Indeed, several Cootamundra ladies were soon seen practising their skill around town and going greater distances escorted by gentlemen cyclists, including J.J. Miller. Young couples who were courting were quick to discover the pleasures of Sunday afternoon cycling excursions.

On June 5th, 1895, at Wilga, Nellie Miller was delivered of her first child, a son. Her confinement went well, and Susannah wept with joy when a handsome baby boy was placed in her arms. He had the fair hair of his grandfather John Miller and the dark-brown eyes of his grandfather Ted Barnes. He was christened Clive by Canon Betts at Christ Church. Clive was a name given to many boys of English ancestry in honour of Lord Clive of India, who in this instance was a very distant relation, a great uncle by marriage of William's paternal grandmother. Because Clive was an especially bonnie baby, everyone in the family called him Bon.

Meanwhile, Littledale station was about to host its second wedding celebration, this time for Margaret Miller, who was engaged to Francis David Porteous Murray, a long-time resident of the town and a founder of the Cootamundra Golf Club. The couple were married in Christ Church by Canon Betts on the 13th of July, 1895. Susannah and her daughters lent a hand with the wedding breakfast in Littledale homestead.

Although no longer Mayor, J.J. Miller remained on the Borough Council, which now served a population of 2,230. Council proceedings were reported in detail by the *Cootamundra Herald*, including a May meeting where discussions were so heated that Alderman Miller invited Mayor Pinkstone to "come outside." Reading the newspaper account, Susannah reckoned the drought needed to end soon to soothe the tempers of Cootamundra residents. Yet the drought continued, with the annual rainfall totalling just over fifteen inches.

In that very dry year Miller & Miller depended on providing assistance with insurance claims to keep the firm in business. Their occasional auctions consisted primarily of abandoned farms and equipment and unoccupied houses and their contents.

It was not an auspicious year for Cootamundra, nor for newlyweds William and Nellie Miller, except for the joyous arrival of Bon.

THIRTY-TWO
Cootamundra Troop

Cast thy burden upon the Lord, and he shall sustain thee...
— PSALM 55:22

Nellie was spending a week on Littledale to give Rebecca Miller some time with her grandson, now a year old, and Susannah missed her daughter's daily visits with Bon. When J.J. wheeled up to Clapham Cottage looking for afternoon tea one day, he found Susannah knitting a little blue jacket.

"That child must have more clothes than any other baby at Coota," J.J. remarked. "My sisters are forever knitting and sewing for him, too!"

"He's such a dear wee boy, how can I not want to do for him?" Susannah didn't add that she was often consumed by thoughts of her own baby boys as she stitched and knitted for Bon.

On an afternoon in the autumn of 1896, whilst he was relaxing in Susannah's sitting room and enjoying a third piece of cherry pound cake, J.J. declared, "I'm planning to be part of a new association. It's time those of us who were born here had an organization of our own. A group of us will be looking for native-born, patriotic men and women to join us. As well as holding social gatherings, readings and debates, our Australian Natives' Association will prepare for future political action."

"No doubt you'll attract members," said Susannah. "There's plenty now who were born here and could be of the same mind." A large group of local leaders established the Cootamundra branch of the ANA on the 11th of April, 1896, and elected J.J. Miller their first President.

Two years later, members of the Australian Natives' Association throughout the colony played leading roles in a new political party, the Federal League, which supported plans for an Australian Commonwealth. Although well aware of the political activities of Free Settlers such as John F. Barnes, J.J. could not have predicted how vigorously the Free Settlers would defend their political status against native-born Australians.

Susannah's concerns were now centred in her husband. At two and fifty years of age, Ted was listless and exhausted. Much as she tried to tempt his appetite, he had little interest in the meals she prepared and no energy for his usual activities. Dr. Brennan saw him regularly and prescribed tonics to revive him and poultices and cough mixtures to relieve the congestion in his chest.

One day, after a lengthy examination of her husband, bedridden at the time, Dr. Brennan accepted Susannah's offer of tea and a currant scone. "As I understand," he said, "Ted has lived at Coota most of his adult life. The dry climate here should have been good for his chest, but his condition continues to worsen. He needs to be examined by pulmonary consultants at Sydney. I'll give you their names and write to them on Ted's behalf."

She would take Ted to Sydney, of course, but what if the consultants required that he stay there for treatment? If he needed to be there, she would stay with him, and then what of their daughters? Nellie and William were well established at Coota, as was Lilla, who had become Librarian at the School of Arts. Hilda was teaching music at Cootamundra School and keeping company with Alick Miller, although she was only seventeen and too young to marry him. Susannah was certain that Nellie and William would make room for Lilla and Hilda at Wilga whilst she and Ted took Goog, Peeler and little Frida with them to Sydney. But she was getting ahead of herself. First, the trip to Sydney to meet with consultants.

In Sydney Ted was diagnosed with chronic pulmonary congestion, and more trips followed for further examinations. A move to the city became essential. Susannah had a quiet weep to herself when it came time to advertise Clapham Cottage for sale. She had lived in Cooper Street for more than one and twenty years and had given birth to all her children there. On March 7th, 1896, a small notice appeared in the *Cootamundra Herald*.

> SALE OF PROPERTIES OF E.P. BARNES—leaving the district. Clapham Cottage, Cooper Street, directly opposite Public School. Brick, dining room, drawing room, sitting room, five bedrooms, dressing room, bathroom, kitchen, pantry, scullery, stable, buggy house and outhouses, shrubbery and garden. Gas and water laid on . . .

On May 13th a *Cootamundra Herald* report included the following:

> FAREWELL—MR. E.P. BARNES, JP
> . . . Mr. Barnes was one of the pioneers of this town, and he was the junior member of the firm of Messrs. J. and E. Barnes, of the Cootamundra store (now Messrs. Nelson and Nelson's), the first merchant establishment of Cootamundra. He was a member of the Vigilance Committee, founded in 1877, also was returning officer for the first aldermanic election, and chairman of the milling company. He is now a Justice of the Peace, deputy sheriff's officer, coroner, a member of the local land board, presiding-officer in parliamentary elections; has for some years held office as treasurer of the Show Association, the Turf Club, been a member of various committees, and for years has held the office of Churchwarden in connection with the Church of England; and he was generally a promoter of amateur engagements on the stage or in athletics, &c. . . . He will thus leave a few vacancies to be filled.

The good people of Cootamundra were not about to let Ted and Susannah Barnes leave without arranging farewell gatherings for them. Despite his declining health, Ted struggled to be convivial and appreciative at these events. In July the men who had served with him in many community endeavours met at the Court House to laud his accomplishments and make a presentation to him. In reporting on the occasion, the *Cootamundra Herald* said in part:

> PRESENTATION TO MR. E.P. BARNES, JP—On Friday morning, at the invitation of some friends, Mr. E.P. Barnes attended at the local Court House, where he was presented with a purse of sovereigns, in recognition of his past services to the town and district. . . . Mr. Barnes asked them to forgive him for not making a long speech. . . . He said Cootamundra would always have his best and heartiest wishes. . . . He looked forward to the welfare of the town and District as much as he did his own welfare. (Applause). . . . Mr. Barnes was pleased to hear Mr. Pinkstone's reference to Mrs. Barnes, who, he felt, had been a power of good in the way of assisting the destitute. (Applause). At the request of Mr. Barnes, those present adjourned, and joined him in a parting glass of wine.

And so Ted and Susannah Barnes left the western slopes of New South Wales in hopes of improving Ted's health. Some treatments for his pulmonary congestion would take place in the Blue Mountains west of Sydney. Veiled in the vapours of eucalypts were mountain sanitaria where pulmonary patients were treated on screened verandahs in the fragrant, misty air. As they travelled by coach into the mountains for Ted's first sanitarium stay, Susannah found herself on a winding road where mists wafted across the ridges like a delicate blue scrim over a scenic backdrop. Tall, tree-shaped ferns fanned out over the road, their branches filtering the strong sunlight into shadowy patterns. Everywhere the trees were noisy with the calls of cockatoos and parrots. Susannah, a long-time resident of a dusty western town, was enchanted by this mountain atmosphere.

September 1st, 1896

Dear Book,

I have missed confiding in you. I know I am a grown woman, a wife and mother, yet I long for a confidante. Lilla and I used to be so close, but Jack White is paying court to her now, and I feel bereft of her company.

I scarcely know where to begin to describe my new life.

Our wedding was more splendid than I had ever anticipated. Dear Mamma and Papa and all my Coota friends and relatives, bless their hearts, made the day perfect for us. I will not comment on honeymoon details, except to say we enjoyed our visit to Sydney, and Willie was a most considerate and gentle bridegroom.

Willie and I have decorated and furnished Wilga quite satisfactorily. Truth to tell, Willie leaves all domestic responsibilities and decisions to me. Clever as he is with things mathematical, he seems more interested in his scores with the Cootamundra Bowling Club than in our household expenses. I know I am capable of keeping track of our finances myself, having had the benefit of all that tutoring in arithmetic from Mrs. Wolstenholme. Willie believes in a distinct separation between men's and women's work, unlike my father, who was always quick to give my mother a hand. I must say Willie is a great help in amusing Bon.

J.J. and Willie are now busy at Miller & Miller with the new Income Tax, assisting businesses in organizing their records and completing returns, something they have time for because their auctions are infrequent in the ongoing drought.

Bon is the centre of my existence. He's such a sturdy, earnest little boy, healthy, vigorous and observant of everything around him. He walks confidently now, and I have to be alert to supervise him.

I'm expecting again, in late February or early March. A girl this time, I hope.

I miss dear Mamma and Papa dreadfully. I doubt they will ever return to Coota because Papa's health shows no signs of improving.

We're spending next weekend on Littledale. J.J. is having a rabbit shoot on the station in anticipation of Scalp Day a month from now. He is Stock Director for the District and expects to pay bounties on over

7000 scalps, an ugly but necessary business. Whilst Willie goes shooting with the men and Bon is fussed over by his Grandmamma Miller and his aunts, perhaps I will be able to work on a painting. I'll take my easel and oil paints with me and hope for a quiet moment to myself.

I shall tuck you away until next time, Dear Book.

Nellie Barnes Miller

At yuletide that year Lilla and Hilda were invited with William, Nellie and Bon to Christmas dinner in Littledale homestead. Hilda was spending every weekend on the station, gallantly courted by Alick Miller. Susannah stayed with Ted and the younger girls at Sydney for Christmas. She came back to Coota every few months to visit for several days, but she was never away from Ted for too long.

During one such visit she confided to her daughters that she was expecting a child. Nellie, Lilla and Hilda were astonished, although they would never say so. Given the state of their father's health, they could only conclude that their parents' attachment over twenty-five years was far stronger than any health concerns.

On March 1st, 1897, at Wilga, Nellie and William had a daughter, a tall, attractive baby with William's dark hair and grey eyes. She was strong-minded from the first, "like her Aunt Mary Jane," said Rebecca Miller. Nellie and Willie named their daughter Bertha Gordon.

In the following month, leaving Frida in the care of Goog and Peeler at Sydney, Susannah returned to Cootamundra for her confinement. On April 19th, 1897, in her forty-sixth year, she gave birth to a pretty baby girl, Florence Esther. Susannah was delivered of her last child by Dr. Hull and Nurse Scholz, who had delivered Nellie's children. Baby Florence, who was an aunt to Bon and Bertha, was seven weeks younger than Bertha and later became Bertha's playmate.

In the continuing dry weather the APH&I Association at Cootamundra decided to organize a show only once a year. After an absence of exhibitions in the previous three years, high hopes were held for the Spring Show in 1897.

September 24th, 1897

Dear Book,

Such feelings of accomplishment! I submitted two oil paintings to the Arts Competition at the Spring Show. To my great astonishment, the smaller painting, depicting seven cows drinking in a wide, meandering stream under a cloudy sky, won First Prize! Willie actually prefers the second, larger painting, a haunting representation (my description) of a full moon in a cloudy sky over a farm. Perhaps the unusual nature of these paintings, black and white oils on opaque glass, attracted the attention of the judges.

I protected the backs of my two glass paintings with folded pages of the Cootamundra Herald, and Willie framed the pictures for me. Willie later fastened my First Prize certificate to the back of the winning entry before hanging both paintings in our drawing room at Wilga. He never fails to point out my works of art to any visitors.

Painting gives me such satisfaction that I feel I must keep on with it, even though caring for a small son and baby daughter has me struggling to find the time and solitude to do so. Thank Heaven for Sunday afternoons on Littledale, when Mother Miller and Willie's sisters take over my children, and I have a chance to paint.

Good night, Dear Book.

Nellie Barnes Miller

J.J. Miller was now appearing at Wilga once a week for dinner. Although he and William had spent all day together at Miller & Miller, the two of them spent hours in the sitting room or on the verandah, talking business and politics. Nellie thought J.J. missed the frequent conversations he had had with her mother.

Decisions of the Borough Council, of which he was no longer a member, were causing J.J. considerable concern. He told William and Nellie he was going to put himself up for election to a new governing body, one that would represent the District. In August he was elected to the newly formed District Council, which became a rival body to the Borough Council in public matters.

With escalation of the struggle between the Boers and British in South Africa, newspapers throughout the colony speculated on an upcoming war. Britain announced she would be depending on men and horses from the colonies to fight alongside her soldiers against the Boers. British commanders declared their preference for Australian volunteers, whom they regarded as experienced horsemen and good marksmen, accustomed to living rough. William Miller, a superb rider and a good shot, would have been an ideal volunteer for service in South Africa had he not been married with children.

Many a town, Cootamundra amongst them, mounted a troop of the First Australian Horse to train for the conflict. Members of sports clubs and groups of school chums commonly joined up together for training with their local troop. When the conflict in South Africa, later called the Boer War, began in 1899, those selected for overseas service sailed westward with their horses from Sydney to South Africa.

On the 27th of September, 1897, William joined the Cootamundra Troop of the First Australian Horse along with his brothers, J.J. and Alick. Their distinctive uniforms, made in England and described in detail in the *Herald*, were myrtle green with black facings. They wore hats of matching green with a plume of black coque feathers and were armed with breech-loading carbines and cavalry swords. Their superior officer was Captain (later Colonel) Mackay, son of Alexander and Annie Mackay of Wallendbeen station.

William rode Arabi, his handsome dark bay mount, part Trakehner and part Arab. Probably because of his superior horsemanship, demonstrated over the years in point-to-point competitions, William Miller was soon commissioned and promoted to Lieutenant Commanding. Nellie told Willie she thought him even more handsome in his Lieutenant's uniform with its sabre and sabretache. His responsibilities included outfitting and equipping the Cootamundra Troop, scheduling camps and supervising training. Encampments were normally held on weekends, and the training attracted hundreds of local spectators.

Troopers Alick and J.J. Miller did not have Willie's responsibilities in the Cootmundra Troop. Alick was busy running Littledale station with the help of his older brother Compton and younger brother Nevil, now age two and twenty. J.J. Miller had become absorbed in the activities of the new Federal League at Cootamundra, which had developed from the Australian Natives' Association. The league strongly backed the upcoming Commonwealth Bill, which was designed to federate the colonies of the Australian continent. Members of the Australian Natives' Association, including J.J. Miller, spoke at meetings in support of a federated Australian Commonwealth and were gratified when Cootamundra voted by a wide margin on June 3rd, 1898, to approve federation.

J.J. then turned his attentions to the upcoming New South Wales elections. "I'm attending the Federal League Conference at Gundagai next week," he announced to William one morning at Miller & Miller. "I'm hopeful of sufficient endorsement to win the Federal League candidacy for Gundagai Constituency." William, as always, was supportive of his older brother's ambitions.

At the Gundagai conference J.J. Miller became a candidate for the Federal League and set out to unseat Free Settler J.F. Barnes, who had been the Member for Gundagai in the colonial legislature for nine years. The *Gundagai Times* whole-heartedly endorsed J.J. Miller's candidacy, printing a "Character Sketch" that recounted his birth and upbringing in New South Wales, his accomplishments as Mayor of Cootamundra and his many contributions to the betterment of Cootamundra District, particularly with regard to agricultural and pastoral concerns. The *Times* article stated in part:

> Mr. Miller is a clear and forcible speaker, can easily express himself with facility, has a pleasing presence, and always commands respect, even from those who differ from him. ... Mr. J.J. Miller, should he become the Gundagai representative, will always be an important element in the deliberations of Parliament, whether in minor or in the broader questions of national life. His private character is pure and

untarnished, single-minded and resolute, of strictest integrity, and an example to many of his compeers . . .

Here was a stellar endorsement indeed, which the *Cootamundra Herald* confirmed by its support of J.J.'s candidacy. John James Miller, the Federal League candidate, launched a vigorous campaign to defeat the incumbent, his Lodge brother, MLA John Frederick Barnes, who was backed by the Free Settlers. Yet on August 13th, 1898, when election results for the 18th government of the colony of New South Wales were announced, Free Settler J.F. Barnes had retained his seat as MLA for Gundagai. He had prevailed over his Federal League opponent, J.J. Miller, by a ratio of 6 to 5.

Astounded at losing the election after such an encouraging campaign, J.J. returned to his work on the Cootamundra District Council. He was elected Mayor of the District the following year.

Meanwhile, Nellie, a young mother of two small children and expecting her third baby, now scarcely saw her husband, so occupied was he with the Cootamundra Troop. William's conversations with his wife were of a military nature, describing training drills he was devising for his men and their horses. In the spring of 1898, he announced to Nellie, "I'm organizing a camp for over one hundred men on the weekend of October 13th to 16th. Behind the grandstand at the racecourse there's plenty of space for manoeuvres and some shade for spectators and the men and their horses. You'll enjoy watching the marching drills and target shooting, the jumping competitions, lemon cutting, tent pegging and cleaving the Turk's Head," he told her. Nellie had some idea of these events because she had heard Major Mackay discussing them with Willie on his many visits to Wilga.

"Willie, I'm not planning to attend," said Nellie, who looked forward to a weekend of visiting and painting on Littledale station whilst her husband devoted himself to his military duties.

"I'm sure one of your sisters will look after Bon and Bertha whilst you see to Sunday luncheon for the family, who will surely all be there," answered her husband. Much as she looked forward to a restful time on Littledale, Nellie was never one to shirk her wifely duties. Although six months along with her third child, she immediately began to plan a meal for a hot day. Nellie was certain Lilla would care for the children whilst Hilda and Willie's mother and sisters helped her with the luncheon. She must get preparations started.

William had looked forward to having his camp inspected by Major Mackay, but the Commanding Officer was still recovering from measles and sent word he could not attend. Nevertheless, the troopers put forth their best efforts for their Lieutenant Commanding and the spectators, and William declared himself satisfied with both the training and his wife's luncheon.

In the stifling heat of January 21st, 1899, Nellie gave birth at home to her third child, a daughter, who was called Coramundra. She was a healthy baby, but very slow to move or speak. Much to her family's sorrow, Coramundra was mentally handicapped. Looking after Bon, Bertha and Cora became more difficult in the month following Cora's birth because the town water supply had been reduced to one hour each day. Grateful as she was for the underground water storage tank at Wilga, Nellie felt increasing strain in caring for her family.

Because J.J. often arrived at Wilga and sat talking to Willie at length, Nellie was aware of how restless her brother-in-law had become. Nellie learned that since arriving at Cootamundra with his family in 1874, J.J. felt he had contributed as much as he could to the development of Littledale and the betterment of the town and District. At the age of nine and thirty, he was in the prime of life and looking for new challenges, but opportunities no longer seemed available to him at Coota. Nellie also knew that J.J.'s defeat in the colonial elections by her uncle, John Barnes, had stung him badly. J.J. Miller had been certain he would be elected MLA for Gundagai Constituency. The voters had decided otherwise.

Nellie and Willie were not surprised when, as summer approached, J.J. began to talk of moving to Sydney. He had made several trips to the colonial capital that year and on one occasion had purchased two town lots at Hurstville in south Sydney.

"I purchased the properties as an investment," he explained. "One of them has a house on it named Wennoe, and on the second lot I'm having a house built which I'll call Parkstone, for the place at Poole in England where my father was raised."

December 12th, 1899

Dear Book,
With dear Mamma so far away, Mother Miller has become like a real mother to me, and Littledale, as you know, has always felt like my second home. Now great changes are about to take place, and already I am struggling with feelings of loss.

After years of drought, Littledale is no longer the prosperous enterprise it once was, yet it must provide for Rebecca, Mary Jane, Sarah and Jessie as well as Alick, Compton and Nevil. I know that Nevil, like Alick, is planning to be married. Both men will bring their brides into Littledale homestead, and J.J. says he feels responsible for providing a new home for his mother and unmarried sisters. A generous intention and a necessary move, to be sure, but how wrenching for them to have to leave the family homestead after all these years.

Alick is now in charge of Littledale, assisted by Nevil, his youngest brother, who is engaged to be married next year to Mabel Constance Betts, daughter of Canon Betts. Willie has told me that although the homestead at Littledale might accommodate two families, he's not certain the station can support them. Compton has never seemed enthusiastic about Littledale. He remains on the station, but has leased a property for himself in Inglis County.

Willie will be returning soon from his Lodge meeting, a gala occasion this evening because a new Worshipful Master is to be installed.
Until next time, Dear Book.

Nellie Barnes Miller

During the month of December 1899, Cootamundra honoured J.J. Miller with farewell tributes, and every event was reported in the *Cootamundra Herald*. At nostalgic meetings of friends and associates, he was lauded as a successful grazier and auctioneer on Littledale station, a respected all-round stock judge, a Past Worshipful Master of Masonic Lodge St. John, a former Alderman and Mayor of Cootamundra, a former member of the District Council and Mayor of the District, a founding partner of Miller & Miller, a founder and supporter of social, sporting, political and agricultural organizations, particularly the APH&I Association and the Farmers' and Settlers' Association of New South Wales, and Lay Reader and Churchwarden at Christ Church of England. Patriotic music and stirring speeches set the tone for memorable gatherings leading up to J.J. Miller's departure for Sydney.

Nellie's painting of cows in a stream, 1897

THIRTY-THREE
Sydney

I will be glad and rejoice in thy mercy; for thou hast considered my trouble; thou hast known my soul in adversities.
— PSALM 31:7

The Miller Christmas party in Littledale homestead in 1899 was a farewell to J.J., complete with sentimental songs and nostalgic recitations. The next week he moved to Sydney, accompanied by his mother Rebecca and his sisters Mary Jane, Sarah and Jessie. William felt deserted and said as much. He and J.J. had been lifelong companions, with William happily following his older brother in childhood activities and adult enterprises and faithfully supporting his political ambitions.

The ongoing drought was continuing to devastate stations in the District as well as trade in town. William still went to Miller & Miller each day, but without the encouraging presence of J.J., his heart was not in the business. Nellie was grateful that Willie had other interests to keep his spirits up. He was organist at monthly meetings of Masonic Lodge St. John and one of the volunteer organists at Christ Church, where he spent several hours each week practising on the church organ. When he had charge of the choir, he rehearsed the music with them on the Thursday evening prior to the Sunday service, paying particular attention, according to choir member Lilla, to proper phrasing and staying on key.

"He's such a taskmaster," said Lilla to Nellie. "He hears every note of our four-part harmony, corrects our breathing and diction, and chastises anyone who sings off-key. I'll admit he does bring out the best in us."

William, like J.J. before him, was now Stock Director of the District and thus Receiver of Scalps, a role which involved him in all kangaroo, rabbit and wild dog shoots. Absorbing most of William's time, however, were his duties with the Cootamundra Troop as Lieutenant Commanding. In lieu of serving in South Africa himself, William assigned his horse, Arabi, to Jim Juleff, son of Cootamundra's bootmaker. The young trooper was accepted for overseas service, and Arabi went with him. Nellie was heartsick when she learned that the elegant Arabi was being sent to war, but William seemed proud that his mount had been selected for service in South Africa.

In Sydney J.J. Miller became an organizer of a farmers' co-operative and in his spare time set out to make a name for himself as a free-lance journalist. He submitted articles to the *Sydney Morning Herald* and sent dispatches to local newspapers around the colony. His topics were varied and interesting: sightseeing in the Blue Mountains, boating excursions to picnic sites around Sydney Harbour, cycling at Manly Beach, touring Randwick Encampment at Sydney and having tea with Colonel and Mrs. Mackay, and watching contingents of men and horses board ships for South Africa. In an early dispatch to the *Cootamundra Herald*, he wrote at length about the departure on January 17th, 1900, of the SS *Surrey*. On board was the Second NSW Contingent with men from the Cootamundra Troop, including Jim Juleff and Arabi, William's horse, "now the property of the Queen," with his regimental number burnt into a hoof "as proof of ownership," reported J.J.

May 12th, 1900

Dear Book,
We are about to celebrate another union of the Barnes and Miller families! My dear little sister, Hilda, who has been courted for years by Alick Miller, will marry him on May 29th in Christ Church, with Canon Betts officiating. She is not yet of age and, as I did, will need Papa's permission to marry, which I know he will readily give.

Wonder of wonders, our Papa, though he is dreadfully ill, is coming for the wedding! He and Mamma are planning to stay on with us at Wilga because dear Mamma wants to be here for my confinement.

I'm grateful to be having an easy time of it with this next baby because little Cora needs so much care.

I would write more, Dear Book, but I am quite exhausted and I must sleep when I can.

Nellie Barnes Miller

On June 27th, 1900, Nellie's fourth child and second son, William, was delivered by Dr. Hull and Nurse Scholz at Wilga. The family marvelled at how much Bill, as he was known, resembled his grandfather Ted Barnes in looks and temperament. Despite being "a Barnes baby," as his Granny Susannah called him, William had a Miller Christian name, which was also the name of his father, his paternal great-grandfather and a paternal great-uncle in Poole, England.

Soon after Bill's birth, as winter was setting in, Ted's respiratory condition worsened, and Dr. Hull told Susannah that her husband was not well enough to return to Sydney. On July 28th, 1900, Ted Barnes, age six and fifty, died at Cootamundra. His funeral service was held at Christ Church and his burial was in the Church of England section of Cootamundra Cemetery. In a lengthy obituary the *Cootamundra Herald* said in part:

> Mr. Barnes was remarkable for his good nature, his love of home and family, and was a very cheerful giver according to his means toward any worthy object. The funeral took place on Monday afternoon, and it brought a large collection of people together, of the town and country. The services were conducted by Canon Betts in the Church of England and at the grave. The choir sang his favourite hymn, "How Bright These Glorious Spirits Shine," Miss Jessie Miller playing the organ. The Mayor (Mr. J.T. Stratton, J.P.) and the aldermen attended, and the flag at the Town Hall was at half-mast from Saturday till Monday. The School of Arts was closed till Tuesday night as a mark of respect to one of its founders and best friends, his daughter, Miss Lilla Barnes, being the

librarian. Deceased leaves a widow and seven daughters—Mrs. W. Miller, Mrs. A. Miller (Littledale), and Misses Lilla, Ivy, Bertha, Frida and Florence Barnes . . .

August 30th, 1900

Dear Book,

Such grief. Although our darling Papa was very ill and had been suffering for many years, his death came as a shock. Dear Mamma was so brave, consoling all of us when I am certain her heart was breaking.

Dear Mamma, Goog, Peeler, Frida and Florence stayed briefly at Coota after the funeral, but they have returned to Sydney. I had hoped and prayed that dear Mamma would come back here to live, but she says she feels quite settled at Sydney and believes the city offers more opportunities for the girls. Of course, J.J. lives at Sydney and visits her often.

If it weren't for Hilda on Littledale, I would anticipate being quite lonely when Lilla marries Jack White, whose family has Merribindinyah station near Bethungra. Lilla is my bosom friend as well as my sister, and I shall miss her intensely.

Enough of my concerns, Dear Book. I must be grateful for my husband and my four beautiful children, and cease pining for what cannot be.

Nellie Barnes Miller

On Federation Day, January 1st, 1901, the government that had been elected in 1898 declared the colony of New South Wales an Australian state. A crowd of thousands, which included J.J. and Susannah, celebrated in Centennial Park at Sydney. At the Opening of the first Parliament, which took place at Melbourne on May 9th, the Speech from the Throne was read by a royal representative, the Duke of Cornwall and York, who was later to become King George V.

John Frederick Barnes, Member of Parliament for Gundagai, had thus become a Father of Australian Federation. J.J. declared to Susannah that if he had been elected MP, he would have organized a grand celebration at Cootamundra, which had voted strongly for federation.

The new federal government was providing J.J. with topics for his freelance articles. On the question of a site for a national capital, he joined many others in writing passionately in favour of a location on the western slopes of New South Wales. Cootamundra was the ideal choice, J.J. declared. The place that became the Australian Capital Territory many years later was Canberra, a town on the western slopes some one hundred miles southeast of Cootamundra.

March 27th, 1901

Dear Book,
A brief note before I have some much-needed sleep. Cora has been particularly restless today, and I am worn out.
   The congregation at Christ Church has just been informed by Canon Betts that the church is now completely clear of debt and may be consecrated. The service of Consecration is set for April 28th, and all current and past parishioners are invited to attend. Papa and dear Mamma worked so hard to build Christ Church and complete its interior; how well I remember all those bazaars, refreshment tents and flower shows. Dear Mamma must want to see the church consecrated.
   I have written to urge her to come with the girls. Perhaps J.J. will come with them.
   Good night, Dear Book.

Nellie Barnes Miller

In the winter of 1901, J.J. Miller was nominated as the Federal League's candidate from Gundagai in the first elections of the Australian Federation. Although he resided at Sydney, he was a property owner in Gundagai Constituency and eligible to represent the constituency in Parliament. He spent weeks out west and campaigned even more vigorously than he had in the colonial elections of 1898. His efforts proved fruitless, however. The voters again elected the incumbent, John F. Barnes, this time as Member of Parliament for Gundagai. Stunned by the electorate's decision in 1898, J.J. was crushed by this second defeat in 1901.
   Nellie was now witnessing behaviour in Willie similar to J.J.'s restlessness before he left Cootamundra in 1899. One evening, unable to endure

his moodiness any longer, she demanded to know what was on his mind. "I cannot see any purpose in continuing at Miller & Miller," he blurted. "Alick is willing to have a go at it, and with some auctioneering and the insurance and income tax businesses, he'll be all right. As for Littledale, Nevil is capable of running the station on his own, if it comes to that. I'm going to Sydney next week to get J.J.'s advice. I don't want to leave Coota, especially Wilga, but there's no future for us here."

This response was more definite than Nellie had expected. Willie sounded as determined to leave Cootamundra as J.J. had two years previously. The ongoing drought conditions were having an effect on all their lives, and Nellie believed Willie's two-year separation from J.J. was also significant. Even before her husband set off for Sydney, she was certain they would be moving there.

She must find the energy to pack up the family's belongings. As soon as Willie returned from Sydney, she would write to her mother, who was sure to come and help. She had a distant memory of a poem on a card given to her by Grandmamma Barnes; one of its lines said, "Ever strive to see the sunny side." Being close to her family at Sydney was surely "the sunny side" of having to leave Cootamundra.

December 27th, 1901

Dear Book,
So much to write about!
   I feel well settled here at Ashfield in West Sydney, where dear departed Papa was born. Willie, however, has been away for long periods of time in Queensland, on the look-out for opportunities there.
   We had such a Christmas! Willie and I invited J.J. and his mother and sisters to join us on Christmas Eve. I served a buffet of savouries and Christmas sweets with wine and cordial, and afterwards, as usual, dear Mamma went to the pianoforte. Before she could play a note, J.J. got down on one knee beside her and asked her to marry him!
   She murmured, "Yes," and the whole room exploded in shrieks of joy. J.J. kissed her (a lengthy kiss!) and placed a lovely ring on her finger. (She had removed Papa's rings to her other hand; I reckon she knew

J.J. was going to propose.) Jessie Miller took Mamma's place at the pianoforte, and the remainder of the evening featured romantic songs and recitations of poetry, many toasts to the happy couple, and as the wine flowed, some blushingly dubious stories from Willie and J.J. about brides and grooms.

J.J. and dear Mamma are to be married on April 11th (our wedding anniversary) in Saint Stephen's Church at Kurrajong at the edge of the Blue Mountains. The officiant will be the Reverend Maurice Gray, now retired, whom we all know from his days at Christ Church, Cootamundra.

I'm very pleased that J.J. and dear Mamma are to be married; they have been such good friends for so many years. J.J. is one and forty, and his bride has turned fifty, but they are both so full of youthful exuberance over their wedding that it's hard to tell!

Because Hilda and I are married to Miller men, little Frida and Florence are J.J.'s sisters-in-law by marriage. They are also now his stepdaughters and they asked if they might call him Papa. He agreed enthusiastically.

So two Miller brothers, Willie and Alick, are married to two Barnes sisters, Nellie and Hilda, and our widowed mother, Susannah, is to be married to J.J., the eldest Miller brother. Now that I think of it, J.J., who is my brother-in-law, will also be my stepfather! And Hilda and I will have a new sister-in-law, dear Mamma! I pity anyone in a future generation who attempts to get us all sorted!

Good night, Dear Book.

Nellie Barnes Miller

The year 1902 was proving especially difficult for residents of Cootamundra, including the Barnes and Miller families. Another year of severe drought was again the overwhelming factor in the lives of those on the western slopes. Littledale and Miller & Miller, as well as the family's development interests around Cootamundra, were seriously affected. During a succession of fires in January, a twenty-ton stack of hay was destroyed on the Shaftesbury property of John Barnes at Jindalee.

After their April wedding and a honeymoon at Lady Robinson's Beach, duly noted in the *Cootamundra Herald*, which sent good wishes, J.J. and Susannah established themselves at Newtown, a suburb of Sydney. J.J. was a Freemason of Southern Counties Mark Lodge, and Susannah became a member of its Ladies' Auxiliary. Together they were involved in Masonic fundraising and social events.

In May 1903, Susannah was thrilled by the arrival of two more grandchildren. In Kernbank at Ashfield on the 5th of May, Nellie and Willie had their fifth child, a baby girl who was christened Elinor Susie and known in the family as Lel. Her cousin twice over, Selwyn Archibald Miller, son of Hilda and Alick, was born three days later at Cootamundra. He was a brother for two-year-old Joan Alexandra, who could not say Selwyn and called him Boy Dear. In time Boy Dear was shortened to Boyd, which was the name used by Selwyn's family and friends for the rest of his life.

Trooper A.A. Miller, 1898

THIRTY-FOUR

The Aorangi

*Be of good courage, and he shall strengthen your heart,
all ye who hope in the Lord.*

—PSALM 31:24

Once they were settled at Newtown, an inner west suburb of Sydney in Marrickville District, Susannah and J.J. Miller joined the congregation of Saint Stephen's Church of England. The church, which featured an organ of renown, had been designed by Edmund Blacket, architect of numerous colonial churches. The newly married Millers took part in all the activities at Saint Stephen's, Susannah offering her particular expertise to the Bazaar Committee and the choir.

At Newtown she often found herself thinking back to Ted and their courtship at her pianoforte in London, her subsequent voyage to New South Wales, her wedding at Balmain and her arrival at Cootamundra. She reflected on the people she had known at Coota: her mother-in-law, Elizabeth Barnes, for one, who left England in 1840 to seek a better life for her family, only to have her husband murdered in the colony; her close friend and new mother-in-law, Rebecca Miller, an assisted immigrant from Ireland who achieved a farm of her own, now managed by her youngest sons; and dear Ted, the years they had together at Cootamundra, their community and church activities, the births of their thirteen children and the burials of a daughter and five sons. The deaths of those babies would never leave her.

Susannah was beginning to feel a contentment with her new life, widowed, but now married to an old friend. Yet whilst she was enjoying her newly married state, her husband was unsettled and preoccupied. Susannah put J.J.'s behaviour down to his political disappointments. He had been so eager to represent Gundagai Constituency in the colonial and federal governments, but twice the voters had rejected him. The continuing drought on the western slopes was a worry, too. Her husband, like many landowners, was concerned about its effects on his family and his property. They had recently learned that Nevil Miller was transporting all the Littledale stock to Moss Vale near Bowral to save the animals from starvation.

Several of J.J.'s Masonic friends at Sydney spoke of leaving Australia and making a new start overseas. They had been men of substance and influence in the colony and had not found commensurate status in the federation. "I must say I'm sympathetic to their plight," said J.J. one evening, "and I'm interested in their emigration plans."

"Your situation is much different, though," said Susannah. "You have commitments here at Sydney, and we have family ties to keep us in New South Wales." He did not answer her.

Susannah wondered if J.J. felt constrained by his life at Sydney. Perhaps he longed for the limitless possibilities of his younger days on the developing western slopes. A man of quick mind and abundant energy, her husband needed something to lift his spirits and provide him with a fresh goal. To have a successful life together, Susannah believed she and J.J. required a shared focus, a new project to which they could devote their energies.

On a pleasant September day in 1903, with Frida and Florence in school, Goog and Peeler away at Brisbane, and J.J. going straight from his office at the co-operative to his monthly Masonic Lodge meeting, Susannah had some time to herself. She spent the morning baking a batch of bread and making a pot of pumpkin soup. After lunch she went into the sitting room to relax in her easy chair and read her latest copy of the *Cootamundra Herald*, which was mailed to her each week.

The news from Coota continued to be dismal: further effects of the lengthy drought on activities in the town; more farmers like Nevil Miller moving their stock out of Cootamundra District in search of adequate grazing; well-established properties being abandoned by their destitute owners. She turned to the next page of the *Herald*. The paper had a reputation for reporting in detail each event in the town and District, and Susannah began to read a long column about a scandalous hearing at the Cootamundra Court House. The Petitioner, a well-known resident, sought a divorce from his wife, the Respondent. At the end of the day-long hearing, the Justice, one of Ted's fellow Magistrates, granted the Petitioner a provisional order for divorce, a *decree nisi*.

Susannah stopped to ponder what she had just read. She was familiar with the couple because they had been neighbours at Coota. She was aware that during the husband's frequent, lengthy trips to Europe, his wife had been alone and dependent upon the company of friends. Susannah had often seen the lady in her stylish cycling costumes with split skirts setting out on excursions with various gentlemen companions.

Certainly, the couple's divorce was a rare occurrence. One never spoke of divorce, although one might know of divorced persons. Mrs. Wolstenholme, for example, had divorced her husband (for very good reason, according to witnesses) and gone on to establish Maybanke College.

Susannah continued to peruse the report in the *Cootamundra Herald* and was horrified by what she read next. During the hearing several witnesses had testified that during her husband's absences, the Respondent had developed particularly close relationships with certain gentlemen, who were named. One of the gentlemen named was Susannah's new husband.

For several minutes Susannah sat in shocked disbelief. Then it occurred to her that beyond political defeats, devastating droughts and diminished opportunities, the real cause of J.J.'s unsettled and preoccupied state of mind had been his knowledge of the impending divorce hearing and its inevitable disclosure of his involvement.

Adding to her immediate consternation, she knew the *Herald* report, no doubt avidly read by residents of Coota, was sure to be reprinted in newspapers across New South Wales. Out on the western slopes, here at Sydney, perhaps anywhere in Australia, the scandalous news of a divorce hearing at Cootamundra, including the involvement of J.J. Miller, was about to become widely known. Realizing the impact of the *Herald* article not only on J.J., but also on their families, she collapsed in tears, venting her feelings of disillusionment and anger.

Furious as she was, she nevertheless gathered her wits and began to consider their situation. How on earth could they find a solution to the distressing circumstances they now faced? A drastic remedy was called for: a fresh start in new surroundings. Yet, with the certainty of widespread publication of the *Herald* report, such a remedy did not seem possible within Australia. The afternoon dimmed into evening as she struggled to find any answer to this dilemma.

She had never waited up for J.J. when he was out in the evenings, but this night she made an exception. When he joined her in the sitting room on his return, he bent down to kiss her. She handed him the relevant page of the *Cootamundra Herald* and went to bed. Her husband slept alone in the sitting room that night.

In the morning J.J. spoke to his wife at length about the pleasures of the lady's company on cycling excursions at Cootamundra and at Manly Beach. He admitted to Susannah that enjoying a close companionship with a married lady during her husband's absences did put him in a questionable position. Susannah's reply to J.J.'s lengthy speech was scorching. Her fierce attacks on his reckless behaviour and complacent explanation completely unnerved him. Aware of Susannah's strength of purpose, J.J. fully expected her to banish him from her life and continue on without him. He should have realized, having known Susannah all his adult life, that she was a loyal, generous and warm-hearted woman. He begged her to forgive him, and, compassionately, she freely did so.

What remained now was finding a way forward. Susannah sent J.J. off to work and, rather than continuing to mull over their situation, began her household chores. Although it was not washday, she stripped the bed and vigorously scrubbed sheets on her washboard. As she did so, she remembered a recent Sydney newspaper article that, ironically, gave her hope. She stopped scrubbing and located the paper in question.

The article, reprinted from a newspaper in Canada, described the city of Winnipeg in the province of Manitoba and its Grain Exchange, which was urgently in need of experienced auctioneers.

Susannah knew as little about Canada and Winnipeg as she had thirty years earlier about New South Wales and Cootamundra. She had heard that Canada was a large and cold land, and from the newspaper article she learned that the city of Winnipeg was a railway hub located in the centre of the country at the eastern edge of a vast grain-growing prairie. Susannah consulted an atlas and saw that, in addition to a voyage across the Pacific Ocean, there would be a lengthy train journey through the mountains and across the prairie to Winnipeg.

As she rinsed sheets, wrung them out and pegged them on the line to dry, her initial feelings of hope were obliterated by the realization of what such a move would mean: saying farewell forever to her children and grandchildren; leaving her friends and all the connections she had made in New South Wales; selling their home and possessions to pay for their emigration, and setting out on an ocean voyage and a train journey for a life in the middle of Canada. Granted that J.J. had been interested in his friends' intentions to emigrate, but would he be keen on going to Winnipeg?

Despite her many misgivings, that evening she showed her husband the information about the need for auctioneers at the Winnipeg Grain Exchange. Not only was J.J. interested, he was also immensely grateful for her willingness to make a new start in Canada. Gathering her courage, Susannah suggested a telegram be sent at once to the Grain Exchange, offering the services of an experienced auctioneer. The Exchange replied promptly by wire, promising J.J. employment on arrival. Susannah and J.J. immediately booked passage on the SS *Aorangi*, proceeded to sell most of what they owned, including Susannah's beloved Broadwood pianoforte, and began to pack their belongings. When she found it all overwhelming, Susannah reminded herself that she had wanted to find a shared focus for their marriage. This particular focus, however, was much beyond her original intention. Her prayers for God's support were frequent and fervent.

September 30th, 1903

Dear Book,
A month from now J.J., Frida, Florence and dear Mamma will be on the other side of the Pacific Ocean in a much colder clime than they have ever known.

   I shall not forget dear Mamma's anguish when she told me what she and J.J. were planning to do. She asked me to forgive J.J. and understand the necessity of their decision, but I confess, Dear Book, my forgiveness and understanding come hard because dear Mamma is having to leave us forever for a life very far away. She and I both began to cry when she spoke of her family and friends and her home and possessions she was about to abandon.

   I can't write anything more, except to say that I shall pray for courage on the day J.J. and dear Mamma board the Aorangi.

   Good night, Dear Book.

Nellie Barnes Miller

With her sides freshly scrubbed and her brass gleaming in the spring sunshine, the SS *Aorangi* was ready for a voyage across the Pacific Ocean. Her lines were tied to bollards on a Sydney dock, and she lay waiting for passengers to board her on the morning of October 6th, 1903.

The ship would proceed from Sydney to Brisbane and thence to Suva in Fiji. She would steam across to Honolulu, Hawaii, and onward to Victoria, British Columbia, before proceeding on the following day a short distance across a strait to Vancouver. There, on October 29th, 1903, the Miller family would disembark and board a train for the journey to Winnipeg. Susannah recalled that her sailing voyage from London to New South Wales had taken fully three months. Steam had supplanted sail, and when Susannah left the same Sydney Harbour that had welcomed her in 1873, engines, not winds, would take her across the ocean. On this voyage she was thirty years older and leaving behind so much more.

Despite Susannah's anguish at their decision to emigrate, she had promised herself that she and J.J. would start afresh in Canada, set down roots and work to establish themselves in a Canadian community. Perhaps they would be amongst the founders of a church as they had been at Coota. She would, of course, have a new pianoforte. She was also determined that their goodbyes would be cheerful. On the dock to see them off were Nellie and William, who had left their children for the day in the care of Rebecca and Mary Jane Miller at Hurstville. Susannah had long known that Nellie was a sensitive girl and for her sake was trying to remain calm and reassuring.

Nellie felt settled at Ashfield, Susannah knew, but William was still talking of moving to Queensland. Susannah reckoned that after his brother's departure from Sydney, William would leave New South Wales and take his family north to a new life. As well, she was aware that money had always been a concern for them because William was a dreamer who seldom gave his attention to the reality of family finances, and this was a constant concern for Nellie.

Frida and Florence, ages eleven and six, were dancing on the dock with excitement, full of childish enthusiasm for a new adventure. The little girls were not old enough to share their mother's feelings for Australia. They were too young to appreciate that their paternal grandparents had arrived in New South Wales in 1841 and had been pioneers in developing properties and businesses on the western slopes. Their father had been born in New South Wales and had been one of the pioneers of a town and a founder of a church. Thirty years ago their mother had come from London to marry him, establish a home, give birth to thirteen children and bury six of them at Cootamundra. What was important to Frida and Florence that day was sailing on a ship across an ocean.

Susannah was leaving behind five daughters and her grandchildren, causing pangs of separation even before she boarded the ship. Lilla and Hilda, like Nellie, were married to men who had responsibilities in Australia. Lilla, who had wed Jack White the previous year, lived on Walhalla, their sheep station near Mitta Mitta; Hilda was settled with Alick and their children on Littledale. Goog and Peeler, her unmarried daughters, would not be left in Australia for long because as soon as she was able, she planned to book passage for them.

Susannah smiled at her eldest daughter, who was hugging Frida and Florence. She sought comfort in the knowledge that William, despite his plans to settle in Queensland, had never been apart from J.J. for long. This alone gave her hope that Nellie and her family, finances permitting, would one day join them in Canada.

The "All Aboard!" sounded, and Susannah and J.J. embraced Nellie and William and followed the two scampering little girls aboard the ship. Clutching tightly wound paper streamers to toss across to those they left on shore, the family stood at the port rail whilst the vessel slipped her lines. The *Aorangi* gave an enormous bellow to announce her departure, sending Frida and Florence into screams then giggles. With streamers wafting and flags flying, the *Aorangi* moved out into Sydney Harbour, swung around, and steamed towards Sydney Heads, the Pacific Ocean and Canada.

Epilogue

In Australia—
Rebecca Miller and her daughters Mary Jane, Sarah and Jessie continued to share Wennoe and Parkstone at Hurstville. Rebecca's other daughters, Elizabeth and Margaret, also stayed in Australia. Elizabeth and Edward Webster raised four children; when Elizabeth was widowed, she married the Rev. Harry Arnold. Margaret and Frank Murray had four children and settled in Tasmania.

Nevil Miller married Mabel Betts, with whom he had six children. Born on Littledale, Nevil remained on the station for his lifetime. When he was a widower, Nevil married Lucy Mary Spencer. In the early twentieth century he rode a cream filly, Zephyr, a descendant of John Miller's mare, Kate.

Compton Miller, who had been elected to the Cootamundra District Council, left for Canada to live with J.J. and Susannah and become secretary of their church. He stayed in Canada only a short time, returning to Australia to live with his sisters Sarah and Jessie at Hurstville. When he was forty-seven years of age, he married Louie Baker and fathered four children.

Thomas, John, George, William and Beth Barnes, their spouses and families, continued to reside in Australia.

Arabi, Lieutenant William Miller's dark bay mount, ridden by Trooper Jim Juleff, was killed by a sniper at Kroonstadt, South Africa. Jim Juleff survived.

Clapham Cottage became the home of the Town and Country Women's Club, where members can relax and enjoy lunches, guest speakers and social occasions.

Littledale station, which was developed into a three-thousand-acre property, remained in the Miller family for 113 years. In the twentieth century it was worked by Nevil Miller and his grandson John Miller. In 1988 Littledale was sold to the Australian television personality and race horse breeder Mike Willesee, who established Transmedia Park Stud. Willesee sold the property in 1995 to Woodlands Stud, owned by the Ingham brothers, who restored the Millers' 1877 Littledale homestead. In 2008 Woodlands Stud at Cootamundra became part of an international Thoroughbred breeding and racing operation, Darley Australia.

In Canada—
Although Susannah and J.J. Miller had intended settling in Winnipeg, Manitoba, they did not go as far as the prairie city. Whilst aboard the *Aorangi*, J.J. learned from other passengers that the province of British Columbia was in the midst of a land boom. Before the family disembarked in Vancouver at the end of October 1903, J.J. had decided to forgo his employment at the Winnipeg Grain Exchange. Ever the entrepreneur, within days of his arrival in Vancouver he opened an office on Hastings Street and obtained a licence as a real estate auctioneer.

J.J. soon prospered in real estate and in 1908 bought a large city lot in the Grandview district, where, on behalf of the city, he had been the auctioneer of building lots totalling $14,000. On his property on Salsbury Drive, he built a large home, Kurrajong, at a cost of $30,000. In that same year, 1908, he was elected the first President of the Vancouver Exhibition Association, the founding organization of the Pacific National Exhibition, which honours him with a fountain on Miller Drive in the exhibition grounds. On August 15th, 1910, at the invitation of J.J. Miller, Prime Minister Wilfrid Laurier opened the first Vancouver Exhibition.

In 1909 J.J. was commissioned to auction building lots in the coastal township of Prince Rupert, and within four days his auctioneering had resulted in a sale totalling $1,142,060. A thirty-third degree Mason in the Scottish Rite, J.J. was a founding member of Lodge Southern Cross No. 44 in Vancouver and was well respected in Masonic Lodges across Canada. In the spring of 1911, he took Susannah, Frida and Florence on a four-month train journey across Canada and south to New York; they then voyaged across the Atlantic to tour France, Wales, Scotland, Ireland and England. In London they attended the coronation celebrations of King George V. Dispatches from J.J. Miller to the *Vancouver World* newspaper became a book, *Vancouver to the Coronation*. In 1916 he served as Alderman for Ward Four in Vancouver.

J.J.'s continuing gratitude to Susannah for her initiative and forbearance in leaving Australia was heartfelt and sincere, and during his long and eventful life in Canada, he frequently expressed his warm admiration for his capable wife.

As Susannah had predicted, after she and J.J. left Sydney, William Miller took Nellie and the children to Queensland. They stayed little more than a year, having received encouraging letters from J.J. about real estate opportunities in Vancouver. Accompanied by young sons Bon and Bill and sisters-in-law Goog and Peeler Barnes, William arrived in Vancouver aboard the SS *Aorangi* on March 17th, 1905.

Four-year-old Bill Miller, seasick for the entire voyage, never forgot being nursed all the way by his aunts, Goog and Peeler. Meanwhile, Nellie returned to Cootamundra, where, on May 9th, 1905, Dr. Brennan and Nurse Scholz delivered her of a third son. Three months later, on August 7th, Nellie boarded the *Aorangi* at Sydney with young daughters Bertha, Cora and Lel and the infant Croydon for a twenty-five-day voyage across the Pacific Ocean. She joined her husband and sons, her mother, sisters and J.J. in Vancouver on September 1st, 1905. Susannah, of course, was overjoyed at her arrival. Three more children were born in Vancouver to Nellie and William: Lionel, Myee and Huntley.

William was also successful in real estate and in 1909, on Napier Street in Grandview, built Wilga, a large home enhanced by a lawn tennis court. He read extensively about his new country and wrote "Letters from Canada" to the *Cootamundra Herald*, extolling Canada's natural features and abundant opportunities. Like his paternal grandmother in Dorsetshire, Margaret Mary Maskelyne Miller, William was a student of astronomy, and in Vancouver he published a monograph entitled "The Moon and Whence It Came."

In December 1911, William and Nellie left Bon, Bill, Lel, Croydon and Lionel in the care of Susannah and J.J. and returned to Australia for an extended visit, accompanied by daughters Bertha, Cora and Myee. They spent Christmas that year on Walhalla station with Lilla and Jack White and their four children.

Alick and Hilda Miller and their children, Joan, Selwyn and Ivy, lived on Littledale and in Cootamundra until 1908, when they emigrated and joined their relatives in Vancouver. They established a general store in Grandview and named their Grandview home The Cottage.

Goog Barnes married Thomas Dowling in 1906, a year after her arrival in Vancouver; they had seven children, including twins. Peeler Barnes married Harold Chafe in 1911 and raised four children in neighbouring Washington state at Tacoma, USA. Frida Barnes married Herbert "Bert" Dyer in 1912 and had two daughters. She subsequently divorced her husband and in 1921 married Harold Miller, of a different Miller family, and had two sons. The youngest Barnes daughter, Florence, married Rowland "Bob" Jenkins in 1919 and had two children.

The Miller families were amongst the founders of Saint Saviour's Anglican Church in Grandview. At the opening of the Vancouver Exhibition in 1910, Susannah and her daughters established a Church of England Refreshment Tent as a fundraiser for Saint Saviour's.

Nellie and William at Wilga and Hilda and Alick at The Cottage lived near Susannah and J.J. at Kurrajong. The three families met frequently in one of their homes for dinners, which, according to Bill Miller, always included nostalgic conversations about life at Cootamundra followed by enthusiastic games of bridge. Susannah and J.J. were generous hosts at Kurrajong. Their extended family and guests were treated to Susannah's sumptuous meals and her performances at the pianoforte. "Believe Me, If All Those Endearing Young Charms" was a favourite request.

Acknowledgements

This saga of my Barnes and Miller ancestors in colonial New South Wales was only possible with the help of many interested relatives. I wish to thank David and Patti Miller, Steve Miller, Sharon Miller, David Martin, Tanya Jorgenson, Elizabeth and Terry Plenty, Susan Knox, Gordon Miller, Trevor and Donna Miller, Carolynne Miller, Ann Miller, Ted and Helen Bowly, and Doug and Jane Campbell for their many contributions. They offered their Barnes and Miller knowledge, photographs and research, and their individual interests and experiences in ships and the oceans of the world, horses and ranching, nineteeth-century educational, medical and legal matters as well as story suggestions. My Australian cousins, Ted and Helen Bowly, researched details for me, and Ted, Helen, Doug and Jane enabled my visit to Cootamundra and Littledale. I am grateful to each of these relatives for participating in this presentation of the lives of our ancestors in colonial New South Wales.

The Venerable Louis Rivers, the Reverend Carole Neilson and the Reverend Raymond Murrin of Saint Christopher's Parish in West Vancouver assisted with church details in the book, and I have greatly appreciated their advice and encouragement.

To Ted and Doris Holdaway go my thanks for their Barnes and Miller research and photographs of Littledale, and I thank Evelyn Baker for her knowledge of farming and crocheting. I am also grateful to patient friends and relatives who read my first drafts and made valuable comments. I am much indebted to three supportive family historians: Barbara Lynch helped with initial editing through to publication; Norah McLaren, who is a Dowling and related by marriage to Goog Barnes Dowling, knew members of the Barnes and Miller families in Vancouver; Margaret Ramsay offered her editorial suggestions, assistance with the pictures and years of encouragement.

In Cootamundra, Patricia Caskie, a former *Cootamundra Herald* editor, opened her files to me, directed me to other sources, promptly answered my numerous questions, and searched through the *Cootamundra Herald* archives for articles concerning the Barnes and Miller families. My sincere thanks to Pat for all her assistance and especially for her generous permission to use material from her definitive publications, *Cootamundra: Foundation to Federation* and *Cootamundra 1901–1924: Past Imperfect*.

I am indebted to Kevin J. Passey, author of *Lachlan Landmarks*, for his detailed account of raids and ambushes by Ben Hall's gang across western New South Wales.

The Kurrajong Tree would not have reached publication without the work of Naomi Pauls, editor, and Patty Osborne, designer. My heartfelt thanks to both of them.

My husband, Stewart Martin, has earned my warmest gratitude for his unfailing patience during those many hours when my mind was far away in nineteeth-century New South Wales.

Illustration Credits

Illustrations are from Miller family photographs and from the collection of Dr. William Miller, with the exception of the following:

page 10   Modern map of Cootamundra area. Shire of Cootamundra.

page 283   Slab church. From "The First 100 Years: Cootamundra Anglican Parish Centenary," by J.L. Tregea (1980).

◈

page I   John and Elizabeth Barnes, c. 1850s, courtesy of Mrs. Doreen Higgins. From *Lachlan Landmarks*, by K.J. Passey (Gippsland Printers, 1986).

page II   Christ Church of England, Cootamundra, 1878, sketch by Graeme Inson (1939), first published in the *Cootamundra Herald*. From *Cootamundra: Foundation to Federation*, by Patricia Caskie (Annwel Enterprises, 1991). Used with permission.

page III   J & E. Barnes Store, Cootamundra, 1881, first published in the *Liberal*, October 19, 1887. From *Cootamundra: Foundation to Federation*, by Patricia Caskie (Annwel Enterprises, 1991). Used with permission.

page III   Margaret Miller, BA, Sydney University, 1886. From *Cootamundra District: A Photographic History, Vol. 5* (Cootamundra Local History Society, 2007). Used with permission.

page V   Mayor J.J. Miller and his sister, Mayoress Miss M.J. Miller. From the *Sydney Mail*, September 24, 1892.

Appendix

The Family of Elizabeth King Ellen Barnes

John Barnes   m. 1833 Elizabeth King Ellen
(1812–1863)   (1802–1886)
b. Bletsoe,   b. Shaftesbury
Bedfordshire, England   Dorsetshire, England

Issue:
Thomas Alfred—stockman, merchant, Postmaster
        b. 1836, Stepney, London
        m. 1866, Isabella Stinson
        d. 1902, Murrumburrah, Australia

John Frederick—miner, cabinetmaker, publican, merchant, Justice of the Peace, Borough Councillor and Mayor, Member of the Legislative Assembly, Member of Parliament
        b. 1837, Stepney, London
        m. 1860, Jane Marshall
        d. 1915, Hurstville, Sydney, Australia

Elizabeth Jane and Mary Ellen—twins, died in early infancy
        b. 1839, Stepney, London
        d. 1839, Stepney, London

George Robert—merchant, Postmaster
        b. 1840, Stepney, London
        m. 1872, Agnes Crisp
        d. 1920, Murrumburrah, Australia

William John—stockman, Inspector of Conditional Purchases
                        b. 1842, Concord, NSW
                        m. 1862, Janet Brown
                        d. 1926, Glebe, Sydney, Australia

Edward Prior "Ted"—merchant, Postmaster, Returning Officer,
    Justice of the Peace, Coroner, Churchwarden
                        b. 1844, Ashfield, West Sydney, NSW
                        m. 1873, Susannah Gordon
                        d. 1900, Cootamundra, NSW

Elizabeth Mary Maria "Beth"—wife and mother
                        b. 1846, Ashfield, West Sydney, NSW
                        m. 1881, Harry Ellen
                        d. 1924, North Sydney, Australia

The Family of Rebecca Nixon Miller

John Miller   m. 1857 Rebecca Nixon
(1824–1881)   (1836–1920)
b. Margate,   b. Drumquin
Kent, England   Tyrone, Ireland

Issue:

Mary Jane—Borough Mayoress, church organizer
           b. 1858, Berrima, NSW
           Spinster
           d. 1916, Hurstville, Sydney, Australia

Emily Elizabeth—teacher, wife, mother
           b. 1859, Berrima, NSW
           m. 1883, Edward Godfrey Webster
           m. 1927, Rev. Harry Arnold
           d. 1946, Auburn, Sydney, Australia

John James "J.J."—grazier, stock and station agent, auctioneer, insurance agent, Borough Councillor and Mayor, District Councillor and Mayor, Lay Reader, Churchwarden, real estate agent, author, Alderman
           b. 1860, Berrima, NSW
           m. 1902, Susannah Maria Gordon Barnes
           d. 1950, Vancouver, Canada

William "Willie"—bank clerk, stock and station agent, auctioneer, insurance agent, pianist, chorister, organist, Lay Reader, real estate agent, author
           b. 1863, Pejar, NSW
           m. 1894, Susie Ellen "Nellie" Barnes
           d. 1944, San Jose, USA

Margaret Mary Maskelyne, BA—teacher, wife, mother
           b. 1864, Pejar, NSW

       m. 1895, Francis David Porteous Murray
       d. 1952, Tasmania(?), Australia

Sarah Ann—teacher
       b. 1865, Tarago, NSW
       Spinster
       d. 1955, Burwood, Sydney, Australia

Eliza Gore Gilmore—died of whooping cough
       b. 1867, Tarago, NSW
       d. 1868, Tarago, NSW

Jessie Annie—pianist, organist, governess, suffragist
       b. 1869, Tarago, NSW
       Spinster
       d. 1954, Hurstville, Sydney, Australia

Compton South—grazier, District Councillor
       b. 1871, Tarago, NSW
       m. 1918, Louise Baker
       d. 1968, Kogarah, Australia

Alexander Archibald "Alick"—grazier, auctioneer, stock and station
  agent, insurance agent, storekeeper
       b. 1873, North Goulburn, NSW
       m. 1900, Hilda Prior Barnes
       d. 1941, Vancouver, Canada

Edward Lanfear—died of diarrhoea
       b. 1874, Jindalee, NSW
       d. 1875, Jindalee, NSW

Nevil Maskelyne—grazier, inventor, District Councillor
       b. 1875, Cootamundra, NSW
       m. 1900, Mabel Constance Betts
       m. 1939, Lucy Mary Spencer
       d. 1958, Cootamundra, Australia

The Family of
Susannah Maria Gordon Barnes Miller

Edward Prior "Ted" Barnes   m. 1873 Susannah Maria Gordon
(1844–1900)   (1851–1927)
b. Ashfield, West Sydney,   b. London, England
NSW   In 1902 at Kurrajong, Australia,
   Susannah married J.J. Miller.

Issue:
Susie Ellen "Nellie"—artist, wife, mother
     b. 1874, Cootamundra, NSW
     m. 1894, William Miller
     d. 1927, Vancouver, Canada

Lilla Maria—organist, librarian, wife, mother
     b. 1876, Cootamundra, NSW
     m. 1902, Jack White
     d. 1959, Richmond, Australia

Eva—died of diarrhoea
     b. 1877, Cootamundra, NSW
     d. 1878, Sydney, NSW

Hilda Prior—pianist, teacher, wife, mother
     b. 1879, Cootamundra, NSW
     m. 1900, Alexander Archibald Miller
     d. 1977, North Vancouver, Canada

Ivy Fenner "Goog"—wife and mother
     b. 1881, Cootamundra, NSW
     m. 1906, Thomas Dowling
     d. 1958, Vancouver, Canada

Bertha Jane "Peeler"—wife and mother
        b. 1884, Cootamundra, NSW
        m. 1911, Harold Chafe
        d. 1982, Tacoma, USA

Edward Gordon—drowned
        b. 1885, Cootamundra, NSW
        d. 1887, Cootamundra, NSW

Twin sons—stillborn—1887

Edward John—died of diarrhoea
        b. 1889, Cootamundra, NSW
        d. 1889, Cootamundra, NSW

Lewis Ernest "Mickey"—died of influenza
        b. 1890, Cootamundra, NSW
        d. 1891, Cootamundra, NSW

Elfrida Mary "Frida"—wife and mother
        b. 1892, Cootamundra, NSW
        m. 1912, Herbert "Bert" Dyer
        m. 1921, Harold Miller
        d. 1962, Vancouver, Canada

Florence Esther—wife and mother
        b. 1897, Cootamundra, NSW
        m. 1919, Rowland Wilfred "Bob" Jenkins
        d. 1988, Vancouver, Canada

Glossary

accoucheuse. Midwife.
antimacassar. Covering on the back of upholstered chairs to protect against hair oil.
Archdeacon. Clergyman who is second to the Bishop.
bail up. To hold up and rob.
Bishop. Clergyman consecrated to have charge of a Diocese.
bombazine. Twilled fabric of worsted wool yarn and silk, often in black for mourning.
boxbark hut. Shelter made of the thick bark of box eucalypts.
bushranger. Predatory outlaw living in the Australian bush.
cambric. Fine linen or cotton cloth.
Canon. Honorary title given to a Church of England clergyman for service to a Diocese.
cassock. Long, close-fitting robe, frequently black, worn by clergy.
castor. Finely granulated white sugar.
Celestial. Chinese person, from the historical name for China, the Celestial Empire.
chancel. Part of a church between the nave and sanctuary, often with choir stalls.
cholera. Infectious, often fatal bacterial disease with severe intestinal symptoms.
Collect. Short prayer used at a particular time or event.
collier. Coal miner.
cope. Cape-like vestment for clergy; the heavier version is worn outdoors.
crack. Colloquial term for Irish conversation, from *craic*.
Curate. Clergyman serving as an assistant in a parish.

Deacon. Clergyman who has passed the first level of Ordination.
demerara. Light-brown raw cane sugar.
Diocese. Territory comprising parishes under the care of a Bishop.
donnybrook. Free-for-all fight, named for the site of a country fair near Dublin.
Doxology. Short hymn of praise and thanksgiving.
dropsy. Abnormal accumulation of fluid in body tissues; edema.
duff. Steamed suet pudding.
dunny. Outdoor toilet or privy.
emancipist. Transported convict who has served his or her sentence and received freedom.
Free Settlers. British immigrants and their families who settled in an Australian colony of their own free will, in contrast to convicts or native-born Australians.
fustian. Thick, twilled cotton cloth.
gorse. Spiny evergreen European shrub with yellow blooms, also called furze or whin.
grazier. One who grazes livestock on a substantial property.
guinea. Gold coin equal to twenty-one shillings.
half a crown. Coin worth two shillings sixpence or one-eighth of a pound sterling.
hessian. Strong, coarse cloth of hemp or jute.
Irish Draught. Large, strong horse for hunting or light draught work, often crossed with Thoroughbreds.
jackeroo. Apprentice hand on a sheep or cattle station.
keening. Irish wailing at a death.
kurrajong. The useful tree *Brachychiton populneus*. Its densely leaved domed shape offers shade. Aborigines use its roots for food and weave its tough, stringy bark into fishing nets. Also, the town of Kurrajong in the foothills of the Blue Mountains, New South Wales.
macadam. Rolled layers of small, broken stones mixed with tar, used in road building.

nave. Main part of a church, where the congregation is seated.
New South Wales Corps. British military unit recruited for the colony to provide defence, convict supervision, policing and judicial services.
Nonconformist. Protestant who does not belong to the Church of England.
Overseer. Supervisor of a station, convicts or steerage passengers.
papist. Colloquial term for an adherent of Roman Catholicism.
phthisis. Progressive wasting disease, for example, *phthisis pulmonalis* (tuberculosis).
point-to-point. Cross-country horse race.
poke. Small, sturdy pouch, used as a purse for gold by successful miners.
portmanteau. Stiff suitcase opening into two equal compartments.
quadrille. Five-part dance performed by four couples arranged in a square.
queen of puddings. Bread pudding topped with jam and meringue.
Riley ballads. Irish ballads in which a man leaves his love and when he returns, tests her faithfulness.
roll-up. Colloquial term for rounding up and dispersing a group.
Rum Corps. Soldiers of the early New South Wales Corps who privately engaged in the rum trade.
sable folk. Colloquial term for Aborigines.
sabretache. Cavalry commander's flat satchel with long straps across the chest, worn on the left.
saltbush. Drought-resistant plants that are used for grazing in arid areas.
sanctuary. Part of a church within the altar rail.
scripture cake. Fruit cake made from ingredients found in the Bible.
scurvy. Disease causing swollen, bleeding gums, skin eruptions, general weakness and possible death, the result of Vitamin C deficiency.

scurvy grass. *Cochlearia anglica,* small plant of the cabbage family, rich in Vitamin C, found in saltwater marshes.
selector. One who has selected and purchased a property for agricultural use.
sheep scab. Infectious skin disease caused by parasitic mites; controlled when dipping began.
skillion. Lean-to hut.
skivvy. Colloquial term for the lowest grade of female domestic servant.
sociable. Open carriage with facing side seats.
sovereign. The monarch, or a gold coin worth one pound sterling.
station. Large property devoted to sheep, cattle and/or farming.
stone. Fourteen pounds or approximately 6.35 kilograms.
stone boat. Sturdy sledge for hauling stones or heavy items.
stuff material. Woollen fabric.
surcingle. Strap around a horse or any beast of burden, securing a saddle or pack.
surplice. Loose white garment, usually of cambric, worn by clergy and choirs.
Ulster. One of the five provinces of early Ireland. It included the counties of what is now Northern Ireland (Antrim, Armagh, Down, Fermanagh, Londonderry and Tyrone) as well as Cavan, Donegal and Monaghan.
ultimo. Last month.
vestry. Small room near a church sanctuary where robes (vestments) are kept.
Vicar. Clergyman who is paid a stipend to care for a parish.
wattle. Any of the numerous acacias, with honey-scented yellow blossoms.
whip. Horseman particularly skilled in driving teams of horses.

Sources

Chapter epigraphs are from the Book of Psalms in the King James Version of the Bible. Prayers are from the edition of *The Book of Common Prayer* used in the Church of England during the reign of Queen Victoria. Church music is from various editions of Anglican hymnals.

References to life in Cootamundra and quotations about events in the town and Cootamundra District are from Dr. William Miller's memorabilia and Ted and Helen Bowly's collection, from reports in the *Cootamundra Herald*, and also from two publications by Patricia Caskie: *Cootamundra: Foundation to Federation* and *Cootamundra 1901–1924: Past Imperfect* (both listed on next page).

Poems and Songs
"The Ash Grove"—Translation of the traditional Welsh song "Llwyn Onn"
"The Banks of Claudy"—Traditional Irish Riley ballad
"Believe Me, If All Those Endearing Young Charms"—Irish air, Thomas Moore & Sir J.A. Stevenson, 1808
"The Flower of Sweet Strabane"—Traditional Irish ballad
"Flow Gently, Sweet Afton"—Scottish air, Robert Burns & J.E. Spilman, 1837
"Little Jim, the Collier Boy"—Victorian-era poem, Edward Farmer
"Red Is the Rose by Yonder Garden Grows"—Traditional Irish song
"Tramp! Tramp! Tramp!"—American Civil War song, George F. Root, 1864
"The Wild Rover"—Traditional Irish song

References

Appleton, R. & B. (1992). *The Cambridge Dictionary of Australian Places*. Cambridge University Press. An extensive listing of Australian locations with the origin and pronunciation of their names and their historical backgrounds.

Australian Biographical and Genealogical Record 1842–1899, Vol. 3. (1988). Sydney: State Library of New South Wales. An informative biographical dictionary of pioneers, compiled for the Bicentennial of Australia. The families of John Barnes and John Miller are included.

Australian Dictionary of Biography 1788–1850, Vol. 1, A–H. (1966) Melbourne: Melbourne University Press. A biographical source of notable Australians, including Caroline Chisholm.

Australian Dictionary of Biography 1851–1990, Vol. 5, K–O. (1974). Melbourne: Melbourne University Press. A biographical source of notable Australians, including George Robert Nichols.

Australian Handbook. (1897). Sydney: Gordon & Gotch. A compendium of facts about settlements in the Australian colonies.

Caskie, P. (1991). *Cootamundra: Foundation to Federation*. Cootamundra: Annwel Enterprises. The story of the development of the town and District from 1861 to 1901. With its detailed pages researched from the *Cootamundra Herald* as well as from archives and historical publications, this book presents activities and achievements of Cootamundra pioneers, including contributions of the Barnes and Miller families.

Caskie, P. (2000). *Cootamundra 1901–1924: Past Imperfect*. Cootamundra: Annwel Enterprises. A continuation of the story of Cootamundra. Researched primarily from the *Cootamundra Herald*, the book mentions members of the Barnes and Miller families.

Clark, C.M.H. (1962). *A History of Australia* (Vols. 1–6). Melbourne: Melbourne University Press. Definitive source of Australian historical information, comprising six volumes.

Cootamundra Herald. 181 Parker Street, Cootamundra, NSW. As a record of the daily activities of the town and District from 1877 to the present, the *Herald* preserves the history of Cootamundra. Patricia Caskie is a former editor.

Cootamundra Local History Society. *Cootamundra District: A Photographic History, Vol. 5*. (2007). Cootamundra: Atlas Printing Works. A collection of annotated photographs of people and buildings in the town and District from the late nineteenth into the twentieth century. Photographs include Margaret Miller, Cohen's Trade Palace and the interior of Christ Church.

Cronin, L. (1987). *Key Guide to Australian Wildflowers*. Kew, Victoria: Reed Books. A handbook of six hundred species, identified and meticulously illustrated.

Cronin, L. (1988). *Key Guide to Australian Trees*. Kew, Victoria: Reed Books. A handbook of 249 species, identified and meticulously illustrated.

Crowley, F. (1980). *Colonial Australia 1841–1874* and *1875–1900*. Melbourne: Thomas Nelson. Collections of wide-ranging articles reflecting life in the Australian colonies from 1841 onwards. Each article has a brief historical preface.

Foote, A. (1948, February 14). "When Prince Rupert Was Auctioned Off." *Vancouver Sun*. A newspaper article recalling the real estate activities of J.J. Miller.

Freeman, P. (1980). *The Woolshed: A Riverina Anthology*. Melbourne: Oxford University Press. A description of woolsheds on old sheep stations in the Riverina District. Wallendbeen station and Alexander and Annie Mackay's home, Rose Cottage, are included.

Gilmore, Dame Mary, Benjamin, Phyllis, & Ellen, H.E. (n.d.). [Letters to the editor]. *Sydney Sun-Herald*. Correspondence concerns details of the Barnes family and the death of Johnnie O'Meally.

Hanson, W. (1889). *The Pastoral Possessions of New South Wales, 1889*. Sydney: Gibbs, Shallard & Company, Government Printers. Lists of state-owned pastoral areas in 1889 and their leaseholders. Compton Miller is named as leaseholder at Leybourne in Inglis County.

Hassam, A. (1994). *Sailing to Australia*. Manchester: University Press. Detailed information on emigrants' experiences aboard sailing ships.

Hirst, J.B. (1988). *The Strange Birth of Colonial Democracy: New South Wales, 1848–1884*. North Sydney: Allen & Unwin. The story of achievement of responsible government in the colony. The roles of George Robert Nichols, Caroline Chisholm and Ben Hall's gang are included.

Hughes, R. (1986). *The Fatal Shore*. New York: Vintage Books, Random House. An exhaustive volume describing convicts' experiences in New South Wales.

Jervis, J. (1962). *A History of the Berrima District, 1798–1973*. Sydney: Library of Australian History with the Berrima County Council. Descriptions of Berrima District's geographical features and pioneer activities. John Miller and Adam Windsor are included.

Lee, I. (1906). *The Coming of the British to Australia, 1788 to 1829*. London: Longman's Green, & Co. Contributions of the first explorers and settlers.

Mariners and Ships in Australian Waters. State Records Authority of New South Wales: Shipping Master's Office; Passengers Arriving 1855–1922. New South Wales Archives, Sydney Records Centre. Included is the manifest of the *Commissary* of Aberdeen, arriving in Sydney from London, November 19th, 1873, with Miss Susannah Gordon aboard.

Miller, J.J. (1912). *Vancouver to the Coronation*. London: Watts & Co. An account of a 1911 holiday journey taken by J.J., his wife Susannah and her daughters Frida and Florence from Vancouver across Canada to New York and thence to France,

Wales, Scotland, Ireland and England, culminating in the coronation celebrations of King George V.

Miller, J.J. (1929). "Early History of the Parish of Cootamundra." Manuscript in possession of the author. A memoir by the eldest son of John Miller, pioneer churchman and founder of Christ Church, Cootamundra. J.J. Miller lived at Cootamundra from 1874 until 1899 and writes from personal experience about early Christ Church services, parishioners and clergy.

Palmer, R. (1986). *The Oxford Book of Sea Songs*. Oxford: Oxford University Press. An annotated collection of sea chanties from the sixteenth to twentieth centuries, including "The Sailor's Alphabet," "Eighty-eight Sir Francis Drake" and "Nelson's Death and Victory."

Passey, K.J. (1986). *Lachlan Landmarks*. Morwell: Gippsland Printers. A thorough account of sites associated with bushranging in the western districts of New South Wales. Details of Ben Hall's gang and the murder of John Barnes are included.

Reports of Vessels Arrived—Shipping Reports of 1841 and 1854 (June to December). New South Wales Archives. Ledgers giving details of ships arriving, their cargoes and passengers. Listed are the *Abbotsford*, carrying the John Barnes family, and the *Caroline*, including steerage passenger Rebecca Nixon and her Record of Assisted Immigration.

Rushen, E. & McIntyre, P. (2008). *The Merchant's Women*. Spit Junction: Anchor Books Australia. Experiences of two hundred courageous women who sailed aboard the *Bussorah Merchant* in 1833 from England to New South Wales, seeking new lives in the colony. Included is the sister of John Barnes, Susanna Eliza Barnes Nichols.

Scrimgeour, G. (Ed.). (2006). *Sailing Tables for the Pacific: Canadian-Australasian Line—Northbound*. Postal History Society of Canada. Included are the departure and arrival dates of the SS *Aorangi* on her voyages from Sydney to Vancouver in 1903, 1905 and 1908.

Soodlum's Irish Ballad Book. (1982). London: Oak Publications. A collection of Irish ballads with words, music, notes on composers and photographs of bygone days.

Sutton, R. (Ed.). (1974). *For Queen and Empire: A Boer War Chronicle—75th Anniversary*. Ryde: Council of the New South Wales Military History Society. An account of Australian participation in the South African War. William Miller's horse Arabi and Trooper Jim Juleff are mentioned.

"Sydney, 1837." (1897, June 19). *Town and Country Journal*. A lengthy newspaper feature printed in honour of the Diamond Jubilee of Queen Victoria's reign, describing Sydney as it was when Queen Victoria ascended the throne, four years prior to the arrival in Sydney of John and Elizabeth Barnes and their children.

Taylor, P. (1988). *Station Life in Australia: Pioneers and Pastoralists*. Sydney: Allen & Unwin. Descriptions of the lives of squatters and selectors in early Australia.

Tregea, J.L. (1980). "The First 100 Years: Cootamundra Anglican Parish Centenary." Manuscript in possession of the author. A brief description of the buildings and clergy serving the Anglican Parish of Cootamundra during its first hundred years. The history begins with the work of Stipendiary Lay Reader John Miller.

Littledale homestead, 1996

About the Author

Elinor Martin was born in Vancouver, Canada, and grew up in West Vancouver, where she attended school. After graduating from the University of British Columbia, she became a secondary school teacher.

She had memories of listening to stories about the Barnes and Miller families and attending numerous family gatherings, including J.J. Miller's birthday parties. On her retirement in 1993 from teaching, she sorted her father's memorabilia, compiled the genealogy of the Barnes and Miller families, and spent many years researching nineteenth-century New South Wales and her ancestors' lives in the colony. With the help of cousins in Australia, she continued her research there and visited Cootamundra and Littledale. Her memories and investigations have resulted in *The Kurrajong Tree*.

Elinor is also the author of *Celebrating 70 Years of Ministry: A History of the Parish of Saint Christopher, West Vancouver, B.C., 1933–2003*, for which she was given a West Vancouver Heritage Achievement Award.

She and her husband, Stewart, live in West Vancouver and have a son, a daughter and a granddaughter.

www.ingramcontent.com/pod-product-compliance
Lightning Source LLC
Chambersburg PA
CBHW020939230426
43666CB00005B/91